Political Parties in Canada

McGraw-Hill Ryerson Series in Canadian Politics

General Editor — Paul W. Fox

Politics: Canada, 3rd Ed.; Paul W. Fox
Canadian Foreign Policy; D. C. Thomson & R. F. Swanson
The Constitutional Process in Canada, 2nd Ed.; R. I. Cheffins & R. N. Tucker
Political Party Financing in Canada; K. Z. Paltiel
One Man—One Vote; W. E. Lyons
Nationalism in Canada; P. Russell
Political Parties and Ideologies in Canada; W. Christian & C. Campbell
Canada: A Socio-Political Report; R. Manzer
Pressure Group Behaviour in Canadian Politics; A. Paul Pross
Canada in Question: Federalism in the Seventies; D. V. Smiley
Political Parties in Canada: C. Winn & J. McMenemy
Government in Canada; T. A. Hockin

Forthcoming

Canada in Question: Federalism in the Seventies, 2nd Ed.; D. V. Smiley
Canadian Politics: Exercises in Analysis; J. Jenson & B. Tomlin
Politics: Canada, 4th Ed.; Paul W. Fox

Political Parties in Canada

by
Conrad Winn
Department of Political Science
Carleton University
Ottawa, Ontario

John McMenemy
Department of Political Science
Wilfrid Laurier University
Waterloo, Ontario

McGraw-Hill Ryerson Limited
Toronto   Montreal   New York   London
Sydney   Mexico   Panama   São Paulo
Johannesburg   Düsseldorf   New Delhi
Kuala Lumpur   Auckland

Political Parties in Canada

ISBN 0-07-082260-3

2 3 4 5 6 7 8 9 10   AP   5 4 3 2 1 0 9 8 7

Printed and bound in Canada

We gratefully acknowledge the following for granting permission to reprint material (numbers refer to pages where reprinted material appears in this book): Canadian Political Science Association, Ottawa, and Dr. Jean Laponce, 2; Longman Canada Ltd., Toronto, 50–51; University of Toronto Press, 52, 122; Clarendon Press, Don Mills, Ontario, 53; extracts from *Political Change in Britain* by David Butler and Donald Stokes reprinted by permission of Macmillan Administration (Basingstoke) Ltd., Houndmills, Basingstoke, Hampshire, England, St. Martin's Press, Inc., New York, 83–84; *Canadian Review of Sociology and Anthropology*, Montreal, 78; Cy Gonick, 79; Tables reproduced by permission of Statistics Canada, 77, 78, 79; Figures reproduced by permission of Information Canada, 92–97, 214, 218; extract from Denis Smith in H. G. Thorburn (ed.), *Party Politics in Canada* (1972) reprinted by permission of Prentice-Hall of Canada Ltd.; T. H. Qualter, 116; James Lorimer and Co., Toronto, 146; Macmillan Co. of Canada Ltd., 153–154; Table 9–2 reproduced by arrangement with Holt, Rinehart & Winston, Inc., New York, 154; extract from *The Diefenbaker Interlude* by Peter Regenstreif reprinted by permission of Longman Canada Ltd., Toronto; Richard D. Irwin, Inc., Homewood, Illinois, and George Allen & Unwin Ltd., Hemel Hempstead, England, 212; Dr. Dale Poel, 211; Table 12-2 reproduced by permission of Queen's Printer, Toronto, 219; extract from *Renegade in Power: The Diefenbaker Years* by Peter C. Newman reprinted by permission of The Canadian Publishers, McClelland & Stewart Ltd., Toronto, 235; Appendix calculated from report of the Chief Electoral Officer, various years, 281.

ACKNOWLEDGEMENTS

We are fortunate to have received the intellectual and other kinds of assistance from a number of colleagues, friends, students, and professional associates. In addition to our co-authors and contributors, we would like to thank Professors Welf Heick, Henry Jacek, Robert Jackson, Roman March, Vincent McHale, Joseph Scanlon, and Michael Whittington; Sen. Keith Davey, David Lewis, John Laschinger, Finlay MacDonald, Clifford Scotton, and Blair Williams of the federal parties; Gordon Galbraith, Patrick Gossage, and Fred Schindeler in the federal government; and Malcolm Daigneault and Craig Oliver along with their colleagues in the CBC and CTV. Professors Irwin Gillespie, Peter Johansen, Reginald Whitaker, and Max Saltsman, MP, took time to read parts of the manuscript. Professor John Meisel, Professor Paul Fox, and Geoffrey Burn, then of McGraw-Hill Ryerson, were kind enough to comment on an earlier version of the manuscript and make many vital suggestions. For assistance in data analysis or otherwise, we would like to thank the following present and past students: Roy Brosky, Chester Burtt, Bruce Macnaughton, John Summers, Charles Yolleck, and especially Pegi Dover and Robert Seed. For kindness in the domain of typing, thanks are due to Miss Betty Smith and Mrs. Arvis Oxland, secretaries in the Wilfrid Laurier Political Science Department, and to Mrs. Pearl Fisher and Mrs. Betty Weiss at the Carleton Department. Finally, Wilfrid Laurier University and the Canadian Radio-Television Commission made available research grants which, although used primarily for other purposes, did provide data which were re-analysed in the context of this work.

v

CONTENTS

Foreword

It is one of the ironies of Canadian political science that, although much has been said about the significance and role of political parties in our system and a large amount has been written about certain aspects of partisan activity, there has been a striking shortage of scholarly works which have examined the way in which our federal parties actually function in the system.

Thus, we have had available, for instance, many good biographies and autobiographies of our politicians, a number of conventional political histories, an increasing number of studies of individual federal and provincial parties and movements, and a mounting flow of behavioural analyses. But, with the exception of Professor Hugh Thorburn's useful collection of articles entitled *Party Politics in Canada*, Professors Frederick Engelmann and Mildred Schwartz's original work which has now been revised and republished under the title *Canadian Political Parties: Origin, Character, and Impact*, and Professors William Christian and Colin Campbell's recent book, *Political Parties and Ideologies in Canada*, no monograph has scanned the broad spectrum of Canadian political party activity. As surprising as this deficiency may be, its inconvenience has been even greater, especially for instructors who have been seeking a good sourcebook for their students.

Consequently, I was very pleased when Professors Winn and McMenemy and their contributors took on the task of writing a book on this important subject. I was even more pleased when I finished reading the final draft of their work because it seems to me that they have done a first-class job.

The merits of the book are many. First, it provides a straightforward, readable, historical description of both major parties and minor parties in the federal sector. This in itself is a benefit, even if a student goes no further. Second, it has a provocative thesis which it argues consistently and persuasively (Those readers who are not convinced will at least be provoked).

Third, the book builds its argument by working its way steadily through the various components of the party system: historical lineage, political cleavages, representation, party personnel and structures, and decision-making. Fourth, the examination of each of these factors is analytical, scholarly, resourceful, and comparative. That is to say, the authors invariably peel away the rhetorical clichés, dig down, often ingeniously, to discernible facts, then compare the data for the respective parties in order to draw conclusions.

Fifth, the book is well organized. It is structured on an input-throughput-output model whose parts fit together very neatly. The basic hypothesis in the input section is tested at the end in the output section. Every chapter and section has a succinct introduction and a summary conclusion which are very convenient for pedagogical purposes.

Sixth, the book is innovative. I particularly like Section V which examines party outputs in an effort to determine to what extent each party has been true to its ascribed and self-proclaimed identity depicted earlier as inputs. Chapter by chapter, Section V reviews each of our three major federal parties' policies in regard to biculturalism, redistribution of income, trade and resources, and external affairs.

Seventh, the book is assertive and contentious. It assaults conventional wisdom and sacrosanct partisan beliefs at almost every point. Thus, although the two principal authors accept that our major political cleavage has been bicultural, one of their contributors, Professor Chi, challenges this view by presenting a Marxist class interpretation.

However, this article is only the beginning of the heresies. Some of the authors' claims will upset orthodox believers of various kinds, especially partisan politicians — but no doubt academics also. For example, some intellectuals will be greatly disturbed to be told that neither the "Whig" theory nor the "Red Tory" interpretation of Canadian political development is true. Professor Stevenson attacks both views:

> Both interpretations magnify and distort the real differences between the Liberal and Conservative parties. Both implicitly attribute to the parties a degree of consistency, homogeneity, and ideological coherence that neither one has ever displayed. Both ignore or suppress any evidence that might cast doubts on their oversimplified assumptions. Both beg the question as to whether political parties really exercise decisive influence on Canadian foreign policy at all. In short, both conventional interpretations are good propaganda but bad history and bad social science.

Politicians, and perhaps some professors, will also bristle when they read in Chapter 11 that federal Liberals have not been as francophile and the Conservatives as anglophile as many partisans claim. "In the domain of domestic policy," writes Professor Winn, "the Conservative party was not found to be consistently anglophile. Furthermore, French-speaking Liberal prime ministers appeared to be the weakest defenders of French-Canadian interests."

Moreover, according to Chapter 13, our parties have actually differed very little in their trade and resource policies:

> When in power [federally or provincially], all parties appeared to be influenced by questions of feasibility... This pragmatic reality not only invalidates the Christian and Campbell argument about the alleged continentalism of the Liberals and the nationalism of the Conservatives, but it also invalidates any suggestion that party policies reflect directly different geographic or class bases of support.

But if all this causes a gorge or two to rise, Chapter 12 may produce apoplexy. After examining the evidence, Professors Winn and McCready come to the conclusion that "there are no major or significant differences in the redistributive behaviour of all the parties. . . In fact, the welfare state as we know it does not redistribute wealth greatly. A number of government programs which are thought to be progressive are in fact neutral or regressive. Consequently, "partisan attitudes towards the welfare state [are] poor indicators of a party's redistributive behaviour."

Finally, the authors tackle the question of why our parties are so similar. Why, for instance, are bicultural cleavages not reflected in different outputs? Their answer is simple, but searing: essentially because party members are so poorly informed on issues that they cannot pack enough punch to influence policy-making by their leaders, elites, and civil servants. To improve the quality of the rank and file, their research facilities must be vastly increased and the media must do a better job of reporting news and opinion. Indicting the media for a mediocre and trivial performance, Winn and McMenemy throw out a challenge and offer a few suggestions.

This brief review of the book's merits should be sufficient to demonstrate that it is not merely a routinely pedestrian account of Canadian political parties. Far from it. The book can be read in two ways, either as a text replete with basic information, or as a provocative interpretation of the Canadian political party system. Personally, I like the combination of the two elements. I imagine that students in particular will find that learning is much easier when leavened with a large infusion of yeast. We have waited a long while for a book on Canadian political parties. Now we have one which is very stimulating as well as highly informative.

PAUL W. FOX
General Editor

November 4, 1975
University of Toronto

CHAPTER 1
INTRODUCTION

A common approach to the analysis of political parties is to describe their internal characteristics. The parties may be compared according to their organization, membership, leadership style, decision-making process, or other characteristics. Our book touches on these questions. However, rather than examining the parties primarily in terms of their internal attributes, the book focuses on the place of parties in the larger political system and in the ongoing political process. Hence, how parties express political cleavages, the significant differences in sentiment among the general population, becomes an important question. It is also relevant to explore how the mass media and elections influence the parties. Finally, it is important to examine how the policies of the parties reflect the joint impact of the political cleavages, the mass media, and other factors.

In brief, the book accepts the conventional wisdoms about the differences in style and electoral support of the parties, but rejects the conventional wisdoms about differences in policy. The opening chapters express the common view of the Liberals and Progressive Conservatives as pragmatic parties and the CCF-NDP and Social Credit as parties of principle. The apparent orientation to success of the larger parties is attributed to their origins as parliamentary coteries seeking the rewards of office; the orientation to principle of the smaller parties is attributed to their beginnings as extra-parliamentary groups created in times of upheaval. The book also accepts the conventional wisdom about the parties as manifestations of political cleavage. The Liberals do receive special support from French Canada, the Conservatives from English Canada, the NDP from some of the western provinces, and the NDP and Social Credit from the lower strata of society. However, the book departs from accepted scholarship by suggesting that these differences in style and electoral support have a negligible effect on policy. Thus, implemented programs exhibit few systematic differences from one party government to another. The book also suggests that elections, the mass media, and other components of the political process encourage similarities rather than differences in party policy.

The text is organized on the input-throughput-output model. The category of inputs includes the historical origins of the parties and political cleavages in society. Inputs are modified or transformed by throughputs, the representational process and party organization. The outputs are the attitudes and policies of the parties, their policy dispositions.[1]

Section I is devoted to the origins of the parties. The major, parliamentary parties are contrasted with the minor, movement parties. The parliamentary parties took shape in the nineteenth century to fill newly created parliamentary offices, while the movement parties arose

1

later to protest the inadequacies of incumbent office-holders. The untroubled origins and longstanding success of the Liberal and Conservative parties are offered as a partial explanation for their greater concern with electoral practicality than with principle or program. By contrast, the greater sense of principle and lesser flexibility of the New Democratic party and, to a certain extent, of the Social Credit party are explained partly by their traumatic origins as protest movements, when their missionary disdain for parliamentary artifice and electoral manipulation took root.

Our perception of party history as an input derives from the tendency of organizations to acquire institutional memories, to adhere to older patterns of authority, and to encourage newcomers to adapt to older forms of behaviour. To borrow an analogy from biology and psychology, political parties can be "imprinted" with older patterns of behaviour at an early stage in their existence. An illustration of imprinting is provided by the Conservative party's apparent affinity for autocratic leaders during the period prior to Robert Stanfield. Thus, Conservative king-makers had repeatedly sought replicas of the arrogant Sir John A. Macdonald in the hope that his electoral success, unparalleled in Conservative party history, would thereby be repeated. Of course, the leadership traits which were virtuous in the nineteenth century were not necessarily admired in the twentieth.

The subject of Section II is political cleavages. Separate chapters are devoted to the bicultural, geographic, and class conflicts. The decision to emphasize these particular divisions was made on the basis of our own prior analysis and was buttressed by some cogent quantitative research undertaken by Jean Laponce. In one particular study of voting behaviour, Laponce identified statistically the best socio-economic predictors of partisan choice in federal elections between 1949 and 1968. He summarized his findings simply:

> . . . the Conservatives are rich and Protestant, the Liberals Catholic and French, the NDP is working class and Protestant. Canada is thus no exception among western industrial nations. Its party system is organized around the usual regional, religious, and social class oppositions to which is added a specific linguistic cleavage.[2]

Although our own research employed different techniques, our findings conformed with those of Laponce. The three basic Canadian schisms emerged in a study of national voting preferences and in a study of municipal and provincial voting in one Ontario city.[3] Bicultural and class cleavages also emerged in a study of attitudes and beliefs among Ontario MPPs.[4]

Historically, the greatest impetus in the study of cleavages came from European, notably Scandinavian, researchers. The works of Stein Rokkan, for example, are landmark studies of the relationship between cleavage structures and party systems.[5] Canadian academics have examined individual cleavages which arise, for example, from English vs. French loyalties, from urban vs. rural location, from continentalist vs. nationalist affinities, and from collectivist vs. individualist belief. In a study first published in 1933, Escott Reid produced statistical evidence from election returns to show the marked dependence of the Liberal and Conservative parties on francophone and anglophone voters respectively.[6] In the 1950s and 1960s, the bicultural, geographic and class cleavages received attention in the extensive writings of John Meisel and later in the work of Peter Regenstreif and others.[7] Meisel and Regenstreif combined a sensitive understanding of crises in Canadian history with the use of simple statistics from opinion surveys to illustrate the presence of these and other social divisions.

While our treatment of cleavages had a substantial literature to synthesize, the subsequent chapters had a weaker foundation upon which to build. Section III is devoted to the representational process and contains chapters on elections and mass communication. Alan Cairns's famous essay on the electoral system remains a significant examination of the impact of electoral rules on electoral outcomes and party policy.[8] However, there are few significant findings about the partisan or policy effects of the media.[9]

The subject of Section IV is internal party attributes. One chapter is concerned with party personnel, another with party structures and decision-making. N. H. Chi and Henry Jacek have reported data on party activists and elites, but few accounts of the internal organization of the parties have been published.[10] The relative absence of information on party organization is unfortunate because the internal structure of party life may have a significant impact on the nature of party policy.

One of the less conventional aspects of the book is Section V on policy dispositions or outputs. While there is a large literature on parties and a growing literature on public policy, few researchers have devoted their attention to the effects of parties on government output. In this connection, David Falcone and Dale Poel deserve recognition for providing some intriguing studies of the significance — or, more aptly, the insignificance — of the factor of partisanship.[11]

Section V is structured in part to reflect the dominant political cleavages in the system. Chapters on bicultural policy and redistributive policy are intended to be counterpoints to earlier chapters on bicultural and class cleavages. The chapter on trade and resources policies was selected because of the intrinsic importance of the topic. Nonetheless, trade and resources policies bear a relationship to regional interests and therefore to the geographic cleavage. The chapter on foreign policy is included on account of its intrinsic importance. Foreign policy does not have a direct relationship to any one cleavage but overlaps with all.

Earlier, we described the organization of the text in terms of a simple, one-way input-throughput-output model. Nevertheless, other more complex and multidirectional relationships are possible. According to the simple I-T-O model, for example, throughputs such as the mass media may influence outputs in the form of changes in electoral outcome or policy. However, throughputs such as the mass media may in fact exercise a direct influence on political cleavages without any change in policy outputs. For example, the press and television could exacerbate the bicultural cleavage by their treatment of bicultural issues without a resulting change in government policies towards the two major cultural groups. In turn, party outputs such as broadcasting legislation could influence throughputs such as mass communication. These and some other patterns of influence are explored in individual chapters.

The original design of the manuscript included an input section on cognitive infusion, or the borrowing of political ideas from abroad. The infusion of ideas from other countries has undoubtedly played an important role in the party system and in policy formation. The historical affinities of Progressive Conservatives for the British Conservative party, of the NDP for British Labour and Swedish Social Democrats, and of the Liberal party under William Lyon Mackenzie King for American Progressivism are well known. Previous and concurrent experiences in the United States, Great Britain, and elsewhere appear to have influenced Canadian practices and laws governing health care, pensions, the franchise, election campaigns, trade unions, and a host of other domains.

The significance of legislative diffusion has been established in the study of policy formation among the American states.[12] However, less attention has been devoted to the study of the international diffusion of laws and political practices or to the study of the diffusion among the jurisdictions within Canada. We chose not to undertake a systematic examination of the impact of cognitive infusion on the Canadian party system because such a task would have been beyond our present resources.

Having discussed the organization of the book, we conclude with a commentary on our motives. The first important impetus for the book came when the two principal authors found themselves in a combined course in Canadian politics at Wilfrid Laurier University from 1970 to 1974. We were frustrated by the vast number of intuitive or speculative interpretations of the party system and by the small number of attempts at empirical verification.

The works of George Grant, Gad Horowitz, and William Christian and Colin Campbell symbolized our dilemma.[13] Their work set forth a number of propositions about the nature of ideological differences among Canadian parties. An assumption shared by all three scholarly efforts is that the Progressive Conservative, Liberal, and New Democratic parties embody conservatism, liberalism, and socialism, respectively. They point to the writings of individual party ideologues and individual party policies as evidence for their positions. However, the authors do not distinguish between party rhetoric and actual performance. Furthermore, the authors give insufficient attention to the practical as opposed to partisan roots of policy. For instance, was Conservative Prime Minister R. B. Bennett's "New Deal" truly evidence of the un-American and collectivist character of toryism? Could the "Canadian New Deal" be an example, instead, of a non-ideological response to dire electoral circumstances and an example of the imitation of American practices? Were the policies proclaimed by Bennett's Conservatives significantly different from the programs subsequently implemented by King's Liberals?

The distinction between collectivism and individualism is central to the work of Grant, Horowitz, and Christian and Campbell. This explanation of party differences has won considerable popularity. For example, G. W. (Jed) Baldwin, the prominent Conservative MP from Alberta, has suggested that the separate identities of the major parties are founded primarily on this distinction. However, while Horowitz believes that the Liberals are the more individualist, Baldwin believes the Conservatives are the more individualist.[14] At least as much empirical evidence supports Baldwin's view as the contrary opinion held by Horowitz and others.[15]

The works of Grant, Horowitz, and Christian and Campbell are well written and a pleasure to read. They add to our fund of knowledge about party history and political thought in Canada. Grant's *Lament for a Nation* is a major contribution to political philosophy and history from a Canadian perspective as well as a model of concise and powerful prose. Grant exercised a significant influence on Horowitz and on the academic nationalists who arose in the late 1960s. The popularity of these works may suggest something to future scholars about the mood among English-speaking Canadian intellectuals during the years of national introspection in the 1960s and early 1970s. In the meantime, none of the works begins to satisfy the canons of scientific proof, so that the hapless instructor seeking to understand the Canadian party system must fall back on his own intuition.

In the absence of much empirical verification, the speculative work of Horowitz and others engendered in us pervasive unease. We sought to reduce this feeling by attempting to be as empirical as possible and by tempering our own speculation with empirical support whenever we were able. With such analysis in mind, we invited several academics to join us as co-authors of individual chapters or as single contributors. Each collaborator was selected because of his empirical bent of mind, because of his hard-headedness, and because of his expertise in a specific domain in which we sought his assistance. N. H. Chi, François-Pierre Gingras, and Garth Stevenson have recognized research specialities in social class, French Canada, and foreign policy. John Weir and Douglas McCready are economists with backgrounds in political behaviour and public policy. John Redekop has a longstanding interest in formal political organization.

Each collaborator was asked to express his own wealth of factual knowledge on a particular subject in a manner which would mesh with the proposed input-throughput-output of the manuscript. The collaborators were also invited to employ their empirical analysis to evaluate the speculative themes in their particular area of speciality.

None of the collaborators found a great deal of correspondence between the facts as they knew them and the ideological analysis proffered by Horowitz and others. On the input side, social cleavages were thought to carry more weight than philosophical disagreements over the relative merits of collectivism, individualism, and other beliefs. On the output side, there was a consensus that few differences among the parties exist and these differences did not conform easily to the notions of those who have sought to explain the party system in ideological terms. Finally, our unwillingness to assign an empirical validity to Horowitz's ideological analysis is not meant to denigrate such analysis. The concepts of collectivism and individualism, for example, will continue to have utmost normative or philosophical importance whether or not they explain the nature of the parties.

CONRAD WINN
JOHN McMENEMY

Notes

1. On the concept of disposition, see Donald T. Campbell, "Acquired Behavioural Dispositions", in S. Koch (ed.), *Psychology: A Study of Science* (New York: McGraw-Hill, 1963).

2. Laponce, "Post-dicting Electoral Cleavages in Canadian Federal Elections, 1949–68: Material for a Footnote", *Canadian Journal of Political Science* 5:2 (1972), 284. See also J. A. Laponce and R. S. Uhler, "Measuring Electoral Cleavages in a Multi-party System: The Canadian Case," *Comparative Political Studies*, 7:1 (1974/75), 3–25.

3. Winn, "Spatial Models of Party Systems: An Examination of the Canadian Case", (University of Pennsylvania Ph.D. dissertation, 1972), and Winn and McMenemy, "Political Alignment in a Polarized City: Electoral Cleavages in Kitchener, Ontario", *Canadian Journal of Political Science*, 6:2 (1973), 230–242.

4. Conrad Winn and James Twiss, "Spatial Models and Party Distances in the Ontario Legislature", forthcoming.

5. See Rokkan, "Geography, Religion, and Social Class: Cross-Cutting Cleavages in Norwegian Politics", in Seymour M. Lipset and Stein Rokkan (ed.), *Party Systems and Voter Alignments* (New York: Free Press, 1967); Rokkan, "Nation Building, Cleavage Formation, and the Structuring of Mass Politics", in Stein Rokkan (ed.), *Citizens, Elections, Parties* (Oslo and New York: Universitetsforlaget and David McKay Co., 1970); Seymour Lipset, "Class, Politics, and Religion in Modern Society", in Lipset (ed.), *Revolution and Counter-Revolution* (New York: Basic Books, 1968); and Richard Rose and Derek Unwin, "Social Cohesion, Political Parties, and Strains in Regimes", in Mattei Dogan and Richard Rose (ed.), *European Politics* (Boston: Little, Brown, 1971). For a recent Canadian study, see John Meisel, "Cleavages, Parties, and Values in Canada", a paper presented to the meetings of the International Political Science Association (Montreal, August 1973).

6. Reid, "Canadian Political Parties: A Study of the Economic and Racial Bases of Conservatism and Liberalism in 1930", reprinted in John C. Courtney (ed.), *Voting in Canada* (Toronto: Prentice-Hall, 1967).

7. See the classic paper by Meisel, "Religious Affiliation and Electoral Behaviour: A Case Study," in ibid. as well as Peter Regenstreif, *The Diefenbaker*

Interlude (Toronto: Longmans, 1965) and Meisel, *Working Papers in Canadian Politics* (Montreal: McGill-Queen's Press, 1972). See also F. C. Engelmann and M. A. Schwartz, *Political Parties and the Canadian Social Structure* (Toronto: Prentice-Hall, 1967) and their *Canadian Political Parties: Origin, Character, Impact* (Toronto: Prentice-Hall, 1975). Both works explicitly relate the party system to the cleavage structure.

8. "The Electoral System and the Party System in Canada, 1921–65," *Canadian Journal of Political Science*, 1:1 (1968), 55–80.

9. See Stephen Clarkson, "Unfair at Any Wavelength", a report to the Canadian Radio-Television Commission (n.d.), and Clarkson, "Policy and the Media", a paper presented at meetings of the Canadian Political Science Association (Toronto, June 1974). See also Engelmann and Schwartz, *Canadian Political Parties*, 119–40.

10. See N. H. Chi, "Class Voting in Canadian Politics", in Orest M. Kruhlak et al., *The Canadian Political Process* (Toronto: Holt, Rinehart and Winston, 1973), 226–47, and Henry Jacek et al., "The Congruence of Federal-Provincial Campaign Activity in Party Organizations: The Influence of Recruitment Patterns in Three Hamilton Ridings", in *Canadian Journal of Political Science* 5:2 (1972), 190–205, and "Social Articulation and Aggregation in Political Party Organizations in a Large Canadian City", *Canadian Journal of Political Science*, 8:2 (1975), 274–98.

11. See David J. Falcone, "Legislative Change and Output Change" (Duke University Ph.D. dissertation, 1974), and Dale Poel, "Canadian Provincial and American State Policy", a paper presented to meetings of the Canadian Political Science Association (Montreal, August 1973), and "The Diffusion of Legislation Among the Canadian Provinces: A Mathematical and Statistical Analysis," a paper presented to the annual meeting of the Canadian Political Science Association (Edmonton: June 1975).

12. See Jack L. Walker, "The Diffusion of Innovations Among the American States", *American Political Science Review*, 63:3 (1969), 880–99.

13. Grant, *Lament for a Nation* (Toronto: McClelland and Stewart, 1965); Horowitz, *Canadian Labour in Politics* (Toronto: University of Toronto Press, 1968); and Christian and Campbell, *Political Parties and Ideologies in Canada* (Toronto: McGraw-Hill Ryerson, 1974).

14. See Richard Jackson, "Conspiracy of the left seen by PC", *Kitchener-Waterloo Record* (October 9, 1974).

15. Chi has shown that Conservative activists are significantly less disposed to public economic intervention and are therefore less collectivist than Liberal activists. See his "Class Voting".

 # SECTION I

Party Origins (Inputs)

The origins of political parties are important because they can affect the way parties behave subsequently. The contemporary differences or similarities among parties may be explained partly by the nature of their birth and the history of their formative years. In this section, we distinguish between parties which arose in the nineteenth century in response to the creation of new offices of political power and those which arose in this century in the context of social tensions and up-heaval. The first group is styled parliamentary parties while the second is classified as fragment or movement parties. Chapter 2 argues that it is in the nature of parliamentary parties to be flexible and pragmatic. The chapter goes on to explain how this greater flexibility is employed to achieve electoral success. Chapter 3 contrasts the relative durability of minor parties which arise from social discontent with the short-lived nature of those which are fragments or splinters of existing parties.

CHAPTER 2
PARLIAMENTARY PARTIES
John McMenemy

Introduction

The historic origins of Canada's political parties have imprinted them with styles of behaviour that have persisted into the present. Like other organizations, parties acquire potent institutional memories and socialize new generations of members and supporters to the myths of the group and the proper forms of behaviour. In terms of the impact of origins on subsequent behaviour, a fundamental distinction exists between the parties of parliamentary origin and the parties formed in response to social tensions outside the legislative environment. Only the two parties of parliamentary origin have formed the federal government. Moreover, each has been pre-eminent for historic periods. The Conservatives were dominant from Confederation to 1896, while the Liberals have been dominant in this century (See Appendix I). This chapter examines the long-term impact of the parliamentary, as opposed to the extra-parliamentary, origins of the Conservative and Liberal parties. It also suggests an explanation of each party's historic pre-eminence.

Interpretations of group behaviour are difficult to subject to empirical testing when the period being examined spans more than a century and such contemporary forms of information as survey data are non-existent. The historic interpretation in this and the subsequent chapter is based on the recorded actions of party leaders in response to important cleavages in Canadian society.

The Progressive Conservative and Liberal parties first took form among officeholders in the legislatures of the mid nineteenth century, although disciplined parties did not exist until the late nineteenth century.[1] The Conservatives began in 1854 as a temporary Liberal-Conservative coalition of Tories and French-speaking bleus in the Province of Canada. As a practical response to the growing dominance of the Tory party, the rural Clear Grits of Upper Canada, the anti-clerical rouges, and the reform element in the Maritimes came together gradually as the Liberal party. Confederation gave an impetus to party solidarity by making the fruits of legislative victory more lush. The changes of 1867 not only established a House of Commons and Senate in the new federal capital, but also provided for separate assemblies in Quebec and Ontario and greater powers for the existing legislatures of the Maritimes.

At their inception, the Liberal and Conservative parties reflected religious, geographic, and other differences among the electors of early Canada. For many incumbent politicians, however, the parties were primarily a means of taking advantage of the new opportunities for power and patronage. In contrast, the CCF, Social Credit, and other "minor" parties arose later when legislative power had already been monopolized by the older parties. These parties took form as popular movements outside parliament during times of social upheaval and were motivated as much and perhaps more by the desire to transform society as by the desire to win elections. Indeed, they were often hesitant and self-conscious about parliamentary victory for fear of committing the sins of the older parties.

Impact of Parliamentary Origin

As a result of their legislative origins, parliamentary parties continue to be more practical, flexible, and manipulative than the newer movement parties. More motivated to achieve or retain power, the parliamentary parties have been more able to manage social tensions for their own benefit, recruit diverse — even incompatible — supporters, and make incongruous alliances. In contrast, the movement parties, the subject of the next chapter, are constrained by the ideals which prompted their creation and which justify their mission to replace the parliamentary parties. Over the long term, this flexibility in treating the mutual suspicions between English and French Canada, between regions, and between business and labour has been the essential component in the electoral success and hegemony of the Liberals and Conservatives.

The pragmatism of the Liberal and Conservative parties is evident in the treatment of personnel and policy matters. For example, each party has depended upon support from members of other parties. In the nineteenth century, Sir John A. Macdonald, the Conservative leader, depended greatly on the assistance of "Liberal ministerialists". These ostensible parliamentary opponents were anxious to curry the favour of any government for the benefit of their constituents and their political career. Macdonald obtained support of staunch opponents on at least two crucial occasions. In 1864, George Brown, the leader of the Reformers in Canada West, agreed to join the Conservatives in a grand coalition to end the political deadlock in the Province of Canada. The coalition was dedicated to the larger project of complete colonial federation. Joseph Howe engineered a successful anti-Confederation movement in Nova Scotia and was elected to the Opposition in 1867. Two years later, after renegotiation of the annual federal subsidy to Nova Scotia, Howe entered Macdonald's cabinet. Such ability to entreat successfully with powerful opponents was crucial to the success of Macdonald's career and to Conservative party fortunes.

In this century, however, it has been the turn of the Liberals to entice politicians and experts from the camps of their opponents. Prime Minister Pierre Trudeau was not a member of the party before his recruitment as a Liberal candidate for Parliament in 1965. Indeed, he had been an outspoken critic of the party and of its leader, Prime Minister Lester Pearson.[2] Marc Lalonde was Trudeau's principal secretary from 1968 to 1972. Elected in 1972, he immediately became an important Liberal minister. Yet a decade earlier, he had been the executive assistant to a Conservative minister of justice. When the Social Credit party dissolved in 1968, one of its two western MPs joined the Liberal party and immediately became a cabinet minister. In 1975, Trudeau appointed a former *créditiste*, now Liberal, MP as Minister of Regional Economic Expansion. In 1964, the twenty-year-old CCF government in Saskatchewan was defeated by a stridently anti-socialist Liberal party. When the new provincial Liberal government dismissed its senior socialist public servants, the federal Liberal government promptly offered some of them refuge in the federal public service. For example, two former Saskatchewan bureaucrats are currently the Liberal-appointed deputy minister of finance and the president of the Canadian Broadcasting Corporation. The latter had been deputy minister of welfare in the huge federal Department of National Health and Welfare.

The flexibility of the parliamentary parties also extends to policy and program. With support in rural Canada in the early decades of Confederation, the Liberal party opposed protectionism and supported commercial reciprocity with the United States. It also opposed Macdonald's program of railway construction. Led by Sir Wilfrid Laurier, the Liberals supported unrestricted reciprocity and suffered for it in the election of 1891. The party's trade policy alienated industrialists who wanted protection for their goods and offended loyalists who saw reciprocity as anti-British. Later in the 1890s, Prime Minister Laurier made his party acceptable among the business class by reversing the traditional stance. In the budget of 1897, the Liberals neatly undercut the Conservatives by introducing the principle of a minimum and a maximum tariff. A chief result of this Liberal protectionism was to give British goods a preference in Canada. In 1903, Laurier personally committed the government to the construction of a second transcontinental railway and fired his minister of railways who opposed the decision. By the election of 1904, the Liberals had acquired Macdonald's railway and tariff policy and could therefore wear the previously Conservative mantle of "party of national development."

In this century, Conservative Prime Minister R. B. Bennett won election in 1930 proclaiming loyalty to free enterprise and promising Canadian manufacturers and producers that he would "blast a way" onto the world markets. A few years later, in the midst of the turmoil of the depression, he questioned the capitalist system and attempted to implement a "Canadian New Deal" to "insure to all classes a greater degree of equality."[3] In 1963, the Liberals changed their longstanding position on nuclear warheads for the Bomarc anti-aircraft missile in Canada. A recipient of the Nobel Peace Price, Lester Pearson had until that time established a close relationship to the "ban the bomb" movement. His wife was a well-known member of the Voice of Women, one group within the movement. Pearson's reversal of defence policy undoubtedly created temporary embarrassment for him. However, he acted on the correct prediction by a few of his Liberal colleagues that reversal of Liberal policy would give greater embarrassment to John

Diefenbaker's Conservative government, increase tensions within it, and accelerate its replacement by a Liberal government.[4] In 1974, the Liberals were re-elected while vigorously opposing the wage-and-price control policy of the Progressive Conservatives; in 1975, the Liberal government implemented controls.

The flexibility of the parliamentary parties is rooted in the inchoate party system of the 1800s. No disciplined party structure and no formal partisan debate existed until late in the nineteenth century. Many candidates were elected as ministerialists, promising to support the leadership clique offering the constituency the greatest material benefit. "Loose fish," complained Macdonald. "Shaky fellows," George Brown called them.[5] Electoral practices discouraged the development of a disciplined party system. Under the open ballot, voters had to declare publicly their support of a candidate. The government-appointed poll officers could find it "necessary" to close polls to ensure "public order" when the vote tally was favourable to the ministerial clique. A system of deferred elections allowed the coalition in power to set the election date in "safe" constituencies first and move afterwards to the more doubtful ones. The government trusted that the spectacle of earlier victories and keen expectations of ministerial favours would sway the doubting voters in the remaining constituencies.

Even after the secret ballot and simultaneous elections were introduced in the election of 1878, the government retained special advantages. It was responsible for drawing constituency boundaries, creating the list of voters, and positioning polling stations. Constituency boundaries could be gerrymandered in order to minimize the effect of opposition voting strength and maximize the effect of government strength. The voters list could include fictitious individuals who would "appear" on election day to cast a vote for the government candidate or exclude blocks of voters known to be opposed to the government. Polling stations could be positioned in areas of government strength and distant from hostile communities.

In the contemporary period, these forms of electoral corruption have largely come to an end. However, the practicality and fundamental similarity of the Liberals and Conservatives have not diminished greatly. The atmosphere of practicality persists in the form of so-called brokerage politics. According to a classic definition of brokerage politics, the two parties act as "middlemen who select ... ideas ... they think can be shaped to have the widest appeal and ... try to sell a carefully sifted and edited selection of [them] to enough members of the electorate to produce a majority in the Legislature."[6] Brokerage politics is usually justified by liberal and conservative social scientists on the grounds that the pragmatism of the major parties helps to moderate and modify the diverse interests of a heterogeneous country.[7] Left-wing social scientists, however, express concern that the brokerage atmosphere obscures matters of social class and other issues deemed important.[8]

Movement parties do not display this atmosphere of practicality as extensively as the parliamentary parties. The movement parties arise in times of social crises to articulate grievances. Their leaders and adherents may not seek political office wholeheartedly at first. Instead, the aims of the movement party may be limited to obtaining only sufficient representation to impress the governing parliamentary party. If the party is primarily interested in radical social reform, political power is seen as a long-term goal and less important than educating the public. Whatever its objectives, the movement party may be satisfied with the election of only a handful of members, at least at the outset.

Bicultural, geographic, and class cleavages in society have profoundly affected the party system (See Section II: Political Cleavages). In this chapter, we shall examine the success of the parliamentary parties and the historic pre-eminence of one party over the other with particular reference to the bicultural and class cleavages.

The Quebec Basis of Pre-eminence

One of the more important electoral facts in Canadian history is that Quebec, the second most populous region and the only predominantly French and Catholic province, has a tendency to vote as a block. Without preponderant support from Quebec, the Conservatives could not have dominated the Canadian legislature between 1867 and 1896. Since then, Liberal pre-eminence has been based on the maintenance of a *Québec solide*.[9] French Canadians have a propensity to vote for a single party of cultural defence because of an anxiety about their subordinate position in the country. This position dates from the British conquest and their anxiety arises from the history of colonial regimes and from the intermittent outbursts of anti-French and anti-Catholic sentiment since Confederation (see Chapter 4: Bicultural Cleavage).

Support in Quebec is not an absolute requirement for victory. In 1957, John Diefenbaker secured a slim plurality of seats without significant representation from Quebec. In the election held less than one year later, Quebeckers elected 50 Conservative MPs to 25 Liberals. However, that Conservative hegemony under Macdonald and Liberal hegemony from Laurier to Trudeau were based on disproportionate support from Quebec suggests the value of strength in that province.

Over the range of Canadian history, both parties have contained immoderately anti-French and anti-Catholic elements in the English-speaking provinces. Among Catholics in Quebec, the Conservatives have had an equally strong pro-clerical wing while the Liberals have had an equally strong anti-clerical one. To secure victory in Quebec, the national leaders of the successful party must suppress the expression of anti-French sentiment among their supporters in English Canada and must prevent their supporters in Quebec from becoming embroiled in church-related conflict. The parliamentary leaders of the successful party must also include in their numbers one or more highly regarded spokesmen for Quebec. Hegemony has been certain to exist when one of the parliamentary parties satisfied all of the preceding conditions, while the other satisfied none.

On the level of propaganda, the pre-eminent party declares itself to be the party of national unity. To the French constituency, this myth means the party will protect French Canada's special interests; to the English-speaking constituency, the myth means the party will defend against extreme separatist tendencies in French Canada. To both cultural groups the myth of national unity implies that the opposition party is a source of ethnic and religious dischord. The pre-eminent party leadership does not hesitate to confirm the suspicion of ethnic and religious hostility in the opposition party through exaggeration and misrepresentation in its propaganda.

In the nineteenth century, Macdonald's relationship with Sir Georges-Etienne Cartier resulted in both the success and the later failure of the Conservative party. Macdonald and Cartier appreciated the nationalism of French Canada as well as the ambitions of English-Canadian businessmen. Advising the English-speaking population of Lower Canada in 1856, Macdonald said: "You struggle like the Protestant Irish in Ireland . . . not for equality, but for ascendancy . . . So long as the French have twenty votes they will be a power and must be conciliated."[10] Cartier knew that English-Canadian acceptance of policies to enhance French cultural identity had to be matched by French support for policies to foster English-led business. Cartier's leadership was important in the Conservative appeal to French-Canadian society because he was a moderate politician with sufficient skill to subdue the mutual distrust among the party's pro-clerical and moderate supporters in Quebec.

When Macdonald failed to unify the Quebec leadership after Cartier's death in 1873, the previously repressed sentiments of the clerically-minded burst into the open. The Quebec wing of the party came under the influence of the extreme ultramontane faction of Catholic opinion. At the head of this faction were the Bishops, who condemned all forms of political liberalism. They denounced the separation of church and state. They vigorously asserted and exercised their right of intervention in the political process. Communicants who voted Liberal were threatened with the loss of the sacrament. The succession to Cartier's position in the party and government was contested by Sir J. Adolphe Chapleau, a moderate, and Sir Hector Langevin, who represented the ultramontane party-church alliance. Langevin eventually displaced Chapleau because of Macdonald's vacillation, but failed to acquire Cartier's credibility among moderates in either Ontario or Quebec.[11]

The dilemma of Cartier's succession was highlighted by the divided attitudes in the Conservative party toward the fate of Louis Riel in 1885. The Métis leader and rebel was found guilty of treason by an English, Protestant jury in Regina. Recalling the death of an Ontario Orangeman on Riel's order in 1870, the Conservative Orange order demanded execution. Mindful that the jury in Regina had acquitted an English-speaking co-defendent of Riel's on grounds of insanity, Quebeckers demanded commutation. Macdonald assumed that party loyalties in Quebec were stable and that opinion in Ontario had to be assuaged. He therefore made the critical decision that Riel hang.

One historian has suggested that, if Macdonald had selected a single Quebec leader to succeed Cartier, the decision on Riel's fate would probably have been different.[12] However, both Chapleau and Langevin supported the decision not to commute Riel's death sentence. In the short run their united position probably precluded a sudden departure of Quebec MPs from the Conservative party. In the long run, however, Macdonald could not heal the split among Quebec Conservatives following Riel's execution, nor could he control the persistent outburst of anti-Catholic, anti-French Orangism in his Ontario wing. In both the Quebec and Ontario sections of the party, moderates lost ground to extremists.

The national pre-eminence of the Conservative party was sustained during the years following Riel's execution, but the signs of weakness were clear. Wilfrid Laurier, a Liberal MP, was already identified by Quebeckers as the leader of the national Liberal party. Before Macdonald's fateful decision, Laurier publicly declared personal sympathy for the violent actions of the rebels. The provincial Conservative government in Quebec was replaced in 1887 by an alliance of dissident Conservatives and Liberals led by the nationalist Honoré Mercier under the banner *parti national*. Mercier characterized the "murder" of Riel as a "declaration of war on the influence of French Canada in Confederation".[13] In the federal election of 1887, the Conservative plurality of 38 seats in Quebec was reduced to one.

Just as the origin of the Conservative party derived from the Macdonald-Cartier alliance in the Province of Canada, so the Liberal party had pre-Confederation roots in a bicultural alliance of moderates in the Province of Canada. In the campaign for responsible government in the 1840s, the coalition of Louis-H. Lafontaine, Robert Baldwin, and Sir Francis Hincks became the forerunner of the Liberal party.

However, with the achievement of responsible government in 1848, the Reform party began to disintegrate under the force of cultural sectionalism. The population in Canada West (Ontario) was larger than in Canada East (Quebec), but there was equal representation in the Canadian legislature from the two sections of the colonies. The English-speaking Reformers of Canada West demanded representation based on population. French Canadians in Canada East naturally feared that an English-speaking majority in the legislature would enact a series of anti-French policies. These fears were justified in view of the latent hostility toward the French and Catholic culture among the rural-based Grit supporters of the Reform party in Canada West. Consequently, French Canada switched its political loyalties from the Reformers to the Conservatives.

After 1854, the Reformers from the two sections of Canada found it impossible to cooperate with each other, let alone challenge the Macdonald-Cartier party. Reform leader George Brown's vituperative attacks on "French domination" and his affection for British institutions were matched in extremism by the Reformers of Canada East. Designated as the *parti rouge* and led by A. A. Dorion, they expressed

strong anti-clerical and pro-republican sentiments. In the eventual confusion and deadlock of Canadian politics, Brown and Dorion did form a
government, but it lasted only two days.[14] Brown's eventual entry into
coalition with the Macdonald-Cartier government in 1864 assisted not
only the project of Confederation, but also the continued ascendency of
the Conservative party.

In 1873 the Conservative government fell as a result of the CPR
Scandal and was replaced by a Liberal government. The Liberal party
was led at that time by Alexander Mackenzie, who was steeped in the
suspicions of rural, Grit Ontario. This was the time of the *rouges'* sub-
jection to the onslaught of the pious ultramontanes. The Liberal party
was thus hobbled by an anti-clerical Quebec leadership unacceptable
to the large body of Quebec society and an Ontario leadership still
mired in the anti-Catholic Grit opinions of pre-Confederation Canada
West. In 1878, the Conservatives returned to office.

Sir Wilfrid Laurier receives the most credit from historians for
reversing Liberal fortunes.[15] He was aided externally by a liberalized
Vatican and internally by Macdonald's inability to settle on a replacement for Cartier and by the execution of Riel. When Laurier became
leader of the Liberal party in 1887, he sought a new orientation for the
party. While the Conservative party was increasingly dominated by
immoderate elements in both Ontario and Quebec, Laurier gradually
removed the old *rouge* leaders in Quebec and thus dispelled the suspicions of Ontario Liberals and of pious Catholics in Quebec.

The end to Conservative pre-eminence was in the making well
before Macdonald's death in 1891. The defeat of the Northwest rebellion encouraged English-Canadian extremists to pursue their goal of
Anglo-Saxon dominance in the country. In Ontario, a prominent Conservative formed the Equal Rights Association to campaign for the at-
tenuation of French minority rights in education in the province. The
Manitoba School Act of 1890 destroyed similar rights in that province.
This Orangism also destroyed the now debilitated Conservative party.
Should the federal Conservative government intervene in the affairs of
a province and pass remedial legislation? For several years the Conservatives struggled vainly to resolve the conflict.

Laurier's response in the election of 1896 was a model for the new
party of pre-eminence. Moderation and "sunny ways" were his style. In
Quebec, he responded with neutrality and non-involvement in clerical
issues. There, many clericalists supported the Conservatives. In English Canada, he counselled compromise. There, many Orangeman
voted Conservative. But, in 1896, the Liberals came to power and the
Conservative party, dominated by extremists on cultural questions, slid
into the opposition role previously held by the Liberal party.

Conservative hegemony in Quebec in the nineteenth century was
based partly on exacerbating divisions in the opposition Liberal party.
In his last campaign, Macdonald continued to smear the Liberals with
the anti-clerical brush, though this characterization was increasingly
false. Today, Liberal hegemony in Quebec is maintained by an analogous strategy. Conservative support for conscription in World War I and

other foreign policy positions since then have provided the Liberals with evidence for their characterization of the Conservatives as the party of British imperialism. However, Liberal strategists have magnified the importance of such prejudices in the Conservative party (see Chapter 14: Foreign Policy).

In the period after 1891, the Conservatives outpolled the Liberals only once in Quebec. Following that rare event in 1958, Conservative Prime Minister John Diefenbaker failed to attract French-Canadian talent to the party and appointed unimpressive French-Canadians to insignificant portfolios. His ardently proclaimed "unhyphenated Canadianism" illustrated his insensitivity to French-Canadian cultural aspirations.[16] From the 1940s to the 1960s, the party depended intermittently upon the organization of the provincial *union nationale* party for support in federal elections in Quebec. Since that party's decline in provincial politics, the Conservative party has virtually ceased to exist in Quebec.

Robert Stanfield attempted to improve French-Canadian perceptions of his party. However, he was not successful in suppressing anti-French sentiments in his party. In the election in 1972, the Conservatives under Stanfield obtained 18% of the popular vote in Quebec, but only two of the province's 74 federal seats. At the same time, the Liberal government suffered a setback in the rest of Canada. The Liberal setback was publicly interpreted by Prime Minister Trudeau and by Jean Marchand, his Quebec lieutenant, as an "English backlash". This interpretation was unscholarly, but guileful. Once again, Liberal strategists sought to magnify the importance of anti-French and anti-Catholic sentiment in the Conservative party. In the backlash interpretation of the 1972 election, the message to French-Canadians was not to abandon "their" party in the next election as they had done in 1958. In English-speaking Canada, the message was an appeal to moderates to return to the "party of national unity".

This strategy was upheld in day-to-day tactical parliamentary activity. In 1973 the Liberal government encouraged parliamentary debate on the program which stemmed from the Official Languages Act of 1969. The Act extended the provision of federal services in both languages across the country and made bilingualism a more important factor for recruitment to and promotion within the federal civil service. In effect, this legislation meant an enhancement of the French language. The debate was an opportunity for the Liberal government to extol the virtues of the Act and for extreme Conservative backbenchers to publicly display again their hostility to French Canada.

In the election campaign of 1974, the Conservative leadership was again embarrassed by manifestations of extremism. Standfield was compelled to denounce and reject the Conservative candidacy of Leonard Jones, whose vigorous opposition to the Official Languages Act had been central to his career as mayor of Moncton. Jones defeated both the Conservative incumbent and the Liberal candidate. In Ontario and on the prairies, Conservative candidates openly criticized the Act in their personal campaigns. This antagonism was particularly noticeable in the unsuccessful effort to unseat the only Liberal cabinet minister on the prairies. Bicultural conflict was at the root of Stanfield's resignation one year later. Stanfield was perturbed that Conservative support in Quebec had not grown sufficiently to win more seats and that anti-French sentiment remained strong in the caucus.

The importance of a solid Quebec remains clear to Liberals, especially since they were not the sole benefactors of Diefenbaker's failure in the 1960s. The disillusion of Quebeckers was also expressed in their support for the *ralliement créditiste*, a populist party which combined reformist economic objectives with conservative values. Since 1962, the *créditistes* have reinforced the historic displacement of the Conservative party as a force in the federal politics of French Canada. A notable feature of Liberal governments since 1963, however, has been an increased role for French Canadians in the federal Cabinet and public service. The Official Languages Act also reinforced French-Canadian sympathy for the Liberal party. In 1974, the *créditiste* popular vote was halved from 1972 and the Liberals captured four of their fifteen seats.

In summary, the pre-eminence of a political party in national politics depends, in part, on a particular strategy related to the bicultural cleavage in Canada. A political party must capitalize on the tendency of Quebeckers to vote as a block and obtain solid support in that province. The leadership's strategy is to ensure that the Quebec wing of the party is cohesive and integrated in Quebec society. Historically, this strategy has meant being neutral or uninvolved in clerical vs. anti-clerical issues and neither repudiating nor satisfying extreme clericalist demands. At the same time, English-speaking elements of the party must not appear as hostile to French-Canadian society. Meanwhile, the opposition party is portrayed as unsympathetic, if not openly hostile, toward the survival of that community, while the pre-eminent party is styled as the party of national unity. Extraordinary effort is required to change popular perceptions because of the tenacity with which they are held. The advantage, therefore, is with the contemporary party of pre-eminence. A change in the relationship between the Conservative and Liberal parties to Quebec would essentially derive from Liberal error. Accumulated learning since the 1890s makes a change in present French-Canadian perception of the parties unlikely. The Liberal party itself is not on the verge of replicating the Conservative party's fate.

The Class Basis of Pre-eminence

Historically and currently, both parliamentary parties have relied almost exclusively on the economic elite in the Toronto and Montreal regions for financial support.[17] In other competitive party systems, trade unions and cooperative movements are major sources of party funds. In Canada, private firms have been the only major source of funds because trade unions and co-ops are not financially powerful. In the past, money was used to finance local vote-getting organizations.

Expenditures included floating friendly newspapers, paying "campaign workers" to intimidate opposition electors, and making it worthwhile for well-disposed electors to declare their vote. Today, such corruption is largely trivial in extent and the communication system is radically different (see Chapters 7 and 8). Millions of dollars are now required to finance campaigns conducted through the costly medium of television. The class basis of pre-eminence involves the acquisition of the economic elite's goodwill for funds and the projection of a reformist image for votes. In the short term, the Conservatives and the Liberals appear to be having difficulty raising funds from corporations under the revised election finance and tax laws of 1974. It remains doubtful, however, that these legislative changes will seriously alter the class-based formula for electoral success in the long term.[18]

Basically, the two parliamentary parties prefer to discount the existence of significant class differences in Canada. This basic strategem has been made more difficult since the depression of the 1930s and the rise of class-based organizations such as industrial trade unions, co-ops, and movement parties including the CCF-NDP. Beyond disclaiming the significance of class differences, each party has the dual task of proclaiming a commitment to social reform for mass consumption while not threatening the goodwill of their financial supporters.

The necessity to enact redistributive measures cannot be entirely avoided, however. The task in such cases is for the party leadership to portray reformist legislation to the masses as important and egalitarian, but to the economic elite as trivial. The politicians quietly reassure the elite that the measure stabilizes the economic system and protects it from radical reform; they tell the masses that the legislation is radical in order to forestall popular support for the potentially destabilizing socialist party.

If elite objections persist, the measure can be postponed, watered down, or enacted in such a manner as to be practically inoperative. In this century, the Liberal party enacted a national health plan fifty years after it was committed to such action. It was out of power for only ten of those years. The tax reform measures of the 1960s were significantly less redistributive when finally passed than when earlier proposed. The government nonetheless characterized them as significant if only by their continued designation as tax reforms. Existing anti-combines legislation appears radical because it makes certain business operations criminal offences. However, such mountains of evidence are required in protracted court proceedings that the intent of the law is rarely achieved. Occasionally, the federal government launches a concentrated attack on a highly visible but unpopular business. The prosecution in 1973 of K. C. Irving's newspaper empire in New Brunswick was not simply to demonstrate the effectiveness of anti-combine legislation, but also the progressiveness of the pre-eminent parliamentary party. Having redesigned his empire, Irvine was eventually successful on appeal, while the Liberal government could take popular credit for having initiated action. Generally, therefore, having introduced measures which are not fundamentally threatening to the economic elite, the party leadership still portrays them to the masses as important and egalitarian.

At the time of Confederation the links between party politicians and the economic elite in transportation and finance were well-known.[19] Undisguised conflicts of interest abounded. For example, Cartier was solicitor for the Grand Trunk Railway while he was solicitor-general of the Province of Canada. Sir Allan MacNab, a Conservative prime minister in the 1840s, stated openly that "railways are my politics." Similar connections were also found among leading reformers such as Sir Francis Hincks. George Brown's dedication to a transcontinental Confederation was predicated on benefits which would accrue to the economic elite of Canada West.[20] A social historian has termed Confederation a "political institution necessary for the pursuit of an economic project". The "privileged sector was to be that of the railroads" and groups associated with them.[21] Railway construction was an integral part of negotiations on the entry into Confederation of the Maritime colonies and later British Columbia.

To ensure pre-eminence on the class basis, however, parliamentary parties must not appear to be exclusively upper class. The Conservative government's railway policy was linked to party financing by private railway interests in the Pacific Scandal of the 1870s. The scandal resulted in the party's brief respite from power. Two financial syndicates — one each based in Toronto and Montreal — were formed in the early 1870s to compete for the government's generous support in this national project. The government sought unsuccessfully for an amalgamation of the two groups, but, following the election of 1872, it granted the Pacific Charter to a new group, which was in effect the Montreal syndicate. Shortly after the election, a Liberal MP levelled charges of corruption and bribery against Macdonald and Sir Hugh Allan, head of the group which ultimately received the Charter. Although Macdonald had told Allan that he would not promise the Charter in advance of the election, both Macdonald and Cartier had on different occasions sought money directly from Allan. The businessman therefore had reason to believe that a re-elected Conservative government would grant him the Charter.[22] Later that year, abandoned by some of his backbenchers, Macdonald resigned and the Governor-General chose Alexander Mackenzie to head the country's first Liberal government. In an election held early in 1874, the Liberals were returned to office with twice as many seats as the Conservatives.

A world-wide depression coincided with Mackenzie's government. His austerity program and his flirtation with reciprocity with United States did little for Liberal fortunes. In 1878, the electorate responded positively to Macdonald's "National Policy" of railway construction, large-scale western immigration, and tariff increases to return the Conservatives to office. A satisfied economic elite rewarded the Conservatives with fulsome support in their successful campaign in 1882.[23]

In the early years of Laurier's leadership, the Liberals continued to champion reciprocity with the United States. In the 1890s, though, Laurier moderated the policy and sought an alliance with the business community. By 1896, the accommodation between the Liberal party and the economic elite was complete. Laurier's expansionist economic policy was indistinguishable from Macdonald's. At the same time, the economic elite rewarded the two parties with equal generosity. However, Laurier's return to reciprocity in 1911 was fatal: business support was withdrawn and transferred to the Conservative party.[24]

In addition to the goodwill of the economic elite, the class basis of party pre-eminence requires a popular reformist imagery. Particularly in the mass democracy of the twentieth century, a party with an undiluted "big business" image cannot be popular. In this century, the Conservative party has chafed under such an upper class image. A strategic problem for the party since World War II is that it has this unpopular image without comparable support from the economic elite. At the same time, the Liberal party has that group support, but also a popular reform image. Undoubtedly the names of the parties reinforce their popular image. In 1942, Conservatives sought to project a new image by selecting a veteran Manitoba Progressive premier as their leader and designating the party Progressive Conservative.

Under the leadership of John Diefenbaker in 1957 and 1958, the Conservatives clearly projected a populist image in contrast to the boardroom leadership of the Liberal party. Social Credit representation was eliminated from Parliament and the CCF reduced to a corporal's guard. Pierre Trudeau owed much in his victory in 1968 and his near defeat in 1972 first to the strength then to the weakness of his progressive posture. By 1974, the Liberals had governed conservatively during a period of both high inflation and unemployment. However, the inclusion of a wage freeze in the Conservatives' anti-inflation policy in 1974 may have resulted in a swing of urban working-class voters in Ontario from both the Conservatives and the NDP to the Liberals to ensure Conservative defeat.[25]

The progressive image of the two parliamentary parties is illustrated in the posture of Sir John A. Macdonald and William Lyon Mackenzie King toward the trade union movement. In 1872, trade unionists in Toronto struck in demand for the nine-hour day. The employers responded with charges of seditious conspiracy. Macdonald interpreted the situation as a threat to his National Policy, which included immigration and the creation of a skilled labour force. He quickly engineered passage of two labour bills. The first act legalized trade unions and put Canadian workers on the same legal footing as their British counterparts. The second act, also based on British legislation, provided special penalties for criminal actions committed by workers. In justifying both the new status granted unions and the class distinctions introduced into criminal law, Macdonald asserted the wisdom of following the British model. However, the effect of the second law was to satisfy businessmen who were skeptical about his first act. Thus, an alliance was formed between the trade union movement and the party of the economic elite.[26]

From his early years in the civil service, Mackenzie King interpreted the role of government as a "third force" mediating the differences between labour and capital in the public interest. This seeming
neutrality nonetheless contained an effective bias toward the better
organized and financed forces of capital. The Industrial Disputes Investigation Act of 1907, created by King as deputy minister of labour,
equated the prohibition of strikes with an embargo on company lockouts. A dissatisfied work force was expected to maintain production
during a protracted period of conciliation in which the very recognition of the union was an issue.[27] Explaining the class neutrality of the
party he led for thirty years, King described the Liberal party as "broad
enough to include all classes who take a like attitude upon public
questions."[28] He left unsaid which class would be neglected when
public questions involved divergent class interests. The corporate basis
of party finance, the tendency to recruit leaders from the economic and
bureaucratic elite, and the appointment of well-to-do people to the
Senate suggests a bias favourable to the upper class.

The successful class-based strategy of the parliamentary party was
reflected in the cliché of Louis St. Laurent, King's successor, labelling
socialists as "Liberals in a hurry." This slogan from the 1950s implies
that the Liberal party, the contemporary party of pre-eminence, is essentially left-wing, but assures the rich that the redistribution of their
wealth may be postponed indefinitely. This extraordinary ambiguity or
flexibility enables the parliamentary party to enact laws on the basis of
its needs for electoral success or power rather than on the basis of
ideological convictions.

Foreign Policy and the Class Basis of Pre-eminence

The class strategy for pre-eminence is related to Canada's foreign policy. During their respective decades of pre-eminence, each parliamentary party had a sympathetic relationship with the economic elite. Historically, little autonomous entrepreneurial activity has been carried on
in Canada. The Canadian business elite was dependent on British business interests until after the turn of the century when American business interests became the major foreign source of economic initiative.
This shift in external economic dependence occurred as the United
States was replacing Britain as the most dominant national force in the
world. The dominant foreign power of the epoch has reinforced the
domestic strength of its Canadian party ally in return for a beneficial
economic relationship and support in international diplomacy.

At the level of party propaganda, the leadership of the pre-eminent
party describes this imperial relationship as necessary for national survival and the party itself as the political agent of national development.
Simultaneously, the opposition party is charged with being less convinced of Canada's independent future and disposed to a relationship
of inferiority between Canada and another foreign power. By this patriotic myth, the pre-eminent party exaggerates the innocuous affection

of the opposition party to a minor foreign elite and obscures its and Canada's real dependence on the dominant imperial power. Imperial services such as monetary support in times of economic stress, portrayed as national benefits, reinforce the party's pre-eminence.

As the pre-eminent party of the nineteenth century, the Conservatives bore the mantle of nation-builders and rebuked the Liberals for their flirtation with commercial reciprocity with the United States. Macdonald characterized Liberal tendencies to view Canada's future in association with United States as "little Canadianism" at best and as "veiled treason" at worst. Simultaneously, the Conservatives justified the more important dependence on British interests as necessary for the country's very survival. In this century the strategy persists, but party and national roles have changed. Liberal governments have condemned Conservative loyalty to a Britain in decline, while forging dependence on the United States. As the Conservatives had done in the nineteenth century, the Liberals now justify Canadian reliance on the United States as necessary for survival.

In both instances, the Canadian economic elite depended on friendly political relations between Canada and the dominant foreign power. The availability of financial and technological resources for the enhancement of the Canadian economy from Britain, later the United States, reinforced the strength and mutual regard of both Canada's economic and political elites. The imperial relation of the nineteenth century did not require as elaborate a disguise as the Liberals have woven in this century. The late nineteenth century was a proud moment for British imperialism. However, in this century, national self-determination has become a fetish of world diplomacy and was, in Canada's case, the myth by which Liberal governments weaned the country from its British dependence. Consequently, it behooved Liberal governments to minimize Canada's economic and military dependence on the United States by exaggerating Canada's diplomatic independence.[29]

Signs of a shift in both the party of pre-eminence and the source of economic dependence can be seen as early as the 1890s. The country was becoming an industrial nation and increasingly attractive to American businessmen. From its victory in 1896, the Liberal party was in a position to encourage and benefit from this transformation. The party had already sought and obtained American financial support in the election of 1891.[30] Affinity between American business and the Liberal party resulted from its traditional positive attitude to the United States. Laurier's self-immolation on the pyre of reciprocity in 1911 must have impressed Americans. A generation later, the Canadian economy slipped into American control while, in foreign policy, the King-St. Laurent Liberal governments adopted the post-World War II perspective of the United States, notably in Europe, East Asia, and the Middle East.[31] Meanwhile, the traditional connection of the Conservative party with Britain made Americans basically wary of that party. John Diefenbaker's avowed pro-British sentiments in the late 1950s and the Conservative Government's symbolic break with the United States in the 1960s no doubt diminished sympathy the party might have had from the American economic elite and their Canadian branch-plant executives.

The rise of the Liberal party did not stem only from increased American economic activity in Canada. The Conservative party would probably have been almost as pro-American as the Liberal party if it had remained pre-eminent in this century. Symbolically, Conservatives have been more pro-British, but the shift from British to American dependence extended beyond the economy. Similar changes also took place in the education and communication systems and in cultural values. New York and Washington replaced London as metropolitan centres of influence from which Canadians generally acquired their social goals and models of behaviour.

As a pragmatic necessity, both parties currently obtain funds from many American subsidiaries. But in 1891, Macdonald had successfully inveighed against the "veiled treason" of the Laurier Liberals. "A British subject I was born, a British subject I will die," he declared on the hustings.[32] Laurier's fatal revival of reciprocity twenty years later at best anticipated the future loyalties of Canada's economic elite. At that time the equity of British investors in Canada still surpassed American equity and the Canadian elite remained fearful of American penetration. It was the next generation of Liberal governments under Mackenzie King that altered the source of foreign economic dominance and the loyalty of Canada's economic elite. King's patriotic myth was not one of membership in empire, but of free partnership in a community of nations. This ostensible internationalism assisted or, more accurately, rationalized the transfer of Canada into the American empire.

Since the mid-1960s, a mood of economic nationalism among the public, including some prominent Liberals, presented the Liberal leadership with a dilemma. The party had to deal with nationalist sentiment without alienating the economic elite which, in many sectors of the economy, has become only a managerial extension of the American economic elite. In 1973, both the Canadian Chamber of Commerce and the Canadian Manufacturers Association were critical of the government's mild legislation to establish a board to review foreign purchases of Canadian businesses.

The Liberal party's position continues to be the traditional strategy on foreign policy and the class basis of pre-eminence. The party leadership accepts, with minor qualification, the dependence on the United States as necessary for economic well-being and future development. In this conviction it receives not only the support of the dependent Canadian economic elite, but also the approbation and sustenance of American economic and political leadership which reinforces its domestic pre-eminence. Meanwhile, the British connection, defended by the Conservative party, is portrayed as the real threat to national independence. The Liberals thus reduce the trivial remnants of the older and irrelevant imperialism such as the monarch's likeness on currency and postage. They discuss the merits of republicanism from time to time and react only mildly to the new and powerful imperialism of the United States.

Conclusion

The Liberal and Conservative parties have monopolized the government and chief opposition roles in federal politics. These parties originated in the context of parliamentary activity in contrast to the movement parties, which came into existence later in the context of social change or crisis. Their parliamentary origin gives the Liberals and Conservatives a flexibility lacking in the more rigid movement parties. This flexibility allows the two parties to adapt both policy and organization to meet the requisites for electoral victory.

Each of the parliamentary parties has been pre-eminent for a historic period: the Conservatives in the nineteenth century and the Liberals in the twentieth. The formula for pre-eminence consists of cultural and class components. The party must have the support of French Canadians. This support is obtained by having a Quebec wing which is integrated with Quebec society and an English-speaking section which is sympathetic to French-Canadian survival.

On the class cleavage, the party must obtain the goodwill of the economic elite, which is desirous of protecting its wealth, yet satisfy the masses that it is committed to a more egalitarian distribution of the country's wealth. The several tactics available to achieve this strategic objective may be summarized as obfuscation. Finally, there is an important foreign dimension to this class strategy. When pre-eminent, the Conservatives and Liberals have nurtured and, in return, have been sustained by economic links with Britain and the United States respectively. Ironically, the pre-eminent party has successfully described this major foreign involvement as necessary for the country's survival, while portraying the lesser party's more innocuous foreign disposition as damaging to national unity.

Notes

1. The origins of the parties and events subsequently mentioned here are discussed in detail in many Canadian history books such as Donald Grant Creighton, *Dominion of the North: A History of Canada* (Boston: Houghton Mifflin, 1944), Arthur R. M. Lower, *Colony to Nation: A History of Canada,* 4th ed. rev. (Don Mills, Ont.: Longmans, 1964), and Kenneth McNaught, *The History of Canada* (Toronto: Bellhaven House, 1970). The designations of the parties, particularly the Conservative party, have varied over time. The present name "Progressive Conservative" arose as a result of the selection of John Bracken, a long-time Progressive provincial premier as leader in 1942 of the then-styled National Conservative and before that the Liberal-Conservative party. Lower has constructed a valuable "Family Tree" of Canadian parties in *Colony,* "At end."

2. "Pearson ou l'abdication de l'esprit," Cité Libre, 56 (April 1963), 7–12.

3. J. M. Beck, Pendulum of Power, Canada's Federal Elections (Scarborough, Ont.: Prentice-Hall, 1968), 194, 209.

4. See the account by Judy LaMarsh, one of Pearson's advisors, Memoirs of a Bird in a Gilded Cage (Toronto: McClelland and Stewart, 1968), 17–18, 26–31.

5. Escott M. Reid, "The Rise of National Parties in Canada," Papers and Proceedings of the Canadian Political Science Association, IV (1932).

6. J. A. Corry and J. E. Hodgetts, Democratic Government and Politics (Toronto: University of Toronto Press, 1959), 221.

7. Frank Underhill, "The Development of National Political Parties in Canada," The Canadian Historical Review, 16:4 (1935), 367–387.

8. For a left-wing analysis of brokerage politics, see Chapter 6 below, "Class Cleavage," by N. H. Chi and John Porter, The Vertical Mosaic: An Analysis of Social Class and Power in Canada (Toronto: University of Toronto Press, 1965), 373–377.

9. Alan C. Cairns has demonstrated that the electoral system exaggerates regional voting in parliamentary representation. "The electoral system and the party system in Canada, 1921–1965," Canadian Journal of Political Science, 1:1 (1968), 61–62.

10. A letter published in the Montreal Gazette quoted in J. H. Stewart Reid et al., A Source-book of Canadian History, selected documents and personal papers (Toronto: Longmans, rev. 1964), 143.

11. Lower, Colony, 372, 401–2, 438; McNaught, History, 161–2, 180.

12. McNaught, History, 180.

13. Ibid.

14. The travails of party politicians in the Province of Canada are recounted in Creighton, Dominion, 282–286; Lower, Colony, 300–311; McNaught, History, 117–123.

15. Creighton, Dominion, 383–4; Lower, Colony, 391, 400–402; McNaught, History, 161–2, 187.

16. See Peter Stursberg's account of Diefenbaker in office, Diefenbaker: Leadership Gained, 1956-1972 (Toronto: University of Toronto Press, 1975).

17. K. Z. Paltiel, Political Party Financing in Canada (Toronto: McGraw-Hill Ryerson, 1970), 4–5, 19–42.

18. By late 1975, however, there was evidence of a decrease in contributions from large corporate donors. The Watergate shame in the United States encouraged a general mood of caution among corporate officials. Furthermore, some U.S.-based corporations in Canada were under new instructions from their head offices as a result of unfavourable publicity created by U.S. Senate investigations of the foreign political involvements of American corporations.

19. Creighton, Dominion, 283; Lower, Colony, 286–289; McNaught, History, 107, 113–115.

20. Creighton, Dominion, 291–292.

21. Alfred Dubuc, "The Decline of Confederation and the New Nationalism," in Peter Russell's Nationalism in Canada (Toronto: McGraw-Hill, 1966), 114, 116.

22. See accounts of the Scandal in Creighton, Dominion, 334; Lower, Colony, 363–365; McNaught, History, 150–3.

23. See Beck's account of the two elections, Pendulum, 30–44.

24. Clifford Sifton, one of Laurier's ministerial architects of prosperity, abandoned the party and undertook to organize an anti-Liberal campaign among businessmen and bankers in Toronto who had hitherto supported Laurier. See Creighton, *Dominion*, 431–434; Lower, *Colony*, 433–434; McNaught, *History*, 202.

25. A preliminary interpretation of the 1974 election survey data challenges this widely accepted view, see Jane Jensen et al., "The 1974 Election: A Preliminary Report," a paper presented to the annual meeting of the Canadian Political Association (Edmonton: June 1975).

26. For an account of Macdonald's relations with the trade union movement, see Bernard Ostry, "Conservatives, Liberals, and Labour in the 1870s", *The Canadian Historical Review*, 41:2 (1960), 93–127; "Conservatives, Liberals, and Labour in the 1880s," *The Canadian Journal of Economics and Political Science*, 27:2 (1961), 141–161.

27. For accounts of King's early career and his progressivism, see Robert Craig Brown and Ramsay Cook, *Canada 1896–1921: a nation transformed* (Toronto: McClelland and Stewart, 1971), 119–123. See also H. S. Ferns and B. Ostry, *The Age of Mackenzie King: the Rise of the Leader* (London: William Heinemann, 1955), 46–76, and Robert MacGregor Dawson, *William Lyon Mackenzie King: a political biography 1874–1923* (Toronto: University of Toronto Press, 1958), 136.

28. Canada House of Commons, *Debates* (1922), quoted in Reid, *A Source-book*, 410.

29. For an eloquent and powerful "lament" on Canada's fate in which its role in the American "imperial system" is central, see George Grant, *Lament for a Nation: The Defeat of Canadian Nationalism* (Toronto: McClelland and Stewart, 1965).

30. P. B. Waite, *Canada 1874–1896: Arduous Destiny* (Toronto: McClelland and Stewart, 1971), 223.

31. In his *Dominion of the North* which ends at 1939, Creighton shows little concern with growing dependence on American business. Contrast this with his account of Canada's economic development in *Canada's First Century, 1867–1967* (Toronto: Macmillan, 1970), 180–181, 251–252, 283–287, 321. See also, McNaught, *History*, 191, 214–15, 294–297.

32. Beck, *Pendulum*, 63.

CHAPTER 3
FRAGMENT AND MOVEMENT PARTIES

John McMenemy

Introduction

Movement and fragment parties became an important feature of the Canadian party system in this century. They arose as a result of tensions and crises associated with the three major political cleavages in Canada — bicultural, geographic, and class. Third parties appeared federally during the early decades of the twentieth century, when Canadian society experienced the stresses of industrialization, urbanization, and the transcontinental settlement and integration of a large immigrant population. Some of these parties were short-lived, while others, notably the CCF-NDP and Social Credit, endured because of their popular and group bases of support.

Canada's parliamentary system also assisted the development of third parties. Under the Westminster parliamentary system employed in this country, the focus of electoral activity is the constituency election. The election of only a handful of Members of Parliament gives minor parties a certain legitimacy and credibility. The government is obliged to respond to their criticism and to their procedural motions in House of Commons debate. By contrast, the American practice of separating the executive and the legislature results in costly, winner-take-all contests for the presidency. Because third party campaigns for the White House are practically doomed to failure and are therefore so completely unrewarding, ideological movements and reform groups are encouraged to find a niche in one of the two omnibus parties rather than to maintain a separate existence.

Third parties in Canada have experienced considerable success at the provincial level, yet none has actually come close to forming a federal government. In 1921, the Progressive party elected sufficient MPs to qualify for the opposition role, but refused to accept the responsibility. Movement parties have displaced parliamentary parties in federal elections in some cities, rural areas, and entire provinces.

Just as the genesis of the parliamentary parties has affected their subsequent behaviour, so too the fates of movement and fragment parties have been influenced by their circumstances of birth. In general, third parties in Canada can be classified as fragment parties, populist and socialist movement parties, and mixed fragment-movement parties. Fragment parties such as the Nationalists of the 1900s and the Reconstruction party of 1935 are organizations with leaders who have abandoned their elite position in a parliamentary party. Their new parties articulate popular grievances, but are short-lived because they lack the grass-roots involvement and group affiliation which would sustain them. By contrast, movement parties are the electoral expression of social movements whose longevity is assisted by support from highly-committed followers and affiliated groups. Populist movement parties such as the Social Credit party and the *ralliement créditiste* tend to be leader-oriented and pragmatic. Socialist movement parties — the CCF-NDP — tend to be program-oriented and less pragmatic. The Progressive party of the 1920s was an example of a mixed fragment-movement party. Its parliamentary leader, T. A. Crerar, an MP from Manitoba and a former Liberal Unionist minister, represented the fragment element. The movement faction was a popular organization in Alberta which grew out of an aggressive farmers' movement.

Fragment Parties

Fragment parties exist as a result of conflict within the elite of a parliamentary party. The fragment party is established by an individual who leaves the elite of a parliamentary party after failing to sway it to his opinion in a given conflict. While the fragment party expresses a popular grievance, the party has no mass base of support. The fragment's leadership is out of touch with those groups whose support would give it sustaining power. Moreover, the elitist or aristocratic career of a fragment party leader does not equip him with the talents, connections, or perhaps even the inclination to develop a mass membership organization. Consequently, fragment parties are evanescent and the subsequent political careers of their leaders are often short-lived as well. Given the inherent pragmatism and flexibility of parliamentary parties on personnel and policy questions (see Chapter 2: Parliamentary Parties), an elite personality in a parliamentary party who was in touch with popular groups would likely find himself and his policies accommodated within the party hierarchy. For example, although he was popular with neither Prime Minister Pierre Trudeau nor the welfare wing of the Liberal cabinet, Finance Minister John Turner's fiscal conservativism was accommodated on a range of issues in 1974 and 1975 because of Turner's strong links to party workers and the public.

When an individual resigns from the elite of a parliamentary party as a protest, he at once signals his political weakness. The identity of the resultant fragment party is defined in terms of the founding or leading personality rather than in terms of popular group support. Henri Bourassa was essential to the Nationalists, H. H. Stevens to the Reconstruction party, W. D. Herridge to the New Democracy, and Paul Hellyer to Action Canada. However, no successful party can base its fortunes entirely on leadership. The Liberals were a little more distressed by the Nationalists than by the Reconstruction party, and both the Liberals and Conservatives were inconvenienced a little by the New Democracy. However, even the Nationalist subversion of the Liberal base in Quebec was temporary. In the 1960s, Paul Hellyer left the Liberal party to form Action Canada. However, he soon foresaw the likely fate of his embryonic party and dissolved it. He joined the Conservatives and was subsequently defeated.

The Nationalists

The Nationalist movement was an elite-led fragment party lacking a mass membership organization. Nonetheless, it was a vehicle for some genuine French-Canadian anxieties. The industrialization of Canada brought stressful conditions to a traditional French-Canadian society. The issues addressed by the Nationalists were social and economic as well as the strictly cultural questions of religion and language. The mainstay of the movement was the personality and leadership of Henri Bourassa.[1]

By 1904, Quebec was the crucial power base for the Liberal party. In the election of that year, the party took approximately 55% of the province's vote and more than 80% of the seats. Votes and seats in Ontario were almost evenly divided between the Liberals and Conservatives. The rest of the country contained fewer seats than either of the central provinces. At the turn of the century, it had been commonly assumed that Bourassa would succeed Sir Wilfrid Laurier as Liberal leader. However, as he approached the height of his career, Laurier found that Bourassa represented the greatest threat in his home province. The Nationalist leader was estranged from Laurier and the Liberal party on matters relating to imperialism and the maintenance of French Canada's cultural identity.

Bourassa became the predominant spokesman for French nationalism. He resigned his seat in the Commons over Canadian participation in the Boer War. He vigorously opposed Laurier's compromise on the autonomy bill of 1905 which provided no constitutional guarantees for separate schools in the new provinces of Saskatchewan and Alberta. He objected to the puritanical Lord's Day Act of 1906 and cited it as evidence of Laurier's inability to control attacks on French cultural values. Rejecting federal politics for the provincial arena, he won election to the Quebec legislature in 1908. There, he worked an uneasy alliance with the provincial Conservatives. Although hostile to Laurier and the Liberal party, Bourassa remained neutral in the federal election of 1908, in which the Liberals again took over 80% of the seats in Quebec with 56% of the votes. Two years later, Bourassa founded *Le Devoir*, a newspaper which became an important vehicle and galvanizing force of nationalist opinion.

In the same year, Laurier provided his Nationalist and Conservative opponents with a major electoral issue. Laurier responded to the "German peril" by creating a small Canadian navy. The Nationalists protested that French Canadians would now inevitably be involved in a British war. At this time, Conservative leader Robert Borden publicly opposed the naval defence bill, apparently because of its long-term commitment to British Imperial policy. Borden nonetheless demanded an emergency contribution to the British navy. In the election of 1911, the Conservative party in Quebec worked in close alliance with Bourassa and the Nationalists. Meanwhile, reciprocity was a more important anti-Liberal issue for English-speaking businessmen, who worked against the Liberals by contributing generously to the Nationalist treasury and to *Le Devoir*, its organ.[2]

Laurier's defeat in 1911 was accompanied by Bourassa's failure to achieve the balance of power in the House of Commons. The Liberal bastion of solid Quebec was split and Bourassa's *autonomiste* candidates won most of the seats not won by the Liberals. At the same time, however, the opposition to reciprocity in English Canada was so cohesive that a majority of seats fell to the more imperialistic of the two parliamentary parties.

The Nationalist movement and Bourassa's career rose and fell dramatically in that period. The election in 1917 brought to a head the most serious bicultural crisis in Canada's history; Quebeckers were reunited in the Laurier Liberal party. For English-speaking Canadians, the war effort was a moral obligation, while for French Canadians it was service to British imperialism. Held only a few months after the enactment of conscription, the election of 1917 was predictably schismatic. The polarized politics of wartime Canada had no room for a third party. Bourassa supported the Laurier Liberals, although his aid was unnecessary in Quebec and a liability in English-speaking Canada. The Liberal candidates won 62 of Quebec's 65 seats and almost 75% of the vote. For the first time since Confederation, no French-Canadian Conservative was elected in the province and only 20 anti-Unionist Liberals won seats outside Quebec.[3]

After 1917, Bourassa's influence became restricted increasingly to the readership of *Le Devoir*. In 1921, he supported the Progressive party. However, the spectre of such an alliance to subvert Liberal Quebec proved illusory. Though led now by an English Canadian, William Lyon Mackenzie King, the Liberals took every seat in Quebec with 70% of the votes. The Conservative party obtained less than 20% of the vote. Bourassa was not a candidate in 1921, but was elected as an Independent in 1925 and 1926. Liberal party success has since been based in part on substantial support in Quebec. During World War II, nationalist sentiment flared briefly in response to King's conscription policy. In 1945, the successor to Bourassa's Nationalists, the *bloc populaire*, fielded 35 candidates in Quebec and two in Ontario. However, it elected only two members in Quebec with approximately 10% of the provincial vote.

The Nationalists of the early 1900s objected strenuously to measures which appeared to threaten the cultural identity of French Canada. In 1907, a nationalist-minded Liberal MP demanded that the French language be "placed on a footing of equality" with English in the federal public service.[4] In the following decade, nationalist opinion in Quebec was enraged by the attacks on French language rights in education in Manitoba and Ontario. The restriction on usage and instruction in French in Ontario was particularly objectionable as it affected large Franco-Ontarian communities along the Ontario-Quebec provincial boundary, including Ottawa.[5]

Since World War II, debate over French language rights has replaced religion as the public expression of English-French antagonism. Liberal governments have sought to forestall the creation of a potent political vehicle of French nationalism outside its ranks. A Liberal government created the Royal Commission on Bilingualism and Biculturalism in the 1960s. With the passage and implementation of the Official Languages Act since 1969, the Liberal government has maintained a visibly supportive posture on French language rights and usage in Canada. In 1974, the provincial Liberal government declared French to be the sole official language of Quebec.

The political expression of nationalist sentiment outside the Liberal organization is now channeled through the provincial *parti québécois* led by René Lévesque, formerly a member of a provincial Liberal cabinet. In the provincial election of 1973, the Liberals won almost every seat. However, the PQ, which formed the official opposition with only six seats, received 30% of the vote. An anti-Liberal appeal by the *péquistes* (PQ) for Quebec voters to spoil their ballots in the federal election of 1972 probably accounts for the large number of spoiled ballots — twice the national and three times the Ontario percentage among votes cast. As long as nationalist electoral politics remains basically a provincial manifestation, federal Liberals need not anticipate a Bourassa-style fragmentation of their federal representation.[6]

The Nationalist movement, then, was a fragment party articulating popular grievances related to the bicultural cleavage. Its leader, Henri Bourassa, was a disgruntled member of the Liberal party elite. Without an effective grass-roots organization, the party failed to survive its first election and only temporarily disturbed Liberal hegemony in Quebec. Nonetheless, nationalist sentiment has persisted in French Canada and both the federal and provincial Liberal elites have sought to preclude the appearance of another nationalist political party. Currently, nationalist debate centres on language rights. By adopting the most pro-French language policy which English Canada could tolerate, federal Liberals have limited the electoral expression of Bourassa-style party nationalism to provincial politics. While mass opinion in Quebec has become radical, *Le Devoir* continues as a platform for the nationalism of the elite loyal to Bourassa's federalism. *Le Devoir's* editor became co-chairman of the federal Royal Commission on Bilingualism and Biculturalism. In this decade, the paper has refused to support the PQ in elections. Consequently, the *péquistes* felt obliged to found their own nationalist newspaper, *Le Jour*.

The Reconstruction Party, the New Democracy, and Action Canada

The depression of the 1930s prompted the creation of two ill-fated fragment parties, the Reconstruction party and the New Democracy movement. In 1969, relatively modest economic problems impelled the creation of a fragment organization called Action Canada, which rose briefly and with less success. Led by disaffected members of a parliamentary party elite who possessed neither mass nor group support, none of these fragment parties acquired even the influence of the Nationalists. The Reconstruction party did not survive its dismal performance in 1935, the New Democracy barely contested the election of 1940, and Action Canada was dissolved before it contested a single election.

In 1934, H. H. Stevens resigned from R. B. Bennett's cabinet after the Conservative prime minister objected to his minister's charges of profiteering by large retail stores and packing houses. Stevens withdrew his resignation in return for the chairmanship of a select parliamentary committee on price spreads and mass buying. The committee received widespread attention as Stevens's criticisms were substantiated. Rebuked later by Bennett, Stevens resigned from the cabinet and became a member of a royal commission which examined his complaints and reported recommendations in line with his views. The government's legislative response to the depression was feeble, partly because of constitutional limitations on the federal government, but also because of the strength of business influence on Bennett. As a result, Stevens resigned from the Conservative party to form the Reconstruction party. The Reconstruction program was of course based on Stevens's earlier recommendations for coping with unfair competition and profiteering.[7]

The election of 1935 marked both the beginning and the end for the party. Its electoral experience highlighted not only the fate of fragment parties in Canada but also of parties with small, spatially diffused electoral support.[8] Compared to the new CCF and Social Credit parties, the Reconstruction party did well in terms of the popular vote. It had few candidates in Saskatchewan and Alberta. However, in Ontario where there were no Social Credit candidates, it received 11% of the vote to the CCF's 8%. Reconstruction candidates also obtained a healthy 14% and 10% of the vote in Nova Scotia and New Brunswick respectively, where there were neither CCF nor Social Credit candidates. Nationally, the Reconstruction party received twice as many votes as Social Credit and only a few thousand votes less than the CCF. However, party strength was concentrated sufficiently in only one of 174 contested constituencies to give it a victory. Stevens was the party's sole successful candidate.

Five years later, Bennett's brother-in-law and confidant, W. D. Herridge, was moved for reasons similar to Stevens's to leave the Conservative party and sponsor another fragment party, the New Democracy. This movement also lacked organization and had only a handful of candidates from Ontario westward in the election of 1940. In Alberta, the New Democracy and Social Credit became intertwined. Outside Alberta the party received only token support; Herridge lost his own contest.[9]

The Reconstruction party and the New Democracy arose in response to class-related grievances. As fragment parties, they were publicly defined in terms of a personality who had been associated prominently with one of the parliamentary parties. While Stevens and Herridge might articulate widespread and keenly felt grievances, the lack of mass membership and organizational support contributed significantly to their failures. Competition from socialist and populist movement parties was a further hindrance to the Reconstruction and New Democracy movements. Moreover, like Henri Bourassa, after the dissolution of the Nationalists, neither Stevens nor Herridge managed to re-acquire their earlier status in public affairs.

In 1972, a disaffected Liberal cabinet minister abandoned a similar attempt to form a fragment party. Paul Hellyer had been a serious contender for the leadership in 1968. But he resigned from the cabinet in 1969 and left the Liberal party two years later to form Action Canada. Like Stevens and Herridge before him, Hellyer offered a non-socialist response to economic grievances occasioned by high unemployment and high inflation.[10] Hellyer abandoned Action Canada as a political vehicle before the subsequent election in 1972 and found refuge in the Conservative party. No doubt he divined that a political fate similar to Stevens's and Herridge's awaited him if he pursued his fragment party project. Nonetheless, his plurality from his last election as a Liberal in 1968 was severely reduced in 1972; he was defeated by his Liberal opponent in 1974. Like Henri Bourassa three generations earlier, Hellyer turned to journalism.

Movement Parties

In contrast to fragment parties which articulate popular sentiment but originate within the hierarchy of a parliamentary party, movement parties originate in society. Moreover, group support for movement parties has resulted in sustained, if attenuated, electoral success. However, unlike Britain, where Labour displaced the Liberal party in this century, no Canadian movement party has posed a serious challenge to either of the parliamentary parties at the national level. As long as the most salient political division is the bicultural division, class- and region-based movement parties cannot achieve more than minor status in Parliament. Class parties will not acquire major status until the mass of French Canadians, who constitute the largest single block of voters, are confident that their cultural integrity is sufficiently protected from assimilation. At the national level, class parties also face the frustration that much welfare and labour legislation is provincial; as well, they are frustrated by an electoral system which diminishes the impact of small parties with spatially diffused support (see Chapter 7: Elections). In

Britain, a unitary state, the rise of class cleavage and the decline of religious cleavage enabled the mass-based and trade union supported Labour party to displace the less effective of the two parliamentary parties.[11]

There are important differences among Canada's movement parties. The populist Social Credit and *ralliement créditiste* are pragmatic organizations relative to the socialist Cooperative Commonwealth Federation, now the New Democratic party, which is more value- and program-oriented. The pragmatism of Social Credit has enabled its leadership to respond to regional values, thereby achieving success as a regional or provincial party. However, Social Credit's ability to articulate regional grievances has made it correspondingly unsuccessful on a national level. Meanwhile, recent provincial successes notwithstanding, the systematic and universal values of the socialist party have historically made it difficult for the CCF-NDP to respond as easily to distinctive regional attitudes. However, the central place afforded the international value system has resulted in a compatible nation-wide leadership. The recent provincial successes of the NDP derive from the weaknesses within the incumbent regimes, from the recently acquired talent of provincial socialist leaders for responding to local grievances, and from anti-East sentiment in the western periphery of the country. Certainly, the success is not derived from widespread adoption of the international values of socialism.

The Populist Party

The Social Credit party was successful in Alberta, where farm organizations had a history of militant activism. The evangelist William Aberhart joined this agrarian activist tradition with church-related support for Social Credit during the depression years. The Social Credit movement advocated a peculiar program of monetary reform; however, its strength was in the agrarian group support inherited from the United Farmers of Alberta and popular enthusiasm created by Aberhart's demagoguery. As a political movement, Social Credit became an alternative to the Conservative and Liberal parties and to the now ineffective provincial UFA government, which had forged links with the new socialist CCF.[12]

From 1925 Aberhart preached a literal interpretation of the Bible on weekly radio broadcasts emanating from Calgary. Converted to Social Credit's economic doctrines in 1932, he became the first person to exploit radio broadcasting for political purposes in Canada. In his weekly sermons broadcast from the Prophetic Bible Institute, Aberhart publicized the Social Credit movement as a vehicle of religious and political salvation. Study sessions on Social Credit were held in church halls as Aberhart garnered Mormon and fundamentalist support in Alberta.

In 1934, Aberhart's educational movement became a political party. In the provincial election of 1935, Social Credit won 54% of the vote and 89% of the seats, so Aberhart became premier of Alberta. In the federal election two months later, the party received 47% of the vote in Alberta and 88% of the seats. The party had candidates only in the western provinces and received only half of the national vote gathered separately by the CCF and Reconstruction parties. Yet, Social Credit won 17 seats compared to 7 for the CCF and 1 for the Reconstruction party. Almost 30 years of Social Credit representation in Parliament was based on this sectional strength in Alberta and later in British Columbia.[13] In Alberta, Social Credit retained provincial office until 1970. In British Columbia, Social Credit has controlled the province for all but three years since 1952.

From 1935 to 1958, the party had minor representation in the House of Commons. Most Socred MPs came from Alberta with occasional representation from British Columbia. The federal caucus of 19 MPs in 1957 was the party's largest. However, less than one year later, the Diefenbaker landslide obliterated Social Credit representation in the House. The Social Credit candidates still won 20% of the popular vote in Alberta in 1958, but the "Diefenbaker candidates" garnered about 60% of the vote and won all the seats. During the 1960s, the Conservatives maintained federal dominance in Alberta and, since the dissolution of the western Social Credit party in 1965, the Conservatives have monopolized federal representation from that province.

In 1962, Social Credit erupted in Quebec, electing 26 MPs. As was the case in Alberta, Social Credit's popularity resulted from its response to genuine popular grievances in a style sympathetic to regional cultural values. The efforts of thousands of party members and the popular appeal of the regional leader, Réal Caouette, were important factors in *créditiste* success. While Aberhart pioneered the political use of radio, Caouette was the first Canadian politician to exploit television successfully. As in Alberta, the party in Quebec was a political vehicle for the expression of sectional and class bitterness among rural and small-town inhabitants toward the economic and political leadership of the country. "You don't have to know all about Social Credit before you vote for it," Aberhart had told Albertans in 1935. "*Vous n'avez rien à perdre. Votez créditiste*," exhorted Caouette almost thirty years later. In addition, the rise of Social Credit in Quebec was facilitated by the weakness of the second parliamentary party in the region, the Conservatives. Since 1962, *créditiste* MPs have assiduously concerned themselves with the welfare of their constituents to insure re-election. In that year, the *créditistes* displaced the Conservative party as the second party in Quebec in terms of seats won. A year later, the *créditistes* also displaced the Conservatives in popular vote.[14]

The western and Quebec-based sections of the party had leaders who were compatible with their regional supporters, but not with each other. The eastern and western elites of the movement were never successfully integrated. Friction developed between Caouette and Robert Thompson, the formal leader. Even the two Social Credit provincial premiers divided their federal support between Caouette and Thompson. Meanwhile, Diefenbaker's "prairie populism" bolstered the Conservatives in the West and thus precluded the re-assertion of the western Social Credit movement in federal politics. At the same time, Diefenbaker's "unhyphenated Canadianism" strengthened the créditistes in Quebec at the Conservatives' expense. As leader and prime minister, Diefenbaker elevated a number of Western-Canadian politicians to national prominence and recruited a large reservoir of western MPs to the Conservative party. He refused to grant comparable status to French-Canadians in his large caucus. Even after his involuntary departure from the leadership in 1967, he continued to symbolize western populism in the Conservative party. This populism is also represented by such Albertan MPs as Eldon Woolliams and Jack Horner.

In 1965, Caouette separated his ralliement créditiste from the Social Credit party, which dissolved before the election that year. Since then, the Conservatives' share of the popular vote in Quebec has surpassed the créditistes' share in three of the four elections, but the wide distribution of those votes has produced fewer Conservative seats than créditiste. In 1974, the popular vote in Quebec for the créditistes, regrouped once more as the Social Credit Party of Canada, was halved to 18% compared to the Conservatives' 21%. The créditistes, however, still won 11 seats to the Conservatives' 3. Since then, Caouette, an ailing leader, has sought to prepare his son for the succession to leadership.

In summary, the populist movement parties are distinguished by a pragmatism and leader-orientation which permits the exploitation of regional cultural characteristics in their expression of class and sectional interests. Unlike socialists, populists are not constrained by a wide, international dissemination of beliefs, conventions, and documents which are supposed to establish for all time the movement's principles. Populists are hence more able to appeal to purely regional or ethnic anxieties. The religious fundamentalism of Aberhart suited Alberta better than the cross-cultural appeal of secular socialism. In Quebec, the traditionalism of Caouette was more congruous with conservative-catholic culture than the socialism of the NDP, which had been repeatedly repudiated by the church. However, the populist party has had to bear the costs of an incompatible national leadership as well as inconsistent and unpredictable policies. Because of a leadership oriented to regional values and customs, the populist party is not likely to become a major national force and is vulnerable to dissolution upon the retirement of the leader and the possible succession of someone incompatible with the regional cultural environment. The vulnerability of populist parties is shown by the swift declines of provincial Social Credit in Alberta and of the union nationale in Quebec upon the departures of Premiers E.C. Manning and Maurice Duplessis.

The Socialist Party

The socialist party has been more successful than the populist party in terms of broad, national support, the cohesiveness of that support, and the national integration of its leadership. Also, socialists in Canada have benefited from the legitimacy of socialism abroad, particularly in

Western Europe and Scandinavia. This internal strength and external legitimacy have not automatically resulted in electoral popularity. United within by an international value system, the socialist movement has not been able to exploit class and regional grievances among a population for whom traditional cultural loyalties remain politically potent. The national weakness of the socialist party is directly related to the weakness of class as a determinant of national party support. If the class cleavage were an important determinant of support, the cohesive and integrated socialist party could be a major electoral force.[15]

In Quebec, the socialist party has been unable to distract French Canadians from their traditional anxiety about cultural survival. Also, socialists in the past had to contend with the hostility of the Catholic church, which is now too weak to be relevant in an electoral sense. Thus, when the parliamentary parties lost working-class support in Quebec in the early 1960s, it was lost largely to culturally indigenous *créditiste* candidates or to non-voting. Only when the two cultural groups attain an equal footing and the cultural apprehensions of French-Canadians have lessened might the socialist party attract large-scale French support.

Marked class distinctions exist in Maritime society. However, the population there appears unwilling to abandon traditional party loyalties and jeopardize established patterns of patronage by voting socialist. Dissatisfied Maritimers leave the region for a "better life" in Ontario. Historically, the socialist party has been popular on the prairies, particularly in Saskatchewan, as an anti-eastern and anti-big business party. However, because of its small population, few parliamentary seats are allocated to the prairie region. Only in Ontario and British Columbia, where most of the unionized working class reside and where a large number of seats are at stake, have the political importance of class and the affiliation of some unions with the party given socialist strategists hope for growth.

While an increase in class-based voter behaviour would undoubtedly improve the party's fortunes, the socialist leadership modified the party's commitment to economic change around 1960. Since then, it has concentrated on the improvement of electoral organization. Originally called the Cooperative Commonwealth Federation, the socialist party was an amalgam of farm, labour, and intellectual groups. Meeting in Calgary in 1932 and Regina in 1933, the founders of the CCF defined their party as anti-capitalist and socialist and chose Labour MP J. S. Woodsworth as leader.[16] The Regina Manifesto of 1933, the basic document of the party until 1956, committed the party to public ownership of industries and government planning to achieve "genuine democratic self-government, based on economic equality."

As a federation of many groups and movements, the CCF was structured to permit grass-roots participation in policy debate and leadership selection. CCFers thus rejected the model of the parliamentary parties which, in their view, were dominated by cliques of eastern politicians and businessmen. In general, the regular involvement of a membership highly committed to the socialist legacy of the depression has brought cohesion to the party. The intense involvement of members has also denied the CCF elite a flexibility comparable to that of the elite in the parliamentary parties. The transformation of the CCF to the New Democratic party in the years 1958 to 1961 can be viewed as a departure from the party's democratic norms. In one sense, the change to the NDP was a monumental revision of socialist goals conceived and directed by the party leadership.

The CCF elite sought to divert their party from its apparent fate as a moribund party of protest. The party had achieved its summit in 1945. Three years earlier, an obscure CCF candidate had defeated Arthur Meighen, a former Conservative prime minister, in a federal by-election. In September 1943, most of the respondents in a national Gallup poll favoured the CCF. In the same year, the party formed the official opposition in Ontario and in 1944 formed an administration in Saskatchewan that lasted twenty years. However, the federal CCF never improved on its performance in 1945 when it elected 28 MPs with 15% of the popular vote.

The Winnipeg Declaration of 1956 became the basic document signalling a redefinition of socialist goals. The mild reformism of the Declaration contrasted with the radicalism of the Manifesto. While capitalism was still seen as immoral, the socialist movement no longer aimed to eradicate it but to regulate it in order to achieve an improved quality of life. The left wing of the CCF feared that this redefinition of goals signalled the end of socialism. However, the moderation of socialist ideology was an international phenomenon. Socialist parties in Germany, the United Kingdom, and elsewhere underwent similar changes. Within Canada, trade union leaders became a more important force in the operation of the new socialist party. Participation of rank-and-file union members as delegates to subsequent NDP conventions pointed to more vigorous trade union association with the socialist party. In contrast with the CCF, the NDP has concentrated much of its resources on constituency and poll organization, assuming that superior electoral organization would balance the costly advertising campaigns of the parliamentary parties.

From 1969 to 1972, a left-wing faction styled the "Waffle" unsuccessfully challenged this strategy.[17] For a decade, the party leadership had been increasingly preoccupied with electoral victory. David Lewis, who had been a dominant official in the party since the 1940s, performed a major role in this CCF-NDP transformation. At a party policy convention in 1969, he led a successful attack on the dissident faction, condemning its attempts to place the party in an "ideological strait jacket." At the party's federal leadership convention two years later, Lewis was compelled to endure a humiliating four ballots before winning the final run-off against James Laxer, the Waffle candidate; an academic, Laxer remained Lewis's last opponent in a group of candidates that had included several MPs. In 1972, the Waffle members withdrew from the Ontario NDP when forced by the provincial executive to choose between continued party membership and the group's separate identity.

By 1975, it was highly questionable whether the new socialist strategy had been successful. Provincial parties formed the governments of Manitoba and Saskatchewan. Defeated in a bid for re-election in 1975, the party in British Columbia nonetheless retained about 40% of the popular vote; the party in Ontario barely formed the opposition in the same year with only 27% of the vote. However, the party's share of the popular vote in federal elections still did not exceed 18%. The balance of power which the party held with 32 MPs from 1972 to 1974 exaggerated the party's real electoral strength. In 1974, the NDP's popular vote fell to 16% and the caucus was halved. Lewis lost his seat and resigned the leadership. One opinion survey in 1975 indicated that NDP support was still below 18%.

From this performance, it appears that the managerial strategy of the NDP leadership, stressing electoral organization over the development of socialist policy options, was paralleled by a pragmatic attitude on the part of the unionized industrial working class. In 1974, this crucial component of party support in Ontario may have abandoned the NDP for the Liberals to protect their favourable labour-management negotiating arrangements from a possible Conservative wage freeze.[18] Even when industrial unions such as the United Automobile Workers of America or the United Steelworkers of America were weak and powerless associations thirty years ago, union members did not commit themselves overwhelmingly to the CCF. Now confident in the strength and permanence of their union, workers are no more inclined to commit themselves to one party. Rank-and-file unionists have traditionally preferred a "secular" bargaining approach to party politics instead of a "religious" commitment to the socialist party.

In summary, various movements and organizations coalesced during the depression to form the socialist CCF. The party failed to become a major force nationally because the class division remains a minor political cleavage. Because of its distinctive values, the party has nonetheless possessed a high level of cohesion between the members and a nationally integrated leadership. These characteristics explain the endurance of the party in the face of electoral failures. However, repeated electoral reversals did not rest easily with the leadership and the transformation of the CCF to the NDP was an attempt to moderate the policy and restructure the Canadian left to make it more appealing to the electorate.

The Mixed Fragment-Movement Party

The Progressives of the 1920s were a mixed fragment-movement party divided internally on aims and strategy. Its fragment component consisted of its parliamentary leadership and supporters in Manitoba. The movement component was based in Alberta. Its leader, T. A. Crerar, was a prominent Manitoba Liberal who had served as the Minister of Agriculture in the Unionist (Conservative) government during World War I. Through independent political action and parliamentary bargaining, Crerar and his supporters hoped to make the parliamentary parties, particularly the Liberals, more responsive to western needs.

The Albertan faction was composed of the popular United Farmers of Alberta and inspired by Henry Wise Wood, a clergyman turned farmer organizer. Wood and his supporters were reluctant to take part in party politics. Their populist goal was to replace the parliamentary party system with representation based on occupational groups. The party never healed its internal split. Nationally the Progressives suffered the swift demise of a fragment party, but its movement element survived in Alberta and to some extent in Ontario. In the early 1930s, Progressive parliamentarians participated in the birth of the CCF and voters in Alberta who had supported the Progressives propelled the Social Credit into national prominence.[19]

The Progressive party originated on the prairies where sectional and class consciousness had been developing since the turn of the century.[20] The West was being populated with Americans and Europeans who had experienced radical politics in their immediate past and had high expectations for their future on the Canadian prairies. However, the protectionist policies of successive federal governments did not make the natural handicaps of marginal farm life easier to endure. High tariffs favoured eastern commerical interests to the detriment of the debtor-society on the prairies. Through cooperative activity, western farmers became conscious of their collective interests as well as their weakness in federal party politics. Western MPs were a distinct minority among eastern majorities in the disciplined caucuses of the Liberal and Conservative parties. Moreover, both parties were financed by the eastern economic elite. The defeat of the Liberals on reciprocity in 1911 confirmed to many in the West the need for a third party. The momentum for independent political action by westerners, however, was temporarily sidetracked by the outbreak of World War I.

The critical year was 1919. In the spring, Crerar resigned from the Unionist cabinet because of inadequate reductions in the tariff. Rather than rejoin the Liberal caucus, he and eight members sat as independents. Western Liberals were further alienated by the succession to the leadership of Mackenzie King, an Ontario Liberal, and by the refusal of the convention to reject the principle of tariff protection. The Winnipeg General Strike and the Government's military and legislative responses heightened class and regional tensions in Western Canada as well.[21] In the same year, the United Farmers of Alberta decided to contest provincial elections not as a disciplined party, but as an occupational pressure group in which individual representatives would be responsible primarily to the constituency association. In Ontario, the United Farmers actually formed the provincial government with the support of members of the Independent Labour party.

Early in 1920, a meeting of organized farmers in Winnipeg decided to take direct federal political action. Wood sought electoral representation by occupational group, while Crerar advocated a new, but conventional, party. This conflict was not resolved. A group of 11 agrarian MPs designated themselves as the National Progressive party, choosing Crerar as their leader.

In 1921, the Liberal government in Saskatchewan barely escaped defeat at the hands of the Progressives, while the United Farmers captured the government of Alberta. In the federal election of that year, the Progressives elected the second largest group of MPs — 61 from the prairies and one each from British Columbia and New Brunswick. King formed the first minority government in Canada. The Conservatives formed the opposition by default: the more numerous Progressives refused to assume a parliamentary role which would implicate them in a party system they were dedicated to abolish. Wood's anti-party views won out over Crerar's. Consequently, Crerar's leadership was made impossible, for he could not negotiate with a government which knew he did not dominate his caucus. Furthermore, the rules of the House of Commons at that time did not easily accommodate a third party and Liberal and Conservative leaders were ill-disposed to procedural changes to allow the Progressives much participation in debate.

The fragment-movement division within the Progressive party sealed its fate. Given its origins and aims, the fragment element was the most susceptible to frustration and defeat. By the end of 1922, Crerar had resigned as leader and two Progressives had defected to the Liberal party. In 1924, the so-called "ginger group" among Wood Progressives broke with the caucus and joined with the two Labour MPs. Other withdrawals took place and by the election of 1925, the Progressive party had obviously disintegrated as a political force in federal politics.[22] Curiously, that election resulted in a stronger position for the Progressives in a parliament of minorities, although they had less than half their strength of 1921. This parliament was short-lived, however, and after 1926 the party ceased to be important. The movement element in Alberta was the most tenacious. In 1926 and 1930, the party continued to gain one-third of the vote in Alberta and elect a majority of MPs from that province, although the candidates were then designated as United Farmers of Alberta.

Despite appearances in 1926, western disaffection with the Liberal and Conservative parties persisted. In 1929, the economy of western countries collapsed and in the ensuing years destitution and near starvation swept the prairies. During this time, the shades of the Progressive party — the "ginger group" alliance with the Labour MPs, the UFA-Progressive MPs, and grass-roots willingness to support independent political action — took new form in support for the socialist CCF and populist Social Credit.

As for the parliamentary parties, the Liberals remained more popular than the Conservatives on the prairies until 1958. In 1957 and 1958, the Conservatives, led by John Diefenbaker, a western populist, put the Liberals in considerable jeopardy in Western Canada, destroyed the Social Credit movement there, and hastened the restructuring of the CCF. Since then, the Conservatives have remained more popular on the prairies than the Liberals, who have projected a Central Canadian bias in leadership, party financing, and economic policy. In the province which carries the populist legacy of Wood Progressivism and the Social Credit movement, the Conservatives have almost monopolized federal representation since 1958 and completely monopolized it in

1972 and 1974. In Saskatchewan and Manitoba, the NDP has managed to retain a base of support with roots in the western revolt of half a century ago.

The Progressive party, then, was a mixed fragment-movement party. It originated in response to class and sectional grievances in Western Canada. The party suffered from a split personality: its parliamentary leadership responded to popular grievances in the style of a fragment party, while its popular support base in Alberta manifested the style of a populist movement party. The factions proposed incompatible objectives for the party. The fragment element, led by a Liberal and former Unionist cabinet minister, sought to re-invigorate the party system, whereas the populist movement section sought to destroy it. The Progressives did not endure four years in parliament as a cohesive group. The fragment element soon left party politics or drifted back to the Liberal party. The movement faction, with its grass-roots base of support, persisted and eventually participated in the founding of two successor movement parties.[23]

Conclusion

Movement and fragment parties arose in this century in response to popular cultural, class, and sectional grievances. Some have successfully challenged the Liberal and Conservative parties at the provincial level and in some regions in federal elections, but none has displaced either of these elite-based parliamentary parties. While each responded to popular grievances, these third parties have manifested important differences. Some have been elite-led fragments of a parliamentary party; others could be classified as populist and socialist movement parties. The Progressives were a mixed fragment-movement party.

Fragment parties are created, led, and dominated by an individual who has abandoned an elite position in a parliamentary party because of serious differences with the leadership on questions of popular concern. These elite-led organizations lack the grass-roots involvement and group support necessary to sustain them. If the leader of the fragment party had possessed the kind of popular support he later sought as the head of a new party, he would probably have been accommodated earlier by the leadership of his parliamentary party. Fragment parties, therefore, are short-lived because they lack this mass support. None has survived to contest two consecutive elections as a credible force.

Movement parties have endured because of support from highly committed group and individual supporters. Both the leadership and membership of movement parties are rooted in sectional and class-aggrieved communities not easily accommodated by elite-dominated fragment or parliamentary parties. From 1911 to the present on a large scale, farmers and organized labour have supported political action independent of the parliamentary parties.

There are two types of movement parties. The populist party has been leader-oriented; the socialist party has been value- and program-oriented. The leadership orientation of the populists has resulted in a political vehicle which responds more easily to distinctive regional customs and preferences. Committed to universal values and even specific cross-national policy proposals, the socialists are often unwilling and incapable of responding to regional cultural distinctiveness. As a consequence, until recently the populists have had greater electoral impact than the socialists. However, the populist movement party has not been as cohesive a political force as the socialist party and has been more susceptible to factional strife and disintegration than the socialist party.

While movement parties have been successful in several provinces, none has seriously threatened to replace either of the parliamentary parties at the national level. This weakness results from the relative unimportance of class politics in federal voting. Ironically, sectional grievances in the western periphery, particularly against the Conservatives, resulted in historic support for the movement parties, but the Conservative party has lately become a vehicle of anti-core sentiment in that region.

This and the preceding chapter have examined the effect of party origins on subsequent behaviour. A common theme is that the extra-parliamentary formation of the movement parties continues to limit the freedom of action available to these parties. The parliamentary parties, in contrast, did not emanate from social upheavals and therefore have fewer historic memories to honour. The elites of the parliamentary parties have had less need to accommodate a core of ideologically committed followers who might decry ideological reversals.

The varying flexibility of the parties may produce two kinds of consequences or outputs: differences in party strategies and differences in implemented party policies. Even without solid statistical evidence, we are convinced that Liberal and Conservative leaders have greater tactical manoeuvrability than the leaders of the NDP and Social Credit. One cannot easily imagine NDP leaders emulating Liberal leader Lester Pearson's about-face when he replaced vehement opposition to nuclear weapons for Canada with vehement support in order to embarrass the disunited Conservative government of John Diefenbaker.

Actual government policy is another matter. Unlike electoral rhetoric and party manifestoes, actual government policy cannot be drafted on the spur of the moment. Unlike party promises, government programs must take into consideration problems of financing, the role of the bureaucracy, and the reactions of groups who have a vested interest in no change. What appears to be a clear difference in the flexibility available to the movement and parliamentary parties may vanish when actual government policies are examined. Chapters 11-14 on policy outputs will provide some clue as to whether the policies of the movement parties are in fact more inflexible and therefore more predictable than the policies of the parliamentary parties.

Notes

1. The only biography of Bourassa in the English language leaves consider-able room for further work. See Casey Morrow, *Henri Bourassa and French-Canadian Nationalism: Opposition to Empire* (Montreal: Harvest House, 1969). H. Blair Neatby's study of Laurier's relationship to Quebec includes a valuable analysis of Bourassa and the Nationalists. See *Laurier and a Liberal Quebec: a study in political management* (Toronto: McClelland and Stewart, 1973). Few historians stress the economic context in which the Nationalist movement thrived. However, historians who do so are Robert Craig Brown and Ramsay Cook in *Canada 1896–1921: a nation transformed* (Toronto: McClelland and Stewart, 1974), 127–143, and Joseph Levitt, *Henri Bourassa and the Golden Calf: The Social Program of the Nationalists of Quebec (1900–1914)* (Ottawa: les Editions de l'Université d'Ottawa, 1969).

2. "The tactics used in Canadian elections often raise ethical questions; none more so than these arrangements of 1911." See J. Murray Beck's account of the election campaign in *Pendulum of Power: Canada's federal elections* (Scarborough, Ont.: Prentice-Hall, 1968), 120–135.

3. Beck, *Pendulum*, 136–148. See also Brown and Cook's account of "the Clash of Nationalism," *Canada 1896–1921*, 250–274.

4. Armand Lavergne, H. of C. *Debates* (Feb. 25, 1907), 3642. Quoted in Neatby, *Laurier*, 164–165.

5. This dispute over language rights took place during the tense binational clash over the war effort. See Brown and Cook, *Canada, 1896–1921*, 252–262.

6. Federal defeat does not necessarily follow from provincial defeat in Quebec. Maurice Duplessis defeated the Taschereau and Godbout Liberals in 1936 and 1943 with the *union nationale*, which consisted of remnants of the Conservatives and some reform Liberals. The federal Liberals retained their ascendancy in Quebec during Duplessis's nationalist regime. The authoritarian and corrupt *union nationale* administration, on which the federal Conserva-tives depended in vain for their Quebec campaigns, disintegrated following Duplessis's death in 1959. On Duplessis, see A. R. M. Lower, *Colony to Nation: a history of Canada*, 4th ed. (Toronto: Longmans, 1964), 531–533. On the man and his regime, see Herbert F. Quinn, *The Union Nationale* (Toronto: Univer-sity of Toronto Press, 1963).

7. On Stevens and the Reconstruction party, see J. R. H. Wilbur, "H. R. Stevens and R. B. Bennett, 1930–34," *Canadian Historical Review*, 43:1 (1962), 1–16, and "H. R. Stevens and the Reconstruction Party," *Canadian Historical Review*, 45:1 (1964), 1–28.

8. See Alan C. Cairns, "The electoral system and the party system in Canada, 1921–1956," *Canadian Journal of Political Science*, 1:1 (1968), 59–60. See Chapter 7, Elections, below.

9. See Mary Hallett, "The Social Credit Party and the New Democracy Movement: 1939–1940," *Canadian Historical Review*, 47:4 (1966), 301–325.

10. Paul T. Hellyer, *Agenda: a plan for action* (Scarborough, Ont.: Prentice-Hall, 1971).

11. D. Butler and D. Stokes, *Political Change in Britain* (New York: St. Martin's Press, 1971), 95–111.

12. Standard works on the Social Credit movement include John A. Irving,

The Social Credit Movement in Alberta (Toronto: University of Toronto Press, 1959), and C. B. Macpherson, *Democracy in Alberta* (Toronto: University of Toronto Press, 1953). See also Lipset's review of Macpherson and Macpherson's reply in *Canadian Forum* (Nov., Dec., and Jan., 1954–1955).

13. Cairns, "The electoral system." See below, Chapter 7, on the effect of the electoral system on electoral outcomes.

14. On the Social Credit movement in Quebec, see Maurice Pinard, *The Rise of a Third Party* (Englewood Cliff, N.J.: Prentice-Hall, 1971), and Michael B. Stein, *The Dynamics of Right-Wing Protest: a political analysis of Social Credit in Quebec* (Toronto: University of Toronto Press, 1973).

15. On the academic level of explaining the party system, socialists have had to contend with the "law of third parties," which declares such organizations to be ill-fated minor parties. On the level of party propaganda, Liberals contend that "socialists are Liberals in a hurry," while both parliamentary parties warn voters that a vote for the socialist party is a "lost vote." See Kenneth McNaught's essay on this "law," "The multi-party system in Canada," in Laurier Lapierre et al (ed.), *Essays on the Left: Essays in honour of T. C. Douglas*, (Toronto, McClelland and Stewart, 1971), 43–49. The "law of third parties" applied to the Canadian party system has intellectual roots in political science and history textbooks of the 1940s. See R. MacGregor Dawson, *The Government of Canada*, revised by Norman Ward (Toronto: University of Toronto Press, 1963), Ch. 21, and J. A. Corry and J. E. Hodgetts, *Democratic Government and Politics*, 3rd ed. (Toronto: University of Toronto Press, 1959), Ch. 8. See also F. H. Underhill, *Canadian Political Parties* (Ottawa: The Canadian Historical Association Booklets No. 8, 1956). Ironically, Underhill was a major participant in the drafting of the socialist Regina Manifesto.

16. On the origin and early years of the CCF, see Kenneth McNaught's biography of the party's first leader, *A Prophet in Politics: a biography of J. S. Woodsworth* (Toronto: University of Toronto Press, 1959). There are several works on the CCF including Gad Horowitz, *Canadian Labour in Politics* (Toronto: University of Toronto Press, 1968), S. M. Lipset, *Agrarian Socialism: the Cooperative Commonwealth Federation in Saskatchewan* (Berkeley, California: University of California Press, 1959), Dean E. McHenry, *The Third Force in Canada, the Cooperative Commonwealth Federation 1932–1948* (Berkeley, California: University of California Press, 1950), Walter D. Young, *The Anatomy of a Party: the national CCF, 1932–1961* (Toronto: University of Toronto Press, 1969), and Leo Zakuta, *A Protest Movement Becalmed; a study of change in the CCF* (Toronto: University of Toronto Press, 1964).

17. For documentation on the issue and the struggle in the NDP until 1970 compiled from a "Waffle" perspective, see Dave Godfrey and Mel Watkins (ed.), *Gordon to Watkins to You: A Documentary: the battle for control of our economy* (Toronto: New Press, 1970).

18. Opinions conflict on this aspect of the election of 1974. See Cliff Scotton, "1974 Federal Election," a report to the Federal Executive Council, New Democratic Party (Sept./Oct., 1974), and Jane Jenson et al., "The 1974 Election: A Preliminary Report", a paper presented to the annual meeting of the Canadian Political Science Association (Edmonton, 1975).

19. See W. L. Morton, *The Progressive Party in Canada* (Toronto: University of Toronto Press, 1950), and Paul F. Sharp, *The Agrarian Revolt in Western*

Canada (Minneapolis: University of Minnesota Press, 1948). On Wood, See W. K. Rolph, *Henry Wise Wood of Alberta* (Toronto: University of Toronto Press, 1950). There is no biography of Crerar.

20. See Brown and Cook's examination of the formative years of the western revolt, *Canada 1896–1921*, 144–161, 309–328.

21. The government replaced the police force with the military and the RCMP. The federally authorized arrest later of strike leaders led to a strikers' march in defiance of a mayoral prohibition. The RCMP and soldiers dispersed the marchers, but one spectator was killed and thirty wounded. The government amended the Immigration Act to permit the deportation of British-born aliens and amended the Criminal Code to permit prosecution for "loosely defined sedition" (McNaught, *History*, 228) "on the weakest of evidence". (Lower, *Colony*, 504). On the general strike, see D. C. Masters, *The Winnipeg General Strike* (Toronto: University of Toronto Press, 1950), McNaught's *A Prophet in Politics: a biography of J. S. Woodsworth* (Toronto: University of Toronto Press, 1959), and D. J. Bercuson's *Confrontation at Winnipeg*, (Montreal: McGill-Queen's Press, 1974).

22. The farm-labour government in Ontario was defeated in 1923.

23. Because the focus of our book is to explain significant aspects of the party system and the political process, the Communist Party of Canada is not discussed. Founded in 1921 as an underground organization, harassed and outlawed for a time, the party consistently followed the policies set by the Communist Party of the Soviet Union. The Canadian party elected only one MP and he was convicted of conspiracy in a Soviet-directed espionage enterprise in the 1940s. In the 1950s, the party lost many members and leaders as a result of revelations of Stalin's tyranny. In the 1960s, the party experienced the schismatic effect of Sino-Soviet differences. For a history of the origins of the party, see William Rodney, *Soldiers of the International: a History of the Communist Party of Canada, 1919–1929* (Toronto: University of Toronto Press, 1968).

SECTION II

Political Cleavages (Inputs)

Many considerations can motivate the choices made by electors. For some voters, the criterion is the candidate; for others, the party; for still others, the party leader. While the range of electoral motivations is almost limitless, nevertheless very few issues motivate, divide, or polarize a sizeable portion of the electorate. Of these political cleavages in Canada, the most important are bicultural, geographic, and class. The presence of these cleavages, but not necessarily their relative importance, makes Canada typical of most industrialized democracies.

Chapter 4 looks at the cyclical nature of English-French, Protestant-Catholic tension in Canadian history and how the parties have been vehicles for this tension. Chapter 5 introduces the concept of a core-periphery cleavage to explain regional tensions in and outside the party system. Chapter 6 combines Canadian government statistics on inequality of income and some Marxian concepts to show the presence of class differences. It then explores how class cleavage is expressed or submerged in party politics.

CHAPTER 4
BICULTURAL CLEAVAGE
François-Pierre Gingras and Conrad Winn

Introduction

The reality of two Canadian nations or cultures has required a special vocabulary. "Races," "ethnic groups," and "cultures" describe what Lord Durham and French-Canadian nationalists have termed "nations." At different times in history, French speakers have been called *canadiens*, French Canadians, or *québécois*, while their English-speaking counterparts have been called "the British party," *les anglais*, English Canadians, or simply Canadians. Through the efforts of the Royal Commission on Bilingualism and Biculturalism, some English Canadians have come to speak of anglophones and francophones. According to that same commission, the two peoples represent different ways "of being, thinking and feeling . . . driving force(s) animating . . . significant group(s) of individuals united by a common tongue, and sharing the same customs, habits and experiences."[1] However, on a world scale, English and French cultural differences are small. French and Irish Catholics share the same religion; workers in Quebec and British Columbia both bargain for higher wages; towns in Quebec and Nova Scotia have the same dearth of employment; Montreal and Toronto confront similar problems in transportation and housing. Nonetheless, English and French Canadians have strikingly separate feelings of identification, especially in times of crisis.

The sentiments of French and English, Catholics and Protestants, have been manifested in different patterns of electoral and legislative behaviour since the onset of parliamentary practice in the eighteenth century. The following passages present a survey of the bicultural cleavage in the period from the Conquest to the Union of the Canadas, in the period of the Union, and in the period from Confederation to the present. Finally, the chapter examines the special role of French-Canadian political leadership in the party system.

1763: Genesis of Conflict

The roots of bicultural differences lie with the Conquest. The acquisition of New France in 1763 provided an enticement for British settlement. Soon after their arrival, the British merchants cast their eyes back across the Atlantic and petitioned the King for, among other things, the summoning of an elected assembly:

> . . . for the better security of your Majesty's dutiful and loyal subjects . . . we beg leave almost humbly to petition that it may please your Ma-

jesty, to order a House of Representatives to be chosen in this as in other of your Majesty's provinces; there being a number more than sufficient of loyal and well affected Protestants . . . to form a competent and respectable House of Assembly.[2]

The purpose of this request was less than democratic, as the then attorney-general of Quebec observed in his report:

An assembly so constituted, might pretend to be a representative of the people there, but in truth it would be representative of only the 600 new English settlers, and an instrument in their hands of domineering over the 90,000 French. Can such an assembly be thought just or expedient, or likely to produce harmony and friendship between the two nations? Surely it must have a contrary effect.[3]

The colonial administration did not recommend the creation of an assembly and the King's "new subjects" were not yet to receive a voice in the government:

. . . it might be dangerous in these early days of their submission, to admit the Canadians themselves to so great a degree of power . . . they would be very unlikely for some years to come to promote such measures as should gradually introduce the Protestant religion, the use of the English language, of the spirit of the British laws. It is more probable they would check all such endeavours, and quarrel with the governor and council, or with the English members of the assembly, for promoting them.[4]

From the inception of British North America, there existed bicultural conflict with the two cultures separated by language, religion, law, tradition, as well as material conflict of interest. These social tensions gave rise to political coteries. The British soon referred to the pro-*canadien* sympathizers as the "French party" and to advocates of British rule as the "British party." The Constitutional Act of 1791 divided the colony into Upper and Lower Canada and provided an appointed legislative Council and an elected Assembly. The Assembly in Lower Canada became the focus of conflict. Because of its strength among the majority of French-speaking members, the *parti canadien* acquired numerical predominance. However, the English, Tory, or British party acquired power as a result of its relationship with the Governor, officialdom, and the merchants of the Château clique. According to one English settler who sat in the Assembly between 1796 and 1800, "The Government and Commerce of the Colony [were] in the hands of the English."[5]

Devoted to economic progress, the British settlers sought to implement a program of modernization. They sought reforms in administrative law and mortgages, as well as the creation of banking institutions, the abolition of seigneurial tenure, and the improvement of transportation and communications. The British party did not consider economic reform to be an immediate instrument of assimilation because they assumed that the French would simply be drowned in waves of immigration expected to follow economic upturn. However, the rural French population quickly perceived the threat of assimilation. Their antagonism to reform stemmed from their traditionalist view that "commerce brings dishonour on the human species in shrouding elementary notions of Morality."[6] Their concern also arose from their nationalist anxiety that "the administration of public affairs [would be] carried on in English, by Englishmen, or men of English principles [as] the first step, and the most efficacious one towards the anglicization of the province."[7]

A conjuncture of several social processes enabled the French population to manifest their antagonism with the increasing dynamism that culminated in the uprising of 1837. At the mass level, economic decline in the countryside provided some sources of grievance. Falling world prices for agricultural exports, the decline of the fur trade, population pressures caused by high birth rates and Loyalist immigration, land pressures caused by land grants to non-producing speculators, and a wheat fly epidemic helped generate widespread discontent and a frustrated rural proletariat in quest of space. At the elite level, the ruling parish curés faced competition from a growing segment of notaries, lawyers, physicians, and journalists. The new professionals who led the *parti canadien* and, after 1826, the *parti patriote* saw nationalism, political reform, and economic conservatism as a means of outbidding the curés for the support of the rural masses. Fernand Ouellet, whose interpretation is not shared unanimously, views the motives of the new professionals with skepticism, if not cynicism:

> A large number of them anti-clerical liberals, often agnostic, with democratic pretensions, they defended the seigneurial régime, the common law of Paris ('la Coûtume de Paris'), and Church privilege, and they condemned capitalism. In reality they were only progressive so long as their liberal principles served their class interests and their nationalist plans.[8]

The immediate political stimulus for the uprising of the *patriotes* was the unwillingness of London to create a more representative form of government. Although French Canadians constituted 90% of the population of Lower Canada, the oligarchical nature of the political system deprived them of opportunities for making policy and for supplying goods and services to the government. Gilles Paquet and Jean-Pierre Wallot, an economist and a historian respectively, have presented some government statistics for the period between 1794 and 1812 to show that the *canadiens* occupied less than one-third of salaried positions in the public sector and received a declining and minority share of government positions.[9]

Monumental indignation describes best the reaction of many British settlers in Lower Canada to demands for more representative government. They would no longer "submit to the domination of a party averse to Emigration, to commerce, to international improvements, and to all those interests which may be regarded as British."[10] The disorganized French-Canadian insurgents were easily put down by troops and volunteers from various points in the Canadas.

French-Canadian nationalists sometimes draw parallels between the rebellion of 1837 and the kidnapping and other terrorist activities of the *Front de libération du Québec* in 1970. To dramatize this connection, the FLQ named some of its cells after French-Canadian heroes of 1837. Parallels are also often drawn between the *parti patriote* and the *parti québécois.* The PQ was founded in 1969 by the Quebec independence movement and now constitutes the official opposition to the Liberal government in the Quebec provincial legislature. In fact, there are similarities between these two periods. Both the *parti patriote* and the *parti québécois* arose in times when economic expectations were not matched by opportunities. The economy of Lower Canada declined for the reasons already cited. Since 1967, the economy of Quebec failed to keep pace with the rising expectations brought about by increased urbanization, widespread acceptance of television-dictated styles of living, and the quiet revolution of the 1960s, during which significant political and social reforms helped to pull Quebec out of its backwardness.

The nationalist movements of the two periods were spurred on by the persistence of economic inequality between English and French. Both movements won support among the frustrated lower strata, the working class of east-end Montreal in the twentieth century and the rural proletariat in the nineteenth. Both movements embodied the extremes of modern and traditional thought. The secular, sometimes anti-clerical, *patriotes* sought to modernize the political system by introducing parliamentary democracy; nonetheless, they wanted to preserve traditional economic roles and some church privileges. The secular, sometimes anti-clerical, *péquistes* seek to modernize the economic, social, and educational systems, while expressing such past themes of French-Canadian Catholicism as ancestor worship, love of the soil, and, occasionally, anti-semitism.[11]

Union of the Canadas

Rising binational conflict and the disturbances of 1837 required some kind of constitutional remedy. The francophone population of Lower Canada was to be submerged in a larger united province. Lord Durham reasoned in the following way:

> If the population of Upper Canada is rightly estimated at 400,000, the English inhabitants of Lower Canada at 150,000, and the French at 450,000 the union of the two provinces would not only give a clear English majority, but one which would be increased every year by the influence of English emigration; and I have little doubt that the French, when once placed . . . in a minority, would abandon their vain hopes of nationality.[12]

Durham's thought was strong on formal logic, weak on political psychology. He failed to anticipate that the sense of threat among French Canadians would spur cohesion, that the absence of ethnic anxiety among the English would permit the expression of internal conflict, and that the French could constitute a balance of power in such circumstances.

In fact, French Canadians had already shown a high level of cohesion from the early 1800s in their practice of electing a united group of members to the Assembly of Lower Canada. This practice was reinstated in the new regime of 1841. In the first parliament of the Province of Canada, 17 of the 18 French-Canadian members clustered around La Fontaine, Morin, and other advocates of constitutional reform. During the early 1840s, a succession of governors appointed by the Conservative government in London invited mainly Conservatives to form ministries in the union parliament. However, the absence of Conservative support among French-Canadian members produced a high degree of ministerial instability and turnover. Once the Liberal party was elected in Great Britain, the principles of responsible government were acknowledged, and Reformers in Canada East and West were able to form a majority government under Baldwin and La Fontaine.

The achievement of responsible government coincided with other changes which together removed the allegiance of French Canadians from the Reform to the Conservative party and set the stage for Sir John A. Macdonald's long hegemony. The achievement of responsible government by itself weakened the link between Reformers in the two Canadas. Both wings had shared a desire for constitutional change, but only Canada West possessed much enthusiasm for economic and social reform. Furthermore, the achievement of responsible government was followed by the resignation of Baldwin as leader of the Reform party in 1851 and the subsequent succession of George Brown. An ardent Presbyterian who spoke against separate schools, against "French domination" of the Union, and in favour of "rep by pop," Brown could only diminish the credibility of his *rouges* allies in Canada East and help solidify the fledgling alliance of Cartier and Macdonald. Canada West had accepted parity of representation with Canada East when the latter's population was the larger. George Brown and others wanted "rep by pop" now that the West was the more populous. Within French Canada, Reformers in the *parti rouge* and later in the *parti démocratique* were deprived of their platform of responsible government and fell back upon anti-clericalism, then a losing battle.

The patterns of bicultural conflict and cooperation which appeared in the Province of Canada presaged the politics of post-Confederation Canada. French Canada would continue to experience a greater sense of ethnic threat than English Canada. French Canada would therefore be more cohesive in her political representation and would hold the balance of power in the federal Parliament. With a comparative unconcern for non-cultural matters, French Canada would accord support to the party which welcomed French Canadians into positions of leadership and which inhibited the articulation of anti-French sentiment or policy (see Chapter 2: Parliamentary Parties). Finally, through much of Canadian history, the party meeting failure in French Canada was the one which would take a position on disputes within Catholicism that foreswore the allegiance of religious moderates. Thus, the *rouges* and their successors did not win the conversion of Catholic moderates until Laurier put a damper on the more anti-clerical elements in his party and until Cartier's death led to the leadership of Quebec Conservatives by the intensely theological, ultramontane clergy.

The Union of the Canadas was intended at least in part to assimilate the French. The French were obliged to make some significant sacrifices. The Union took place when the public debt in Upper Canada was large and the debt in Lower Canada was negligible. Lower Canada accepted equality of representation in the Union Parliament despite her greater population. Now that her population was smaller, Lower Canada would receive diminished representation in the federal Parliament created by Confederation. Nevertheless, whatever French Canada's apparent sacrifices, the plan for her assimilation did not succeed. Hardcore advocates of English supremacy could fulminate:

> The Union has completely failed in its purpose. It was enacted with the sole motive of reducing the French Canadians under English domination. And the contrary effect has resulted! Those that were to be crushed dominate.[13]

Post-Confederation Canada

Although Canada is commonly accorded the year 1867 as a birthdate, the existence of ongoing English-French relationships during the previous century meant that the country did not begin with a *tabula rasa* at Confederation. In spite of the B.N.A. Act, which sought to allay fear by delimiting constitutional responsibility, Canada's future was constrained by a long history of economic inequality and political wariness separating the "two founding races." In the century after Confederation, each culture has contained elements alert to evidence that the latest government policy, economic change, or social process might tip the balance of power in favour of the opposition. The plethora of issues which have provoked at least some cultural anxiety include the Jesuit Estates Act in Quebec, the Métis rebellion, the fate of Riel, the Boer War, military policy prior to and during both world wars, relations with fascist Italy, immigration, provincial education policy, the federal role in education, foreign aid, and relations with blocs of foreign countries according to their linguistic or religious character.

Chapter 11 examines the attitudes of the federal parties on a cross-section of issues which affected the bicultural balance of power. This chapter focuses on those issues which provoked the greatest bicultural concern. Generally, the strongest tensions were stimulated by crises relating to education and to war.

The first major issue in education was the Jesuit Estates Act (1888).[14] Ontario Orangemen vigorously opposed the Quebec legislation, which gave compensation to the Jesuit Order for property seized at the Conquest and which also gave assistance to Protestant schools. The most controversial issue in education was undoubtedly the Manitoba Schools question. The province's education had been established originally by Catholic settlers from Quebec. Because Catholic schools predated Confederation, they were subject to the protection of the B. N. A. Act. However, waves of Ontario immigrants in the 1880s and 90s became a power base from which the Ontario Orange Lodge could convince the Manitoba government to abolish Catholic and French language schools. Similar inroads on French and separate schooling claims were made in Saskatchewan, Alberta, and Ontario. In the case of the western provinces, Prime Minister Laurier's plans for parallel Catholic and Protestant education on the Quebec model were skuttled by vehement Protestant opposition. In Ontario, the Orange wing of the provincial Conservative government attempted to abolish French language schools through "Regulation 17," implemented by the Department of Education in 1912.

Although disputes over education did little for Canadian unity, the question of war, either internal war involving the Métis or external war overseas, aroused tension as well. The failure to satisfy the desire of the Métis for self-government in the Northwest and the consequent rebellion provoked the fiery indignation of Orangemen in Ontario and outpourings of sympathy for the insurgents in Quebec. For French Canada, the Métis were not simply another victim of Anglo-Ontarian despotism, but a French-speaking kindred culture. The long deliberations over Riel's fate and his eventual execution further exacerbated tensions. In Quebec, editorial indignation and fiery oratory were this time accompanied by mass demonstrations addressed by Laurier and other prominent French-speaking leaders.

After Laurier acceded to power in 1896, English-French mistrust was provoked by the Boer War and by the two world wars. Laurier attempted to achieve a compromise solution on the Boer question, by which Canada would supply a small number of volunteers for British service. However, French-Canadian nationalists feared that any military aid would act as a precedent for future British claims for assistance. Their suspicions were not groundless. During the subsequent world wars, Canada supported Britain against the wishes of French Canadians with a generosity which included the supply of conscripted forces.

Cultural mistrust at the time of World War I was fomented not merely by the issue of conscription itself, but also by the insensitivity of Sir Robert Borden's Unionist government and by the culmination of longstanding disputes over education in the provinces. As his Minister of Militia, the prime minister selected Sam Hughes, who had been in the forefront of the anti-French, anti-Catholic crusade of the 1880s. Meanwhile, the army resisted the creation of French-speaking regiments or the promotion of French-Canadian officers and appointed at least one Protestant clergyman as a recruiting officer in Quebec. In education, Regulation 17 had been implemented in Ontario before the outbreak of the war and French schools in Manitoba were abolished during the course of the war. The conjuncture of these events provoked the following outcry from Henri Bourassa, Laurier's leading nationalist opponent:

> In the name of religion, liberty and faithfulness to the British flag, the French Canadians are enjoined to fight the Prussians of Europe. Shall we let the Prussians of Ontario impose their domination like masters, in the very heart of the Canadian Confederation, under the shelter of the British flag and British institutions?[15]

English-French relations survived the cultural provocations of World War I partly because Quebec was still a rural society. Only a small share of her population belonged to the socially mobilized sector capable of nationalist political behaviour. Comparatively few people lived in cities and were exposed to mass education or mass media. The *canadiens* identified as much with their locality or church as with the French-Canadian nation. By World War II, Quebec was highly urbanized and socially mobilized. Despite MacKenzie King's sensitive handling of conscription, the government provoked almost as much disturbance as had been caused during Word War I both by Borden's abrasive management of military needs and by the movement against French-language education in the provinces.[16]

The different wartime styles of the Borden and King governments coincide with the different bases of support for the two major parties. In this century, Liberal partisans have tended to be French speaking and Catholic, while Tories have been disproportionately English and Protestant. Two landmarks in electoral research identify this bicultural cleavage: the works of Escott Reid and John Meisel. In his noted essay on parties, subtitled "A Study of the Economic and Racial Bases of Conservatism and Liberalism in 1930," Reid argued that the major parties were best distinguished by ethnicity ("race").[17] The more French the inhabitants of a locality, the more Liberal; the more English, the more Conservative. In 1953, Meisel conducted a survey of Kingston, showing that Catholics had a 41:1 probability of voting Liberal rather than Conservative. He also discovered that one-fourth of Conservative respondents spontaneously attributed their preferences to anti-Catholic or anti-French feelings. According to Meisel, the pattern remains essentially the same in the 1970s: "the gap in party attachments between anglophones and francophones [being still] startlingly wide."[18]

The attachment of French Canadians to the Liberal party is usually attributed to a critical change during the federal elections of 1887, 1891, and/or 1896. As the distinguished historian, Arthur Lower, has expressed it, ". . . a realignment of political forces [took] place that was to serve as the basis of Canadian life for another half-century."[19] According to common understanding, the execution of Louis Riel, the decline of Catholic schooling in Manitoba, strife between ultramontane and moderate Conservatives in Quebec, and the selection of a French-Canadian Liberal leader all contributed to a permanent new attachment for the Liberal party in Quebec. French Canadians allegedly became concerned about the influence of the Orange Lodge and sensitive to the inability of federal Conservatives to protect their position within Confederation. In that frame of mind, French-speaking Canadians became ready converts to the Liberal party in appreciation for the prominence it accorded to members of their group.

The preceding interpretation is so widely accepted among social scientists that it is rarely argued and apparently never debated. Among historians, there exists some disagreement about the relative import of the alternative causes of realignment, but not about its timing and form. Thus, historians have devoted their energies to arguing about the relative impact of some or all of the following stimuli on Tory misfortune in Quebec: Riel,[20] militant protestantism,[21] Anglo-Saxon "racialism,"[22] Laurier,[23] Manitoba's schools,[24] secret U.S. funding of Quebec Liberals,[25] Tory dissension,[26] economic recession,[27] and shortfalls in Tory patronage.[28]

Widespread support for the thesis of an abrupt or critical realignment of parties is attributable at least in part to the preoccupation of academics with the distribution of seats instead of the actual distribution of votes. In the eighteen years between 1882 and 1900, the Conservative share of ridings in Quebec declined from 79% to 12%. However, this change is at least partly explained by the vagaries of the first-past-the-post system of balloting, by which moderate Conservative losses in popular vote in Quebec (from 52% in 1882 down to 44% in 1900) became huge losses in representation (see Table 4-1).[29] In the allegedly "critical" election of 1896, the Conservative party won only 25% of the seats in Quebec. But the party secured 46% of the Quebec vote, a proportion which exceeds the national share of the vote received by the Conservatives in almost every election in the last seventy-five years. The ease with which votes and seats can be confused is shown by Mason Wade in his classic book on French Canada. Wade writes that "Quebec in 1896 . . . *voted* more than three to one for Laurier."[30]

Table 4-1

Liberal and Conservative Seats and Votes (%)
for Quebec and Ontario, 1882–1904

	Quebec		Ontario	
	Seats	Votes	Seats	Votes
1882 Conservative	79	52	60	50
1882 Liberal	20	42	40	49
1887 Conservative	51	49	60	51
1887 Liberal	49	49	40	49
1891 Conservative	43	51	52	49
1891 Liberal	57	48	48	49
1896 Conservative	25	46	47	45
1896 Liberal	75	54	47	40
1900 Conservative	12	44	60	50
1900 Liberal	88	56	40	49
1904 Conservative	17	42	56	50
1904 Liberal	82	56	44	50

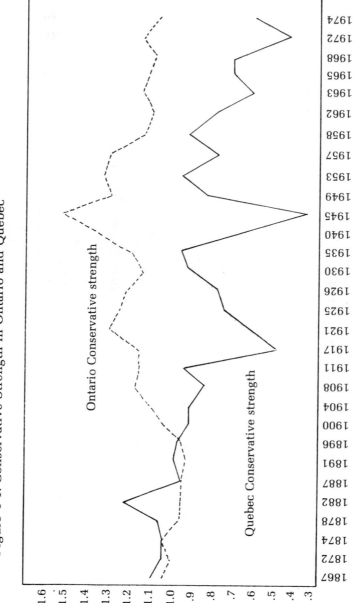

Figure 4-1. Conservative Strength in Ontario and Quebec*

*Strength equals Conservative proportion of provincial vote divided by Conservative proportion of national vote.

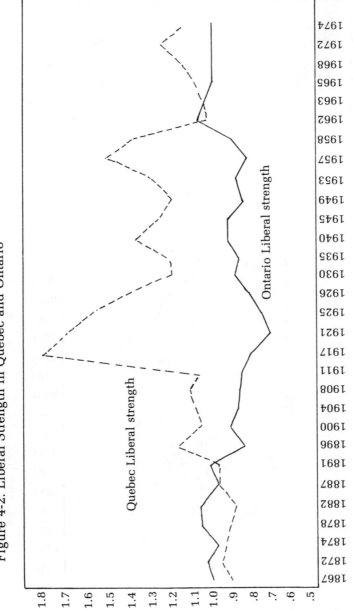

Figure 4-2. Liberal Strength in Quebec and Ontario*

*Strength equals Liberal proportion of provincial vote divided by Liberal proportion of national vote.

Figures 4-1 and 4-2 portray the pattern of support for the Liberals and Conservatives in Ontario and Quebec in federal elections from 1867 until the present. Neither chart documents an *abrupt* reversal of support at the end of the nineteenth century. Instead, the pattern of curves suggests a gradual or secular realignment, beginning in 1896 and achieving marked intensity during the world wars and to some extent in the early 1970s.

A statistics-minded reader might question the use of Figures 4-1 and 4-2 to disprove the portrait of an abrupt realignment on the grounds that an aggregate unit as large as the whole of Quebec might disguise underlying subprocesses. The ostensibly "gradual" realignment of Quebec might have consisted of the transit of French and English Quebeckers in opposite directions. A moderately rapid realignment of French Quebeckers towards the Liberal party may have been obscured by a very rapid flow of the less numerous English Quebeckers towards the Conservatives.

In order to evaluate this possibility, the voting behaviour of Anglo-Protestant townships in Quebec was examined.[31] Figure 4-3 portrays the behaviour of Hampden and Bury townships in the region Southeast of Montreal. The population of Hampden was 91% English, while the inhabitants of Bury were 89% Protestant. Neither township increased its support for the Conservatives during the period. Figure 4-4 compares the voting behaviour of all townships with 70% or more English or Protestant inhabitants. No evidence supports the supposition that English and French Quebeckers travelled in opposite directions. On the contrary, the decline in Conservative support among English speakers seems to parallel the decline across Quebec as a whole. This fact takes further credence away from the thesis of an abrupt bicultural realignment.

As mentioned, however, some gradual realignment did take place, beginning as early as 1887 and culminating in 1917. In addition to the political factors already referred to, economic grievances may have played an important role in driving French Canadians away from the Conservative party. The Quebec economy was in decline in the final decades of the nineteenth century, while the New England states to the south were experiencing a boom. It is estimated that as many as 350,000 Quebeckers emigrated in the decade 1881–91.[32] Migration eased off in the years before World War I as U.S. authorities began to erect barriers. It is possible to conjecture that emigration acted as a surrogate for political revolt against the Conservatives. Certainly, the early opportunities for and later unavailability of emigration coincided with the gradual and subsequently dramatic realignment of electoral forces. Furthermore, there is a pressing need to reconcile the documentary findings of historians, who show that French-Canadian journalists and professionals turned against the Conservatives in the 1880s and 1890s, with the electoral data, which show that Quebec voters did not fully repudiate the Conservatives until later.

Because of the assumption of homogeneity within the two cultures in our review of the bicultural cleavage since Confederation, it is ap-

Figure 4-3. Conservative Popular Vote (%)
in two Anglo-Protestant Townships
in Quebec

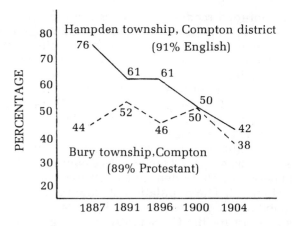

Figure 4-4. Conservative Popular Vote (%)
Quebec and in Subset of
Anglo-Protestant Townships*

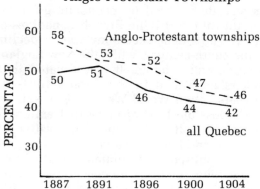

*Subset includes all townships with 70% or more
English or Protestant population according to 1881
census

propriate to express a few caveats. French Canadians make the frequent error of treating "English Canadians" as a residual category: all those who are not French are English. Likewise, English-speaking Protestants sometimes fail to perceive any distinctions among Catholics. In terms of electoral behaviour, English-speaking Catholics do not seem to have deviated from the pattern of bicultural cleavage. In fact, English Catholics are an even stronger basis of support for the Liberal party than French Catholics. In English-speaking cities such as Hamilton and Kitchener, the Knights of Columbus are an important and sometimes predominant element in Liberal party organization. However, the coincidence of English and French Catholic voting behaviour should not be taken as evidence that the two groups share identical positions on the bicultural cleavage. Some English-speaking Catholics have been deeply hostile to such objectives as French-language education. In the first decades of this century, conflict between the Irish and French over control of the University of Ottawa and other Catholic institutions led Irish Catholics to display a wry ecumenicalism by joining the Orange Lodge in the movement against bilingual schools in Ontario. The coincidence of English- and French-Catholic voting behaviour should also not be taken as evidence that religion is as strong a source of cleavage as language. Increasingly, evidence shows that religion persists as a division primarily because religion and partisanship are both inherited. Voting differences between Catholics and Protestants appear to reflect vague historic issues, while voting differences between anglophones and francophones reflect contemporary feeling.[33]

As a final caveat, we note that the bicultural cleavage has operated within parties as well as between. Hitherto unpublished data made available by Roman March show that, at the Liberal leadership convention of 1968, Trudeau could count on the first ballot preferences of most French-Canadian delegates, while other delegates preferred his English-Canadian adversaries (see Table 4-2). Similar divisions exist within the other parties. For example, Claude Wagner, the only French-Canadian candidate for the Conservative leadership in 1976, entered the convention with substantial support from Quebec.

The Role of French-Canadian Leaders

The preceding sections examined in a summary way the patterns of bicultural cleavage which emerged in various political forms from the Conquest to the present. The purpose of this section is to look at the special effects on the party system produced by the presence or absence of French-speaking party leaders.

The question of French-Canadian party leadership is important because Quebec's tendency to elect blocks of MPs has rendered French-Canadian support essential to any party aspiring to form the Government. Only five times since 1867 has a party managed to control Parliament without polling a majority of French-Canadian votes: these instances include the coalition administration of 1917 and

Table 4-2

First Ballot Preferences (%)
at Liberal Leadership Convention, 1968

	Trudeau	All other candidates	Uncommitted	No.
French-Canadian Delegates	56	40	4	679
Other Delegates	33	64	3	1779

Source: Based on surveys made by the Trudeau and Hellyer organizations prior to the first convention ballot. Data made available through the generosity of Professor Roman March, McMaster University.

Diefenbaker's minority governments of 1957 and 1962. In over half the elections held from 1896 to the present, the winning party's seats in Quebec exceeded its majority over the opposition in the House of Commons. During the same period, the Liberal party's edge over its main opposition in Parliament[34] was, half the time, smaller than its edge over the Conservatives in Quebec.[35] To express it more dramatically, if *la belle province* had never been a part of Canada, the federal Liberals would not have won half the elections they did win after 1895. In the period since Confederation, the Conservatives would have been in office for 64 years and the Liberals for 44 years, instead of the actual 45 and 63.

The high proportion of seats held by federal Liberals in Quebec since 1896 (see Table 4-3) obscures the fact that French-Canadian electoral behaviour is governed not just by sympathy for the party of Laurier, King, St. Laurent, Pearson, and Trudeau, but also by reluctance to support the English and generally Protestant-dominated party of Tupper, Borden, Meighen, Bennett, Manion, Bracken, Drew, Diefenbaker, Stanfield, and Clark. In the period after French Canada's so-called bandwagon prank of 1958, the 48% average popular vote for the Liberals in Quebec is hardly evidence of frenzied enthusiasm. The Liberals were able to regain their stranglehold on seats largely because their opposition was divided.

In the context of their weakness in Quebec, it is striking that the Conservatives not once provided an opportunity for a French Canadian to become prime minister, even though they had fourteen leaders since 1867. At the 1976 leadership convention, Claude Wagner almost became leader, but was narrowly defeated by Joe Clark, a less experienced politician from the West. By contrast, of the seven Liberal leaders, all but one destined to form a cabinet (Edward Blake), three were French Canadian. An intriguing question is to what extent the Tories' inability or unwillingness to place francophones in positions of authority accounts for their lack of electoral success in Quebec and across the country.

Table 4-4 contains the results of a test of Hypothesis I, that French Canadians — or, more accurately, Quebeckers — will prefer a party led by a French-Canadian over one that is not. The hypothesis accounts for 12 out of 13 cases; a French-led Liberal party outpolled an English-led

Table 4-3

Seats and Votes (%)
for Quebec by Selected Periods

A. Seats

	Liberals	Conservatives	Social Credit	CCF/NDP
1867–1891	39	60		
1896–1911	77	22		
1917–1957	88	8		
1958	33	67		
1962–1974	69	9	21	0

B. Votes

	Liberals	Conservatives	Social Credit	CCF/NDP
1867–1891	47	52		
1896–1911	55	44		
1917–1957	61	27		
1958	46	50		
1962–1974	48	22	21	7

Conservative party all but once in a sample of 13 elections. It is noteworthy that the Liberals outpolled the Conservatives in Quebec only 11 out of 17 times when led by an English Canadian. It is also striking that the Liberal vote was exceeded outside Quebec on 7 of the 12 occasions when they were led by French Canadians, a feature which illustrates the link between the cultural origins of party leaders and their electoral bases of support.

In almost three-fifths of the elections since Confederation, the leaders of both parties have been anglophones, so that in these instances francophones can rise to positions of lieutenancy at best. The

Table 4-4

National Origins of Party Leaders
and Distribution of Votes in Quebec

Liberal Leaders	Conservative Leaders	Total number of elections	Party polling a majority of votes in Quebec According to Hypothesis I*	Actual number of elections Liberals	Conservatives
Fr. Cdn.	Eng. Cdn.	13	Liberals	12**	1
Eng. Cdn.	Fr. Cdn.	0	Conservatives	—	—
Fr. Cdn.	Fr. Cdn.	0	No Prediction	—	—
Eng. Cdn.	Eng. Cdn.	17	No Prediction	11	6

Hypothesis I true	= 12
Hypothesis I untrue	= 1
No prediction	= 17
Total number of elections	= 30

*Hypothesis I: French Canadians are more likely to vote for a party whose leader is French Canadian than for a party whose leader is English Canadian.

**Outside Quebec, the Conservatives polled more votes than the Liberals in 7 of these elections.

French-Canadian right-hand man of an English-speaking party leader can usually be identified when the House of Commons is in session. It takes no special gift to assign such a role to Georges-Etienne Cartier or Ernest Lapointe. Sometimes, however, the situation is unclear and one is obliged to examine electoral campaigns and the perceptions of lieutenancy conveyed by the French-Canadian press during the month or so before polling day.

By this method, the 17 elections in which the two party leaders were anglophones were divided into 6 in which both parties had francophone lieutenants, 7 in which only the Liberals possessed one, and 4 in which only the Conservatives possessed one. Table 4-5 presents the analysis of Hypothesis II, that an anglophone-led party with a francophone lieutenant will be more successful in Quebec than an anglophone party without such a lieutenant. The hypothesis accounts for all relevant cases. Binational leadership — at least in terms of a French-Canadian Lieutenant — appears to be essential to securing the French-Canadian vote.

Table 4-5

Distribution of Votes in Quebec and Presence of French-Canadian Lieutenants when Party Leaders are English Canadians

French-Canadian lieutenant in			Party polling a majority of seats in Quebec		
Liberal Party	Conservative Party	Total number of elections	According to Hypothesis II*	Actual number of elections Liberals	Conservative
Yes	No	7	Liberals	7	0
No	Yes	4	Conservatives	0	4
Yes	Yes	6	No prediction	4	2
No	No	0	No prediction	—	—

Hypothesis II true	= 11
Hypothesis II untrue	= 0
No prediction	= 6
Elections to which Hypothesis II does apply: 17	

*Hypothesis II: When party leaders are English Canadians, French Canadians are more likely to vote for a party having a French-Canadian lieutenant then for a party having no French-Canadian lieutenant.

However, how important is French-Canadian leadership to a party's overall success? Our third hypothesis is that French Canadian leadership is essential to victory, and the data in Table 4-6 appear to uphold our contention. The Liberals never once formed a government without at least a French-Canadian lieutenant while the Conservatives managed to do it just three times out of nine, including the coalition government of 1917.

While the presence of a French-Canadian spokesman is virtually essential for electoral success, it is not a sufficient condition for victory. A party must not merely be sensitive to Quebec's aspirations, it must also be alone in that sensitivity. Because of the Liberal party's obvious

Table 4-6

National Origins of Party Leaders, Presence of a French-Canadian Lieutenant, and Parties Forming the Government

Liberal Leader	F.C. Lieut.	Conservative Leader	F.C. Lieut.	Total number of elections	According to Hypothesis III*	Actual Lib.	Cons.
Fr. Cdn.		Fr. Cdn.		0	No prediction	—	—
Fr. Cdn.		Eng. Cdn.	Yes	5	(a) Liberals	4	1
Fr. Cdn.		Eng. Cdn.	No	8	(a) Liberals	5	3
Eng. Cdn.	Yes	Fr. Cdn.		0	(a) Conservatives	—	—
Eng. Cdn.	Yes	Eng. Cdn.	Yes	7	No prediction	5	2
Eng. Cdn.	Yes	Eng. Cdn.	No	7	(b) Liberals	7	0
Eng. Cdn.	No	Fr. Cdn.		0	(a) Conservatives	—	—
Eng. Cdn.	No	Eng. Cdn.	Yes	3	(b) Conservatives	0	3
Eng. Cdn.	No	Eng. Cdn.	No	0	No Prediction	—	—

Hypothesis III(a) true = 9   untrue = 4
Hypothesis III(b) true = 10   untrue = 0
Total   true = 19   untrue = 4

*Hypothesis III:
   (a) A party whose leader is French-Canadian is more likely to form the Government than a party whose leader is English-Canadian.
   (b) When both major parties are led by English Canadians, the presence of a French Canadian as lieutenant increases the chances of a party forming the Government.

intimate concern for French-Canadian sensibilities, recent efforts by the NDP and the Conservatives to promote French Canadians to positions of leadership have not been fruitful. For a period in the 1960s, the NDP could boast as its Quebec lieutenant an amiable, charismatic leader in the person of Robert Cliche. But Cliche was defeated in a middle- to working-class urban French riding by Eric Kierans, an anglophone. In the 1970s Robert Stanfield could boast the lieutenancy of Claude Wagner, an ex-provincial justice minister. But, the Conservatives were not immediately more successful as a result.

Conclusion

The purpose of this chapter was to review the pattern of bicultural conflict in a summary way from the Conquest to the present in order to illustrate some of the historical antecedents for current mistrust and grievance. We attempted to show how cultural mistrust was an essential feature of each period. In the past two centuries, hardly a decade has passed in which a French-Canadian nationalist movement has not decried on ethnic grounds a government policy or socio-economic condition. Hardly a decade has passed without some expression of English-Canadian fear of "French domination" and without some English-Canadian appeal to those defeated in 1760 to finally submit. The bicultural cleavage has significantly affected Canada's constitutional changes: in 1791 when the existence of bicultural differences in

British North America demanded some decentralization of authority, in 1841 when rebellion in Lower Canada showed that French Canadians wanted to exercise the decentralized authority in their own interest, and in 1867 to break a deadlock in the Union Parliament created in part by equal representation from Canada East and Canada West.

Each constitutional modification was designed to improve a political situation judged untenable. A great irony is that the group, which according to many was to be submerged, assimilated, or otherwise defeated, has managed not only to survive, but also to exercise a considerable influence in federal politics. The preceding statistical analysis showed the extraordinary importance of French-Canadian support for a party's electoral success, although, of course, it is not to say that French Canadians as a group were ever able to call the tune alone. At all times, English-speaking Canadians outnumbered French-speaking Canadians in Parliament and held a comfortable majority of cabinet posts and senior civil service positions.

An irony for the future is that the party most identified with French Canada's interest — the Liberal party — may undermine its own position if and to the extent that it actually satisfies the many political, economic, and cultural concerns of its major constituency. If bicultural grievances are satisfied, the bicultural cleavage might be more easily supplanted by regional and/or class cleavages, from which the Liberal party need not necessarily gain. Thus, Liberal government support for French-Canadian interests is congruous with the basis of Liberal electoral support, but it would not necessarily be congruous with Liberal self-interest if French-Canadian anxieties were fully overcome. On the other hand, if French-Canadian anxieties are not overcome, the movement for Quebec independence would probably increase the number of its supporters, thus threatening even more than ever the stability of the country, a prospect cherished by neither the Liberals nor any federal political party.

A frequent assumption in political science is the rationality of voters. Either voters consciously support the party which serves their interests or, as a corollory, parties reward their supporters. If this assumption were valid, one could assume that Liberal governments consistently implemented programs more favourable to francophones than their Conservative counterparts. Expressed simply, a francophone input would yield a francophone output. Chapter 11, Bicultural Policy, will examine if this input-output relationship holds.

Notes

1. Royal Commission on Bilingualism and Biculturalism, *Report*, I (Ottawa: Queen's Printer, 1967), xxxi.

2. Cited in J. H. S. Reid, K. McNaught, H. S. Crowe, *A Source-book of Canadian History* (Toronto: Longmans, 1964), 51–52.

3. Cited in ibid., 52.

4. Ibid., loc. cit.

5. Observations on the Government of Canada, by John Black, in a letter to

the Duke of Kent (October 9, 1806), in W. P. M. Kennedy, *Documents on the Canadian Constitution 1759–1915* (Toronto: Oxford University Press, 1918), 246.

6. Translated from *Le Canadien* (December 12, 1807).

7. *Quebec Mercury* (November 24, 1806).

8. Translated from Ouellet, "Le Nationalisme canadien-français: De ses origines à l'insurrection de 1837," in Fernand Ouellet et al., *Constitutionalism and Nationalism in Lower Canada* (Toronto: University of Toronto Press, 1969), 10.

9. *Patronage et Pouvoir dans le Bas-Canada (1794–1812)* (Montréal: Les Presses de l'Université du Québec, 1973), Tables XIV to XVI.

10. Letter of John Molson et al. to Craig (November 22, 1834), in Public Archives of Canada, Secretary of State's Papers, Lower Canada, cited in D. C. Creighton, *The Commercial Empire of the St. Lawrence* (Toronto: Ryerson Press, 1937), 294.

11. On the links between Roman Catholicism and anti-semitism in Quebec during the 1930s, see Lita-Rose Betcherman, *The Swastika and the Maple Leaf* (Don Mills, Ont.: Fitzhenry and Whiteside, 1975).

12. *Lord Durham's Report on the Affairs of British North America*, II, edited with an introduction by Sir C. P. Lucas (Oxford: Clarendon Press, 1912), 307.

13. Sir Allan MacNab, speaking during the debate on the Rebellion Losses Bill (April 1849).

14. For an overview of several schooling crises, see D. G. Creighton et al., *Minorities, Schools, and Politics* (Toronto: University of Toronto Press, 1969).

15. Quoted in Ramsay Cook et al., *Canada* (Toronto: Clarke, Irwin, 1967), 172.

16. See R. MacGregor Dawson, *The Conscription Crisis of 1944* (Toronto: University of Toronto Press, 1962), and J. W. Pickersgill's account in *My Years with Louis St. Laurent: A Political Memoir* (Toronto: University of Toronto Press, 1975).

17. "Canadian Political Parties: A Study of the Economic and Racial Bases of Conservatism and Liberalism in 1930," in John C. Courtney (ed.), *Voting in Canada* (Scarborough, Ont.: Prentice-Hall, 1967), 72–81.

18. John Meisel, "Howe, Hubris and '72", in *Working Papers on Canadian Politics*, enlarged edition (Montreal: McGill-Queen's University Press, 1973), 218. Meisel's 1953 study is "Religious Affiliation and Electoral Behavior: A Case Study" in Courtney, *Voting*, 150.

19. Arthur R. M. Lower, *Colony to Nation: A History of Canada* (Don Mills, Ont.: Longmans, 1969), 402.

20. J. W. Dafoe, *Laurier: A Study in Canadian Politics* (Toronto: McClelland and Stewart, 1965), 25–7.

21. Lowell C. Clark, "The Conservative Party in the 1890s," *Canadian Historical Association Reports* (1961), 58–74.

22. Ibid.

23. Lower, *Colony to Nation*, 401.

24. Paul E. Crunciman, "The Manitoba School Question and Canadian Federal Politics: A Study in Church-State Relations" (doctoral dissertation, University of Toronto, 1968).

25. P. B. Waite, *Canada 1874–1896* (Toronto: McClelland and Stewart, 1971), 223.

26. John T. Saywell, "The 1890s", in J. M. S. Careless and R. Craig Brown (ed.), *The Canadians 1867–1967*, (Toronto: Macmillan, 1967), 111, and Robert W. Cox, "The Quebec Provincial Election of 1886", (McGill University Thesis, 1948), passim.

27. Saywell, "1890s," 125–6 and Waite, *Canada*, 276.

28. Ibid.

29. On the influence of the first-past-the-post method upon electoral outcomes, see Chapter 7.

30. *The French-Canadians, 1760–1911*, I, rev. ed. (Toronto: Macmillan, 1968), 437. Italics ours.

31. This study was assisted by John Summers and Charles Yolleck, then students at Wilfrid Laurier University.

32. See Gilles Paquet, "L'Emigration des Canadiens français vers la Nouvelle-Angleterre, 1870–1910: Prises de vue quantitatives," *Recherches sociographiques*, V (1964), 319–70.

33. See William P. Irvine, "Explaining the Religious Basis of the Canadian Partisan Identity: Success on the Third Try," *Canadian Journal of Political Science*, VII (September 1974), 560–63.

34. The Progressives in 1921, the Conservatives in all other instances.

35. For the Conservatives such an extreme dependence upon Quebec occurred only in 1872.

CHAPTER 5
GEOGRAPHIC CLEAVAGE: CORE VS. PERIPHERY

Douglas McCready and Conrad Winn

The late Professor Walter White provided helpful suggestions for the writing of this chapter.

Introduction

Although the scholarly literature makes much ado about class cleavage in industrial societies, these societies are marked by geographical cleavage as well. Even France, well-known for its divisions between wealthy and poor and believers and non-believers, is divided into its geographic core and its periphery. To the resentment of the remainder of the country, Paris contains a quasi-monopoly of industrial activity, higher education, advanced research, mass communication, entertainment, high-brow culture, political ceremony, and political power.

Despite its different history, the United States also exhibits an unequal spatial distribution of goods, services, and benefits. Like Paris, the strip from Boston to Washington possesses an extraordinary concentration of corporate wealth (Wall Street), mass communications (Manhattan), education (Ivy League), research (Boston-Philadelphia), and power (Washington). The inequality between core and periphery has produced political conflict both between and within the parties. So long as the Republican party was governed by the old families of New York, New England, and Pennsylvania, the Southern periphery remained safely within the Democratic party. In the 1960s, the Goldwater phenomenon opened the GOP to the new rich of the mid and southwest periphery and the Democratic party lost its monopoly in the southern periphery.

The geographic cleavage in Canada is akin to that in the United States. The Toronto-Ottawa-Montreal triangle possesses a quasi-monopoly of corporate power (Bay and St. James Streets), mass communication (CBC and CTV), highbrow culture (Stratford, the National Museums, National Arts Centre), entertainment (National Film Board, C.N.E., Man and His World), education (McGill, Queen's, Toronto), and political power. Of course, Canada is different from the United States in the sense that Canada is a subordinate, somewhat dependent, state.[1] For example, Central-Canadian elites do not receive all their training at their own universities, but supplement their educations with advanced work at American and sometimes British institutions. However, the proximity of the American core to the Canadian core, of Boston and New York to Montreal and Toronto, bolsters the position of Central Canada within Confederation.

There is a similarity not only betweeen the Canadian and American cores, but also between their peripheries. In recent years, the Canadian West, especially Alberta, has exhibited a sense of aggrieved status deprivation similar to the sentiments of some of the newly rich states of the American mid and southwest. Like Barry Goldwater in his rise within the Republican party, John Diefenbaker encountered considerable resistance among the core-based rulers within the Conservative party. Like Goldwater, Diefenbaker was an outsider on geographic, not to mention ethnic grounds. Diefenbaker came from Saskatchewan rather than Ontario or even historic Nova Scotia, while Goldwater emerged from Arizona rather than New York or New England. In their names, the two leaders revealed German rather than British ancestry.[2]

Like Goldwater, as well as Richard Nixon, Diefenbaker felt obliged to use symbolic patriotism as a means of undermining the position of his party's core-based elite. For Goldwater and Nixon, Wall Street, Nelson Rockefeller, and the eastern seabord families were insufficiently patriotic, insufficiently anti-communist. In Diefenbaker's darkest moments, his nemesis, Dalton Camp, Bay Street, and some of the Ontario Tories were portrayed as servants of American interests. Of course, the analogy between Diefenbaker and the conservative western-based Republicans is limited strictly to conflict rooted in geography. Diefenbaker is conspicuously more libertarian, more egalitarian, and less ethnocentric than his American counterparts. Contrast the loathing for Franklin Roosevelt of conservative Republicans, the veiled racism of Goldwater and Nixon, and the veiled anti-semitism of Nixon and Agnew with Diefenbaker's admiration for Roosevelt, his preference for black Africa over white supremacist South Africa, and his affection for Israel.

This chapter is divided into two parts. First, the chapter examines the spatial, political, economic, and communication disparities between the peripheral provinces and the central provinces, especially Ontario. Second, the chapter explores how these regional differences are expressed through the party system.

Geographic Inequality

The prototypical modern nation-state normally possesses a core distinguished by a high concentration of people, industry, wealth, decision-making, and the varied services and benefits which accrue to such a position of privilege. The capital is usually at the centre of the core. The residual space is known as the hinterland or periphery.[3] It takes no special genius to identify London and the southeast as the core of Great Britain and Wales, the Midlands, the Northeast, Scotland, and other areas as the periphery. In Canada, it is obvious that the Maritimes, the western provinces, and the Arctic region constitute the periphery.[4]

Delineating the Canadian core is more of a conundrum. Unlike London or Paris, but somewhat like Washington, Ottawa lacks a non-governmental source of influence. Its population is small and its economic base almost entirely bureaucratic. Rather than revolving around "Bytown," Canada's industrial heartland is found among Toronto, its satellite cities, and to a lesser extent in Montreal. Toronto and Montreal, rather than Ottawa, possess the important stock exchanges, banks, corporate offices, plants, respected newspapers, publishing houses, artists, broadcasters, and production plants for broadcasting and film.

For the preceding and other reasons, it makes sense to identify the core as "the Macdonald-Cartier Freeway," the "Golden Horseshoe," or even as Quebec and Ontario together. Although the city of North Bay does not have the same economic and political position as Toronto or London, Ontario, a sufficiently strong provincial sentiment in Canada justifies treating the provinces as undivided entities. Furthermore, readily available statistical data for the provinces shows in a dramatic way the special position of the two central provinces in Confederation. Some of the focus of the succeeding passages will be to illustrate with economic statistics the predominant position of Ontario and Quebec.

At the outset, we acknowledge a weakness in our analysis — the question of Quebec. As the statistics will show, Quebec's position is ambiguous. By some criteria, Quebec belongs to the core; by others, it does not. Furthermore, its economic performance or centrality has a peculiar character. While considerable power is located in Quebec, much of the economic power and some of the political power is in the hands of Anglo-Quebeckers. Finally, Canadians' perceptions of Quebec's membership of core and periphery are probably asymetric, with non-Quebeckers more likely to see the province as part of the core.

A usual but not necessary attribute of a core is spatial centrality. In the case of France, for example, the core is substantially central in terms of distance and the networks of transportation. The capital's centrality provides it with the best location for communication with the elements of the periphery, while the periphery acts as a multipurpose buffer against the outside. The Canadian core is centrally located with respect to internal communication. For reasons of distance, Central Canada can communicate more easily with the West and the Maritimes than the two peripheries can with each other. However, unlike the French core, the Canadian is not buffered, but is exposed to the American core more than any other Canadian region. To the extent that Canada adopts a policy of independence from the southern neighbour, the proximity of the two cores is probably an added burden for the Canadian core. Policy-making in Ottawa is more accessible and therefore more open to American influence than policy-making would be in an alternative capital at, say, Churchill, Manitoba, on the western shore of Hudson's Bay. On the other hand, to the extent that Canada pursues a policy of dependence on the United States, the special proximity of the Canadian core enhances its position within the Canadian system. American economic, cultural, and other "branch plants" enter and locate in the region most convenient to themselves.

While the proximity of the American core strengthens the position of the Canadian core directly in terms of economic benefits, the American core also enhances the Canadian core by serving as a model to be emulated and by providing ideological justifications or rationalizations for the Canadian case. For example, the relative concentration of television production and diffusion in New York City served as a model and a justification for the location of CBC and CTV facilities in Montreal and Toronto. The CBC need not give serious consideration to the regional dispersion of production because, except for the case of California, no such practice exists south of the border.

In the United States, the concentration of endeavour in the Northeast is justified in terms of conscious and unconscious beliefs about the superiority of the core and the inferiority of the hinterland. Like most other American beliefs, these views undoubtedly find their way into Canadian culture. The superiority complex of the Northeast Americans is not so strong as that of some Frenchmen. In France, some believe that there is Paris and then "the desert." Nevertheless, Spiro Agnew, the resigned U.S. Vice President, struck a chord in the hinterland when he spoke of the East's "effete intellectual snobs", as did President Gerald Ford when he reluctantly assisted New York City in its financial plight in 1975.

Not only are the Canadian and American cores linked to each other, but the Eastern and Western Canadian peripheries are also linked to the corresponding peripheries of the United States. Halifax, Moncton, and St. John, N.B., are all closer to Maine than to Ontario. The western provinces are closer to the northern states of the mid and far west than to the cities of Central Canada. Seattle, Washington, is more than twenty times closer to Vancouver than is Ottawa. In terms of direct air miles, Vancouver is closer to San Francisco, Los Angeles, and even the Mexican border than it is to the Golden Triangle.

The links between the Canadian and American peripheries undoubtedly enhance the hinterland identification of the Canadian periphery. This identification is especially true for the Canadian West. On account of easier access and because the American West is larger and more important than Maine, there has been greater communication between the Canadian and American western peripheries than between the Maritimes and Maine. The Canadian West was especially influenced by the American West because the American frontier was settled first. The populist and reformist movements of the western half of the continent have shared a common mood of anti-eastern resentment. The American and Canadian movements nourished each other with similar notions about the exploitative character of the cities of their respective core regions. In the Canadian case, the non-socialist movements of the West — particularly, Social Credit in Alberta — assimilated American populist ideas and followed the leadership of several American expatriots.

While location is one characteristic of the typical core and periphery in a political system, population density is another. Cores are densely inhabited and Central Canada is no exception. From Confederation, Quebec and Ontario possessed the bulk of the country's population. In 1867, Central Canada's population could justify 81% of the seats in the House of Commons and 67% of the seats in the Senate. Despite the addition of six provinces, Ontario and Quebec retain today three-fifths and one-half, respectively, of the seats in the Commons and Senate.

These figures conceal the actual political weakness of the peripheral provinces. The periphery tends to be under-represented in the important cabinet portfolios, in the bureaucratic ranks, and in federal-provincial consultations. The significant social, defense, and economic ministries tend to fall to Ontarians, and recently, to Quebeckers as well. Even John Diefenbaker, unequalled champion of the hinterland, felt obliged to assign the key Finance and Trade and Commerce posts to members from Ontario when he was prime minister. In the bureaucracy, only Ontario is over-represented, while the periphery tends to be under-represented. To add insult to injury, the federal government seems to value more highly the input of provincial governments from the core than from the periphery. In 1973, for example, 75% of bilateral federal-provincial meetings involved Quebec and Ontario.[5]

Historically, Quebec lay somewhere between Ontario and the periphery in terms of political power. Although under-represented in important portfolios and in the bureaucracy, Quebec has exercised a much greater influence than the periphery by means of "anticipated reaction." The Ontario-dominated, or at least English-dominated, cabinets of both world wars were obliged to postpone conscription for fear of subsequent repercussions in Quebec. Similar considerations helped to delay the liberalization of divorce law and the appointment of Jews to federal cabinet.[6] In recent years, Quebeckers have actually come to occupy the powerful ministerial and bureaucratic positions characteristic of a core region. At the time of writing, francophones were in charge of Information Canada, the Economic Council of Canada, the Unemployment Insurance Commission, the Canadian International Development Agency, the Science Council, the Department of Secretary of State, Air Canada, the Ministry of State for Science and Technology, the Ministry of the Solicitor General, the National Library, the Canada Council, the Armed Forces, the RCMP, and the supply half of the Department of Supply and Services.

The political inequality of the Canadian core and periphery is partly a reflection of an inequality in physical access. Even if Ontario were not more populous and no more developed economically than other provinces, it would still be easier for Ontarians to communicate with, learn about, satisfy, and gain admission to bureaucratic and ministerial circles in Ottawa. The personal displacement costs are simply lower for a resident of Kingston or Guelph than for a resident of Calgary or Charlottetown.

For French Quebeckers, the cultural inhospitality of Ottawa has been a special factor, a proxy for distance. The city has been a determinedly English-speaking town. As recently as the 1960s the nation's capital refused to install bilingual road signs. However, federal government policy to locate office complexes in Hull and to organize the two sides of the Ottawa river into a de facto bilingual district may make the capital more hospitable to Quebeckers and help integrate Quebec into the core.

Although the political status of Central Canada reflects geographic considerations, it also reflects economic considerations. By some criteria of economic development, Ontario and even Quebec are far more advanced than the remainder of the country. The position of the core is especially strong in the sense of economic decision-making and power. Not only are the majority of the economic institutions of the federal government in the core, but most of the significant institutions of the private sector are in the core as well. Almost all the headquarters of Canadian banks, insurance companies, trust companies, stock exchanges, and related institutions are found in the core. Likewise, the American and other multinational corporations tend to locate their Canadian head offices in the core.

Unfortunately, no census of corporations in Canada exists. Consequently, it is difficult to make accurate summary statements about the location of corporate head offices. Nevertheless, in 1973 the federal government undertook a survey of federally incorporated companies. The data, presented in Table 5-1, show the obvious dominance of Central Canada. More than 90% of these firms have headquarters in Ontario and Quebec.[7]

Table 5-1

Federal Corporations Registered with
the Department of
Consumer and Corporate Affairs, 1973

Newfoundland	1
Nova Scotia	8
Prince Edward Island	0
New Brunswick	9
Quebec	1,335
Ontario	655
Manitoba	60
Saskatchewan	9
Alberta	74
British Columbia	35

Source: Information Canada by telephone. This information is not usually kept, but was available because of a special survey done in 1973. The unusually high number of federal registrations from Quebec may occur because companies wish to be treated under common law rather than Quebec's civil law.
Note: See Note 7.

One economic correlate of the location of corporate head offices in the core is the concentration of corporate income in that region (see Table 5-2). Ontario and Quebec, respectively, account for about 45% and 23% of the total. Ontario's portion of corporate income significantly over-represents the province's share of the population. Quebec's portion of corporate income is also large compared to the other provinces, but its portion actually under-represents its population, particularly its francophone population.

By itself, the regional distribution of corporate income does not have a dramatic effect on the income of Canadians in different regions. Despite the concentration of head offices and corporate income in the core, some of the peripheral provinces have been able to sustain high per capital incomes (see Table 5-3). Two very aggrieved provinces, British Columbia and Alberta, have sustained especially high incomes. In five of the eight election years in the period 1926-57, B.C. achieved the highest per capita income in the country. In the period since, the per capita incomes of the two westernmost provinces have exceeded the incomes of all other provinces but Ontario. The Blishen socioeconomic profile of the provinces portrays a similar pattern, with Ontario achieving the highest score and the Maritime provinces the lowest (see Table 5-4).[8]

Table 5-2

Corporation Taxable Income: 1969
(in millions of dollars)

	Newfoundland	Nova Scotia	P.E.I.	New Brunswick	Quebec	Ontario	Manitoba	Saskatchewan	Alberta	B.C.
Agriculture, forestry, and fishing	0.2	1.4	0.1	0.8	2.2	12.0	0.8	1.7	5.9	26.6
Mining	4.4	3.3	—	0.7	60.7	65.3	13.8	9.4	59.8	22.3
Manufacturing	8.5	33.3	2.5	37.7	684.6	1434.8	76.2	27.4	128.6	368.8
Construction	7.1	7.3	0.7	4.6	45.9	120.5	15.5	12.1	40.3	40.9
Transportation	15.5	17.7	2.0	10.3	118.5	200.4	18.8	29.8	76.3	78.3
Wholesale Trade	6.4	12.6	1.5	10.9	157.0	278.4	26.2	14.1	52.5	73.2
Retail Trade	7.1	18.8	1.5	13.6	82.1	192.8	25.3	18.5	55.4	72.9
TOTAL Non-financial industries	51.9	99.8	8.3	82.1	1234.2	2439.6	191.6	119.6	450.1	727.8
PER CAPITA (in dollars)	100.97	129.95	75.45	131.36	206.25	327.38	195.61	124.61	288.34	352.10
AS % OF CANADIAN	1.0	1.8	0.2	1.5	22.8	45.1	3.5	2.2	8.3	13.5

Source: Ministry of Industry, Trade, and Commerce, *Corporation and Labour Unions Returns Act: Report for 1969; Part 1: Corporations*, Table 5, (Ottawa: Information Canada, 1972).

Table 5-3

Per Capita Personal Income by Province
for Election Years 1926-72

	NFLD.	N.S.	P.E.I.	N.B.	P.Q.	ONT.	MAN.	SASK.	ALTA.	B.C.
1926	—	291	241	278	363	491	465	437	488	524
1930	—	317	227	281	394	532	424	264	387	547
1935	—	243	174	201	284	397	282	197	248	407
1940	—	339	232	285	375	549	400	310	399	536
1945	—	625	446	544	622	931	721	646	705	889
1949	507	742	553	691	848	1188	1030	964	1050	1182
1953	668	961	644	839	1139	1555	1251	1322	1400	1583
1957	825	1120	778	989	1334	1812	1419	1178	1503	1841
1958	836	1157	830	1025	1357	1856	1545	1297	1624	1811
1962	987	1334	1065	1169	1573	2062	1721	1644	1761	1975
1963	1036	1389	1074	1233	1630	2156	1736	1807	1807	2065
1965	1238	1562	1257	1431	1880	2436	1961	1883	2028	2377
1968	1654	2060	1718	1893	2394	3146	2598	2278	2698	2914
1972	2477	2990	2478	2810	3403	4366	3557	2991	3749	4086

Source: Statistics Canada, *National Income and Expenditure Accounts*, 1, Catalogue No. 13-531, (forthcoming publication) (Information Canada, Ottawa.)

Table 5-4

Blishen Index by Province, 1961

	Mean Socio-Economic Index of the Labour Force	Rank in National Class Hierarchy
Newfoundland	35.58	10
Nova Scotia	37.27	7
Prince Edward Island	35.59	9
New Brunswick	36.76	8
Quebec	38.48	5
Ontario	39.61	1
Manitoba	38.78	3
Saskatchewan	38.15	6
Alberta	39.20	2
British Columbia	38.72	4

Source: Adapted from Bernard R. Blishen, "A Socio-Economic Index for Occupations in Canada", *Canadian Review of Sociology and Anthropology*, IV (February 1967), 53.

The concentration of economic decision-making in the core has not visibly improverished the West, but may have deprived the West of opportunities for still greater income and participating in economic policy-making. There is no foolproof evidence that head offices in the core formulated corporate policies to satisfy primarily the needs of their own region. Yet, the prevalent economic and business reasoning supports such an argument. For example, on grounds of efficiency and reliability, it is natural for banks to favour creditors in their own region. This widely accepted mode of thinking gives some credence to the oft repeated western grievance that the Central Canadian banks borrow in the West but prefer to lend to client firms from the core. Similarly, it makes sense for existing firms to add manufacturing capacity within ready access of the head office, of major markets, of major supplies of skilled labour, and of sources of technological innovation. For the multinational or Canadian firm with headquarters in Montreal or Toronto, it therefore makes sense to add capacity in the core. As for transportation, senior corporate executives and planners are located in the core, interact in the core with the executives of other industries, and therefore would be expected to be more aware of the anticipated growth and needs of the core.

Cy Gonick, an economist, pamphleteer, and leader of the left faction in the Manitoba NDP, has framed a stronger, Marxian version of this analysis. According to Gonick,

> . . . in Canada the flow [of wealth] is from the provinces to Ontario, and from Ontario to the United States. The provinces are hinterlands of Toronto. Toronto (and to a lesser degree . . . Montreal) acts as the financial headquarters of American branch-plants. Provincial capitals, in turn, house the local branches and serve their own hinterlands. The provinces are colonies within a colony. They provide cheap pools of labour for Ontario.[9]

The Politics of Geographic Inequality

While it is easy to identify the objective economic, political, and communication disparities between the core and periphery of a country, it is a harder task to isolate the political consequences of these disparities. Not all geographic differences in political behaviour are inherently spatial. For example, the apparently "regional" differences in the political comportment of Quebec and Ontario are less regional than bicultural. It happens that the two regions possess relatively homogeneous populations of the two main cultural groups. However, if francophones and anglophones were randomly dispersed in Central Canada instead of being concentrated as they are now, the bicultural cleavage would probably persist even without a regional character. Thus, any conflict between the inhabitants of the two regions of Central Canada stems from bicultural rather than purely locational or spatial considerations.

The following passages are concerned with political cleavages which are inherently locational. Admittedly, it is a difficult task to isolate intrinsically geographic conflict from other conflicts because many conflicts possess spatial attributes. The political alienation of the western provinces from the Canadian core illustrates the intermingling of inherently spatial factors with inherently cultural factors, even if

they are often portrayed as spatial. In terms of their economic development and in terms of their current economic and political power,
the western provinces can be understood partly as "internal" colonies
within Confederation.[10] The western provinces were created at
Ontario's behest and continue to be very much subject to decisions
made in Ontario and Quebec. Nonetheless, some of the West's resent-
ments are cultural rather than spatial in origin. Unlike the provinces
east of Manitoba, the western provinces were settled after the rise of
socialist movements in Great Britain and Europe. The western
populace therefore included a disproportionate number of citizens
socialized to view society in terms of conflict and prepared to question
the legitimacy of Canada's political and economic rulers, who happened to reside in the core. The most revolutionary act in Canadian
history during this century, the Winnipeg General Strike of 1919, did
take place in the periphery, but it was led by immigrants who had
acquired their social outlooks in the British labour movement or
through British Methodism. The Methodist Rev. J. S. Woodsworth, who
helped lead the strike and subsequently led the CCF, manifested this
cultural influence.

Although it is difficult to isolate geographic conflict from other
conflicts correlated with it, it is nevertheless possible to hazard some
generalizations about the political relationships between cores and
peripheries. First, like the former European colonies of Africa and Asia,
the "internal" colonies constituting the periphery of a country tend to
be more left-wing than would be expected on class or economic
grounds.[11] In the case of the international political system, Marxian
theory predicted that communism would come first to the most developed industrial states. Instead, communism was unsuccessful in the
industrial core of the international system, the North Atlantic area,
while flourishing in the semi-industrialized periphery of Russia,
China, Vietnam, Cambodia, Cuba, Guinea, Syria, and Iraq. Within
Canada, solely economic considerations would lead to predictions of
greatest success for the left in Ontario and to some extent in Quebec as
well. Instead, the left has been particularly successful in the semi-
industrialized West, where the so-called "objective" bases of intrare-
gional class conflict are weak. Internationally, communism is partly an
expression of hostility to the North Atlantic core.[12] Domestically, the
left is partly an expression of hostility to the national core.

Secondly, like the ex-colonies of the third world, "internal" colonies are less likely to adopt left-wing political behaviour when they
lack a certain minimum level of economic performance and therefore a
minimum level of economic expectations.[13] Internationally, the left
arose in wealthy Cuba and Chile and not in impoverished Bolivia,
where the peasantry saw Che Guevara as something less than a saviour.
In Canada, the left is successful in the wealthy but vulnerable western
provinces, yet unsuccessful in the poor provinces of the Atlantic
region.

The domestic political behaviour of Norway, Britain, and France
illustrate these two propositions about the behaviour of peripheries. In

these countries, the strongholds of the left are found in the periphery, while the parties of the centre-right reside in the core. In Norway, the distant north has a persistent record of radicalism and was the first region to elect Labour members to the *Storting*.[14] In Great Britain, Wales, Scotland, and the English northeast are the strongholds of the left. The workers of Glasgow and the miners of Wales and Durham are part of the legend of the Labour movement. In the mid-1960s, Labour could count on only 40% of the vote in the southcentral region of England, but on 51% in Scotland, 59% in the northeast, and an amazing 72% in Wales.[15] In France, the core is located in the north and the sourthern periphery, the *midi*, is the backbone of the left. In the 1965 election for President, the unsuccessful socialist candidate, François Mitterand, won in 24 *départements*, only one of which (his own) was neither in the southern periphery of the *pays d'oc* nor on its borders.[16]

In France, it is commonplace to view the south, overall, as the bastion of the left, and occasionally of the radical right, and to view the northern core as the home of the centre-right. However, the French periphery is not homogeneous. The economically advanced components of the *pays d'oc* such as Toulouse and Marseilles are heavily *rouge*, more so than their urban counterparts in the north. By contrast, the economically retarded sectors of the south vote for the incumbent centre-right parties. These sectors are characterized by a lack of opportunities for employment, which drives out active youth and raises the age of the overall population. According to one French political scientist, "One can see developing a welfare mentality, which consists of voting systematically for the party in power, the general dispenser of loans and subsidies."[17]

France is a particularly helpful analogy for the Canadian case. The leadership of the left in both countries (François Mitterand, Ed Broadbent) may come from the core, but electoral strength resides in the periphery, particularly the developed periphery. Like the retarded regions of France, the Maritimes give allegiance to the mainline parties capable of providing assistance through the Department of Regional Economic Expansion or by other means. According to Regenstreif, some Maritime ridings follow one of the major parties out of historic loyalty, while others chose between the two after a careful assessment of the nation-wide outcome.[18] Like the poor *départements* of the south of France, the Maritime provinces have a dearth of employment and experience the outmigration of the active young.

Of course, not all of the behaviour of the Maritimes is accountable in terms of the characteristics of depressed peripheries. In recent years, the Atlantic provinces have given unexpected support to the opposition Conservatives, partly out of loyalty to a favourite son, Robert Stanfield, and partly out of appreciation for the efforts of the Diefenbaker government to identify with the Canadian periphery. Until 1972, Newfoundland was loyal to the Liberal party as a result of the power of Joseph Smallwood, the ex-Premier, whose links to the federal Liberals were cemented before Newfoundland joined Confederation.

While the behaviour of the Maritimes approximates that of the poor southern *départements* in France, the behaviour of the western provinces resembles the developed *départements* in the *midi* and the periphery in Britain and Norway. Like Glasgow and Marseilles, Winnipeg and Vancouver are bastions of the left. The two Canadian cities are historic sites for socialist and even communist activity. Between 1900 when many Labour candidates sought federal office and when the CCF contested its first election, the independent Labour and Socialist candidates in Manitoba and British Columbia polled proportionately far more votes than their counterparts in Central or Eastern Canada.[19] In 1935, the CCF secured one-third of the popular vote in British Columbia and one-fifth of the vote in Manitoba and Saskatchewan, but less than 10% of the vote in industrialized Ontario and almost no vote in Quebec. Communist candidates have continually secured election to local positions in Winnipeg.

The importance of the west for the CCF-NDP can be seen in the nature of its formation, leadership, and myth. Many of the early organizational meetings took place in Calgary and Regina. For almost forty years, the parliamentary leaders of the CCF-NDP came from the West: J. S. Woodsworth, M. J. Coldwell, and T. C. Douglas were westerners. The party's sacred texts are the Regina Manifesto and the Winnipeg Declaration, the more eastern document being the more moderate.

The contemporary moderation of the Atlantic provinces and the overt political alienation of the West conform with the historical behaviour of the two regions. The East's only significant act of alienation was its hesitation to join Confederation. However, through coaxing, connivance, railroad and financial consessions, Macdonald was able to win over Howe and his region. Compared to the rest of Canada, the economic fortunes of the East have steadily declined since 1867. Circumstances of this kind normally induce moderation and acquiescence.[20] By contrast, the alienation of the West is a growing phenomenon of this century, accelerated by the boom-and-bust nature of the western economy. The western wheat economy provides its region with unusual opportunities for the acquisition of wealth along with an unusual vulnerability to external economic forces. This vulnerability was compounded by the West's dependence on Central-Canadian institutions for credit and for transportation and by the West's indirect subsidy to the centre as a result of the tariff haven provided to Ontario- and Quebec-manufactured goods.

The West experienced two boom-bust cycles of political import. Between 1910 and 1919, the price of wheat rose from $.69 per bushel to $2.32. In the next two years, wheat fell to $1.55 and $.76. In the latter year, 1921, the West spawned its first generation of new parties. Federally, the Progressives won more than a fifth of the national vote with 61% in Saskatchewan, 53% in Alberta, and 44% in Manitoba. Provincially, the United Farmers took office in Alberta. In the next five years, the price of wheat rose again to more than a dollar per bushel and popular support for the Progressives declined. However, wheat fell to a new low of $ .32 in 1932 and the Social Credit and CCF parties were formed.[21]

In all the western provinces but Alberta, the CCF-NDP became the principal alternative to the mistrusted, core-based Liberals and Conservatives. The CCF formed the government in Saskatchewan in 1944, providing a provincial base for federal victories in that province. In 1969 and 1972, the NDP won provincial elections in Manitoba and British Columbia. Alberta proved an exception to the thesis of left-wing voting. However, the provincial and federal rise of Social Credit in Alberta was actually assisted by the early, almost premature, success of socialism in that province. The United Farmers of Alberta were in power when the depression began. In 1933, the UFA adopted a socialist program and affiliated with the national CCF. Since the UFA had been in office, voting UFA-CCF in Alberta was not an alternative to the status quo — only a vote for Social Credit would be.[22]

The success of the ideologically right-wing Social Credit in the Canadian periphery undermines our thesis about the left-wing tendencies of non-depressed peripheries, but only slightly. While peripheries tend to promote left-wing behaviour, they also have a more general tendency to ideological polarization. In France, the left has been especially strong in the *midi* periphery, but the less popular, semi-fascist *poujadist* movement has also received a larger than normal share of support in the *midi*. In Britain, the Labour movement and Enoch Powell's racialism appear to vie for support in some of the same peripheral regions. Like the right-wing Republicanism of Gov. Ronald Reagan in California, western Social Credit is an example of the radical right in the periphery. In its marked anti-communism, authoritarianism, and its traces of ethnocentrism and anti-semitism, Social Credit embodies some of the elements of fascism. Of course, Alberta and British Columbia no longer elect Social Credit Members of Parliament. The region nonetheless continues to spawn politicians of the radical right, most notably Jack Horner, the Conservative MP from Alberta.[23]

Before concluding our case for a relationship between peripheral location and left-wing behaviour, it is important to present quantitative evidence that the lesser preference of the western provinces for the parties of the centre or centre-right cannot be explained in terms of class. In their work on Britain, Butler and Stokes demonstrated the independent effect of region on voting by providing 2 × 2 tables isolating the effect of class. Some of their data is combined with responses from the 1965 Canadian national survey in order to compare the core-periphery effect in both countries (see Table 5-5).[24] In the Canadian case, Quebec is excluded from the core to control statistically for the bicultural cleavage. To include Quebec would overstate our case. It makes more sense to attribute the low NDP vote in that province to French Canada's suspicion of an English party which was once led by two Protestant clergy, J. S. Woodsworth and T. C. Douglas, than to Quebec's hostility as a core province to a political party of the periphery.

Most obviously, Table 5-5 shows the greater strength of the left in Britain. The table also shows one striking similarity and one difference.

Table 5-5

Labour and NDP Voter Identification (%) by
Self-Perceived Class in Cores and Peripheries of
Britain and Canada

	Canada (all-party vote)		Britain (2-party vote)	
	Ontario	West	Southeast	North
Middle Class	8	15	20	26
Working Class	20	27	67	74

The left-wing vote increases in both social classes in the respective peripheries of both countries. However, left-wing support rises proportionately more in the Canadian periphery than in the British, suggesting that location may be more of a factor in support for the NDP than in support for Labour.[25]

The NDP is not the only party to receive support in the West. The West has a long history of attachment to the Liberal party. Even Saskatchewan, now known for its socialism, was once famous for the Liberal "machine" of Jimmy Gardiner. A considerable part of the West's affinity for the Liberals is explained by the issue of the tariff. Ever since John A. Macdonald's National Policy, the Conservatives were committed, at least rhetorically, to a high customs barrier in order to protect the infant industries of Central Canada. Dependent on the import of farm machinery into their region, westerners would absorb the costs of the high tariff policy through higher prices for Canadian manufactures. The Liberals were committed, at least rhetorically, to a policy of low tariff. Until the accession of Diefenbaker to the leadership of the Conservatives, the apparent differences between the major parties on the tariff and the apparent affinity of the Conservatives for Central-Canadian business were sufficient reasons for the West to remain loyal to the Liberals.[26]

By 1957, the long rule of the King and St. Laurent governments must have taught the Prairie provinces that the major parties did not really differ on the tariff question. Canada still had a tariff. In 1957, one of the major parties was led for the first time by an avowed champion of the hinterland. It is not surprising, therefore, that the West should have switched its allegiance from the Liberals to the Conservatives.

An important question to ponder is whether the West's support for the Conservatives is fundamentally regional in character or can be explained by another factor. In the case of the NDP discussed above, a substantial portion of its support in the West cannot be explained in terms of class, but must instead be attributed to peripheral resentment. By contrast, the considerable support for the Conservatives in the West appears to be explicable in terms of other factors. In Canada the Conservatives receive disproportionate support from English-speaking Protestants and, like conservatives in other countries, receive disproportionate support from small-town and rural inhabitants. It happens that the western provinces contain a very high proportion of the voters who would typically vote Conservative in any province, Ontario included.

Table 5-6 contains some evidence to confirm that the West votes strongly Conservative because its population is English-speaking and non-urbanized rather than for intrinsically geographic reasons. The table compares Conservative popularity in Ontario and the West in towns (population 1,000 to 30,000) and in rural areas (under 1,000). If the West votes Conservative for intrinsically geographic reasons, popular support should be greater in the West than in Ontario among both towns and rural areas. The table shows no such pattern.

Table 5-6

Support for the Progressive Conservatives
in Ontario and the West (1965 CIPO Poll)

	Towns (pop. 1000-30,000)	Rural Areas (Pop. under 1000)
Ontario	26%	36%
West	25%	32%

Even if this particular CIPO survey under-represented Western affection for the Progressive Conservatives, additional evidence would be needed to demonstrate that the West is inherently more Conservative than Ontario. It is clear that the Right Honourable Member from Prince Albert, Saskatchewan, continues to display a great deal of personal magnetism. It is equally clear that western voters see Diefenbaker as a spokesman for their region. To discover how much of Conservative voting in the West is owed to partisan affection and how much is owed to admiration for the Chief would require waiting until he retires from politics, though the West may continue its support, since Joe Clark, the new leader, is from Alberta.

Conclusion

The traditional approach to the geographical factor in political behaviour has been to examine the behaviour of individual provinces or regions. There is some merit to this approach and there is a good literature in this genre.[27] At the risk of missing some important details and facts, we chose instead to make some generalizations about the most important aspect of conflict rooted in geography, the core-periphery cleavage.

We began by demonstrating the objective economic, communication, and political aspects of the disparities in the power and influence of the Canadian core and its peripheries. We looked at the distribution of corporate profits, corporate decisions, and government decision-making; as well, we looked at the effect of core-periphery differences in the United States on her northern neighbour. The chapter then turned to the political manifestations of core-periphery disparities. Using analogies from international politics and comparisons with Britain, France, and Norway, we suggested that location in the periphery acts as an independent source of left-wing behaviour and voting. Not by geographic accident, therefore, did Canada's major left-wing party, the CCF-NDP, and its sister protest parties rise in the West, nor is it accidental that the NDP continues to benefit from a disproportionate support in the region.

While peripheries seem to accord special support to the left, they also tend to be ideologically polarized, extending some support to the radical right as well. It is not surprising, therefore, that many of the pressures for greater law and order in the 1970s seem to emanate from the Far West, nor is it surprising that the most articulate opponents of socialist tendencies in government tend to be western politicians such as Jack Horner, MP.

In terms of public policy, we might expect that the parties supported by the West — the pre-Diefenbaker Liberals, the post-Diefenbaker Conservatives, and the CCF-NDP — would implement policies most favourable to that region. For example, we might expect recent Conservative governments actually to lower the tariff and recent core-based Liberal governments to raise it. This might be a reasonable expectation if Canadian politics were a simple input-output system and if federal politicians — eastern, western, or from the core — were able to implement policy in a rationally calculated way. Chapter 13, on tariff and resource policies, explores how much historical evidence can support this kind of reasoning.

Notes

1. There is a large literature on Canada's dependency on and vulnerability to the United States. See Ian Lumsden (ed.), *Close the 49th Parallel* (Toronto: University of Toronto Press, 1970); James Steele and Robin Mathews, *The Struggle for Canadian Universities* (Toronto: New Press, 1969); and Abraham Rotstein and Gary Lax, *Independence: The Canadian Challenge* (Toronto: McClelland and Stewart, 1972).

2. See John Diefenbaker, *One Canada*, I (Toronto: Macmillan, 1975), and Peter Stursberg, *Diefenbaker: Leadership Gained, 1956–1962* (Toronto: University of Toronto Press, 1975).

3. On the concepts of core and periphery, see Norman Pounds and S. S. Ball, "Core Areas and the Development of the European State System", *Annals*, American Association of Geographers, LIV (1964), 24–40; Roger E. Kasperson and Julian V. Minghi (ed.), *The Structure of Political Geography* (Chicago: Aldine Publishing, 1969), 69–186, passim; Richard L. Merritt, "W. Berlin — Center or Periphery", in Richard L. Merritt and Stein Rokkan, (ed.), *Comparing Nations: The Use of Quantitative Data in Cross-National Research* (New Haven: Yale University Press, 1966); and Daniel Lerner, "Some Comments on Center-Periphery Relations", in ibid.

4. For an examination of the core-periphery cleavage in Canada, see John Meisel, "Cleavages, Parties, and Values in Canada," a paper presented at the

IXth Congress of the International Political Science Association (Montreal, August 1973). The paper appears in amended form under the same title as Sage publications paper 06-003. For a study emphasizing federal-provincial relationships, see Simon McInnes, "Federal Systems and Centre-Periphery Analysis: The Canadian Case," a paper presented at the XLVIth Meeting of the Canadian Political Science Association (Toronto, June 1974).

5. Ibid. The calculation by McInnes was based on a sample size of 109.

6. The persistence of medieval prejudice in Quebec is suggested by the decision of the province's Press Council to condemn *Nouvelles Illustrées* (circulation 75,000) for anti-semitic headlines. Its sister paper, *Le Journal de Montréal* (circulation 140,000), was also condemned for employing news columns for commercial purposes, disguising advertisements as news stories. See *The Globe and Mail* (January 21, 1975), 8.

7. An attempt was made to collect data on provincial incorporations and head offices. While all provinces can give data on new incorporations, provinces such as British Columbia have no record of those corporations which disband. Federal data on head offices define a head office as being "in a separate location from the ordinary place of output." Since many companies have their head offices near or at their plant location and since these are not counted, that data is not reported here.

8. For survey evidence on regional perceptions of economic well-being, see Mildred A. Schwartz, *Politics and Territory: The Sociology of Regional Persistence in Canada* (Montreal: McGill-Queen's University Press, 1974), 87.

9. Gonick, "Socialism and the Economics of Growthmanship," in Laurier Lapierre et al., *Essays on the Left: Essays in Honour of T. C. Douglas* (Toronto: McClelland and Stewart, 1971), 135–59.

10. For the concept of internal colonialism, see Michael Hechter, *Internal Colonialism: The Celtic Fringe in British National Development* (Berkeley: University of California Press, 1975). For a Canadian argument, see C. B. Macpherson, *Democracy in Alberta* (Toronto: University of Toronto Press, 1953).

11. See John H. Kautsky, *Political Change in Underdeveloped Countries: Nationalism and Communism* (New York: John Wiley and Sons, 1967), 3–123.

12. See Kautsky, *Political Change*.

13. On the effects of economic growth and economic expectations on political alienation, see James C. Davies, "Toward a Theory of Revolution," *American Sociological Review*, XXVII (1962).

14. See Stein Rokkan, "Geography, Religion and Social Class: Cross-cutting Cleavages in Norwegian Politics," in Seymour M. Lipset and Stein Rokkan (ed.), *Party Systems and Voter Alignments* (New York: The Free Press, 1967), 367–444. Norway's western periphery deviates from the general pattern by voting Christian rather than left, radical right, or even centre-right. Rokkan explains this behaviour in terms of the confounding influence of the region's religiosity. See his section on the West's "cultural distinctiveness," ibid.

15. See David Butler and Donald Stokes, *Political Change in Britain* (Toronto: Macmillan, 1969), 135–50.

16. See Michel Grosclaude, "Deux Comportements Politiques," in Robert Lafont (ed.), *Le Sud et le Nord: Dialectique de la France* (Toulouse: Edouard Privat, 1967), 181–204.

17. Ibid., 201. Our translation.

18. Peter Regenstreif, *The Diefenbaker Interlude: Parties and Voting in Canada* (Toronto: Longmans, 1965), 164, 167.

19. See J. Murray Beck, *Pendulum of Power: Canada's Federal Elections* (Scarborough: Prentice-Hall, 1968).

20. Davies, "Revolution."

21. See Seymour M. Lipset, *Agrarian Socialism: The Cooperative Commonwealth Federation in Saskatchewan* (Garden City, N.Y.: Anchor Books, 1968), Chapter 2, for a study of the economic setting in the west.

22. See Lipset's analysis, ibid., 153–55.

23. The Liberal caucus has also contained the occasional spokesman for the extreme right. In the 1930s and early 1940s, some Liberal candidates on the west coast appealed openly to racist sentiment, seeking to tar the CCF with favouring legal equality for Asian Canadians. See James Morton, *In the Sea of Sterile Mountains: The Chinese in British Columbia* (Vancouver: J. J. Douglas, 1973), 295. Also, see Ch. 6, Note 42.

24. Butler and Stokes, *Britain*, 138. The British Core (Southeast) included London, Middlesex, Surrey, Sussex, Berkshire, Buckinghamshire, Dorset, Essex, Hampshire, Hertfordshire, Isle of Wight, and Kent. The northern periphery included Cheshire, Cumberland, Durham, Lancashire, Northumberland, Westmoreland, and Yorkshire. We gratefully acknowledge the assistance of Dr. John Meisel, who made available the 1965 national data.

25. In Chapter 6 below, Professor Chi argues that, in a middle-class society such as Canada, self-perceived or self-reported class is a poor method of measuring the class status of respondents in a survey. Irrespective of their income or occupation, too many respondents believe themselves to be middle class. Self-perceived class is used in this study primarily because it is the easiest way of comparing Canadian voting behaviour with British behaviour. Nevertheless, other measures of class yield similar findings about the independent effect of western location on voter support for the NDP. Among respondents with grades 1-8 education in the 1965 national survey, regional support for the NDP was 16% in Ontario, 26% on the Prairies, and 33% in British Columbia. For upper status respondents with 14 or more years of education, the comparable percentages were 9, 14, and 13.

26. See Chapter 13, below, for an argument that the tariff policies of the major parties were not really different.

27. For some provincial or regional studies of institutions and behaviour, see J. M. Beck, *The Government of Nova Scotia* (Toronto: University of Toronto Press, 1957); M. S. Donnelly, *The Government of Manitoba* (Toronto: University of Toronto Press, 1962); Hugh G. Thorburn, *Politics in New Brunswick* (Toronto: University of Toronto Press, 1961); Walter D. Young, *Democracy and Discontent* (Toronto: McGraw-Hill, 1969); C. B. Macpherson, *Democracy in Alberta: Social Credit and the Party System* (Toronto: University of Toronto Press, 1953); Donald C. Rowat (ed.), *Provincial Government and Politics* (Ottawa: Carleton University Bookstore, 1973); and Martin Robin (ed.), *Canadian Provincial Politics* (Scarborough: Prentice-Hall, 1972), and David Bellamy et al. (ed.), *The Provincial Political Systems: Comparative Essays* (Toronto: Methuen, 1976).

CHAPTER 6
CLASS CLEAVAGE

N. H. Chi

I am indebted to Conrad Winn, Leo Panitch, and Khayam Paltiel for having read an earlier draft of this paper and offering many valuable suggestions.

Introduction

Almost all political scientists agree that the substance of politics consists of political cleavages, conflicts of interest, or "contradictions," to use Marxian language. As two liberal-democratic scholars have expressed it, the activity of politics involves

> the selection of the preference . . . for society [so as] to exploit the authority and force of society in realizing these choices over the objections of those whose preferences must remain unrealized.[1]

The conflict may be resolved with or without the use of force. When violence is present, Marxists speak of an "antagonistic contradiction". Otherwise, the contradiction is "non-antagonistic."[2] Maoists and liberal-democrats have different approaches for insuring that contradictions within a system remain non-antagonistic. To turn an "antagonistic contradiction" into a "non-antagonistic" one, the Maoist model relies on an extensive program of political education or indoctrination.[3] Meanwhile, the liberal-democratic or free market model requires a system of political bargaining in which politicians act as mediators or brokers between competing interests.[4] Irrespective of one's ideology, to understand a political system requires a study of the dominant conflict or "primary contradiction" and the ways in which that conflict is resolved.

An apparent conflict may emerge between different religions (e.g. Northern Ireland) or between regions (e.g. The American civil war). According to Marxist theorists, however, these religious or regional conflicts are fundamentally economic in nature. In Northern Ireland, for example, the conflict between Roman Catholics and Protestants receives its impetus from class differences with Catholics found in large numbers in the working class. The "primary" contradiction in an industrialized system such as Canada is the revolutionary one between capitalists and proletarians. As Karl Marx observed, "all struggles within a state . . . are merely the illusory forms in which the real struggles of the different classes are fought out among one another."[5]

In Canada, the bicultural and geographic cleavages may provoke more widespread and more intense popular feeling than class conflict. That is why this book accords more importance to the first two cleavages. From a neutral, non-ideological perspective, the editors' choice of emphasis may make as much academic sense as a personal preference for class analysis. However, a political by-product of giving greater attention to non-class issues is to serve the interests of the more privileged. The power base and the economic interest of the dominating class could be undermined if the less privileged majority of voters thought and behaved according to their class interests. Whether on the election hustings or in the classroom, to downplay class differences is to encourage the Canadian worker to be loyal to capitalism and to view the major parties as representative of all economic classes.

Thus, the Canadian proletariat displays a certain degree of "false consciousness." Canadian workers remain unaware that the bureaucracy, the media, the political parties, and the remaining superstructure of Canadian society tend to serve the interests of the capitalist class. Voters lack a sufficient class perspective in considering various political issues. On the contrary, they tend unduly to emphasize non-class factors, such as ethnic conflicts, regional disparities, and provincial autonomy.

Understandably, liberal-democratic theorists in the West do not share the Marxian focus on social stratification. They do not see class conflict in western democracies as either pre-eminent in importance or revolutionary in character.[6] The political right goes so far as to hail the end of class ideology in the West, at least in North America.[7] The non-communist left, including liberals, social democrats, and some socialist revisionists, sees the electoral process as a "democratic class struggle" between those who have a lot and those who do not have enough.[8] Unlike orthodox Marxists, the non-communist left does not wish to abolish private ownership entirely, but to minimize class conflict by minimizing disparities of income and wealth.

Until recently, the Cold War discouraged the use of class analysis as an appropriate tool of analysis for serious-minded political scientists.[9] The tension between the Soviet and American blocs impeded the widespread use of Marxian tools in western social science. Threatened by McCarthyism, some scholars may have feared for their livelihoods. Other scholars may have hesitated to criticize their own systems out of patriotism or a fear of being suspected of "ideological treason."[10] Still others may have modified their radicalism out of a recognition that Marx's humanistic values were not necessarily monopolized by the ostensibly Marxist countries. Undoubtedly, the emerging portrait of Stalin's tyranny in the 1950s had a shattering effect on the morale of Marxists in the West.

However, the subsequent depolarization and moderation of the Cold War have removed Marxism from the "black list," at least in the academic world. It may still be true that it is "indecent to employ the term [class] in well-bred society."[11] However, the 1960s and the 1970s have witnessed a revitalized interest in class analysis, even in the United States.[12] Class analysis was not restored merely because of the distant passing of U.S. Senator Joseph McCarthy and his witch hunt. The re-introduction of class analysis was also a reaction against the traditional approach in social science, apparently unable to offer an adequate answer to such contemporary problems in American society as race, crime, and political violence and corruption. This change in scholarly theory may be seen as a reflection of a widespread feeling of self-doubt in the Western World. While a number of young western thinkers look toward Marxism for inspiration, it is an irony to note that the Soviet society built in the name of Karl Marx is moving toward the form of a corporate state with an organization not so different from that of ITT or General Motors.[13]

The Orthodox Approach vs. the Reality of Class Politics

Like American academics, Canadian scholars have not shown a great interest in class analysis. Furthermore, Canadian political scientists have largely imported from the United States the labels of classical liberal economics to describe political behaviour. Western countries in general and Canada in particular are described as heterogeneous, pluralistic systems in which political demands for government services and the supply of such services are freely exchanged. Canadian academics borrow the fundamentals of their theory of politics from their American counterparts. However, these scholars claim to have a different ideological position and propagate the idea that the Canadian system is a "mosaic" in contrast to the American "melting pot." Thus, the Canadian mosaic is portrayed as a bargaining process between two or more cultures striving to maintain their own identities. To emphasize the fairness of the Canadian system, politicians are compared to stock-brokers. Just as stockbrokers handle purchases and sales in a more or less neutral way, politicians are presumed to process government transactions without bias or prejudice for or against any political group or class.

First introduced by H. McD. Clokie in 1944, the concept of "brokerage politics" has reappeared uncritically in almost every Canadian textbook since. Like Adam Smith's "unseen hand," our political brokers are supposed to mediate conflict between competing interests in the political marketplace. However, few academics have asked which interests are mediated and which may be left out of the broker-age process altogether. Remarkably, little research has been done on how government decisions are made and who benefits from them. Indeed, it is generally assumed by Canadian scholars that the political brokers mainly resolve conflicts arising from non-class issues.

Recently, a number of Canadian scholars revised the Wall Street model by adopting the consociational theory imported from the Netherlands.[14] Consociational theorists believe that politics should be removed from the influence of the mass public and that the leaders of different ethnic, religious, and regional groups should have more freedom of action to accommodate each others' interests. This new theory of elite accommodation deviates from the classical notion of the market, where numerous buyers and sellers have complete freedom of competition. Instead, the consociational view of politics reflects a market system dominated by a few monopolies. Even so, the fundamental question remains unanswered: whose interests are being accommodated by the elites?

For years, the prevailing view of the Canadian system as mosaic politics, brokerage politics, or the politics of elite accommodation was rarely challenged. Development of class analysis was greatly hindered by the dearth of information about the class nature of Canadian society. Sociologist John Porter provided the first successful challenge to the non-Marxian orthodoxy in 1965. His sardonically entitled book, *The Vertical Mosaic*, provided profuse statistical information on the power elite in Canada. Armed with new data, Porter inveighed against the "quasi-religious dogma"[15] of brokerage politics. John Meisel had previously questioned "the still widely held myth that Canadians form a classless society."[16] But faced with the common problem of little research into the class basis of Canadian politics, Meisel quickly backtracked. In his retreat, Meisel duly noted that "the most distinctive feature of the [Canadian] party system is . . . [its task] of promoting a sense of national community. This is the key to an understanding of Canadian parties and elections."[17]

Meisel and other mainstream political scientists overlook the fact that the political cleavages which appear to be unrelated to class are rooted in the economic structure of the Canadian system. The separatist cry of the *White Nigger* is not merely the cry of *québecois* threatened with cultural extinction. *White Nigger* is also the cry of the revolutionary, who interprets his economic history as continual exploitation by the Anglo-Scottish banking and industrial elite of central Canada.[18] The behaviour of Premier Peter Lougheed of Alberta embodies more than the mere desire for regional autonomy. Lougheed's vehement support for high oil prices serves not merely Alberta's interests, but the American oil companies as well. The anger and political alienation of the Prairie farmers is not a question of culture shock.[19] The western farmers are simply vulnerable to the high freight rates and restrictive lending policies of railroads and banks that are not primarily Western Canadian or agricultural in their focus. The nationalist movement in English Canada is not merely a psychological or cultural phenomenon. The active nationalism of a few Canadian entrepreneurs gives substance to the quip that the Committee for an Independent Canada is essentially a Committee for Indigenous Capitalists.[20]

The presistence of these various cleavages prompts one to ask whether the popular and academic neglect of the class factor has succeeded in creating a better integrated society. The answer can hardly be an unequivocal "yes." Canada is not much better integrated than a century ago. French-English relations are no more amicable, nor westerners less alienated. It is true that economic progress has brought an increase in real per capita income which doubled in the years between 1951 and 1971.[21] However, during the same period, "progress" brought a remarkable and disturbing increase in the level of inequality of income (see Figure 6-1). Except for the years 1951-57, the gap between rich and poor grew wider in the form of a parabolic curve.

An unequal distribution of income is one of the expected costs of a system founded on the belief that material success is available to those who are diligent. The cost would be bearable if those who tried to "make it" were duly rewarded. Yet, in a system of increasing inequality, many must try harder merely to maintain a relative position in the hierarchy of wealth. The traditional expectation of upward mobility through hard work may result in frustration and competition may intensify. Those who find that "hard work" is unrewarded may be tempted to resort to political radicalism, crime, or other non-conventional means to obtain the highly cherished material incentives. Alternatively, they may be tempted to drop out of the "rat race" altogether.

It is not surprising, therefore, that the pattern of inequality in Canadian society has been approximated by the pattern of labour unrest (see Figure 6-1). In the years between 1951 and 1971, the rising level of inequality in the distribution of income coincided with a pattern of growing labour unrest in the form of strikes and lockouts. From a non-Marxian perspective, the relationship between inequality and labour unrest may be seen as mere coincidence. For non-Marxists, in-

Figure 6-1.   Labour Unrest and Inequality

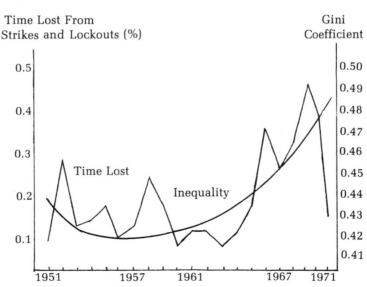

*Labour unrest is defined in terms of workdays lost as a percent of the estimated working time of the total labour force. Inequality is defined by the accepted measure, the Gini coefficient. The Gini coefficient varies from 0 to 1. The value of the coefficient rises as a smaller and smaller percentage of the population possesses an increasingly large share of the attributes being measured.

creasing labour unrest may be the result of urbanization, the fragmentation of the labour movement, or television-dictated styles of living. A non-Marxist might argue that life in the city creates the impersonal social relationships fomenting industrial conflict, that the fragmented organization of Canadian trade unions inhibits large-scale agreements, and that television has encouraged strife by displaying life-styles beyond the material reach of most of the population.

These arguments have some validity. However, in addition to sharing some of these interpretations, Marxists would also see meaning in the coincidence between inequality and unrest. They would infer that workers resorted to industrial protest to maintain their relative position in the hierarchy of wealth. They would conclude that the economic system has become wasteful in terms of the human cost of inequality and in terms of lost productivity as well as that the class struggle has become intensified.

Figure 6-2.   Mental Health and Inequality

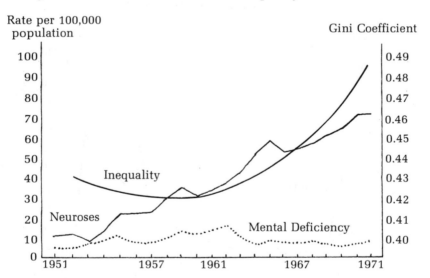

Note that from 1957 to 1971 the two curves representing "inequality" and Neurotic Behaviour have the same shape (i.e., there may be a close relationship between the two variables). On the other hand, it appears that "Inequality" is not related to "Mental Deficiency", which remains more or less constant during the period under study. The two mental health indices are based on the number of "first admissions by diagnosis". Cases which are not serious enough to be admitted to mental institutions are not counted due to lack of data.

Source: *Canadian Perspective* (Statistics Canada, 1974), 49, 156.

Strikes and lockouts are not the only costs of rising inequality. Strikes are a practical attempt to recapture an economic position. However, a society characterized by mosaic thinking may encourage the individual to blame himself rather than the system for his falling behind. Canadians have been taught that their society offers equality of opportunity, that it is legitimate to harbour great expectations, and that a failure to sustain a relative position is the personal failure of an inadequate individual. However, in reality Canadians confront growing inequality and increasing stress for those who seek upward mobility. Marxists anticipate that the victim of the widening gap may find it difficult to reconcile the discrepancy between dogma and reality.

The victim might respond by having few expectations and therefore little outrage or alternately by having great expectations and directing outrage against the system. Because of the influence of mosaic dogma, however, Marxists might expect the victim to blame her or himself. The effect of the dogma of classlessness would be that the potentially revolutionary desire to blame the system is transformed into feelings of self-blame, self-rejection, and guilt. Psychological or

Figure 6-3.   Inequality and Alcoholism

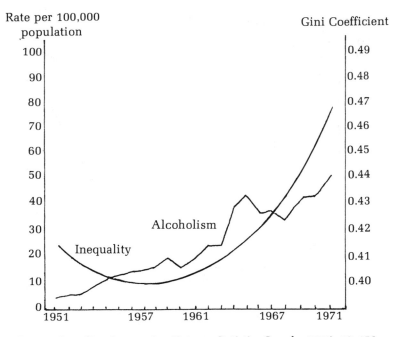

Source: *Canadian Perspective* (Ottawa: Statistics Canada, 1974), 49, 156.

physical dropout in case of failure becomes both a cause and a result of ongoing false consciousness. According to Marxian theory, alienation from the political system is replaced by alienation from oneself.

The thesis that mosaic ideology and the classless mythology transform political alienation into personal alienation receives some support from existing data on rates of maladaptive behaviour such as alcoholism, severe neurosis, and suicide. All three forms of mental disturbance are manifestations of counter-productive, self-destructive attempts to handle alienation. Killing oneself is the ultimate form of self-depreciation; in our reasoning, it is the ultimate cost of the "rat race." From a Marxian perspective, it is not surprising that the rates of all three forms of personal alienation have risen and followed the rate of inequality (see Figures 6-2 to 6-4). Nor is it surprising that, of the three maladaptive behaviours, the pattern of suicide approximated the pattern of inequality the most closely.

One should not infer from the data presented in Figures 6-1 to 6-4 that there is a class difference in the rates of alienation. In the absence of empirical facts, one might be tempted to argue that the downtrodden are more alienated than the privileged. However, this kind of speculation is unnecessary within Marxism. Inequality, according to Marx,

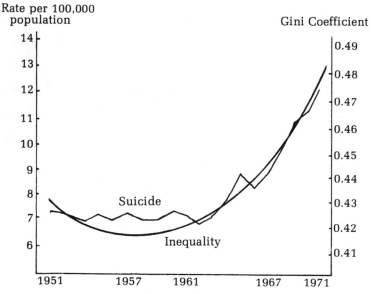

Figure 6-4.   Suicide and Inequality

Rate per 100,000
 population   Gini Coefficient

Source: *Canadian Perspective* (Statistics Canada, 1974), 52, 156.

results from the exploitation of one class by another. Every member of a system of exploitation is alienated from every other. The exploiter feels alienated because he finds himself caught in the inexorable drive for capital accumulation; the exploited feels alienated because he or she is the victim of the system of exploitation. Both the exploiter and the exploited live in a dehumanized environment and alienation is not the trademark of the proletariat alone. Yet, in the case of the exploited, when alienation is expressed in the form of maladaptive behaviour, it reflects a false consciousness because blame is internalized rather than directed against the system.

In fairness, the data presented in Figures 6-1 to 6-4 do not demonstrate the validity of the Marxian thesis of alienation, that inequality leads to system-directed or self-directed hostility. Far more data and a far more complex research design would be required for confirmation. However, the data are suggestive. They help illustrate the reasoning behind the Marxian theory of alienation. At a minimum, the data do not invalidate the Marxian thesis.

To summarize, we observed that Canadian political science was woefully deficient for ignoring class analysis and class-related conflicts. The absence of class analysis in Canadian scholarship could be understood in terms of the pressure of the Cold War and in terms of the prevalence of mosaic thinking. By portraying the Canadian system as a classless society founded on the laudable principle of equal opportunity, mosaic scholarship discouraged its practitioners from examining class-related problems. Mainstream political scientists overlooked the real and growing nature of class inequality. They also overlooked the human and economic costs of inequality. In Marxian analysis, mosaic thinking in Canada was an intrinsic part of the superstructure of the capitalist system, whose stability depended on widespread feelings of false consciousness among workers. Thus, the continued stability of our capitalist system required that workers interpret their economic setbacks in personal rather than political ways. So long as economic setbacks are interpreted politically, it is desirable that the interpretations be ethnic or locational rather than based on class.

Class in Political Behaviour

Just as orthodox political scientists have overlooked the class nature of material benefits in Canadian society, they have under-estimated the class content of mass electoral behaviour. There are two basic styles of academic opposition to the class analysis of voting, and these styles are best portrayed as active vs. passive resistance. The prevailing passive style of resistance involves avoiding the class issue entirely. Indeed, passive resistors may avoid all generalizations about voters, claiming that the data are either insufficient or confusing. A case in point is R. MacG. Dawson: in his basic textbook, Dawson argues that the evidence about electoral behaviour is contradictory and consequently all generalizations "are difficult, if not dangerous."[23]

The pre-eminent active resister is Robert Alford. In his basic reference on the politics of the Anglo-American countries, Alford argues bluntly that class does not matter in Canada. He asserts that "political parties are identified as representatives of regional, religious, and ethnic groupings rather than as representatives of national class interests."[24] According to Alford, "party loyalties are not mediated by identification of the parties with stable economic interests and by class organizations which support a party and are identified with it."[25]

Though Alford's view prevails, it is not supported by everyone. In a study of urban voting in the 1965 federal election, Wallace Gagné and Peter Regenstreif found that party support was differentiated along class lines.[26] In her study of religion and voting in Ontario, Lynn McDonald encountered and took note of some class influence on electoral behaviour.[27] In their studies of two Ontario ridings, John Wilson[28] and James Simmons likewise discovered evidence of class cleavage among the electorate.[29] Unfortunately, all the studies whose findings are incompatible with Alford's are limited either to a single riding, to a single province, or, in the case of Gagné and Regenstreif, to urban areas.

To challenge the orthodox view with success requires the nationwide class analysis of voting behaivour. The analysis should show which class supports which party as well as the conditions which hamper or facilitate the development of class politics at the mass level. Since Canadian voting behaviour and party loyalties are notoriously unstable, the analysis should minimize the transitory effects of new leaders, the outbreak of intra-party factionalism, and other short-term factors. For example, the arrival of dynamic new leaders such as John Diefenbaker in 1956 and Pierre Trudeau in 1968 could disturb temporarily the normal or long-term loyalties of many voters.

In order to minimize the effects of transitory disturbances, the present study will employ six national surveys conducted by the Canadian Institute of Public Opinion in the years 1961-73. This period of thirteen years is long enough to avoid being too sensitive to very short-term factors such as the introduction of a new leader yet it is short enough to avoid entangling the analysis in the possibility of a slow, long-term, undetected change in voter behaviour. All six CIPO data sets are pooled after reweighting the individual surveys so that all surveys are treated equally, even if their original samples varied in size.

Four federal parties are considered: the Liberal, Progressive Conservative, New Democratic (or CCF), and Social Credit parties. The provinces are grouped into four regions: the Atlantic provinces, Quebec, Ontario, and the West. The respondents are also divided into three religious groups (Protestants, Catholics, others) and three linguistic groups (English, French, others).

The most intractable of the variables is, of course, social class:[30]

1. Social class may be defined in Marxian terms on the basis of ownership of the means of production. Either the respondent possesses some ownership of the means of production or he does not.
2. Alternatively, class may be defined in terms of social status. Accord-

ing to this procedure, individuals are ranked according to the superior or inferior status ascribed to them by members of their society.[31] This is a favourite method among North American sociologists who do not wish to be tarred with Marxism.

3. Social stratification can also be conceived in terms of power.[32] Rank is assigned to individuals "according to the criterion of authority and not according to the criterion of material advantage or prestige."[33]

4. Class can be treated in terms of subjective feeling following W. I. Thomas's famous dictum that "if men define situations as real, they are real in their circumstances."[34] The fundamental datum in class analysis becomes each individual's self-perceived class position.[35]

5. Finally, there is an institutional, organizational, or interest group approach. Union membership becomes an index of class because "the labor union contributes to maintenance of polarization [of class conflicts]"[36] and because "union members are in general more likely to maintain their identification with the working class than are other people of similar occupational status."[37] With this conception of class, respondents in a survey are divided into two groups, "union" and "non-union."

Undoubtedly, each of the class indices presented above is related to another. Those who possess the means of production tend to have prestige, power, wealth, and the awareness that they belong to the upper strata. By contrast, those who work on a plant floor lack these attributes. Nevertheless, some indicators of class are not so fruitful as others. For example, in a society characterized by the classless myth and false consciousness, the subjectivist approach, based on self-perceived or self-reported class, is inadequate simply because so many voters believe that they belong to the middle class. An effective approach might be to employ several indicators. However, in practice the combined CIPO dataset permitted social class to be defined in only two ways: whether the respondent was a blue collar labourer and whether he belonged to a union.

In this study, the parties are compared according to the internal class composition of each party. A party can be said to represent a given class if a very high percentage of its supporters come from that class. An alternative technique of measuring the class character of a party would be to examine how successful the party was at attracting support from a given class. While this alternative approach has merit, it has some striking liabilities. In particular, a very large successful party — such as the Conservative party under Diefenbaker in 1958 or the Liberal party under Trudeau in 1968 — could attract majority support from every social class. Could such a party represent the interests of every class? The answer would be "yes" if the Canadian political system did not operate along class lines. We showed in the previous section that striking evidence exists of inequality of income in the system. There is also considerable evidence elsewhere that the elites of the different parties can be distinguished along the left-right continuum.[39] Hence, it would be naive to believe that a particular party could represent all social classes.

At best, a party leader practising political brokerage might try to satisfy the demands of each class according to the electoral power of that class. At worst, he would neglect the interests of the *minority* class *within* his party. "Representativeness" can be defined crudely in terms of the percentage of each class of voters within each party. Thus, no matter how many votes that a party has collected from among blue collar workers, if the working class is numerically dominant inside that party, the interests of the workers can occupy a privileged position among the priorities of that party. Instead of comparing how effectively different parties attract support from different classes, a more useful mode of class analysis is to compare the class profile of each party in order to discover which class predominates within which party.

The voter profiles of the federal parties, presented in Figure 6-5, provide some empirical evidence of a class character in Canadian mass politics. Not surprisingly, neither major party achieves a strong base among the low status occupations. Although each regularly outpolls the NDP across the nation, neither possesses a majority or plurality among manual workers. Furthermore, the Liberal profile displays only 2% more workers than the Conservative profile. By contrast, the NDP has a recognizable working-class base. Among NDP voters, 54% are blue collar workers. In the case of union members supporting the NDP, the profile is almost twice as strong as the profile of either the Conservatives or Liberals.

Of course, the strength of the NDP among workers simply reflects its origins. The party was formed out of the bosom of the Cooperative Commonwealth Federation precisely in order to cement links with the trade union movement (see Chapter 3: Fragment and Movement Parties). The high hopes encouraged by the public opinion polls of World

Figure 6-5. Working Class Profiles of the Four Federal Parties

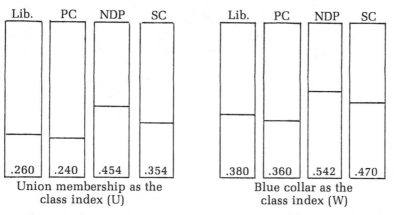

Lib.	PC	NDP	SC
.260	.240	.454	.354

Union membership as the
class index (U)

Lib.	PC	NDP	SC
.380	.360	.542	.470

Blue collar as the
class index (W)

Note: The lower part of each bar represents the proportion of a party's supporters belonging to the working class.

Figure 6-6. Working-Class Profiles of the Four Federal
Parties by Regions

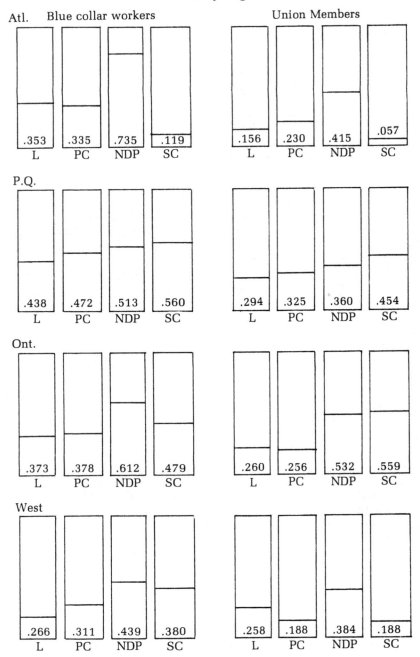

Atl.   Blue collar workers   Union Members

.353   .335   .735   .119   .156   .230   .415   .057
 L   PC   NDP   SC   L   PC   NDP   SC

P.Q.

.438   .472   .513   .560   .294   .325   .360   .454
 L   PC   NDP   SC   L   PC   NDP   SC

Ont.

.373   .378   .612   .479   .260   .256   .532   .559
 L   PC   NDP   SC   L   PC   NDP   SC

West

.266   .311   .439   .380   .258   .188   .384   .188
 L   PC   NDP   SC   L   PC   NDP   SC

War II and by the victory of the British Labour party in 1945 came to an end with the Diefenbaker landslide of 1958. The CCF caucus was reduced to eight members. The New Party — after 1961 the New Democratic party — would be affiliated to sympathetic unions and benefit from their manpower and resources. Two unions in particular, the Steel Workers and the United Auto Workers, became central to the party's material welfare.

If it is not surprising that the NDP profile is working class, it may be surprising to some that the Social Credit profile is also somewhat working class. The conventional portrait of Social Credit as right wing or ultra-right wing describes its ideology and goals better than its electoral base. Social Credit depends considerably on working-class support, especially in Quebec (see Figure 6-6).

Working-class support for the NDP and Social Credit reflects their common histories as parties of protest. Both were born in the depression as a response to economic dislocation. Both were ideologically opposed to large corporations and financial institutions. Both protested the Liberal Tweedledum and the Conservative Tweedledee. These similarities are, however, superficial and misleading. The two parties advocate fundamentally different solutions to the problems of economic exploitation. Social Credit wishes to turn back the clock to a pre-industrial economy which was not dominated by large corporations, to a life which appeared simpler, and to a society which was more integrated and more homogeneous. Its reactionary quest for a pre-capitalist system, its simple-minded conception of "free enterprise," and its traces of authoritarianism, zenophobia, and anti-semitism place Social Credit among quasi-fascist parties such as the Poujadist movement in France and the George Wallace movement in the United States.[40]

By contrast, the CCF-NDP exhibits a more universalistic, modern and left-wing approach to the economic and social problems of the post-industrialized society. Yet, if the NDP lacks the primitivism and ethnocentricism of Social Credit, its left-wing nature should not be exaggerated. Like many socialistic parties in the West, the NDP has lost its zeal. It has begun to accommodate itself to capitalism.[41] It may even see itself as the best manager of the capitalist system rather than as the agent of its demise. The *embourgeoisement* of the NDP was reflected in forcing the left-wing Waffle to leave the party. No party can hope to gain respectability and legitimacy in a political culture founded on the myth of classlessness without softening its class-based ideology. Someone more genuinely Marxist than this author would be especially sensitive to the NDP's role in reducing class conflict by means of its moderation.

The purpose of this section was to show that the orthodox scholarly view of classless politics was once again misleading. At the level of mass electoral support lie significant class differences. Social Credit and especially the NDP are substantially more working class than the Liberal or Conservative parties.

The Question of False Consciousness

The preceding profile analysis still does not answer the crucial question of why the two major parties continue to attract more than two-thirds of the working-class votes. Growing economic inequality suggests a weak sense of class consciousness among the working class. A number of working-class voters appear to perceive the Liberal and Conservative parties as representative of all classes. Thus, class conflict is not adequately translated into electoral action. Instead of using their ballots to defeat the major parties at the polls, many blue collar workers express their political alienation in the form of labour unrest. The myth of classlessness and the political superstructure of political parties and government services remain unscathed, in spite of the widening gap between the rich and the poor.

A common problem facing upper-class oligarchies or right-wing parties in different political systems is how to acquire working-class support (see Chapter 2: Parliamentary Parties). If class consciousness motivates proletarian voters, the right-wing party has no chance. Workers always outnumber the members of the privileged class. The traditional method of diluting the proletarian class consciousness is to teach the alienated workers to look toward God for consolation and salvation.

If resignation to God's will does not work, the next best strategy is to divide the working class along non-class lines and to channel the workers' frustration to ethnic, racial, regional, and religious scapegoats (see Chapters 4 and 5: Bicultural Cleavage and Geographic Cleavage). "Don't blame the system," might go the refrain, "blame the Marsians." The "Marsians" are blacks in the American south, "foreigners" in Britain, Jews in Europe, francophones and Catholics in rural Ontario, Ontarians in Alberta, and Asians in British Columbia. Almost every constituency has a suitable scapegoat. The successful ruling elite bolsters its position by displacing towards a vulnerable outgroup the working-class anger which would otherwise be directed against itself. Every attempt is made to augment national solidarity — or regional solidarity in the case of Alberta — because then left-wing critiques are so easily portrayed as disloyal, perhaps even treasonable.[42]

One of the most important questions to be examined in this context is how the intensity of class politics varies among Canadian regions. We presume that the more people vote along the class lines within a given region, the more intense is class politics. In other words, the strength of the relationship between class and party choice becomes a measure of class politics. As a statistical index of class politics, our analysis will employ the Pearson coefficient of contingency. This coefficient is normally used as a measure of the strength of the relationship between two nominal variables (e.g. class and party choice).

Figure 6-7A shows that class politics is most intense in Ontario, which happens to be the most industrialized and urbanized of the provinces. On the other hand, class conflict is weak in the less industrialized and urbanized Atlantic region. Class conflict is also weak in Quebec, where ethnic and religious rivalry has often taken the place of class cleavage.

The intensity of class politics varies not only among regions, but also among various religious and ethnic groups (see Figures 6-7B and C). Class voting is stronger among Protestants and among those who speak English at home, weaker among Roman Catholics and French Canadians, and weakest among voters of minority ethnic background. It appears that culturally marginal voters are not inclined to vote along class lines. To test this hypothesis directly, the sample of respondents is divided into marginal and non-marginal categories. Marginal voters

Figure 6-7.   Intensity of Class Politics:

A. in each region, B. in each religious group, C. in each ethnic group, and D. in marginal and non-marginal groups.

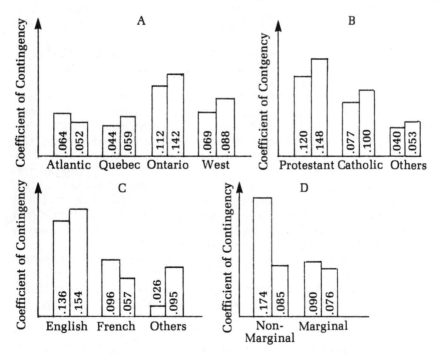

The intensity of class politics rises as the relationship between class and voting becomes stronger, as measured by the Pearson coefficient of contingency. This coefficient is a standard measure of the relationship between two nominal variables, the category to which class and party belong. As in previous tables, class is measured twice. In each pair of bars, the left bar represents blue collar workers and the right, union members.

are those (i) who speak neither English nor French at home, or (ii) who are not Catholic in Quebec, or (iii) who are not Protestant in the other provinces.

Figure 6-7D shows the expected voting behaviour of marginals as compared to non-marginals: marginal voters are less likely to vote along the class lines than non-marginal (i.e. modal) voters. Cultural marginality decreases the intensity of class politics. Interestingly enough, the negative effect of marginality on the development of class consciousness is stronger among blue collar workers in general than among labour union members. When respondents are dichotomized into "union members" and "others", the intensity of class voting is only slightly higher among modal voters than among marginal voters. On the other hand, when "blue-collar" is used as a class index (i.e., when the sample is divided into two groups, "blue collar workers" and "others"), the effect of marginality on class voting becomes striking indeed. In short, cultural marginality is a source of false consciousness, but the labour movement provides a strong counterweight to the effect of marginality.

A variety of phenomena may explain the conservative political effects of cultural marginality. First, as an outgroup and political scapegoat for all kinds of social illnesses in Canada, marginal Canadians are in a precarious position. Feelings of insecurity and fear of discrimination may discourage marginal voters from antagonizing the "establishment." Any party which takes an explicit stand in support of the mosaic system with a promise of tolerance and equal treatment is likely to rally ethnic votes. This faith in the mosaic system is strengthened further by the public opinion leaders of various ethnic groups, who have no reason to disturb the status quo because they themselves enjoy certain privileges in the Canadian society.

Secondly, the relative conservativism and false consciousness of immigrant workers may arise from a misconception of the class structure in the so-called frontier society. Immigrants from the underdeveloped regions of Asia, Africa, or Europe might be forgiven for confusing the lesser inequality in Canada with actual equality. They might also confuse their own improvement of material circumstance with upward social mobility.

Finally, one should note the well-known tendency of immigrants to turn to their churches as a means to maintain their cultural identity. While European workers are no longer under the strong conservative influence of their churches and are more responsive to radical ideologies, immigrant workers in North America are resocialized into various religious doctrines, which put a higher value in law and order than in social change.[43] The psychological effect of joining a proletarian organization may equal joining a church, but the political consequence differs: a proletarian identity with its left-wing orientation instead of a religious identity and political conservation.

Cultural anxieties and the phenomenon of marginality are not the only factors which diminish class consciousness. A major reason for weaker class voting in Canada as compared to the other English-speaking countries may be the confusion caused by the joint influence of the incompatible American and British political cultures. The American influence is expressed as "business unionism" in the organizational form of the AFL-CIO. Dominated by the conservative crafts unions, the AFL-CIO is stridently anti-communist and anti-socialist. Believing that its task is to secure higher wages for its members rather than to improve the political system, the American trade union movement opposes in principle any formal link with a political party. In practice, of course, the AFL-CIO has strong informal ties with the Democratic party. By contrast, the British Trades Union Congress is openly political, openly social democratic in belief, and formally linked to the Labour party. More so than the BTUC or the AFL-CIO, the Canadian Labour Congress is a weak umbrella organization with power vested in the member unions.

The American and British traditions quite naturally work at cross-purposes, helping to diminish the intensity of class politics. The Americans would prefer that Canadian unions bargain with the Conservatives and Liberals and possibly choose the latter as the closest counterpart to the U.S. Democratic party. Although many Canadian union leaders are British-born or trained in the British tradition, they must cope with strong counter-pressure from the U.S. headquarters of the so-called international unions. When the leadership of the Canadian Labour Congress and the CCF worked to cement links in the late 1950s, the AFL-CIO actually mobilized union organizers to oppose these links. Socialists in the Canadian labour movement withstood the pressures of the AFL-CIO and the NDP came to fruition partly as a result of the assistance of the more left-wing United Auto Workers union in the United States.

Conclusion

This chapter began by examining one of the most important features of the Canadian political system — the change in the income distribution during a quarter of a century. Except for the Korean War years, the gap between the rich and the poor increased dramatically at a geometric rate. Rising inequality was accompanied by increases in various social malaises. Admittedly, one may doubt the causal relationship between inequality on the one hand and strikes, neurosis, alcoholism, and suicide on the other. However, if rising inequality does not happen to be the cause of these disintegrative tendencies, the very fact of these tendencies may raise some questions about the effectiveness of the mosaic system and the validity of the orthodox approach in political science.

This chapter not only demonstrated that there are class differences in access to income, but also that there are class differences in party support. It argued that class differences in voting were diminished by false consciousness among the working class and that false consciousness was strengthened by the phenomenon of cultural marginality.

Workers belonging to ethnic or religious minorities were less likely to vote along class lines.

An important question is whether the mosaic politics helps to improve the economic conditions of these marginal workers. How much do they benefit from federal and provincial programs funded to promote various ethnic interests? In principle, all anti-discriminatory programs assist ethnic Canadians. However, this principle does not necessarily mean that the ethnic underdog will have the same share of attention as the ethnic topdog. Special ethnic-minded legislation may have the effect of increasing the gap between the rich and the poor *within* every minority group. The principle of equality of opportunity must be adjusted to take into consideration that motivation and the means of achievement are not distributed equally among classes. How may Quebec workers benefit from the language training program? How often do slum dwellers use the expensive medicare program? Does the regional development program help to alleviate inequality between regions or provide "corporate rip-offs"?[44] Does the promotion of sexual equality help waitresses, salesgirls, and cleaning women or does it serve merely the well-educated ladies of the upper strata?

These questions need to be answered. Yet, orthodox political scientists are too deeply involved in the superstructure of the free enterprise system to notice the artificiality of their theoretical perspective. One may worry to death about national disintegration stemming from regional conflicts — East vs. West, francophones vs. anglophones, etc. However, the fundamental conflict pits the haves against the have-nots. This kind of conflict cuts across all ethnic, regional, language lines.

It is undoubtedly utopian to ask Conservative and Liberal leaders to dismiss their public relations experts, for they have done an effective job "by absolutely avoiding class symbols [in order to make] other symbols more important."[45] This kind of electoral strategy has worked in the past, when popular expectations for fair play were less widespread. The discrepancy between expectations and opportunities was tolerable so long as the society as a whole experienced rapid economic growth. However, the situation faced by Canada in the 1970s is one of increased inequality among its citizens and relative economic stagnation. Class conflict cannot be easily swept away in an era of both double-digit inflation and high unemployment. In 1975, "rough justice" was the official euphemism for "injustice" to explain arbitrary features in the federal government's selective prices and incomes policy. The threat of national disintegration would become indeed serious if a regional movement were radicalized enough by the mounting dissatisfaction of the mass. The total collapse of the *union nationale* and the gradual decline of the *ralliement créditiste* in conjunction with the rise in popularity of the *parti québécois* suggest that non-class politics may not easily achieve its goal of national integration.

In the context of the input-output organization of this book, one might conceivably expect the modest but real class differences in support for the parties to result in modest but real differences in the class character of their policies. However, Marxian analysis would suggest otherwise. Marxian analysis draws attention to the many upper-class biases pervading the political superstructure. The privileged class is aided not merely by the conservative orientation of scholarship, but also by the class orientation of the media, the bureaucracy, and the pressure group system. For example, when Robert Presthus, a liberal democrat, conducted his massive study of interest groups and policy-making in Canada, he found that the pressure group system was differentiated on class lines and that the business class exerted the dominant influence.[46] These entrenched interests in the policy-making process combine with false consciousness at the electoral level to handicap any reform-minded party. If Marxian analysis is correct, one should expect few genuine class differences in the policies of the NDP and the major parties. Chapter 11, devoted to redistributive policy, will help answer this question.

Notes

1. William H. Riker and Peter C. Ordeshook, *An Introduction to Positive Political Theory* (Englewood Cliffs: Prentice-Hall, 1973), 2.

2. Mao Tse-Tung, *On the Correct Handling of Contradictions Among the People* (Peking: Foreign Language Press, 1957).

3. Op. cit. See also James R. Townsend, *Political Participation in Communist China* (Berkley: University of California Press, 1968).

4. Anthony Downs, *An Economic Theory of Democracy* (New York: Harper & Bros., 1957). See also Riker and Ordershook, op. cit., 240–271. For brokerage politics, see H. McD. Clokie, *Canadian Government and Politics* (Toronto: Longmans Green, 1944), 81–83; F. Englemann and M. Schwartz, *Political Parties and the Canadian Social Structure* (Toronto: Prentice-Hall, 1967), 222–239; F. H. Underhill, *Canadian Political Parties*, (Ottawa: Canadian Historical Association, 1967), 4–5; Richard J. Van Loon and Michael S. Whittington, *The Canadian Political System*, 2nd ed. (Toronto: McGraw-Hill Ryerson, 1976), 230ff.

5. Karl Marx and Friedrich Engels, *The German Ideology* (R. Pascal, ed.) (New York: Invernational Publisher, 1967), 23.

6. According to F. X. Sutton's Parsonian analysis, class differentiation does not exist in "intensive agricultural" societies because of the prevalence of ascriptive, particularistic, and diffuse norms or in "industrial" societies where universalistic, specific, and achievement-oriented norms prevent the development of class loyalty and identification. See his "Social Theory and Comparative Politics" in Harry Eckstein and David Apter (ed.), *Comparative Politics: A Reader* (New York: Free Press, 1963), 68–81. See also Seymour M. Lipset, "The Changing Class Structure and Contemporary European Politics," *Daedalus*, 93 (Winter 1964), 271–303.

7. Daniel Bell, *The End of Ideology: On the Exhaustion of Political Ideas in the Fifties* (Glencoe: The Free Press, 1960). See also Gunnar Myrdal, *Beyond the Welfare State* (New Haven: Yale University Press, 1960).

8. Lipset, *The Political Man* (New York: Doubleday, 1950).

9. Frank E. Myers, "Social Class and Political Change in Western Industrial Systems," in Giuseppe Di Palma (ed.), *Mass Politics in Industrial Societies* (Chicago: Markham, 1972), 258.

10. James A. Bill and Robert L. Hardgrave, Jr., *Comparative Politics: The Quest for Theory* (Columbia, Ohio: Charles E. Merrill, 1973), 176.

11. R. H. Tawney, quoted by Myers, ibid.

12. See for example, Johan Galtung, "Structural Theory of Imperialism," *Journal of Peace Research*, 8:1 (1971), 81–117; Tord Hoivik, "Social Inequality — The Main Issues," *Journal of Peace Research*, 5:5 (1968), 119–142; Pierre Jalée, *The Pillage of the Third World* (New York: Monthly Review Press, 1968); Gustavo Lagos, *International Stratification and Under-Countries* (Chapel Hill: University of North California Press, 1963).

13. Alfred G. Meyer, *The Soviet Political System* (New York, 1965).

14. On Clokie's Wall Street Model, see note 4 above. On consociational theory, see Arend Lijphart, "Cultural Diversity and Theories of Integration"; S. J. R. Noel, "Consociational Democracy and Canadian Federalism"; Gerard Bergeron, "Commentaire de la Communication du Professeur Arent Lijphart," *Canadian Journal of Political Science*, IV (1971), 1–21.

15. John Porter, *The Vertical Mosaic* (Toronto: The University of Toronto Press, 1965), 369.

16. John Meisel (ed.), *Papers on the 1962 Election* (Toronto: University of Toronto Press, 1964), 286.

17. Ibid., 287–88.

18. Gilles Bourque and Nicole Laurin-Frenette, "Social Classes and National Ideologies in Quebec, 1960–1970," and Stanley B. Ryerson, "Quebec: Concepts of Class and Nation," in Gary Teeple, *Capitalism and the National Question in Canada* (Toronto: University of Toronto Press, 1972), 185–228.

19. H. E. Bronson, "Continentalism and Canadian Agriculture," ibid., 121–140.

20. L. Panitch and R. Whitaker, "The New Waffle: From Mathews to Marx," *Canadian Dimension*, 10 (April 1974), 51–56.

21. *Perspective Canada* (Ottawa: Statistics Canada, 1974), 138.

22. Ibid., 48.

23. R. MacGregor Dawson, *The Government of Canada* (Toronto: University of Toronto Press, 1970), 414.

24. Robert R. Alford, *Party and Society: The Anglo-American Democracies* (Chicago: Rand McNally, 1963), 251.

25. Ibid., 282.

26. Wallace Gagné and Peter Regenstreif, "Some Aspects of New Democratic Party Urban Support in 1965," *Canadian Journal of Economics and Political Science*, 33 (1967), 529–50.

27. Lynn McDonald, "Relgion and Voting: A Study of the 1968 Canadian Election in Ontario," *Canadian Review of Sociology and Anthropology*, 4 (1969), 129–144.

28. John Wilson, "Politics and Social Class in Canada," *Canadian Journal of Political Science*, 1 (September 1968), 397–412.

29. James W. Simmons, "Voting Behaviour and Socio-Economic Characteristics: The Middlesex East Federal Election, 1965," *Canadian Journal of Economics and Political Science*, 9 (1965), 61–76.

30. James A. Bill and Robert L. Hardgrave, Jr., op. cit., "Class Analysis," Chapter 5, 175–200.

31. W. Lloyd Warner and Paul S. Lunt, *The Social Life of a Modern Community* (New Haven: Yale University Press, 1941), 82.

32. Ralf Dahrendorf, *Class and Class Conflict in Industrial Societies* (Stanford: Stanford University Press, 1959), 138.

33. W. Wesolowski, "Some Notes on the Functional Theory of Stratification," in Reinhard Bendix and Seymour Martin Lipset, (ed.), *Class, Status, and Power* (New York: Free Press, 1966), 69.

34. Quoted by David M. Ralfky, "Phenomenology and Socialization: Some Comments on the Assumptions Underlying Socialization Theory," *Sociological Analysis*, 32 (1971), 12.

35. For an illustration of this approach, see Richard Centers, *The Psychology of Social Classes* (Princeton: Princeton University Press, 1949); James S. Rinehart and I. O. Oraku, "A Study of Class Consciousness," *Canadian Review of Sociology and Anthropology*, XI (August 1974), 197–213.

36. Angus Campbell et al., *The American Voter* (New York: John Wiley and Son, 1967), 208.

37. Ibid.

38. For example, Professor Meisel's 1968 election dataset shows that over 60% of the respondents did not see themselves as members of any social class. Among those who answered the question without further probing, more than 51% believed that they were members of the middle class. If one considers the sample as a whole, only 14.2% of the respondents believed that they were members of the working class or lower class.

39. N. H. Chi, "Class Voting in Canadian Politics," in O. M. Kruhlak, et al. (ed.), *The Canadian Political Process* (Toronto: Holt, Rinehart and Winston, 1973), 226–247; N. H. Chi and G. C. Perlin, "The New Democratic Party: A Party in Transition," in Hugh G. Thorburn (ed.), *Party Politics in Canada*, 3rd ed. (Scarborough, Ontario: Prentice-Hall, 1972), 177–187.

40. John A. Irving, *The Social Credit Movement in Alberta* (Toronto: University of Toronto Press, 1959); C. B. Macpherson, *Democracy in Alberta* (Toronto: University of Toronto Press, 1953); J. R. Mallory, *Social Credit and the Federal Power in Canada* (Toronto: University of Toronto Press, 1954); S. M. Lipset, *Agrarian Socialism* (New York: Doubleday, 1968); Walter D. Young, *The Anatomy of a Party: The National CCF* (Toronto: University of Toronto Press, 1969); R. MacGregor Dawson, *The Government of Canada* (Toronto: University of Toronto Press, 1972), 423.

41. N. H. Chi and G. C. Perlin, op. cit.

42. In the 1935 federal election, Liberal candidates in British Columbia presented an openly racist program. A full-page ad in the *Province* included pictures of the party's candidates on the lower mainland along with the following promises: "The Liberal Party is opposed to giving these Orientals the vote. Where will you stand on election day? A vote for any CCF candidate is a vote to give the Chinaman and Japanese the same voting right you have! A vote for a Liberal candidate is a vote against Oriental enfranchisement." Quoted in James Morton, *In the Sea of Sterile Mountains: The Chinese in British Columbia* (Vancouver: J. J. Douglas, 1973), 245. On anti-Catholic and anti-Jewish sentiment in Ontario, see Larry Zolf, "The New Shape of Canadian Politics, or how

to make the lynch mob work for you," *Saturday Night* (Dec. 1975), 17–21. On anti-semitism in Quebec, see Lita-Rose Betcherman, *The Swastika and the Maple Leaf* (Don Mills, Ont.: Fitzhenry and Whiteside, 1975).

43. Frank E. Myers, "Social Class and Political Change in Western Industrial Systems", op. cit., 263.

44. David Lewis, *The Corporate Welfare Bums* (Toronto: James Lewis & Samuel, 1972).

45. G. Horowitz, "Conservatism, Liberalism, and Socialism in Canada: An Interpretation", *Canadian Journal of Economics and Political Science*, 32 (1966), 170.

46. *Elites in The Policy Process* (Toronto: Macmillan, 1974), 171–77.

SECTION III

The Representational Process (Throughputs)

A political system can have any number and pattern of political cleavages. However, without the means of communication, these latent cleavages cannot be mobilized for political purposes. Without at least the anticipation of elections, the politically mobilized cleavages cannot readily influence policy outcomes by legitimate non-violent means. The processes of communication and election are therefore crucial to the transformation of political differences into policy outputs. The two chapters which follow examine how the mass media and the electoral process affect the success and character of political cleavages and political parties.

CHAPTER 7

ELECTIONS

Conrad Winn

Introduction

The political folklore of western countries holds that the essence of parliamentary democracy lies in the free use of the ballot. The folklore provides for a system of mass communication to convey neutral political information to a citizenry which is then able to make intelligent electoral choices among competing elites. Along with the automobile, Coca Cola, and other attributes of western culture, this political folklore has achieved such international acceptance that the authoritarian, one-party states of Africa, Asia, and Eastern Europe feel obliged to offer at least the form of regular elections and mass communication. East Germany and Czechoslovakia even provide the façade of a multiparty system.

In reality, communists, fascists, and other opponents of liberal democracy look at elections and mass communication with skepticism and cynicism. Their cardinal assumption is that, even if elections were perfectly free and non-coercive, the media socialize or indoctrinate their audience to choose among political alternatives which reinforce the system and differ little from each other. Of course, elections are not considered to be really free, but are for elites to manipulate popular sentiment as a result of a privileged access to mass communication, finances, and organization. To their intellectual credit, the opponents of parliamentary democracy understand some of the actual and potential biases in the electoral and communication processes. An unfortunate consequence of this perceptive understanding is that the opponents of democracy are unwilling to consider truth or individual choice as legitimate objects of communication and elections. In the Soviet Union, the understood purpose of elections is to reinforce an emotional bond between citizens and the state rather than to provide genuine political choice, while the goal of mass communication is to justify current policy preferences, even the whims, of incumbent elites.

By contrast, liberal democrats believe strongly in the possibility and desirability of neutrality and fairness in the election and communications processes. This faith is not accompanied, however, by a great deal of interest in the possible biases in these processes. With few exceptions, narrowly specialized experts have monopolized discussions over the effects of alternative ballots or alternative methods of party finance. The study of the political effects of mass communications lacks even a sizable body of committed experts. J. R. Mallory's book, *The Structure of Canadian Government*, symbolizes well the limited interest of liberal democrats in the political consequences of the communication system.[1] Although the book offers comprehensive chapters on the Senate, the House of Commons, and even on the electorate, it possesses not a single indexed reference to communication.

As a result of the low interest in the electoral and communication biases of parliamentary systems, few have attempted to scrutinize empirically the anti-democratic hypothesis about intrinsic bias or the pro-democratic assumption of benign neutrality. On the basis of our limited knowledge to date, the ensuing sections of this chapter examine the current effects on the party system contributed by the historical development of the franchise, the first-past-the-post ballot, the existence of provincial governments, and patterns of patronage and party financing. Chapter 8 is devoted entirely to mass communication.

The Franchise and the Growth of Political Participation

For a good part of the nineteenth century, the structure of federal elections discriminated moderately, but systematically, in favour of the upper strata and the ruling Conservative party. From 1867 to 1884, the federal franchise was based on provincial laws, which required the ownership of property as a condition of voting. Candidates for the House of Commons were likewise obliged to own property. Prior to 1874, the government of Sir John A. Macdonald also benefited from staggered elections. Instead of holding a simultaneous vote across the country, the Conservatives began balloting in their own bastions, using early successes to coax or intimidate the electorate in marginal or opposition regions. Macdonald's Act of 1885 brought the ballot under federal jurisdiction. However, the Act of 1885 retained a complex set of property and income qualifications along with plural voting, by which citizens could vote wherever they owned property.

The subsequent steps and crises in the expansion of the franchise are outlined in Table 7-1. After 1920, exceptions to the universal franchise applied mainly to Mennonites, Hutterites, conscientious objectors, Indians on reservations and a portion of the Asian population. The last to receive a clear and unequivocal franchise were Mennonites in 1955 and Indians in 1960. Thus, a fully universal franchise has existed only in the past generation.

Under the contemporary universal franchise, there exists no intrinsic bias in favour of certain cleavages or parties. Historically, the swift, uneventful extension of the franchise to the lower strata served to diminish the basis for class cleavage and working class parties. Canada followed closely the practices of Great Britain in extending the suffrage downwards and in extending the legal rights for the political and economic organization of trade unions. Because Canada experienced industrialization and unionization much later than Britain, the effect of the early reforms was to diminish greatly class grievance expressed through the ballot and to help postpone the birth of working-class parties. Socialists failed to contest elections on a nation-wide basis until 1935, thirty-five years after the British Labour party was founded.

Table 7-1

Steps in the Development of the Suffrage

1867—provincial male franchises employing property qualifications and plural voting.

1885—an ostensibly uniform male federal franchise which included complex property qualifications, plural voting, and the disfranchisement of Asians.

1898—return to provincial franchises, most of which were male and somewhat more universal.

1917—Central Europeans were disfranchised while the vote was given to the female relatives of soldiers and to Indians in the armed forces.

1918—Female franchise introduced on the pattern of the existing male franchise.

1920—Quasi-universal franchise, which excluded Asians disfranchised under provincial regulations and conscientious objectors.

1934—Eskimos explicitly disfranchised.

1938—Asian franchise reduced further; he or she could not vote in any province if disqualified under provincial regulations in his or her province of origin.

1948—Asians granted normal franchise.

1950—Eskimos granted the franchise.

1955—Religious conscientious objectors granted the franchise.

1960—Indians on reservations granted the franchise.

Note: Compiled from T. H. Qualter, *The Election Process in Canada* (Toronto: McGraw-Hill Ryerson, 1970).

While the development of the franchise diminished class cleavage, it appears to have exacerbated ethnic tensions. The greatest crisis occurred in 1917, when the predominantly Conservative Union government passed the wartime Elections Act and the Military Voters Act. The franchise was taken away from conscientious objectors, Doukhobors, Mennonites, and all British subjects who were born in an enemy country, who normally spoke an enemy language, or were naturalized after March 1902.[2] Deputy returning officers were even authorized to refuse the ballot to an individual who "by his manner shows that he was born in an enemy country".[3] By contrast, the vote was given to non-residents, minors, and Indians in the armed forces as well as to the female relatives of soldiers. These invidious election distinctions must explain a portion of the strong subsequent attachment of central Europeans to the Liberal party.[4] The election acts of 1917 also exacerbated the bicultural cleavage because the perceived objectives of the acts were to reinforce the wartime British connection.

While historic crises in the expansion of the suffrage have a continuing influence on electoral behaviour, these crises have received little attention. By contrast, electoral malpractice and chicanery, which affect very few ridings, continue to be the subject of intense discussion and gossip during campaigns. One story, shared repeatedly in one guise or another among election workers in Montreal, concerns the former Anglican Bishop of that city. Bishop Farthing apparently arrived early at his poll to be told that all ballots had been used and that the records showed that he had voted.

The main techniques of electoral fraud are multiple voting at one occasion ("ballot stuffing"), impersonating a legitimate voter ("telegraphing"), bribing voters ("treating"), excluding opposing partisans from the voters' lists (false enumeration), enumerating fictitious voters ("padding" the voters' lists), and physical intimidation. Delightful and entertaining rumours abound, but few stories are easily confirmed. Moreover, it is doubtful if chicanery of any kind ever affected the outcome in more than a handful of ridings.

The main impediments to fraud are that chicanery is costly and that incumbent parties, which are in the best circumstance to manipulate elections, are normally in the least need of doing so. Telegraphing, for example, requires at least the benign neutrality of the polling officials who may know personally the voter being impersonated. Furthermore, the telegrapher can only be cost effective if he is sufficiently skillful and mobile to vote at many polls.

Ballot stuffing and false enumeration have occurred primarily in ridings where a traditional one-party dominance is threatened by a candidate with great popularity and weak organization. Both fraudulent activities can only take place with at least the acquiescence of the polling officials and sometimes of the local police. This acquiescence usually requires long one-party rule in a given region. Consequently, ballot stuffing has been more prevalent in provincial elections than in federal. As recently as the 1960s, a Quebec journalist reported in *Maclean's* how she had "sold [her] vote twenty times" to the *union nationale*.[5] In the early part of this century there continued to be sporadic examples in all the provinces of goons seizing federal ballot boxes, voting generously, then returning them to the polling stations. In the more recent period, this practice has surfaced only occasionally in federal elections in Newfoundland.

While ballot stuffing requires connivance and/or intimidation on election day, false enumeration begins weeks before. M. J. Coldwell described false enumeration in the notorious riding of Cartier in Montreal in the following words:

> Altogether some 2000 names have been checked since last Thursday, checked carefully by persons who are reliable and are in some instances supporting their checkings with affidavits which I have on the desk beside me. Out of some 2000 names, 650 ... were found to be false or improperly on the list, a proportion of approximately one-third. For example, a baby seven weeks old listed as a bookkeeper; a little girl five years of age listed as a retired spinster, whatever that may be; a number of non-existent addresses which would make the voter reside over a railway or over a street intersection; seven voters listed at a United Cigar store; seven voters listed for the store which is now the Liberal candidate's committee room; 11 voters listed in a barber shop; six voters listed at a restaurant.[6]

Coldwell concluded that "if a complete check were made of the 42,000 names on the list, we believe that at least 10,000 would prove to be false. . ." The contest that the CCF leader described was a by-election in 1943, yet Cartier continued to be plagued a generation later. In the early 1960s, an NDP candidate of Greek origin complained that thousands of Greek Canadians had been mischievously left off the voters' lists. Similar irregularities in Cartier in 1958 and in three Toronto ridings in 1957 and 1962 were followed by successful prosecutions.

While false enumeration is kept under control by legal sanction, treating is almost unimpeded. Even in the 1940s, bribing voters was more widespread than false enumeration, especially east of Ontario. The provision of nylon stockings to ladies, alcohol to men, and the two or five dollar bill to members of both sexes still forms part of the political culture of the Maritimes. However, it is highly doubtful if treating will remain for long. The sums required for effective bribery at the current standard of living are much higher than the amounts needed a generation ago. Furthermore, bribery is no longer reliable. Political organizers are often compelled to bribe citizens not to vote at all rather than risk a wrong vote.

In a systemic sense, treating tends to diminish the effective divisions between social classes and regions in the country. Class cleavage is moderated as a result of lower electoral support for the NDP owing to its inferior financial position. Geographic cleavage between periphery and core is lessened because of the increased financial dependence of Maritime Liberals and Conservatives upon their sources of funds in central Canada.

From Votes into Seats

Telegraphing and ballot stuffing are messy, onerous, and potentially counterproductive ways of controlling the outcome of elections. Too many accomplices are required; too many laws need to be broken. By contrast, malapportionment and gerrymandering are efficient and not

Figure 7-1. Alternative configurations of voters and electoral outcomes for parties A and B

necessarily illegal. Malapportionment consists primarily of the over-representation of certain regions, usually the countryside to the disadvantage of the city. Gerrymandering is the redrawing of constituency boundaries out of political spite.

Changes in population and settlement require the redrawing of boundaries in order to preserve a uniform number of voters in each riding. While community and local ties are supposed to constitute guidelines for the creation of new constituencies, Figure 7-1 shows clearly that alternative patterns of boundaries will produce different electoral outcomes. In both configurations the proportion of supporters for party A is 60% while the remainder are attached to party B. In configuration I, party A wins all three seats while in configuration II it wins only one.

The potential for the creative use of boundary reconstruction seems obvious. By a kind of iron law of oligarchical corruption, the Conservatives in the nineteenth century were more disposed to gerrymandering, while in the twentieth century their role has been assumed by the Liberals. The Conservative elections acts of 1872, 1882, and 1892 were shameless gerrymanders. In 1882 as many as 46 Ontario constituencies were mischievously redrawn.[7]

During this century, gerrymandering has been sporadic, but nevertheless real. Montreal Cartier, which previously elected Fred Rose, the Communist MP, was elaborately redrawn in 1947 in order to return a Liberal. Further west, the Conservative party's leader and its financial critic both lost their seats, while the riding of Prince Albert, which had spurned Mackenzie King for a CCFer, was redrawn. In 1952, John Diefenbaker, the Conservatives' only parliamentarian in Saskatchewan, found his seat abolished by way of redistribution.[8]

As a result of the Electoral Boundaries Commissions Act of 1964, the delineation of constituencies has become a relatively non-partisan matter independent of Parliament. Gerrymandering seems to have little future. One reason for this permanent change is that public morality has improved greatly. Voters are less tolerant of chicanery, especially when it is grotesque. Even in the classic gerrymander of 1882, the government party found to its dismay that it was almost annihilated in precisely the constituencies it had so laboriously redesigned.[9]

While gerrymandering has not always been effective, malapportionment usually is. Typically, malapportionment follows an extended period of migration from the countryside to the cities and the absence of an electoral redistribution. Because of their greater electoral roots in the countryside, the advantage falls to the more conservative parties. This unfair advantage has played a major role in the long-term dominance of the union nationale, Conservatives, and Social Credit in the provincial systems of Quebec, Ontario and the Far West. For rural-based parties, the advantage of malapportionment over gerrymandering and other malpractices is that the public does not normally perceive the decision to postpone redistribution to be as machiavellian or as self-serving. In fact, malapportionment in favour of the countryside can even be defended in part by reference to the greater difficulties encountered by parliamentarians in serving underpopulated, far-flung constituencies.

Provincial malapportionment is important for the federal party system because of the great dependence of the federal parties on provincial party machines.[10] Nevertheless, malapportionment has not constituted as serious an iniquity in federal elections as in provincial because the greater probity of federal politics has not tolerated enormous delays in redistribution. Furthermore, the unfair effects of federal malapportionment have not always been intended. The Conservatives did benefit in the 1963 election from Prime Minister Diefenbaker's decision to postpone redistribution, although it is unclear by how much. Without providing clear supporting evidence, Peter Newman has argued that as many as 60% of the federal ridings were dominated by rural voters even though only 12% of the electorate lived on farms.[11] The Progressive Conservatives also benefited in 1957 and 1965. However, in these two instances the systemic bias towards the Conservatives stemmed from a lack of foresight among the incumbent Liberals. In 1957, the Conservatives secured more seats than the Liberals despite a lower popular vote. The preceding St. Laurent government had possessed the power to forestall the rural-urban disparity which gave advantage to its opponents. In 1965, the Liberals failed to secure a majority of seats because they were too impatient to await a completed redistribution before calling an election.

According to a study by the Office of the Chief Electoral Officer of Canada, the Liberals would have acquired their majority of 136 seats instead of 131, and the Tories 92 instead of 97.[12] Typically, the urban-based New Democrats suffered the most by the absent redistribution. They would have achieved 14%, or three, more seats. The rural-based Socreds and *créditistes* would have each lost one seat. Had the election been called after redistribution, Walter Gordon, the Liberals' leading strategist as well as economic nationalist, would have been vindicated and would not have felt obliged to resign from the cabinet.

Generally, malapportionment and gerrymandering reinforce the position of the older parties vis-a-vis the CCF-NDP and therefore diminish class cleavage while augmenting the regional and cultural cleavages. In this century, malapportionment has tended to serve the Conservatives and gerrymandering, the Liberals. Although both gerrymandering and malapportionment have often been discussed, neither of these factors has influenced the outcome of elections as greatly as two other aspects of our political process: the winner-take-all nature of the ballot and the federal nature of government.

With the British ballot employed in Canada, electors vote for individual candidates in more than 260 single-member ridings across the country. The candidate with more votes than any other wins the riding, while the party with the most elected members normally wins the election. In principle, if five parties contested an election, if one party received 25% of the popular vote in every constituency, and if the other four parties divided the remaining votes evenly and equally, then the party with 25% of the vote would acquire 100% of the seats. The same distribution of votes would produce a completely different allocation of seats under proportional representation (PR). In the simplest variant of PR, Canada would have a single multimember constituency and each citizen would vote for a party rather than a candidate. In the example given above, the largest party would secure 25% of the seats, the remainder to be divided equally among the other four parties.

The example just given illustrates the marked tendency of the first-past-the-post ballot to discriminate in favour of the largest party (see Table 7-2). Of course, the example is unrealistic because the pattern of national voting is rarely uniform in a spatial sense. There is a normal regional variation in voting and this variation is in turn accentuated by the ballot. In 1968, for example, the Conservatives and Liberals were able to win four-fifths and three-quarters, respectively, of the seats in the Maritimes and Quebec on the basis of slightly more than half of the popular vote. By contrast, the 45% Liberal vote in P. E. I. went completely unrewarded while the 21% vote for the Conservatives and New Democrats in Quebec and Ontario was badly under-represented. In his classic indictment of the first-past-the-post system, Cairns has shown that our ballot consistently accentuated the division between Quebec and English Canada. Between 1921 and 1965, the Liberals gained 752 members in Quebec to the Conservatives' 135, despite a margin in voters of less than 2 to 1.[13]

Table 7-2

Percentages of Votes and Seats
for Government Party, 1921–1965

	% Votes	% Seats		% Votes	% Seats
1921	40.7	49.4(L)	1949	49.5	73.7(L)
1925*	39.8	40.4(L)	1953	48.9	64.5(L)
1926	46.1	52.2(L)	1957	38.9	42.3(C)
1930	48.7	55.9(C)	1958	53.6	78.5(C)
1935	44.9	70.6(L)	1962	37.3	43.8(C)
1940	51.5	73.9(L)	1963	41.7	48.7(L)
1945	41.1	51.0(L)	1965	40.2	49.4(L)

*In this election the Conservatives received both a higher percentage of votes, 46.5%, and of seats, 47.3%, than the Liberals. The Liberals, however, chose to meet Parliament, and with Progressive support they retained office for several months.
Source: Alan C. Cairns, "The Electoral System and the Party System in Canada, 1921–1965", The Canadian Journal of Political Science, I:1 (1968), reprinted in Paul W. Fox (ed.), Politics: Canada, 3rd ed. (Toronto: McGraw-Hill Ryerson, 1970), 197.

Party strategists understand well the different profits to be had in different regions from similar electoral investments. In 1957, the Conservative party made its famous decision to "reinforce success not failure", by concentrating its efforts outside Quebec.[14] In the 1970s, the contest over air routes between the publicly owned Air Canada and the private CP Air showed that the NDP also understands well the costs and benefits of alternative sectional alignments. The New Democrats ought to have supported the crown corporation, especially since the behaviour of CPR in passenger transportation and real estate speculation has not been exemplary according to the canons of socialist morality.[15] However, CP Air carried the affection of the West because of its location in Vancouver, and the NDP allied itself with CP accordingly. The cost to the NDP in seats might have been dear otherwise, even if the party could have been assured an increase of votes in Ontario equal to its expected loss in the West. Cairns has summarized the effects of the first-past-the-post ballot in the following words:

> The electoral system has not been impartial in its translation of votes into seats. Its benefits have been disproportionately given to the strongest major party and a weak sectional party. The electoral system has made a major contribution to the identification of particular sections/provinces with particular parties. It has undervalued the partisan diversity within each section/province. By so doing it has rendered the parliamentary composition of each party less representative of the sectional interests in the political system than is the party electorate from which that representation is derived.
>
> The electoral system favours minor parties with concentrated support, and discourages those with diffuse national [eg. class] support. The electoral system has consistently exaggerated the significance of cleavages demarcated by sectional/provincial boundaries and has thus tended to transform contests between parties into contests between sections/provinces.[16]

The Provinces as Bases of Support

While the first-past-the-post system serves the established parties, federalism assists the NDP. As Pierre Trudeau observed to his then CCF friends, "in the absence of PR it seems obvious that the multi-state system of a federal constitution is the next best thing."[17] In an insightful analysis of federalism and electoral tactics, Trudeau chastized the CCF leaders for their obsession with victory at the federal level. Using Mao Tse-Tung as his point of departure, Trudeau argued that the party needed to be sufficiently flexible to seize new advantages as they arose. "Federalism," observed Trudeau, "must be welcomed as a valuable tool which permits dynamic parties to plant socialist governments in certain provinces, from which the seed of radicalism can slowly spread."[18]

Viable provincial parties are essential for all the federal parties. When the future of a federal party is seen to be bleak, the existence of a provincial party in power can be a great source of morale and resources. Incumbent parties at the provincial level are able to employ at public expense party organizers as well as public relations experts, who proclaim the achievements of their government and hence of the incumbent party. A large portion of pork barrel is provincial. Decisions about liquor licenses, liquor store appointments, liquor purchases, road construction, land development, appointments to government commissions, advertising, drivers' license bureaus, insurance contracts, legal work, and other professional services are undertaken in whole or in part at the provincial level. A successful provincial party helps maintain the allegiance of party workers deprived of rewards at the federal level. For example, Dalton Camp has been able to devote his magnificent energies to the national Conservatives in part because his livelihood has been assisted by advertising contracts from the tourism ministries of Conservative governments in the Maritimes and Ontario and by other government service. [19]

Among the incumbent provincial parties, the Smallwood government in Newfoundland was most faithful to the Liberal parent in Ottawa. Before Newfoundland's union with Canada, Senator Gordon Fogo, the Liberal treasurer, coaxed distillers and brewers into donating one-quarter of a million dollars to the campaign for Confederation. [20] Smallwood was forever grateful. As long as he was premier, he personally appointed all federal candidates and arranged funding and advertising through the provincial Liberal office. [21] During the 1962 campaign, Smallwood even undertook to prohibit Donald Fleming, the Conservative Finance Minister, from addressing the St. John's Rotary club.

The dependence of federal Tories on the Ontario Conservative party is well known. Their past dependence on the *union nationale* in Quebec is less well known. Pierre Sévigny, Associate Minister of National Defence under Diefenbaker, estimates that the UN made possible ten out of the eleven Tory victories in Quebec in the crucial 1957 election. Duplessis unleashed his party machine, deployed government patronage, and even recruited candidates personally. Paul Comtois, Diefenbaker's Minister of Mines, became a candidate at *le chef*'s personal urging. [22] Duplessis's Liquor Police furnished campaign workers under conditions of economic incentive that included special daily bonuses as well as automobile allowances of ten cents per mile. [23]

The interdependence of federal and provincial parties is too large a subject to be detailed here in full. The important point to note is that the proximity to federal power of the Liberals and Conservatives makes them less dependent on provincial allies than the movement parties. For years, Robert Thompson's western-based Social Credit party depended on regular subsidies from the Alberta and British Columbia Socred regimes. In the CCF-NDP, the Saskatchewan wing has consistently provided a lion's portion of membership, finances, and organization assistance. [24] The generosity of the Saskatchewan section resulted from the great morale, organization, and patronage made possible by a party in power. [25] NDP elections in British Columbia and Manitoba in the 1970s augmented further the strength of the national party. Only the *créditistes* of Réal Caouette have been totally self-sufficient and independent of provincial assistance. It is doubtful that the return of Social Credit to power in British Columbia in 1975 will aid the national party.

Origins of Party Resources

While federalism gives the minor parties, especially the NDP, a relative advantage, Canadian practices in the financing of partisan activity place the major parties, especially the Liberals, at a great advantage. In the private sector, the bulk of party resources have come from large corporations. Trade unions have contributed a small portion, while individual citizens who are unconnected to firms or unions have contributed very little. In the public sector, incumbent parties have been able to arrogate to themselves various forms of patronage. The Liberal party possesses a material superiority over its competitors because of its privileged access to corporate coffers and to federal government patronage. This corporate base of party finance may, however, be diminished by the Election Expenses Act of 1974.

Some of the reasons for the greater affection of corporations for the Liberal party are innocent enough. Many firms depend on the federal government in the realms of taxation and contracts. Accustomed to cultivating friendships in the course of their livelihoods, businessmen quite naturally think in terms of political donations as a means of facilitating friendships with policy-makers. On the few occasions where donations have been politely refused — usually in the case of New Democrats — businessmen have been quite genuinely perplexed.

The businessman's belief that a favour deserves a favour in return makes it an easy task for the long dominant Liberal party to acquire donations. Jean Marchand was probably truthful when he assured an interviewer that companies receiving grants from the Department of Regional Economic Expansion "are never solicited, except afterwards, and I do not know by whom."[26] The simple public knowledge that Marchand was both the minister in charge and party leader in the province of Quebec, the largest recipient of DREE grants, undoubtedly eased the tasks of Liberal fund-raisers. Like most Canadian politicians, but unlike Spiro Agnew, Marchand would never threaten reprisal against a recalcitrant firm, nor would he probably ever intervene. It is the businessman's ethic, not intimidation, which makes possible the financing of the Liberal party and to a lesser extent of the Conservative party.

Of course, there have been examples of straightforward corruption. A famous instance involved the Beauharnois Power Company. In order to insure government cooperation, the Company contributed handsomely to Liberal campaigns in 1921, 1925, 1926, and 1930. The gift in 1930 alone exceeded $600,000. However, this beneficence was exceptional, since until the 1950s the Liberals apparently had difficulty sustaining regular financing.[27] In Newfoundland, Joseph Smallwood's ingenuity enabled him to sell positions in the Canadian Senate even before union with Canada. The first installment was a mere $250.[28]

The realm of advertising and opinion research involves clearly understood quid pro quos. Camp, Foster, and Hayhurst are associated with the Tories while MacLaren and Goldfarb are linked to the Liberals. MacLaren's links with the federal government have been sufficiently prosperous for it to assign to the party the services of George Elliott, a Vice-President. Before the Diefenbaker landslide, MacLaren's special position with the Liberal party was held by Cockfield, Brown. Over a period of a decade, Cockfield, Brown provided the party with a full-time national secretary and, for a time, shared a common Ottawa address. In 1975, the Liberal government's anti-inflation board retained MacLaren Advertising "on a consulting basis" for a $500,000 advertising program.[29] The NDP has benefited from the assistance of Dunsky Advertising. Dunsky established offices in Manitoba, Saskatchewan, and British Columbia to handle the provincial government accounts.

Eric Kierans, who was Postmaster-General under Trudeau, has described the trials and tribulations of attempting to hire the "best" advertising firm if it happens to be Conservative:

> Well, boy, I was really into it. There is a committee of cabinet ministers, a formal committee, that looks after the doling out of government advertising, and they were mad as hell. The contract went into the Treasury Board and it just stayed there for months.[30]

Kierans convinced his Cabinet colleagues to accept Foster Advertising only after demonstrating that all 22 major advertising projects were already in the hands of Liberal firms. If Foster Advertising were granted the post-office contract, Foster could be used as "living proof" that the government was innocent to charges of patronage. However, Foster did not remain "living proof" for long: it lost the contract as soon as Kierans resigned from the cabinet.

While governments employ advertising contracts in order to gain the partisan service of advertising talent, they employ legal patronage and political appointment in order to encourage the candidacies of respected leaders in local communities. Legal patronage is allocated by a committee in the Ministry of Justice.[31] These services consist of mortgage work and prosecution for federal offences such as narcotics abuse. Political appointments include nominations to judgeships, commissions, and the Senate. Expectations for continuing legal work or future appointment often act as incentives for lawyers and other professionals to serve the incumbent party during and between campaigns. These incentives help explain the very high social status of Liberal candidates.

Grants under the Local Initiatives Programme have also been an instrument of patronage. For the fiscal year, 1973-74, Paul Hellyer showed that Liberal ridings received on the average $344,000 in LIP grants, while comparable figures for Conservative and NDP constituencies were $208,000 and $249,000.[32] Of course, Liberal ridings may have exhibited greater economic need. However, when Donald Blake, a U.B.C. political scientist, isolated by statistical means economic from political considerations, he nonetheless found that the constituencies which secured the greatest LIP allotments were those which elected Liberal Members and especially those held by Cabinet Ministers or Liberals with marginal victories.[33]

In recent years, the most significant change in party financing occurred as a result of Bill C-203. Passed in January, 1974, the bill authorizes modest public subsidies for candidates of all parties. More significantly, it requires full public disclosure of the source of funds. If this aspect of the bill is enforced, there may be some far-reaching consequences. According to Finlay MacDonald, Robert Stanfield's chief of staff in 1974, firms which have contributed to the established parties may now feel obliged to assist the NDP as well out of a fear of harming business relations with the provincial NDP governments in the West.[34] The act may also make the provincial parties more dependent on the federal parties, to whom contributions are now tax deductible.

In the latter part of 1975, the major parties found themselves in the invidious position of receiving less financial support than either the NDP or the *créditistes*. This unusual turn of events may have been influenced by the new legislation on election expenses as well as by a changed political climate in the United States. Watergate and the plethora of related scandals brought about a certain mood of caution among corporate executives. In particular, American multinational corporations felt constrained by the unfavourable publicity associated with the U.S. Senate's investigation of their foreign political activity.

Conclusion

The general theme of the preceding passages is that the electoral process tends to favour the development of cultural and geographic cleavages at the expense of class. As Cairns has shown, the first-past-the-post system can make regional electoral appeals cost effective. The development of the franchise has also favoured the bicultural cleavage. On the one hand, the franchise manipulations of 1917 exacerbated ethnic tensions. On the other hand, the smooth extension of the franchise to the lower strata deprived the left of the grievances prevalent in some, less democratic, countries.

The regional tendencies encouraged by the first-past-the-post system were in turn strengthened by federalism. The existence of provincial staging bases — Social Credit and NDP in the West, Conservatives in Ontario, Liberals in Quebec — increased the likelihood that federal victories would have geographic and bicultural attributes. Paradoxically, the existence of opportunities for provincial victory in the West has enabled the most class-oriented party, the NDP, to sustain its federal hopes as a result of benefiting from a geographic cleavage.

The two most important electoral malpractices which persist in this century are malapportionment and patronage. Although malapportionment exists mainly at the provincial level, it affects the federal parties to the extent that they depend on their provincial wings. In particular, malapportionment may have aided the rural-based Social Credit in the West, the Conservatives in Ontario, and the Liberals rather than the *parti québécois* in Quebec. Like malapportionment, patronage affects the federal system from provincial as well as federal origins. The more establishmentarian parties have an advantage because of their greater proximity to federal patronage. However, Social Credit and the NDP have also had access to patronage through their control of provincial governments.

While malapportionment and patronage have political implications, they have ethical implications as well. The visible display of unethical public conduct is hardly a good learning model for society. In the case of the legal profession, one can only wonder how the high ethical standards required to practice law can remain uninfluenced by the different criteria of behaviour needed to achieve government contracts and employment.

Notes

1. (Toronto: Macmillan, 1973).

2. *Statutes*, 7–8, Geo. V, c39, s.1(d) and s.2. For a review of the franchise, see T. H. Qualter, *The Election Process in Canada* (Toronto: McGraw-Hill Ryerson, 1970), 1–45.

3. *House of Commons Debates* (1917), 5621.

4. Although the Liberals benefit from Central European resentment of the Conservative party, they receive little affection among Asian Canadians. Citizens of Asian ancestry were not pleased with the Liberal Act of 1938, which further reduced their franchise, or with their forced resettlement or internment during World War II.

5. Cathie Breslin, "I sold my vote — twenty times," *MacLean's*, (August 13, 1960), 2–3.

6. *House of Commons Debates* (1943), 5093.

7. See R. MacGregor Dawson, "The Gerrymander of 1882," *Canadian Journal of Economics and Political Science* (May 1935), 197–221.

8. See J. R. Mallory, *The Structure of Canadian Government*, 189–90.

9. See N. Ward, "A Century of Constituencies," *Canadian Public Administration* (1967), 1, 110.

10. See also Chapters 9 and 10 below.

11. Peter C. Newman, *Renegade in Power* (Toronto: McClelland and Stewart, 1963), 399n.

12. See William E. Lyons, *One Man–One Vote* (Toronto: McGraw-Hill Ryerson, 1973), 88–90.

13. Alan C. Cairns, "The Electoral System and the Party System in Canada, 1921–65," *Canadian Journal of Political Science*, I:1 (March 1968), 62.

14. See John Meisel, *The Canadian General Election of 1957* (Toronto: University of Toronto Press, 1962), 167–68.

15. For a left-wing indictment of the CPR, see Robert Chodos, *The CPR: A Century of Corporation Welfare* (Toronto: James, Lewis and Samuel, 1973).

16. Cairns, "The Electoral System," 62.

17. "The Practice and Theory of Federalism," in Michael Oliver (ed.), *Social Purpose for Canada* (Toronto: University of Toronto Press, 1961), 373. The work was sponsored by the socialist Boag Foundation and was edited by the first national president of the New Democratic Party.

18. Ibid., 373–4.

19. Robert Nixon, the Ontario leader of the Liberal party, revealed in March 1974 that four of the eleven contracts of Dalton Camp Associates came from the Ontario Ministry of Tourism. Between 1971 and 1974, Ontario Tourism accounts were worth about $2,700,000 to the Camp firm. Yet an Ontario auditor's report showed that "no contract or written agreement was in force at the time of audit." Toronto Star (March 8, 1974), A4. On Camp's connection with the Nova Scotia Government Travel Bureau, see Geoffrey Stevens, Stanfield (Toronto: McClelland and Stewart, 1973), 77.

20. See Peter Cashin, Harold Horwood, and Leslie Harris, "Newfoundland and Confederation, 1848–49," in Mason Wade (ed.), Regionalism in the Canadian Community, 1867–1967 (Toronto: University of Toronto Press, 1969), 250–51.

21. Khayyam Z. Paltiel and Jean Brown Van Loon, "Financing the Liberal Party, 1867–1965," in Committee on Election Expenses, Studies in Party Finance (Ottawa: Queen's Printer, 1966), 155.

22. Pierre Sévigny, This Game of Politics (Toronto: McClelland and Stewart, 1965), 70–71 and 204–205.

23. Peter C. Newman, Renegade in Power (Toronto: McClelland and Stewart, 1963), 287–88.

24. See Khayyam Z. Paltiel, Howat P. Noble, and Reginald A. Whitaker, "The Finances of the Cooperative Commonwealth Federation and the New Democratic Party, 1933–65," in Committee on Election Expenses, Studies in Party Finance (Ottawa: Queen's Printer, 1966), 317–406.

25. Robert Tyre, no great admirer of the NDP, argues that patronage was rife under T. C. Douglas. See his Douglas in Saskatchewan (Vancouver: Mitchell Press, 1962), 144–64.

26. Interview with Arthur Blakeley of the Montreal Gazette, quoted in Walter Stewart, Divide and Con (Toronto: New Press, 1973), 87.

27. This observation depends on the research in progress of my colleague, Reginald Whitaker, whose generosity of spirit is gratefully acknowledged.

28. See Cashin et al., "Newfoundland", 247 and 249.

29. Reginald Whitaker, research in progress. Also, Nicholas Cotten, "Anti-Inflation Board is expected to spend $500,000 on advertising," Globe and Mail (December 6, 1975).

30. Walter Stewart, Shrug: Trudeau in Power (Toronto: New Press, 1972), 167.

31. Interview, Sen. Paul Martin (March 1974).

32. Toronto Star, 5th December, 1973, p. A9. Heward Grafftey and Tom Cossitt, both Conservative MPs, have also made statements about LIP grants as patronage.

33. Donald C. Blake, "LIP and Partisanship: An Analysis of the Local Initiatives Programme," a paper presented at the annual meeting of the Canadian Political Science Association (Edmonton, June 1975).

34. Interview, Finlay MacDonald, (March 1974).

CHAPTER 8
MASS COMMUNICATION
Conrad Winn

Introduction

The communication system is vital to the political process because of
the enormous dependence of modern man on impersonal rather than
personal sources of information. Because politicians are largely inac-
cessible to the ordinary public, citizens are obliged to rely on newspapers, radio, and television for all kinds of political information. Even
party elites depend greatly on the media. Politicians employ the media
to secure information on government activity, on the performance of the
economy, and on shifts in public sentiment as well as to test ideas and
wage electoral warfare. Some evidence of the importance of the communications system is suggested by the reply of Robert Stanfield's
chief of staff to a question on Conservative financial needs:

> Of course, we would be glad to increase our budget by another half a
> million dollars or more. However, a more effective method of working
> with the media would be worth far more to us than an increase in dona-
> tions for which there is no specific, demonstrable need.[1]

The underlying assumption here is that the media are not necessarily neutral, but may favour certain parties, ideas, or interest groups.
Few political observers would reject the possibility that the media may
introduce biases into the political process. Furthermore, there are those
who believe that media biases are neither local nor accidental in nature, but general and systematic. John Porter and other academics on
the left attribute a systematic right-wing bias to mass communication,
while George Grant and some other observers believe the media to
accord a special place to the liberal view.[2] Despite the vital importance
of the media to the political system and to democratic ideals, almost no
systematic, scientific research has been undertaken. Consequently, any
generalization is fraught with uncertainty.

The ensuing sections of this chapter examine in sequence current
speculation about media bias, some empirical evidence about television news, some empirical evidence about the daily press, and the role
of economic factors in political reporting. The section on current
speculative thought elucidates the right-wing view of left-wing bias as
well as the left-wing view of right-wing bias. The section on television
presents some data on the content of news programs produced by
CBC-TV, CTV, and Radio-Canada. The section on the daily press re-
examines some existing data and presents some new data to explore the
relationship between editorial and news partisanship. Finally, the
chapter examines in a speculative way the likely effects of economic
factors on the style and content of political analysis.

Existing Speculation about Media Partisanship

In Canada, the study of mass communication is one of those academic disciplines that cries out for attention but receives almost none. For whatever reasons, the universities and agencies of government have been slow in providing incentives for this kind of inquiry. The few journalism faculties have chosen to remain trade schools rather than become, in part, sponsors of research. As is true in some other fields, some of the more creative individuals have gone south. Indeed, A. Bandura and P. H. Tannenbaum, to name two leading scholars in the field, are expatriot Canadians in the United States.[3] The Canadian deficiency in mass media research may reflect our deficiency in the creation and production of programming. In the absence of farsighted government policies, the local entertainment industry has been unable to provide sufficient capital to retain Canadian talent, which has been obliged to find work in the United States. In one particular field, television comedy, it has been estimated that as many as 40% of the writers employed by the American networks came from Canada.[4]

The absence of a body of systematic empirical research on the media means that much of existing commentary is impressionistic and speculative. The left-wing position is that the owners and publishers of the media are businessmen, whose corporate values are reflected in the entertainment and especially in the news content of their outlets. Porter has shown that the owners of the media tend to be born to wealth. For Porter, therefore, it follows that all the media except perhaps the CBC espouse corporate values and support the Liberals and Conservatives. Because none of the media, except for the separatist *Le Jour*, are owned by their employees, by unions, or by socialist cooperatives, none have supported the CCF or NDP. Nor do they "do very much to bring about the progressive-conservative dialogue of creative politics."[5]

Porter is obviously correct in his assertions about the socioeconomic background of media owners. Unlike a century ago, to publish a newspaper requires considerable personal resources. Furthermore, publishers and editors undoubtedly tend to be Conservative or Liberal in partisanship and establishmentarian in their economic and political beliefs. The Regina *Leader-Post*, the *Winnipeg Free Press*, the *Montreal Star*, and Montreal's *La Presse* are some of the better known Liberal dailies, while the Hamilton *Spectator*, the now defunct *Toronto Telegram*, the *Frederiction Gleaner*, and the *Montreal Gazette* would be numbered among Conservative publications. Historically, the *Toronto Daily Star* was one of the most partisan Liberal papers. Acquired in 1899 at Wilfrid Laurier's initiative, the *Star* remained steadfastly Liberal until 1972, when it expressed editorial sympathy for Robert Stanfield. Many radio and television stations are also owned by admitted Conservatives and Liberals.

To know the ideological orientation of media owners is important information, but it is an insufficient basis for judging the possible reporting biases of the media. The systematic analysis of content is required. In the absence of this kind of information, the thesis that the communication system is skewed to the political right receives some support from hearsay and from a small number of documented cases of bias. After an all-party election meeting, this writer overheard an NDP candidate chastise the election reporter of his local paper for misrepresentation. The reporter became quite indignant:

> Come on, J---! You know better than that. We're quite fair now. You must surely remember the good old days when the _____ never once mentioned the CCF. At least we cover you.

In a series of interviews at a CTV affiliate, some members of the staff insisted that a document of "100 dos and donts" existed to govern local news reporting. The station owner allegedly made it known that the Queen merited coverage, but that great discretion should be exercised with regard to the NDP and a sports columnist the owner considered irresponsible. Pierre Berton has claimed that editors employed by the Thomson chain have come to him with controversial material saying, "We can't touch this; will you?"[6]

La Presse and the *Kitchener-Waterloo Record* provide more clear-cut instances of vested interest and ideological bias. In the mid-1960s, Gerard Pelletier was dismissed as editor of *La Presse* because he opposed the construction of a provincial government steel complex, of which his employer had been appointed a director.[7] Pelletier was known as somewhat reform-minded. In the 1970s the *Kitchener-Waterloo Record* prevented its readership from learning that the city of Kitchener had committed itself to a massive urban development scheme. The *Record*'s publisher had corporate links to the developer involved. The newspaper's role in the subsequent controversy placed it squarely in the camp of Liberal and Conservative aldermen, who favoured the development, and against the outspoken New Democratic politician, who led the opposition to the plan.[8]

The left-wing argument of right-wing bias is not the only view of the possible ideological effect of the media. Albert Campion, then an official of the Ontario Progressive Conservative party, argued before the Senate Committee on Mass Media that there is a "secondary establishment" of columnists, producers, TV commentators, hosts of public affairs programs, who tend to hold centre-left or left-wing opinions. "The news media in Canada are controlled by the political left-wing — or more properly, the liberal left. And when I say this, I'm lumping together small-L-liberals and large-L-Liberals." Campion observed that CBC television's coverage of a speech by the prime minister on August 13 1969, consisted of 30 minutes allocated to Trudeau, 20 minutes to Douglas, and merely 9 minutes to Stanfield, the leader of the Official Opposition.[9]

Just as Porter's observations on the ownership of the mass media have considerable importance, Campion's comments are not to be dismissed lightly either. Campion's observations are basically twofold: that the CBC is biased and that the working press as a whole is biased. Each of these propositions needs to be examined separately.

There is some systematic evidence from abroad, particularly from Great Britain, that journalists do tend to hold liberal, socialist, or other centre or left-of-centre opinions.[10] However, there is no systematic evidence in Canada. Their studied professional disguise of cynical neutrality means that journalists will not readily admit to partisanship. Nevertheless, it may be true that Canadian journalists tend to be centre-left or left-wing in their outlook. Their customary attitudes towards social welfare, personal responsibility, religion, alcohol, women's liberation, and sexual behaviour probably make them more akin to urban New Democrats than to rural Conservatives. They seem likely to hold the "liberal" view on these matters.

If this conjecture is correct, it nevertheless remains to be shown that the views of the working press are fully manifested in their work. There are economic and occupational constraints on bias. The economic constraints of the marketplace take the form of a possible loss of readers or viewers and of the occasional real or anticipated pressure of advertisers. The occupational constraint may take the form of a compromise between the more left-wing views of the journalist and the more right-wing views of the employer. Neither employer nor employee need be consciously aware of the compromise for it to take place. In any organization, it is common for the subordinate to adjust his thinking in the direction of the superordinate as a means to acquiring the rewards of employment.

If there is an implicit understanding between journalist and proprietor, this understanding may take the form of permitting greater radicalism on social matters than on economic or party-related issues. The proprietor may be quick to anger at the prospect of the nationalization of industry, higher corporation taxes, or an NDP victory. He may be no more sanguine about the Women's Liberation Movement, but find little rational reason for depriving the movement of attention. Indeed, there may be rational economic reasons for the media to highlight the women's movement and to employ it as an instrument of marketing. Sex sells. In some respects, Women's Liberation may be another variant of the age-old battle between the sexes.

If this thesis is true, it may explain the considerable support provided to the Women's Liberation Movement by the media as a whole. The sympathy of journalists and the tacit cooperation of their employers may explain the enormous media exposure given to the pro-abortion movement even though the Right-to-Life movement has been far more successful at enrolling members and securing signatures. By contrast, the media have been noticeably silent and conservative on such economic questions as the capital gains tax, corporation taxes, and the price-fixing powers of the legal and medical professions.

The preceding speculative comments were introduced as a means of reconciling Porter's observations about the class background of media owners and Campion's observations about the liberal beliefs of journalists. Campion's other observation was more specific in nature. He suggested that the CBC showed partisan hostility to the Conservative party. The political role of the CBC and indeed of broadcasting in general has received considerable discussion and for this reason is treated separately in the next section.

In between the left-wing argument of right-wing bias and the right-wing argument of left-wing bias lies a middle ground where some observers acknowledge the presence of political bias but consider the distortions to be random rather than systematic in character. The *Toronto Star* provides a classic example of naked self-interest as a motive for the manipulation of news. In the 1940s, the Ontario Conservative government put an end to the right of charitable agencies such as the Atkinson Foundation from operating competitive businesses such as the *Star*. In reaction, the *Star* became more determined than ever to undermine the Tories at both federal and provincial levels. In the federal campaign of 1949, one of the newspaper's banner headlines read:

KEEP CANADA BRITISH
DESTROY DREW'S HOUDE
GOD SAVE THE KING[11]

Needless to say, such extreme and overt examples of partisan commitment have become exceedingly uncommon.

Broadcasting: The Case of Television News

In the Soviet bloc, in France under de Gaulle, and in much of the Third World, government-owned broadcasting networks have served in part or in whole as instruments of propaganda on behalf of incumbent parties and elites. However, in Canada, as in the United Kingdom, law and custom impose a large measure of neutrality on both private and public broadcasters. The impartiality of the Canadian networks is sufficiently real for all political parties to expect fair treatment and for few strong complaints to be actually expressed.

Nevertheless, Campion, the previously mentioned Conservative official, is not the only observer to suggest the possibility of an anti-Conservative bias on the CBC. Nor is Campion's example of the coverage of the speeches of party leaders an isolated example of an imbalance in reporting. In the middle of the 1974 federal election campaign, Stanfield's press secretary revealed that over a period of two weeks the CBC-TV news had devoted 21 minutes 9 seconds to the Liberal leader, 12 minutes 41 seconds to the leader of the New Democratic party, but merely 12 minutes 9 seconds to the Progressive Conservative leader. Speaking for the CBC, Knowlton Nash stated that the imbalance would be rectified.[12] In an interview, Malcolm Daigneault, the news editor, attributed the imbalance to the criteria of news worthiness currently being employed. Daigneault explained that the imbalance occurred because the news department had decided at the outset of the campaign to give priority to platform promises. Stanfield apparently made few promises.[13]

Daigneault's explanation may indeed be truthful. However, allegations of the CBC's liberalism are made possible by a smattering of other evidence. Engelmann and Schwartz note that a study by the Secretary of State's Department showed that an English language public affairs program on the CBC interviewed 18 Liberals as opposed to 8 Conservatives and 5 New Democrats.[14] In 1956, the popular radio host and satirist Max Ferguson produced some radio advertisements for Stanfield in the Nova Scotia provincial election. The CBC obliged Ferguson to discontinue his work on grounds of "non-partisanship." While the decision was neutral in appearance, the effect was not neutral since the private media in that Nova Scotia election were flagrantly pro-Liberal.[15]

A few years earlier, Peter Dempston had been invited to produce a segment of *Capital Report*, a CBC program, but the invitation was apparently cancelled because he joined the Conservative *Toronto Telegram* as a regular correspondent.[16] In 1959, the Corporation's *Preview Commentary* program became so consistently critical of the Conservative government in Ottawa that Diefenbaker felt obliged to threaten the network with reprisal if the practice continued.[17] Perhaps the best known example of the CBC's apparent Liberal partisanship occurred in Spring 1966, when it cancelled the iconoclastic, muckraking public affairs program, *This Hour Has Seven Days. Seven Days* was the most popular serious program in CBC history. However, its investigative journalism proved too embarrassing for the Liberal government.[18] A truly extreme example of political interference occurred during the FLQ crisis, when the CBC permitted its news to be censored.[19]

The most reputable spokesman for the view that the CBC is oriented to liberalism is philosopher George Grant. In a highly regarded work on the Diefenbaker government, Grant writes that "the Conservatives . . . justifiably felt that the CBC, then as today, gave too much prominence to the Liberal view of Canada."[20] In quiet conversation, some officials of the CBC and of the Canadian Radio-Television Commission, the government regulatory body, may concede that the CBC is timid and uncritical of governments, especially Liberal ones. However, they are quick to point out how well served are the Conservatives by the CTV. When Diefenbaker was prime minister, his anger at the perceived Liberalism of the CBC caused private broadcasting licences to be, in Grant's words, "ladled out to prosperous party supporters."[21]

While the CBC is allegedly Liberal and CTV allegedly Conservative, Radio-Canada has been intermittently accused of being somewhat separatist and socialist. The *créditistes* have expressed frequent concern about their own lack of coverage, while federalists in all parties, including Prime Minister Trudeau, have criticized the network for allegedly excessive coverage of separatist activities.

In order to assess the validity of alternative thoughts on the political character of the networks, statistical analysis was conducted of a simultaneous, quasi-random sample of 20 national news programs each on CTV, CBC-TV, and Radio-Canada in the early months of 1974.[22] The search for evidence of partisanship included not only a comparison of the amount of exposure given to the parties but also an analysis of agenda setting. Table 8-1 shows the amount of time allotted to the federal Liberal, Progressive Conservative, and New Democratic parties on the three networks. Table 8-2 shows the amount of time devoted to inflation, non-confidence motions in Parliament, and strikes — three issues which placed the governing Liberals in a relatively invidious position.

Generally, all three networks reported news on the three major parties and on the three public issues in question. All three discriminated against Social Credit. Neither English network reported any news on that party while Radio-Canada allotted only 1.5% of its time. This small allotment was excluded from the data comprising Table 8-1.

From the first of the two tables emerges a portrait of the CBC as fair-minded in a formal sense. Its allocation of time to the parties most closely approximates their representation in Parliament. From Table 8-2 emerges a tentative portrait of the network as anxious, perhaps fearful, of the incumbent government. Compared to the CTV, the CBC devoted less attention to three news stories, inflation, non-confidence motions, and strikes, which might have placed the Liberal party in an awkward or defensive position. These two portraits can be joined together to produce a picture of a crown corporation which is anxious not to offend any respectable group in Parliament, least of all the party with the greatest influence over its budget.

Table 8-1

News Time Allotted to the Federal Parties
on Three Television Networks

	CBC-TV	CTV	Radio-Canada
Liberals	54%	69%	68%
Progressive Conservatives	32%	18%	10%
New Democrats	13%	13%	22%

Table 8-2

News Time Allotted on Three Television Networks*
to Inflation, Non-Confidence Motions, and Strikes

	CBC-TV	CTV	Radio-Canada
Inflation	11%	17%	10%
Non-Confidence	5%	9%	5%
Strikes	4%	8%	5%
	20%	34%	20%

*Percentages are based on time devoted to domestic news stories.

The CTV emerges as a kind of opposition critic (Table 8-2), but not as a spokesman for the Conservative party (Table 8-1). Like many other journalists, the editors at both CBC and CTV apparently believe in assigning priority to news stories which the audience would view as important and exciting.[23] Unlike their counterparts at the CBC, however, the journalists of the private network encounter some pressure for a Conservative slant from the proprietors of the CTV affiliates. The network can resist this pressure on account of its autonomy from the member stations and on account of the regulatory position of the CRTC. The CTV news department is largely free to attend to political leaders and issues according to journalistic criteria, which give priority to spokesmen who are glib rather than reflective or even-handed. The CTV could therefore ignore the more lacklustre copy coming from Stanfield and other Conservatives. In our study, the Conservatives actually received less exposure on the private network than on the public.

Another difference between the two networks is that the CBC must depend financially on the whims of both its audience and the federal government, while the private network depends almost entirely on its audience. Unlike the simpler role of the private network, the CBC occupies a position which is fraught with uncertainty and ambiguity. Because it is publicly funded, it must undertake certain responsibilities which are non-economic. Even so, the knowledge that the corporation undertakes some non-economic activities often acts as a stimulus for public and Parliamentary demands that it undertake further non-profitable activities even if public subsidies are not increased by comparable amounts. In turn, the corporation is frequently condemned for failure to reach standards of performance that are unrealistic in terms of the financial resources made available. To add insult to injury, the CBC must endure parliamentary criticism and cross-pressure on an annual basis because Parliament has not had the good sense to plan the network's appropriations on a more long-term and secure basis.

The different financial positions of the private and the public networks may explain why the private network devoted more attention to inflation and other critical problems (Table 8-2). These issues were foremost in the minds of Canadians. To discuss these issues would necessarily give greater exposure to the governing Liberals, who would be expected to explain or defend their policies. To discuss these issues would also place the Liberals in a vulnerable position. It is doubtful if the private network set out to embarass the government by focusing on economic problems or non-confidence motions. However, in addition to satisfying audience interests, the CTV may have sought to fulfil a role as vigorous defender of the public interest vis-a-vis any incumbent government. This self-image as a kind of media watchdog may have stemmed from philosophical roots and/or from a desire to justify the existence of the private network in the face of CBC's historic claims in broadcasting. Hence, CTV's commercial desire for an audience and its search for a philosophical raison d'etre apparently combined to give its news a more anti-establishmentarian flavour than that of the government network. By contrast, the CBC's continual state of financial uncertainty vis-a-vis the government may have encouraged the network's mood of insecurity to extend from economic to other realms.

Compared to CTV or CBC, Radio-Canada appears to be somewhat less neutral and more partisan. Table 8-1 suggests a marked bias to the left. On the French network, the NDP received almost 70% more exposure than on the English networks, more than twice as much exposure as the Conservatives, and more than 10 times as much exposure as the *créditistes.* Yet the NDP has never achieved representation in Quebec or in French Canada generally. The moderate exposure given to inflation, non-confidence motions, and strikes (Table 8-2) on Radio-Canada may reflect the network's disinterest in English-Canadian and federal issues rather than the establishmentarian flavour attributed to the English-language public network.

In conclusion, the data collected in this particular study lend no support to the notion of the CTV as an instrument of Conservativism, but do lend support to the view that the French language network of the CBC tilts towards the left. Radio-Canada's apparently insufficient coverage of the Conservatives may help to accentuate the bicultural cleavage in the political system by diminishing the salience and therefore the electoral prospects of that party in Quebec.

The data lend some support to the view that the English-language CBC has a pro-Liberal or establishmentarian tendency if one takes the position, which this writer does, that the media ought to give priority to the failures and foibles in incumbent parties and elites. The media ought to pay special attention to the weaknesses of government, to such issues as inflation and strikes, because of the increasing imbalance of forces that favours the bureaucracy and the incumbent party as compared to the opposition parties, citizens' groups, and the press. In recent years, the Cabinet Secretariat and the Prime Minister's Office, not to mention the government departments, have grown by leaps and bounds. Between 1965 and 1975, the PMO increased from a staff of 4 to a staff of about 100, while the Cabinet Secretariat expanded from a complement of 19 to one of 264.[24] Meanwhile, there has been no comparable increase in the resources of the opposition parties and citizens' groups and no comparable increase in the research capacity of the Press Gallery.[25]

To be precise, our data do not establish whether CBC is pro-Liberal or simply establishmentarian. To identify the better of the two explanations requires data on CBC news when the Liberal party is in opposition. Furthermore, because the apparently establishmentarian or pro-Liberal orientation is modest, additional data are required to ascertain whether the tendency is a characteristic of the sample or a long-term trend and whether the tendency is weak or strong. Additional data are required to establish to what extent the apparent behaviour of a given network is influenced by the transient nature of events. For example, did Radio-Canada's attention to the NDP depend on the bilingual ability of David Lewis, party leader during the period in question? More data is also needed to ascertain whether a given partisan tendency arises from the way in which the network collects and organizes its information or whether it arises from actual decisions made by broadcasters about what is newsworthy.

The Daily Press

While television in Canada is formally committed to political neutrality, the same has not always been true of the print media. Through the nineteenth century and the early part of the twentieth, it was widely accepted that the ownership and control of a servile press were necessary ingredients of partisan manoeuvre. Government patronage was an essential source of income for many newspapers. Patronage ranged from secret service money to advertising, subscriptions, and printing contracts. For example, the government of Sir John A. Macdonald directed 100 times as much advertising to the Conservative *Mail* as to the Liberal *Globe*, while the Laurier government allocated 10 times as much to the *Globe* as to the *Mail*.[26] In the middle of the twentieth century, the *union nationale* and Liberal governments of Quebec and Saskatchewan continued to employ advertising and printing as a means of rewarding friends and punishing enemies. However, government contracts are no longer so remunerative and government patronage is no longer so publicly acceptable. If federal patronage continues to exist, it affects mainly the marginal profit ventures such as small community and ethnic publications. It is doubtful, but not certain, that federal government advertising is any longer distributed among the media on a partisan basis. Nevertheless, it would not be counter to human nature for the publishers receiving government assistance to feel some gratitude to the party in power.

It is possible to examine the political character of the press in the second half of the twentieth century with the help of some data published by T. H. Qualter. The most extensive dataset on the Canadian press in existence, Qualter's material consists of a large variety of statistical information on political reporting in a sample of eight Ontario newspapers during the two months prior to the election of 1962.[27]

Qualter's data suggest a modest bias in favour of the ruling Progressive Conservatives and a modest bias against the opposition parties, especially the Liberals. The Conservatives received an average allocation of 44% of party news as compared to 37% of the national vote and 42% of the vote in Ontario. The NDP received 14% of the space as compared to 14% of the national vote and 17% of the vote in Ontario while the Liberals received 34% of the space as compared to 37% of the national vote and 42% of the vote in Ontario. This bias was in turn accentuated by the greater locational priority given to news about the Progressive Conservatives. Almost 15% of Conservative news appeared on the front pages as compared to approximately 10% and 7% for the Liberals and New Democrats, respectively.

It might be tempting to attribute the superior treatment of the Conservatives to a right-wing or to some other form of partisan bias. However, in 1962 the press was not strongly Conservative in its sympathies. In Qualter's sample of eight dailies, five were pro-Liberal and one, the *Globe and Mail*, was essentially neutral. As an incumbent party, the Conservatives may have had an advantage over their rivals in the manufacture of news because of their prestige and because of their monopoly of public relations experts in government employ. In principle, public servants are neutral, but, in practice, some of them provide services, openly or surreptitiously, to incumbent parties, especially one that has been in power for a long period.

The argument that incumbent parties begin with a communications advantage is also supported by the small amount of data available on the press in the 1974 federal election. In a sample of 16 daily papers, the Liberals received 48% of party-related news stories on the front page and 54% of leader-related stories. This compared to 34% and 32% for the Progressive Conservatives and 27% and 19% for the NDP. Yet, in the same papers the Conservatives held an editorial advantage over the Liberals.[28]

Qualter's dataset does more than suggest that incumbent parties begin with an advantage. His data provide an opportunity for examining the relationship of editorial preference to news treatment. His Table III contains data, measured in column inches, on the volume of editorials favourable, unfavourable, and neutral towards each party in each newspaper. His Table V contains information on the number of column inches devoted to each party on the front page of each paper.

To compare statistically the editorial and news partisanships of the sample of papers requires the construction of indices or scales so that each paper can be scored for editorial sympathy towards each party. Accordingly, for each party an editorial index was constructed by adding the amount of editorial space favourable to that party and the space unfavourable to other parties, then subtracting space unfavourable to the first party and favourable to all other parties. Editorial sympathy towards each party was then compared to the amount of space allocated to the same party on the front page for the sample of dailies. Chi square tests were strong, especially for the three largest parties (see Table 8-3).[29] It is therefore reasonable to conclude that editorial and news content are connected, at least for Ontario papers during one election, and that editorial sentiments somehow predict priorities attached to party news.

To discover whether or not the finding was a freak occurrence, the study was replicated with a small longitudinal sample involving two time periods. Editorial and news partisanship were examined in the *Globe and Mail, Toronto Daily Star*, and *Telegram* during the six weeks prior to both the 1958 and 1963 general elections.[30] The advantage of employing these papers is not only that Toronto is the media centre of English Canada, but also that regional influences are excluded or controlled by using only one city. The 1958 election was significant because it produced a landslide for John Diefenbaker's Conservatives while the 1963 election was important because it represented the first victory for Lester Pearson's Liberals in four elections. Although several years and one election intervened between the two periods, the major parties were led by the same individuals.

An additional advantage arises from studying the Toronto papers during these two elections because the proprietors of two of the papers, the *Globe and Mail* and *Telegram*, changed their allegiances from the

Conservative to Liberal party. As Table 8-4 shows, the *Star* remained pro-Pearson and anti-Diefenbaker in both elections, although less anti-Diefenbaker in the second contest. The other dailies reversed their initial pro-Diefenbaker and anti-Pearson sentiments.

Table 8-3

Achieved significance in Chi square tests comparing editorial sympathies with proportion of space on the front page for each party using Qualter's data on Ontario dailies in 1962.

Conservative Editorial Affinity	with	Conservative Space on Front Page	.016
Liberal Editorial Affinity	with	Liberal Space on Front Page	.003
NDP Editorial Affinity	with	NDP Space on Front Page	.014
Social Credit Editorial Affinity	with	Social Credit Space on Front Page	.047

Table 8-4

Editorials favourable and unfavourable to Diefenbaker and Pearson in three Toronto newspapers during the general election campaigns of 1958 and 1963.

The Globe and Mail

	1958		1963	
	D	P	D	P
F	5	0	0	7
U	0	10	12	3

The Telegram

	1958		1963	
	D	P	D	P
F	16	1	1	4
U	0	8	11	2

The Toronto Star

	1958		1963	
	D	P	D	P
F	1	10	0	8
U	28	0	14	0

| D — Diefenbaker | F — Favourable |
| P — Pearson | U — Unfavourable |

Table 8-5 presents data on the two-party shares of headlines, news space, and pictures. In general, the reportorial behaviour of all three papers mirrored accurately the changes in mood of their editorial pages. In the *Star*, the more equitable news treatment of the two parties in 1963 reflected the less volatile sentiments of the editorials. Both the *Globe* and *Telegram* accorded less favoured reportorial treatment to Diefenbaker in the latter election. In terms of headlines and stories, the *Globe* actually assigned a preferred position to Pearson in 1963. That Pearson supplanted Diefenbaker on the news pages of the *Globe* but not of the *Telegram* may be explained by the greater pro-Tory news bias with which the *Telegram* began in 1958.

Table 8-5

Headlines, story space, and photographs accorded Diefenbaker and Pearson in three Toronto dailies during the campaigns of 1958 and 1963.

	The Globe and Mail				The Telegram				The Toronto Daily Star			
	1958		1963		1958		1963		1958		1963	
	Dief.	Pear.	Dief.	Pear.	Dief.	Pear.	Dief.	Pear.	Dief.	Pear.	Dief.	Pear.
1.	19	12	8	12	26	4	21	15	6	19	16	23
2.	396	312	301	335	184	59	201	90	54	162	168	244
3.	45	22	0	0	108	0	17	35	27	86	85	164
4.	5	2	2	2	4	0	6	4	2	9	2	5
5.	10	3	13	12	11	2	11	14	4	15	12	13

1. Total headlines in inches, rounded.
2. Front page stories in column inches, rounded.
3. Stories on front pages of inside sections in column inches, rounded.
4. Number of photographs on front page.
5. Number of photographs on other pages.

How the party biases of editorials come to be manifested in news could result in some fascinating research. In a study of British journalists, Tunstall has suggested that reporters simply read the editorials of their employer.[31] In a frank autobiography of his experiences as a Canadian journalist, Peter Dempston revealed that, in his experience, party biases originated with desk and news editors rather than publishers. As an election reporter with the *Telegram*, Dempston's first assignment was with the Liberal campaign of 1949. He encountered repeated frustrations at having his stories printed until he learned to portray the St. Laurent campaign as uninspiring and ineffective. The most effective way to have his by-line appear was to accompany a pessimistic story on Liberal fortunes with a picture of empty seats at a St. Laurent rally. According to Dempston, the pressure for a pro-Conservative slant came from the desk editors rather than the proprietor, who on one occasion chastized his staff for excessive distortion.[32]

Our analysis suggested evidence, then, of editorial partisanship being somehow related to partisanship on the news pages. The news partisanship of individual dailies can reasonably be attributed to the informal pressures exerted by superordinates on subordinates in most organizations. Nevertheless, in the absence of additional analysis, it is conceivable that the news and editorial partisanship of newspapers are not directly related to each other, but are instead the result of local or community influences. Qualter's data contained no evidence to support Campion's thesis of a left-wing bias.

Economic Sources of Bias

The preceding sections examined the question of partisan bias from the perspective of the possible decisions, choices, or preferences of news gatekeepers. However, not all, nor even the most important, sources of distortion need be personal in nature. In practice, the economics of news-gathering may introduce stronger biases than the apparent behaviour of newsmen. First, the relative costs of news-gathering in Canada impose a distinct preference for news and information which is American in nature or which is acquired and conveyed by U.S. wire services. Secondly, the economics of producing and marketing news programs disposes the industry towards the dramatic, impassioned, and personalized portrayal of events and away from the impersonal unimpassioned discussion of public problems and social conflicts.

Probably the single most important aspect of the Canadian system of mass communication is the economic pre-eminence of U.S. journalism. The Southam press, the CBC, and other chains and networks can afford only a small number of correspondents abroad, whereas the U.S. agencies and wire services ring the globe. As Joseph Scanlon has written in the title of a paper on American journalistic dominance, "Canada Sees the World Through U.S. Eyes."[33]

The high costs of sponsoring news teams abroad and the low costs of using American material are responsible for a great emphasis on U.S. news and on the U.S. reporting of events outside North America. A study of the print media by Scanlon showed that 20% and 15%, respectively, of anglophone and francophone news stories concern the United States. The United Kingdom and France occupy only 4% and 3% of the space of English- and French-Canadian newspapers. The reporting of U.S. news is so financially compelling that U.S. international news occupies more than twice as much space as Canadian international news. Even U.S. domestic national news occupies almost one-and-a-half times more space than Canadian international news. As for news outside North America, most of that originates with American sources.[34]

Because of the especially high costs of hiring film crews abroad and transmitting film over long distances, Canadian television depends even more on U.S. sources than does the printed press. Even Radio-Canada relinquishes its usage of Agence France Press and places its reliance on U.S. sources. For Canadian television, foreign news reporting becomes in substantial measure the task of taping earlier U.S. television broadcasts and re-editing them, with French speech in the case of Radio-Canada. To use content "scalped" from the U.S. networks is sufficiently cost effective for U.S. foreign and domestic reporting to displace potential Canadian foreign reporting as well as potential Canadian domestic reporting. Our study of the national news programs showed that CTV devoted 67% of its news to foreign events and that 42% of this pertained to the United States.

The domination of foreign news-gathering by Americans appears to have three main consequences. First, the United States occupies a position of prominence in reporting, which makes sense for an American audience, but which distorts the news for a Canadian audience. Secondly, the selection of foreign events to be reported satisfies U.S. needs more closely than Canadian needs. For example, the great prominence given by the Canadian media to the Vietnam war over the last decade can only be understood in terms of the sources of the news, because Canada has no historic links with that part of the world. Thirdly, the reporting of foreign events by U.S. agencies tends to portray United States motives with charity and to exaggerate U.S. achievements. Even the *New York Times*, much vaunted for its comprehensiveness and neutrality, falls short of the objectivity which Canadians might deserve in the reporting of foreign events. A study of reporting on Vietnam, which compared *Le Monde*, a moderate French daily, and the *Times*, showed that the latter continually hesitated or failed to report U.S. military or political setbacks.[35]

With respect to the political process, it is possible to conjecture that the domination of Canadian foreign reporting by the U.S. wire services has tended to undermine public confidence in the NDP and in critics of U.S. foreign policy in the other parties. The Pentagon and, prior to Henry Kissinger, the White House tended to express a Cold War view of the world, seeing all foreign disturbances as manifestations of East-West conflict, even when the roots of such troubles were partly local or regional. The American press accepted this portrait of Vietnam and accorded greater attention to military conflict than to the social, psychological, and economic conditions which undermined the Saigon regime. This shortsighted reporting on Vietnam could not help but diminish some of the credibility of New Democrats and other Canadian politicans who condemned American policy for its failure to understand the social causes of popular opposition to the government in the South.

The Vietnam war is past and some journalists have been quick to claim some credit for its end. However, it is relevant to note that, until the latter stages of the debacle, the American and therefore the Canadian press took a rather servile position vis-a-vis the U.S. government. Under the presidency of Lyndon Johnson, subtle and less than subtle manoeuvres influenced the foreign reporting of American journalists.[36] Furthermore, quite aside from any active interference from the White House, the American press was disposed to accept uncritically White House and Pentagon interpretations of U.S. military activity abroad. In 1964, the press accepted at face value President Johnson's protrayal of the Tonkin Gulf incident as an unprovoked North Vietnamese attack on innocent U.S. naval vessels. According to American evidence, however, the U.S. ships were within North Vietnam's 12-mile territorial limit and had been escorting South Vietnamese ships during their attacks on North Vietnamese land installations.[37] In March of the same year, Senator Ernest Gruening made the first speech in the U.S. Senate advocating a military withdrawal from Southeast Asia. Yet not even the *Washington Post* or the *New York Times* reported his message.[38] In 1965, the American press accepted at face value the Pentagon's White Paper on Vietnam, which purported to show that the Viet Cong were then heavily armed by Eastern Europe and China. The press largely ignored the Pentagon's own statistics, which showed that 97.5% of captured Viet Cong weapons were made in the United States.[39] At one stage *Time Magazine* forced the resignation of its Southeast Asia staff by publicly repudiating its reports for alleged lack of credibility and optimism.

The sheer mass of information of U.S. origin influenced the thinking of Canadian journalists and therefore the thinking of their readers and audiences. American reporting of U.S. foreign policy and foreign conflicts has probably achieved a greater impact on Canadian foreign policy than on electoral behaviour. The NDP and critics of U.S. foreign policy in the other parties have probably not paid dearly for their views because the Canadian public is more interested in matters of domestic import than in foreign policy. Nevertheless, the sheer mass of pro-U.S. government information has tended to undermine the confidence of potential critics of United States policy and has weakened the position of those who are openly skeptical. In a remarkable display of candor, the head of Southam News publicly admitted at the end of the Vietnam War that he had previously exercised a kind of censorship. Charles Lynch acknowledged that he had wrongly moved Bruce Phillips from his post as Washington correspondent for Southam to another post with less opportunity to interpret critically United States policy in Southeast Asia.[40]

While the economic structure of journalism in Canada assures a pro-American bias in foreign reporting, the economic structure of our mass communication also has the effect of diminishing the strength of the three principle domestic cleavages. Our media convey so much information about life and politics within the United States that portions of the Canadian public and even some elements of the federal public service have come to believe that black-white relations and other American problems and cleavages are more vital in Canada than the three traditional cleavages or than such obvious Canadian problems as the aspirations of the native population.

It is true that the class and geographic cleavages exist in both countries, but they achieve different political expression. In the United States, class conflict is expressed between the Democratic and Republican parties, while in Canada it is expressed primarily in rivalry between the NDP and the major parties rather than between the two major parties themselves. Furthermore, the core-periphery cleavage differs because the American equivalent of our Atlantic periphery is relatively minuscule and because the periphery of the former Confederate states has no counterpart in this country. It is reasonable to suspect that these differences in the expressions of the class and geographic cleavages would introduce some confusion in Canadian perceptions of Canadian cleavages.

While the American content of the mass media weakens Canadian political cleavages, the dramatic and fictionalized style of news reporting may diminish the cleavages as well.[41] Television news, especially, tends to depict reality as dramatic personal conflicts with readily identifiable protagonists rather than as social problems or conflicts. Conflicts between parties are portrayed as gladiatorial duels between leaders, not as disputes over policies and programs. This emphasis on personal drama is likely to diminish the vitality of long-term disputes over such matters as economic disparities between regions and social classes.

Once again, the economic structure of journalism may explain the priority given to personalities over issues and programs. Television broadcasters in particular feel obliged to structure news in terms of a large number of short stories in order to sustain audience excitement and therefore loyalty. It is also assumed that television must emphasize fast-moving film in order to achieve its fullest potential. These constraints of time and action are more easily satisfied if Parliamentary debate is portrayed as personal rivalries rather than as differences over policy and program. A short, fast-moving story is less compatible with a dispassionate analysis of issues than with an event replete with emotional turmoil, personal accusations, and counter-accusations.

Television's need for mass audiences encourages the fictional and dramatized depiction of reality, but it is doubtful if the complement of current journalists could intelligently depict party policies and government programs, even if there were economic incentives to do so. Over the past century, an increasing share of media budgets has been devoted to technology, with the result that proportionately fewer journalists oversee an enlarged public sector. A century ago, journalists were literate and were therefore among the most educated people in society. Journalists are currently less well educated than most of the senior bureaucrats and politicians on whom they must report. Furthermore, those journalists who are competent because of native ability or training are not permitted sufficient research time to do justice to their tasks.

The uninformed character of Canadian journalism is a serious problem. At the elite level, Canada has lacked the equivalent of such eminent U.S. journalists as Walter Lippman, Harrison Salisbury, James Reston, or the non-conformist I. F. Stone. Indeed, many public servants, politicians, and professors believe that most reporters are poorly educated and ill-informed.[42] Beryl Plumptre has estimated that the first public report of the Food Prices Review Board was not understood by fully 95% of the press in attendance. The board's chief economist was obliged to take aside one reporter to explain the difference between an "asset" and a "liability." Nor was this incident surprising because, according to Plumptre, the economic knowledge of reporters is "mostly very poor."[43]

Some journalists are sensitive to the problem of media quality. In his inimitable style, Larry Zolf has described ordinary journalists in the parliamentary press gallery as "the Ottawa division of the Global Village Idiots. Any highschool dropout and ex-disc jockey who could press a pencil or a pencil mike at some befuddled Ottawa politician caught in another inexplicable vagary was eligible for membership in Canada's journalistic elite corps."[44]

One of the established truths in the modern social sciences is the link between low education and high ethnocentrism, and Canadian reporters are probably no exception to this rule. In a journalism fraternity which is largely Anglo-Scottish, journalistic instinct is sometimes expressed as a kind of Anglo-Saxon nativism involving a limited understanding of or sympathy for people of non-British origin. The occasional undercurrent of British ethnocentrism may have exacerbated English-French and other ethnic differences. In particular, there have been few noticeable efforts to portray French advances in the public sector as legitimate in a bicultural system or as an attempt to recapture a position worsened by the long inhospitality of the federal government to the French fact.

According to Zolf, Trudeau's uncharitable view of English-speaking reporters was influenced most by his assessment of their disposition toward French Canada. Trudeau apparently believed that working journalists saw Quebec as "either a winter carnival or an FLQ circus. If they didn't quite view French Canadians as the White Niggers of North America, they, at their Lily St. Cyr-est best, viewed French Canadians to be as newsworthy (and in the same way) as the black niggers of Watts and Newark."[45] The mention of stripper Lily St. Cyr may refer to the oft repeated remark, first attributed to columnist Douglas Fisher, then an MP, that French Canadian culture amounted to Lily St. Cyr and Maurice "The Rocket" Richard.

The occasional undercurrent of British ethnocentrism may have also affected the treatment of multicultural Canadians. Ukrainian Canadians and others of eastern European ancestry have not always received the respectful attention justified by their concern about political and cultural oppression in the Soviet bloc. Likewise, sufficient legitimacy has not always been accorded to the concern of Jewish Canadians about the threat to Israel posed by some of her Muslim and Soviet-bloc opponents.

The preceding observations do not hold equally true for all journalists or institutions. For example, some criticisms apply more to the media in medium-sized than in large cities. Unfortunately, the nation's capital is not a large city and the quality of its local press sometimes reflects the size of its population. One can only wince at the prospect that a policy-maker might reach a decision on the basis of information provided by or recommendations made by the Ottawa papers.

Conclusion

The chapter began by organizing current speculation about the political effects of the media around the alternative right-wing and left-wing arguments of bias. The chapter presented some evidence in support of the assumption shared by both political poles, that partisan sentiment could influence reporting. Our re-analysis of Qualter's data on a sample of Ontario dailies showed an apparent relationship between editorial and news partisanship.

We found little evidence to corroborate the right-wing view of left-wing bias except for the apparent left-wing bias of Radio-Canada. The most important consequence of this phenomenon might be to reinforce the bicultural cleavage.

The best evidence to support Porter's view of right-wing bias is probably the pre-eminence of U.S. journalism in this country. There appears to be very little anti-NDP bias in Canadian reporting that could not be accounted for by a general bias in favour of incumbent parties. However, the pre-eminence of U.S. news might undermine the NDP in several ways. The spillover into Canada of the American portrait of the Democrats as a party of the left and of the Republicans as a party of the right might encourage potential left-wing voters in Canada to look to the Liberals rather than the NDP. In foreign reporting, the prevalence of a bias in favour of the views expressed by the U.S. government might also undermine slightly the position of the NDP as well as the position of individual critics of U.S. policy, such as Alvin Hamilton, the former Conservative cabinet minister, and Walter Gordon, the former Liberal minister.

Our data on CTV and CBC-TV suggested the possibility of a less establishmentarian or less pro-Liberal slant on the private network. However, this possibility definitely needs more exploration.

Without more research, it is not entirely clear how the structure of cleavages is affected by mass communication. Nonetheless, it is more likely that the class and geographic cleavages have been diminished than that they have been strengthened. The geographic cleavage is weakened because of the centralization of English mass communication in Toronto. The English-language CBC is concentrated in Toronto, while even the western daily newspapers look to the *Globe and Mail* for cues about newsworthiness. The class cleavage is weakened by the American pre-eminence in information and by the emphasis on personalities rather than party programs and issues.

By contrast, the system of mass communication may have accentuated the bicultural division. The English and French networks and newspapers are quite isolated from each other. The French print media depend on Agence France Presse and would therefore be expected to encourage some degree of attitudinal integration between French Canada and France. Both English and French television depend on American services and both would therefore encourage attitudinal integration with the United States. In the case of Radio-Canada, the data suggested the possibility of an anti-Conservative bias and therefore the possibility of accentuating the bicultural cleavage. An alternative interpretation of the French network's apparent bias would be that the bicultural cleavage is weakened in the longterm. By according a privileged salience to the NDP, Radio-Canada encourages its audience to identify with the left and to substitute the upper strata for English Canada as the object of frustration.

Notes

1. Interview, Finlay MacDonald, (March 1974).

2. John Porter, *The Vertical Mosaic* (Toronto: University of Toronto Press, 1968), and George Grant, *Lament for a Nation* (Toronto: McClelland and Stewart, 1965).

3. A. Bandura, *Aggression: A Social Learning Analysis* (Englewood Cliffs: Prentice-Hall, 1973), and P. H. Tannenbaum, "Studies in Film and Television-mediated Arousal and Aggression: A Progress Report," in G. A. Comstock and E. A. Rubinstein (ed.), *Television and Social Behavior*, V (Washington, D.C.: U.S. Government Printing Office, 1972).

4. Ted Kotcheff, speech to the CRTC Symposium on Television Violence (Kingston, August 1975).

5. *Vertical Mosaic*, 484. See Wallace Clement, *The Canadian Corporate Elite* (Toronto: Carleton Library, McClelland and Stewart, 1975), Ch. 7.

6. "Whither the Press and Periodicals?" in D. C. Williams (ed.), *The Arts as Communication* (Toronto: University of Toronto Press, 1961), 52.

7. W. H. Kesterton, *A History of Journalism in Canada* (Toronto: McClelland and Stewart, 1967), 354–55.

8. See Hugh Winsor, "A Power Elite Gets Its Way in Kitchener", *Globe and Mail* (February 8, 1972), 8, and Conrad Winn and John McMenemy, "Political Alignment in a .Polarized City: Electoral Cleavages in Kitchener, Ontario," *Canadian Journal of Political Science*, VI: 2 (June 1973), 231–33.

9. F. C. Engelmann and M. A. Schwartz, *Canadian Political Parties* (Toronto: Prentice-Hall, 1975), 126. For an important document on the media, see also Canada, Special Senate Committee on the Mass Media, *Report*, 3 vols. (Ottawa: Information Canada, 1970), known popularly as the Davey Report.

10. See Jeremy Tunstall, *Journalists at Work* (Beverly Hills, Cal.: Sage Publications, 1974), 121ff. See also E. J. Epstein, *News From Nowhere* (New York: Random House, 1973), and W. L. Rivers, "The Washington Correspondent and Government Information," (doctoral dissertation, The American University, 1960).

11. Kesterton, *Journalism in Canada*, 87. Former leader of the Quebec Conservative party, Camilien Houde was interned, during World War II, for opposing the war effort. In 1949, he stood successfully as an independent.

12. *Toronto Star* (June 22, 1974), A3.

13. Interview (June 1974). By the end of the 1974 election campaign, Conservative and Liberal exposure on CBC-TV news was equal. See the data in Frederick J. Fletcher, "The Mass Media in the 1974 Canadian Election," in Howard Penniman (ed.), *Canada at the Polls* (Washington: American Enterprise Institute, 1975).

14. *Canadian Political Parties.*

15. Dalton Camp, *Gentlemen, Players, and Politicians* (Toronto: McClelland and Stewart, 1970), 219–20.

16. When Dempston queried Marjorie McEnaney, the official in charge of public affairs programs, about the cancellation, she replied, "Oh, we have a regular stable of correspondents in Ottawa who do this program for us. Blair Fraser, Bob McKeown, Ann Francis — and, anyhow, just the very mention of the name *Telegram* and it sounds so Conservative." Peter Dempston, *Assignment Ottawa* (Toronto: General Publishing, 1968), 50.

17. Peter Newman, *Renegade in Power* (Toronto: McClelland and Stewart, 1963), 335–37.

18. See Peter Newman, *The Distemper of Our Times* (Toronto: McClelland and Stewart, 1968), 408.

19. Based on interviews with several former CBC newsmen.

20. *Lament for a Nation,* 19.

21. Ibid.

22. The television data are drawn from a study of television news and national integration supported by grants from the Canadian Radio-Television Commission, Wilfrid Laurier University, and Carleton University. Thanks are owed to my research collaborators, Robert Seed and Chester Burtt. The sample was only quasi-random as a result of the imperfect performance of the local cable company.

23. Several interviews, 1974–75.

24. My gratitude to the office of Colin Kenney, PMO, for this and related information.

25. On the limited research capacity of the Parliamentary Press Gallery, see Anthony Westell, "Reporting the Nation's Business," in G. Stuart Adam (ed.), *Journalism, Communication, and the Law* (Toronto: Prentice-Hall, 1976).

26. See N. Ward, "The Press and Patronage — An Exploratory Operation", in J. H. Aitchison (ed.), *The Political Process in Canada* (Toronto: University of Toronto Press, 1963).

27. T. H. Qualter and K. A. Kirby, "The Press of Ontario and the Election", in John Meisel (ed.), *Papers on the 1962 Election* (Toronto: University of Toronto Press, 1968). Bruce Macnaughton kindly provided computer assistance.

28. Frederick J. Fletcher, "The Mass Media in the 1974 Canadian Election," Tables 9-1 and 9-4.

29. No statistical meaning need be attributed to the tests of significance, which can be treated instead as evidence that the relationship within the sample was not trivial.

30. Much of the ensuing analysis depends on data collection and processing undertaken by Gordon Florence in a course given by the author at Wilfrid Laurier University in 1973–74.

31. Tunstall, *Journalists.*

32. Dempston, *Assignment Ottawa.*

33. "Canada Sees the World Through U.S. Eyes: One Case Study in Cultural Domination" (unpublished paper, Carleton University, Nov. 10, 1973). Reproduced in part under the same title in *Canadian Forum* (October 1974).

34. Joseph Scanlon, "A Study of the Contents of 30 Canadian Daily Newspapers" (Ottawa: Special Senate Committee on Mass Media, October 1969), 29.

35. Geoge Lichtheim, " 'All the News That's Fit to Print' — Reflections on the *New York Times*", *Commentary*, 40:3 (Sept. 1965), 33–46.

36. Reported intermittently in the issues of *I. F. Stone's Weekly* and the *New York Review of Books* for the period.

37. According to Senator William Fulbright, Chairman of the Senate Foreign Relations Committee, U.S. ships were within 11 miles of the North Vietnamese shore. See the discussion in I. F. Stone, *In a Time of Torment* (New York: Random House, 1967), 195–202.

38. See Robert Sherrill, *Why They Call It Politics* (New York: Harcourt Brace Jovanovich, 1974), 294.

39. See Stone's famous "Reply to the White Paper", reprinted in his *In a Time of Torment*.

40. Charles Lynch, nationally syndicated Southam column (Oct. 22, 1974).

41. See the excellent analyses in E. J. Epstein, *News From Nowhere* (New York: Random House, 1973), and CRTC, "Television's Depiction of Reality" (August 1975).

42. For Prime Minister Trudeau's unflattering view of the press, see Larry Zolf, *Dance of the Dialectic* (Toronto: James, Lewis and Samuel, 1973), 16ff.

43. Interview, December, 1975.

44. *Dance of the Dialectic*, 12. Zolf's comments applied to his category of paparazzi, who consisted of ordinary print journalists, wire services personnel, and all broadcasters except for Bruce Phillips, Geoff Scott, Peter Stursberg, and Ron Collister. See *ibid.*, 116–17. For some biting observations by another insider, see Westell, "The Nation's Business."

45. Zolf, *Dance of the Dialectic*, 17.

# SECTION
IV

Internal Party Attributes (Throughputs)

The common purpose of Canadian parties is to win elections. In a mass democracy, organization is necessary to acquire election funds and mobilize voter support. Party leaders allege that organization is also crucial to the recruitment of personnel and policy-making. This section analyzes the personnel of the parties and assesses the impact of formal organization on electoral and non-electoral decision-making. Using the categories of operating elite, secondary elite, and activists, Chapter 9 explores similarities and dissimilarities among the parties' personnel. Chapter 10 describes the constitutional nature of the parties and their decision-making processes.

PARTY PERSONNEL — ELITES AND ACTIVISTS

John McMenemy and Conrad Winn

Introduction

The influence of political parties on the daily experiences of Canadians is not great. Many citizens who possess partisan feelings towards a party do so only in the sense that they are willing to cast a vote on its behalf. By contrast, parties in some European societies exercise a pervasive influence on the non-electoral activities of the population. An individual's employer, trade union, cooperative, literary club, and athletic association might each be associated with the party he supports in elections.

Canadian parties contain passive supporters consisting of reliable voters and party members whose aid is limited to a small annual fee. They also include active supporters or activists. This party personnel includes volunteers in elections, candidates for public office, delegates to party conventions, and party officials. At the highest level of each party exists a small set of decision-makers or operating elite who exert great influence over policy and especially over election strategies. Each party also has a large secondary or residual elite of potential decision-makers.

While parties differ significantly in the composition and influence of their activists and elites, there are also important similarities. In general, the class background of activists is similar among the parties and unrepresentative of the electorate. Meanwhile, the cultural backgrounds of party activists reflect the particular electoral support of the parties. The composition of party elites reflects the dependence of each party on certain groups for special resources.

Common Features of Elites and Activists

While each of the parties proclaims its uniqueness, common ground exists among the parties' elites and activists. Regardless of party, elites and activists tend to hold higher social and occupational status than their followers and the electorate at large. Furthermore, all parties tend to recruit leaders of higher social class where and when the party's electoral prospects are great.[1] Thus, Conservative and Liberal activists and elites may exhibit somewhat greater status than their NDP counterparts and do exhibit higher status than their Social Credit counterparts. Nonetheless, as a whole, activists and elites manifest higher status than the electorate generally.

A study of the Conservative and Liberal national leadership conventions in 1967 and 1968 showed that a majority of delegates had some university education.[2] Almost half held undergraduate or post-graduate degrees. Of the more than 40% who had family incomes exceeding $15,000 annually, more than half had family incomes exceeding $20,000 annually (see Table 9-1). According to the 1961 Canadian census, approximately 3% of the population twenty years of age or more had university degrees and the mean family income was $5,449. In his analysis of data gathered by Hugh Thorburn and others on Liberal and Conservative activists and elites, John C. Courtney remarks that

> ... the typical Liberal or Conservative convention delegate in 1967 or 1968 (and, it is fair to assume, at earlier conventions as well) ... is well

Table 9-1

Socio-Economic Characteristics of
Liberal and Conservative Convention Delegates
and the Canadian Population*

	% Population 20 years old and over	% Progressive Conservative Convention Delegates 1967	% Liberal Convention Delegates 1968
Selected Occupation			
Managerial	8	21	16
Lawyer	0.2	n.a.	20
Professional other			
than lawyer	10	34	14
Clerical	13	2	2
Sales and Service	19	9	7
Farmer	10	4	5
Education			
University started	3.1	10	14
University degree	3	33	37
Post-graduate degree	n.a.	10	7
Total Family Income			
$15,000 − $19,999	—**	17	16
$20,000 and over	—**	27	25

*Compiled from data presented by John C. Courtney, *The Selection of National Party Leaders in Canada* (Toronto: Macmillan, 1973), 106, 124, supplemented by additional census data, 1961.

**The census classifications in 1961 did not correspond to those of the convention delegates' profiles. Census data are nonetheless illuminating: $10,000–14,999 was the total family income for 6.3% of the Canadian population; $15,000 and over for 2.8% of the population.

above-average in both income and education. The chances of his being a middle-aged manager, or a lawyer (or some other professional), are extremely good, but the chances of his being employed in a clerical position, or as a labourer, or a skilled worker are very slight.[3]

Liberal and Conservative candidates for office tend also to be high in socio-economic status. Allan Kornberg has computed socio-economic scores for a sample of federal candidates in the years 1945–1962 (see Table 9-2).[4] Kornberg's data confirm that aspirants for membership in the House of Commons are drawn from the upper occupational and educational strata of Canadian society. Among the elected members, 28% have not been to college, while a majority has professional occupations.[5] In a similar fashion, constitutency level activists tend to belong to the middle class. Not surprisingly, Kornberg found that interpersonal influence in Liberal and Conservative local organizations tended to be based on high personal status.[6]

Table 9-2

Mean SES Scores on a 00 to 96 Scale of Conservative and
Liberal Candidates by Region for the Period 1945–1962

Party	Quebec	Ontario	Other Regions
Conservative	71.8	63.9	58.8
	(N=273)	(N=290)	N=344)
Liberal	77.2	67.5	59.0
	(N=302)	(N=291)	(N=359)

Note: N refers to sample size.
Adapted from Allan Kornberg, *Canadian Legislative Behavior: A Study of the 25th Parliament* (New York: Holt, Rinehart and Winston, 1967), 46.

Members of the Liberal and Conservative elite, such as cabinet ministers and opposition front benchers, have still higher status. Many are members of families with past histories of political activism. Analyzing his national sample of the political elite, John Porter discovered "the beginnings, at least, of a 'political class' in that one-quarter of the entire elite came from families in which some member of an earlier generation had occupied political roles, though not all these roles were at the level of the elite."[7]

This phenomenon of higher status among elites and activists than among followers also applies to the NDP. For a national sample of activists, Table 9-3 shows that almost as many NDP activists have university education as Liberal and Conservative activists. Table 9-4 shows that an actual majority of activists serving the working-class party consider themselves to be middle-class or higher in social status. In fact, many New Democratic activists are professionals. In rural Saskatchewan, it has been known that the party's activists come from the more prosperous farmers.[8] In British Columbia and Ontario, working-class activists and elites are found among the better paid workers and highly remunerated union officials.[9] The leaders of the socialist party have been university educated. M. J. Coldwell was a high school principal and David Lewis a lawyer. T. C. Douglas has a master's degree and Ed Broadbent a Ph.D.

Table 9-3

Education of Party Activists (%)

	PC	Lib.	NDP	SC
12 years or less	67	70	75	100
13 years or more	33	30	25	0

Source: Carleton University Political Science Department's version of Professor John Meisel's 1965 National Survey. For this calculation, activists are those who attended campaign meetings, read party leaflets or reports of election speeches, and attempted to convince others to vote for a particular party or candidate.

Table 9-4

Self-Perceived Class of Party Activists (%)

	PC	Lib	NDP	SC
Middle class or higher	70	63	63	9
Working class or lower class	30	37	37	91

Source: See Table 9-3, above.

The position of Social Credit is more ambiguous. Tables 9-3 and 9-4 portray the party's activists to be by far the most working-class. Nonetheless, at the elite level the phenomenon of higher social status appears to apply to Social Credit as to the other parties. According to Maurice Pinard, three-quarters of *créditiste* candidates hold middle-class occupations compared to less than a quarter of their supporters.[10]

Lawyers are numerous among activists in the three largest parties and especially at the highest level. Between 1940 and 1960, lawyers accounted for approximately one-third of all MPs and almost two-thirds of ministers.[11] Members of the legal profession are successful partly because of the nature of their employment. Their work requires the same verbal and negotiating skills which are important in political life. Furthermore, a large proportion of political work is legalistic. Legalism carries a special importance in a federal system like Canada because differences over the propriety of alternative policies often become disputes over jurisdiction among governments. Thus, federal action in 1974 to tax royalties paid to provincial governments by oil companies became a dispute over constitutional points of law as much as over the distribution of wealth. By contrast, members of other professions are inhibited from entering politics because of the few opportunities for leaves of absence. A lawyer entering politics may formally, at least, leave his firm in the capable hands of a partner. Members of other professions cannot accommodate both private and public careers as easily. Law therefore faces little competition.

The Canadian lawyer has great financial incentives to enter politics. The very act of contesting an election provides him with low cost publicity for his legal practice. A lawyer may become a token candidate in an unwinable seat or give other service to his party in order to maintain a flow of public business to his firm (see Chapter 7, Elections). If elected, the nature of his work enables the lawyer to secure and disguise easily political patronage and other sources of extra income. Public business or private gifts from an unpopular or disreputable client or even outright patronage can take the form of an obscure fee for service to the legal firm from which the lawyer MP receives a retainer. By the nature of their work, teachers and other professionals in politics are more vulnerable to charges of unethical conduct or conflict of interest.

All parties, then, contain elites and activists of higher status than their supporters. In general, party activists and elites tend to have professional occupations. Among the professions, law dominates for reasons related to the nature of political debate in Canada as well as the profession of law itself.

Inter-Party Differences Among Activists

While inter-party similarities appear to reflect a deference among Canadians to high status individuals, inter-party differences among activists reflect differences in electoral preferences. Each party tends to possess activists among these groups from which it draws voting strength. This similarity between electors and activists tends to be true for religion, language, and region, but not very true in the case of social class (see Chapters 4, 5, 6).

In terms of religion and language, an historic cultural cleavage has pitted Roman Catholics against Protestants and French against English. After the 1890s, the Liberal party found increased support among French Canadians and Catholics to the chagrin of Conservatives and, later, of the New Democrats. Social Credit recently achieved some success among French Canadians and Catholics insofar as it was represented by Réal Caouette and his rural populist movement, the *ralliement créditiste*.

The party preferences of different religions sometimes take organizational form. In a number of constituencies, the Liberal party and the Knights of Columbus have been closely linked. Historically, the Conservatives and local Anglican parishes were similarly linked and, less frequently, the CCF-NDP allied with clergy and lay members of the United Church. The party connections of Anglicans and United Churchmen reflect the affinities of the Church of England for the British Conservative party and of Methodism for the Labour party. A study of party organization in Hamilton found that the Liberal party attracted

80% of the city's Catholic activists, but less than one-third of their Protestant counterparts.[12] The national pattern tends to be similar in form although Catholic-Protestant differences may not be so marked. Table 9-5 shows that, nationally, activists in the Social Credit and Liberal parties tend to be Catholic rather than Protestant, while the reverse is true for the Conservatives and NDP.

Table 9-5

The Religion of Party Activists (%)

	PC	Lib.	NDP	SC
No religion	5	0	8	0
Protestant	73	38	57	15
Roman Catholic	22	62	35	85

Source: See Table 9-3 above.

Both the Hamilton study of party organization and an analysis of British Columbia New Democrats found that the NDP attracted an unusual number of activists with secular or agnostic religious views.[13] This religious-political pattern of belief may anticipate the eventual replacement of the historic Catholic vs. Protestant cleavage with a secular vs. religious cleavage, pitting the NDP against one or both of the larger parties.

In terms of region, the deepest electoral roots of the Conservative party are in Nova Scotia and Prince Edward Island. The Liberals are strongest in Quebec, while NDP strength lies in Manitoba, Saskatchewan, and British Columbia. This pattern of electoral success is probably manifested directly in each party's supply of activists. An important exception might be Saskatchewan, where the NDP finds a reservoir of dues-paying members whose number and high level of activity by far outstrip the current level of federal strength in that province. This particular involvement of Saskatchewan in the CCF-NDP reflects the high level of political participation which has been historically characteristic of the province and which received impetus from the cooperative movement.

In terms of social class, Social Credit activists are clearly working-class (see Tables 9-3 and 9-4). Aside from Social Credit, however, the main socio-economic difference among activists probably relates to occupation rather than to social status. Because of the expressed interest of the Conservative and Social Credit parties in the needs of small businessmen, many small businessmen are attracted to these parties. Because of its long rule and its tie to big business, the Liberal party appeals to a disproportionate number of middle to high echelon corporate managers. Because of its control of federal legal patronage, the Liberals can also count on many lawyers as activists. Finally, because of its ties to the trade union movement, the NDP has many activists who are union members and officials.

Inter-Party Differences Among Elites

Party elites contain members of the House of Commons and, in the case of the older parties, Senators as well. The extra-parliamentarian members of the elite may overshadow the parliamentarian members. Appointed parliamentarians in the Senate may be more powerful than elected parliamentarians from the Commons. Party elites normally consist of cabinet ministers and their critics in the official opposition, influential backbenchers on both sides of the House of Commons, senators, party officials, fund-raisers, interest group leaders, special advisors, and provincial leaders. Only the small operating elite exercises influence on a specific issue, but the membership of that fraction of the total elite varies from issue to issue. Thus, officials of the automobile and steelworkers' unions may exercise decisive influence on NDP attitudes towards budgetary legislation without having any impact whatsoever on that party's attitudes towards biculturalism. Curiously, individuals may belong to the operating elite without actually attending its deliberations. For example, these trade union leaders need not participate personally in NDP discussions on monetary or fiscal policy because their views are already known. For the remainder of the operating elite to ignore their views would risk the loss of union assistance during elections. Until energy became a public issue, executives in the oil industry had a comparable role in Liberal decision-making.

The composition of each party's elite reflects in part the nature of its electoral support. Partly because of electoral support on cultural questions, the Liberal and *créditiste* parties have many more French Canadians and Roman Catholics in leadership roles than do the Conservative and New Democratic parties. Partly as a result of regional support, proportionately more individuals come from Ontario and Quebec than elsewhere in the Liberal elite. The *créditiste* elite is overwhelmingly from rural Quebec. The members of the NDP elite are predominantly from industrial urban Ontario and the West, while Conservative party leadership is possibly the most spatially diffuse. In part because of class-based support, the Liberal elite has by far the most upper status. It contains a disproportionate number of millionaires elected to the House or appointed by the party to the Senate. The *créditiste* elite has the lowest status of all party elites, while Conservative leaders are probably somewhat more upper- and middle-class than those of the NDP.

Although electoral cleavages are manifested in the composition of party elites, their significance actually diminishes at the higher levels of the party hierarchy. In particular, the Liberals, Conservatives, and New Democrats are so intent on electoral success that each strives to appeal to a virtual cross-section of the populace. The most rational method of appealing to such a cross-section is to constitute an elite which is representative of as many segments of the electorate as possible. These representatives can interpret the needs of each segment to their party and publicly identify the party with each segment. Not all parties attempt this representativeness because they are not equally intent on attaining electoral success or equally capable of acting rationally, for whatever purpose. Also, the resources to acquire this cross-sectional support are not equally distributed among the parties. By their rate of success, the Liberals are the most resourceful and the most rationally intent on winning elections. Success reinforces success, of course, for government policy and patronage are important resources denied other parties.

The desire of the parties to obscure the significance of electoral support in recruitment of their elites is strongest in the case of bicultural and regional support. By contrast, the relatively mild attempts to reduce the significance of class support probably results from the relative unimportance of that electoral cleavage. Because of their electoral frustrations in Quebec, both the Conservatives and the NDP normally make a great effort to win the allegiance and promote the careers of talented French Canadians from that province. In 1972, Claude Wagner, a former provincial Liberal minister, was apparently offered a wide variety of inducements to become a Conservative candidate. Once elected, he immediately became the second-ranking member of his caucus. However, Joe Clark, an MP from Alberta where the PCs hold all the seats, gained the leadership. The NDP accorded preferred treatment to Robert Cliche, its former Quebec leader. His unsuccessful candidacy in 1968 — and his poor health — terminated his elite standing in the NDP. Recently, the Liberals have had great difficulty in winning seats in the West; as a result, if a western Liberal is lucky enough to get elected, he will likely be appointed to the Cabinet, provided the party remains in power. In the 1960s, the party was so anxious to identify itself publicly with the West that it appointed to the Cabinet Roger Teillet, a Manitoba MP who possessed so little political shrewdness that he subsequently became the first minister to lose the nomination of his own constituency association.[14] The Liberal party successfully wooed Hazen Argue, a CCF MP from Saskatchewan, following his defeat by T. C. Douglas for the NDP leadership in 1961. Argue lost a re-election bid as a Liberal MP in 1963, but was rewarded subsequently with an appointment to the Senate. After the bifurcation of Social Credit into a western and a Quebec section in 1965, the Liberals tried with some success to achieve the conversion of western Social Credit MPs.

With less success, the Liberal party has occasionally attempted to employ elite recruitment to counteract the inroads of the CCF-NDP among working people. During World War II, Mackenzie King included briefly in his cabinet Humphrey Mitchell, a leader from the Trades and Labour Congress. King also attempted to recruit M. J. Coldwell, the CCF leader. In 1965, Lester Pearson was able to entice Jean Marchand, outgoing president of the Confederation of National Trade Unions. Ironically, Marchand obliged the Liberals to find a safe seat for his friend and the party's then vociferous critic, Pierre Trudeau, who became Liberal leader and prime minister three years later.

The foregoing illustrates how Canadian parties strive to make their elites more regionally and culturally representative during times of electoral need. In addition, in their rational drive for electoral success parties promote to elite status — especially operating elite status — individuals who possess special resources which can help achieve success. These resources may be monetary, organizational, personal, or cognitive. Five types of people are able to provide these resources and therefore constitute the operating elite: parliamentarians, party officials, interest group leaders, experts, and successful provincial party leaders. Since each party has different needs, it accords different importance to each of the categories of political leadership (see Table 9-6).

Table 9-6

Importance of Different Sources of Recruitment
to the Operating Elites of Federal Parties

	Lib.	Con.	NDP	Cred.
1. Parliamentarians	Low	High	High	High
2. Party officials	High	High	High	Low
3. Policy specialists	High	Low	Low	Low
4. Interest groups	High	Low	High	Low
5. Provincial parties	Low	High	Low	Low

Because of the demands of the parliamentary system, notably to form a government from MPs, parliamentarians are included in the elites of all parties. However, MPs are relatively less important in the Liberal party, where parliamentary and other political experience is considered to be a lesser virtue. As a result, Liberal MPs have less pre-parliamentary political experience than other members. Furthermore, many Liberal ministers are appointed after very short parliamentary apprenticeships. Some ministers, such as Pierre Juneau in 1975, were appointed before entering Parliament; formerly a senior civil servant, Juneau failed to secure election, resigned from the cabinet, and joined the Prime Minister's Office. Four future Prime Ministers, Mackenzie King, Louis St. Laurent, Lester Pearson, and Pierre Trudeau, joined the Liberal party at the elite level and succeeded to its leadership after a few years of parliamentary experience.

This recruitment to the Liberal operating elite from outside the House and the concomitant low involvement of Liberal MPs in the operating elite derives from the party's lengthy reign. Generally, the Liberal party's parliamentary origin allows for a pragmatic approach to such matters as recruitment. Moreover, the Liberal party has been in power for all but six of the last 41 years. Its leadership perceives itself as a national administration with neither of the major opposition parties as a worthy alternative. It publicly characterizes the Conservative party as a threat to Confederation and considers the NDP a mere thorn in its side. Hence, leadership qualifications in the party consist of managerial efficiency and technical expertise rather than combative and parliamentary skills. While the election to the House of Commons is one path to the operating elite of all parties, for the Liberal party it is chiefly an incidental route necessitated by the parliamentary form of government.

By contrast, certain Conservative MPs can be identified as members of the party's operating elite because of their distinctive representative quality, policy expertise, or regional base. Claude Wagner belonged to the party's operating elite from 1972 to 1974 because he was the party's only French-Canadian MP and a prestigious personality. James Gillies was in the operating elite as the financial critic from 1972 to 1974. His status in the party was based on his links to the corporate core in Toronto and on his career as Dean of York University's Faculty of Administrative Studies. After an uncertain performance in his party's 1974 campaign, Gillies remained in the elite, but was replaced as financial critic by Sinclair Stevens, a millionaire-financier also from Toronto. Generally, western MPs who enjoyed power under Diefenbaker or remained loyal to his leadership were in Stanfield's residual elite, while David MacDonald and other maritime MPs were part of the operating elite because of their long friendship with Stanfield. Joe Clark will likely bring little change: an ex-aide to Stanfield, his leadership coalition came from Stanfield supporters; Diefenbaker loyalists opposed him.

In the NDP, MPs achieve operating elite status on the basis either of their electoral clout or their policy-making talents. At the outset, they have status because they are rare specimens of the party's public appeal. Moreover, the leader lacks the range of sanctions and rewards which the Liberal and Conservative leaders can apply to keep their MPs in line. NDP leaders understand that many of the party's seats are held as a result of candidate appeal and are not safe party seats. Indeed, personal defeats suffered by the two recent leaders of the party should make the NDP leader even more acutely aware of his own vulnerability. David Lewis, the former leader defeated in 1974, may remain in the party's elite, but his influence will certainly decline.

The operating elite of the *ralliement créditiste* is basically its mercurial leader, Réal Caouette. In the election of 1968, for example, Caouette was responsible for formulating both the party's program and electoral strategy. His power results in part from the greater interest of the veteran MPs in constituency rather than parliamentary affairs. Because of their specialized interests and lack of parliamentary expertise, the *créditistes* have sometimes called upon nearby New Democrats in the House of Commons to help draft their motions. A few younger and newer MPs who see their role as developing policy and contributing to national debate represent a potential parliamentarian challenge to Caouette's liberty.[15] In recent years, Caouette has groomed his son to succeed him.

Each party's operating elite also contains non-elected party officials, whose roles usually involve fund-raising and organizing (see Chapter 10, Party Structures and Decision-Making). Between elections, they assist in the management of internal factionalism and dissent. In election campaigns, they constitute the national campaign organization and may supplement or supplant local organizations in marginal constituencies. Each party's officials hold different formal roles. Because of their longstanding rule, Liberal prime ministers have been able to appoint election organizers and fund-raisers to the Senate. Keith Davey, Richard Stanbury, Gildas Molgat, Harry Hays, and John Godfrey are examples of operating elite personnel in the Senate. Because the Senate has a light legislative load, these Liberals have few necessary responsibilities, nor do need they to seek voter support for the retention of their public salary and senatorial prestige. In short, they are free to devote their time to the business of the Liberal party.[16]

Because the Conservatives lack corporate support comparable to the Liberals' and because they have lately lacked the power of senatorial appointment, they have fewer full-time officials. Under Stanfield, Finlay MacDonald, a longtime friend and campaign director, and Malcolm Wickson, party treasurer, were located in the leader's office. The Opposition leader's bureaucracy is generally small. Tenure is temporary and normally dependent upon a relationship to the leader. The role of Dalton Camp as party president in the protracted struggle over the continued leadership of John Diefenbaker was an exceptional instance of an official's independent power.

Lacking much money for campaigns and without a large core of voter support, the NDP is particularly dependent on organization. Consequently, officials in the party are numerous and influential. Indeed, many MPs possess status because of their earlier careers as party officials. David Lewis was a national party officer longer than he was an MP. He had operating elite status in the CCF-NDP as an official long before he was elected to Parliament. MP Les Benjamin and former MPs John Harney and Terrence Grier were full-time party secretaries prior to their public careers. Indeed, Harney was a serious leadership candidate against Lewis in 1971 before he became an MP. Familism has reinforced the importance of officialdom. Both Grace MacInnis, a former MP, and Stephen Lewis, the Ontario leader, have benefited from family members and friends in organizational positions.

Generally, the key *créditiste* organizers in Quebec are loyal to Caouette, allowing him free rein on policy and on many organizing decisions. But Caouette's power is not absolute, as evidenced by his reluctant approval of party entry into Quebec provincial politics. Personalism is a dominant theme in the party. According to *créditiste* officials, their endemic factionalism arises from personality conflicts resulting from ambition or disloyalty rather than from doctrinal differences or electoral defeats.[17]

Policy specialists are most prominent in the Liberal party. As the party of national administration, the Liberals have looked to policy specialists in the senior civil service for leadership as well as policy direction. Mackenzie King was deputy minister of labour prior to entering the party formally as the minister. As prime minister, King took future Prime Minister Lester Pearson from his senior position in external affairs and appointed him to the Cabinet. J. W. Pickersgill, Mitchell Sharp, Maurice Lamontagne, and Pierre Juneau, however briefly, were also civil servants who joined the operating elite of the Liberal party as key ministers. Although they remain nominally non-partisan administrators, some senior civil servants belong to the Liberal operating elite, partly because the Liberals have been in power and partly because of personal attachments.[18]

Recent Liberal prime ministers have found the Prime Minister's Office a convenient site for the entry of policy specialists. Marc Lalonde was in the operating elite of the party as principal secretary to Trudeau from 1968 to 1972. Lalonde's friendship with the leader gave him more power than held by many cabinet ministers of long standing. In 1972, Lalonde achieved election and an important portfolio. He was replaced in the PMO in 1972 by a defeated minister more highly valued by Trudeau than by his local constituents. From 1974 to 1975, now-Senator Jack Austin was Trudeau's principal secretary. Trudeau had earlier brought Austin, a resource company official, into the civil service as a deputy minister in the Department of Energy, Mines, and Resources. As mentioned, the electorally hapless Juneau is now in the PMO.

The NDP does not accord the same status to policy specialists, but the party's need for advice is the point of impact for supporters in universities. Walter Young, Charles Taylor, and Desmond Morton are influential as academic advisors who also held party posts or have been occasional candidates. Initially, Melville Watkins and James Laxer gained operating elite status in the party as policy specialists and party officials. Later, Laxer became Lewis's strongest opponent for the leadership.

The operating elites of the parties also contain representatives of institutions which provide material assistance to the party. The leadership is keenly aware of their aid and therefore sympathetic to their desires. The Liberal leadership has developed close ties to the corporate world and found it a major source of elite recruitment. Since 1963, such powerful Liberal economic ministers as Walter Gordon, C. M. Drury, Eric Kierans, and James Richardson came directly from the corporate world into the operating elite upon their election to parliament. Their individual histories suggest that these men of power came to the Liberal party to administer policy rather than out of a passion for the hustings. With their colleagues from the civil service, they constitute a political leadership which views itself as a natural ruling class rather than as one political force contending with others for the opportunity to rule.[19] With less access to major corporate support, the Conservatives have turned to small or medium-size businesses. Many of their officials, candidates, and some MPs have a small-business background.

The NDP's operating elite contains some trade union leaders. Affiliated unions regularly provide money and organizers to the party, with additional assistance during elections. The unions publicize the party internally and encourage members to vote for the party. The cohesiveness of the labour delegation at leadership conventions in 1971 and 1975 contributed to the victories of Lewis and Broadbent. Dennis McDermott, of the United Automobile Workers, and Joseph Morris, president of the Canadian Labour Congress, are examples of union representatives in the party's operating elite.[20]

In contrast, the *créditistes* do not possess significant institutional benefactors. More than any party, it is financially dependent upon its membership. While this situation puts the party at a disadvantage, it tends to enhance Caouette's position within the party. Since his personal appeal is largely responsible for the party's grass-roots support, he remains the sole leadership figure of any consequence.

Provincial parties represent a historic source of operating elite personnel and organizational support for the Conservative party. Neither the Liberals nor the Conservatives are hostile to the interests of the corporate world. Because the Liberals have obtained a preferential support from the senior echelons of corporate and public bureaucracies, the Conservatives are more compelled to seek support from successful provincial regimes. Since 1940, three of the Conservatives' five leaders have been recruited from the ranks of provincial premiers. Both Stanfield and his major opponent in the leadership convention of 1967 were successful premiers. In 1975, Premiers Peter Lougheed and William Davis were touted as successors to Stanfield. The national party has depended upon leaders, organizers, and fund-raisers of the *union nationale* in Quebec and the Conservative party in Ontario. Since the demise of the *UN*, the party is even more dependent on the successful Conservative regime in Ontario.[21] The NDP may develop similar provincial connections as a consequence of recent provincial victories. In 1961, the party chose as federal leader T. C. Douglas, the only CCF Premier. Following Lewis' resignation, Premiers Schreyer and Blakeney were the only serious leadership possibilities from outside the federal parliament.

Conclusion

In addition to a large number of passive supporters, Canadian parties contain activists and elites. Activists are election workers, candidates, convention delegates, and officials. The residual elite consists of potential decision-makers. The operating elite consists of effective decision-makers. There is some correspondence between the nature of party elites and activists and their bases of electoral support.

Activists in particular tend to reflect the parties' electoral support. The bicultural cleavage is generally manifested in the composition of party activists. Most notably, Conservative activists tend to be Protestant and Liberal activists Catholic. Party activists tend also to be more numerous in the region of the party's greatest electoral support. Unlike the bicultural cleavage and regional divisions, the class cleavage is weakly manifested among party activists in the sense that activists in the NDP, as in other parties, tend to have higher social status than their supporters and than the population at large.

The composition of party elites reflects the electoral cleavages still more weakly than is the case of activists. As a matter of conscious policy, the three larger parties strive to create elites which are somewhat broadly representative of the population, with the result that the bicultural and geographic cleavages tend to be attenuated. Class differences tend to be weak as well. The elites of the three larger parties are well educated and of higher-than-average status. In the case of the parties of parliamentary origin, there is an especially strong role for the legal profession. This decline of bicultural, geographic, and class differences in the demographic profiles of party elites may exercise a moderating force on party policy, forestalling the development of significant policy differences among the parties. The strong presence of the legal profession, even to some extent in the NDP, may also have the effect of giving greater priority to parliamentary manoeuvre as opposed to philosophical principle with the result that long-term party goals and therefore differences may become obscured.

It was also suggested that five categories of people provide resources to help parties secure electoral success: parliamentarians, party officials, interest group leaders, policy specialists, and provincial party leaders. The chapter showed how the parties' elite recruitment varies in each category and how this variation could be explained in terms of the resources and needs of each party.

Notes

1. Despite the populism of the *créditistes*, this generalization is also true for them. See Maurice Pinard, *The Rise of a Third Party: A Study in Crisis Politics* (Englewood Cliffs, N.J.: Prentice-Hall, 1971), 130–32, and Michael B. Stein, *The Dynamics of Right-Wing Protest: A Political Analysis of Social Credit in Quebec* (Toronto: University of Toronto Press, 1973), 124–30.

2. Based on a study by Hugh Thorburn and others, findings on the representativeness of conventions are reported in John C. Courtney, *The Selection of National Party Leaders in Canada* (Toronto: Macmillan, 1973), 105–26.

3. Ibid., 125–26.

4. *Canadian Legislative Behavior: A Study of the 25th Parliament* (New York: Holt, Rinehart and Winston, 1967), 44.

5. Maurice Pinard, *Third Party*, 126–27, and Kornberg, *Legislative Behavior*, 44–46.

6. Allan Kornberg, Joel Smith, and Harold Clarke, "Attitudes of Ascribed Influence in Local Party Organizations in Canada and the United States," *Canadian Journal of Political Science*, 5:2 (1972), 220–29.

7. *The Vertical Mosaic; an analysis of social class and power in Canada* (Toronto: University of Toronto Press, 1965), 394.

8. S. M. Lipset, *Agrarian Socialism: The Cooperative Commonwealth Federation in Saskatchewan: A Study in Political Sociology* (Berkeley: University of California Press, 1967), Ch. 11.

9. Walter Young, "A Profile of Activists in the British Columbia NDP," *Journal of Canadian Studies*, 6 (1971), 19–26.

10. *Third Party*, 129.

11. Porter, *Mosaic*, 391.

12. Henry Jacek et al., "The Congruence of Federal-Provincial Campaign Activity in Party Organizations: The Influence of Recruitment Patterns in Three Hamilton Ridings," *Canadian Journal of Political Science*, 5:2 (1972), 190–205. See also Henry J. Jacek, "Party Loyalty and Electoral Volatility: A Comment on the study of the Canadian Party System," ibid., 8:1 (1975), 144–45, and Jacek et al., "Social Articulation and Aggregation in Political Party Organization in a Large Canadian City," *Canadian Journal of Political Science*, 8:2 (1975), 274–98.

13. Walter Young, "A Profile of Activists in the British Columbia NDP."

14. Beck, J. Murray, *Pendulum of Power* (Scarborough, Ont.: Prentice-Hall, 1968), 402.

15. Such a challenge to Caouette came during debates on the War Measures Act and related matters in 1970. See Donald Murray, "The Ralliement des Creditistes in Parliament, 1970–71," *Journal of Canadian Studies*, 8 (1973), 13–31.

16. Their role is facilitated by the lack of attention given the Senate by the Canadian press, academics, and public. When their role is occasionally publicized, the attention is decidedly negative in tone. For an account of Senator Hays's activities, see "Federal Liberals twisted arms in U.S. head offices for election cash," *Globe and Mail* (July 5, 1973). See also accounts of Senator Godfrey's fund-raising role and his connections with the corporate elite in Geoffrey Stevens, "the fund-raisers (II)," *Globe and Mail* (June 28, 1974). See John McMenemy's article in the forthcoming fourth edition of Paul W. Fox (ed.), *Politics: Canada* (Toronto: McGraw-Hill Ryerson).

17. Stein, *Right-Wing Protest*, 155.

18. On the willingness of Liberal leaders to co-opt senior civil servants directly into the political elite and on the question of personal attachments, see John Porter, *Mosaic*, 407–08, 425–32. See also, John Meisel, "Formulation of Liberal and Conservative Programs in the 1957 Canadian General Election," *Canadian Journal of Economics and Political Science*, 26:4 (1960), 565–67, 572–74. Pickersgill's memoirs from the 1940s and 1950s illustrate the permeable boundary between public service and partisan politics. According to historian Ramsay Cook, "The most revealing aspect of [the memoirs] is the extent to which Pickersgill, though a public servant from 1937 until 1953, acted as though the government of Canada and the Liberal Party were indistinguishable. [In the 1940s] Pickersgill became an integral cog in the Liberal machine despite his membership in the supposedly neutral civil service." "Flashes of modesty — and it will last — but read it with a healthy Newfie skepticism," *Globe and Mail* (October 25, 1975). See also J. W. Pickersgill, *My Years With St. Laurent, A Political Memoir* (Toronto: University of Toronto Press, 1975).

19. The fluid movement of the late Robert Winters in and out of the boardrooms of corporations and Liberal cabinets illustrates this relationship. Second to Trudeau for the leadership in 1968, he returned to the corporate world until his death. Porter examines the origins of this relationship in the career of C. D. Howe. See Porter, *Mosaic*, 430–31.

20. The leadership of the cooperative movement alleges emotional ties with the NDP's social democratic policies. However, the co-op leadership does not provide institutional resources to the NDP comparable to the labour movement and therefore its leadership does not have comparable status in the party's operating elite.

21. George Drew, a Conservative premier of Ontario, served as national leader from 1948 to 1956. At the non-elected level, Eddie Goodman, a lawyer in Toronto, is a major example of an official serving both parties. In 1972, Premier William Davis put the provincial organization publicly behind Stanfield and presumably gained standing and credit with the national leader. In 1975, Davis was included in public speculation about Stanfield's successor.

Chapter 10

PARTY STRUCTURES AND DECISION-MAKING

John McMenemy, John Redekop, and Conrad Winn

Introduction

While all political parties have formal constitutions, these constitutions are an imperfect guide to party life. All constitutions provide for the democratic participation of party members. Nonetheless, all parties are governed in practice by a small group of leaders located primarily in parliament. This hierarchy is especially true of the Liberal and Conservative parties, which were both created in a parliamentary environment. By contrast, the CCF and Social Credit had for a time a significant extra-parliamentary organization and leadership, yet in time the parliamentarians in these parties came to exercise a predominant influence as well. Only the CCF-NDP has continually maintained the appearance of democratic control by its extra-parliamentary membership. The party prescribes conditions for membership, has affiliated groups, and requires a biennial convention — its "supreme governing body" — to deliberate on policy and leadership.

The preceding chapter observed that political parties undertake a great variety of activities, not all of which are conspicuously political. For many party activists at the constituency level, the party is primarily a social unit akin to the church and sometimes indistinguishable from it. Party and church activities alike provide opportunities for making friendships, for establishing links with the community, and for contributing to the social order. For many lawyers and businessmen in politics, partisan activity is a form of economic investment rather than an intellectual or ideological commitment. For still others, politics is a form of recreation.

From the larger perspective of the political system, however, selecting leaders, making policy, and waging campaigns are the three main party activities. In the input-throughput-output model, party structures and decision-making, like party personnel, constitute a throughput mediating the influence of party origins and cleavages in the parties. Thus, the selection of leaders, the continuing parliamentary campaign between elections, the hectic campaign period before every election, and the declaration of party policy can in principle influence the structure of electoral cleavages, the actual outcome of an election, or the nature of government programs and legislation.

Between 1956 and 1976, the Conservatives were led by a Saskatchewan MP and a former premier of Nova Scotia while the Liberals were

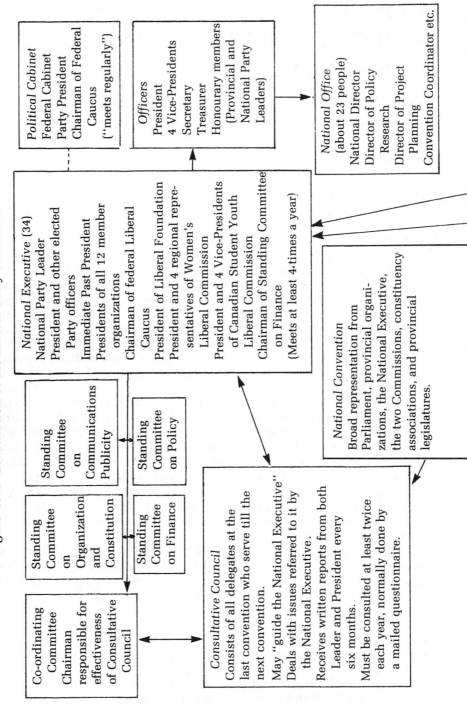

Figure 10-1. Constitution of the Liberal Party of Canada*

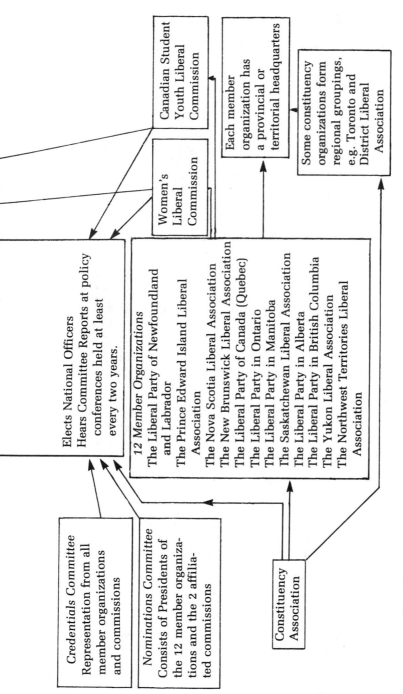

Canadian Student Youth Liberal Commission

Each member organization has a provincial or territorial headquarters

Some constituency organizations form regional groupings, e.g. Toronto and District Liberal Association

Women's Liberal Commission

Elects National Officers
Hears Committee Reports at policy conferences held at least every two years.

12 Member Organizations
The Liberal Party of Newfoundland and Labrador
The Prince Edward Island Liberal Association
The Nova Scotia Liberal Association
The New Brunswick Liberal Association
The Liberal Party of Canada (Quebec)
The Liberal Party in Ontario
The Liberal Party in Manitoba
The Saskatchewan Liberal Association
The Liberal Party in Alberta
The Liberal Party in British Columbia
The Yukon Liberal Association
The Northwest Territories Liberal Association

Credentials Committee
Representation from all member organizations and commissions

Nominations Committee
Consists of Presidents of the 12 member organizations and the 2 affiliated commissions

Constituency Association

Constituency organizations form the delegate base for provincial and national conventions.
Both the provincial and the federal constituency associations belong to the provincial organization.

* The chart is based on the party "constitution" as well as occasional organizational changes described in Liberal Party documents.
The arrows indicate the direction of the flow of personnel.

Figure 10-2. Constitution of the Progressive Conservative Association of Canada*

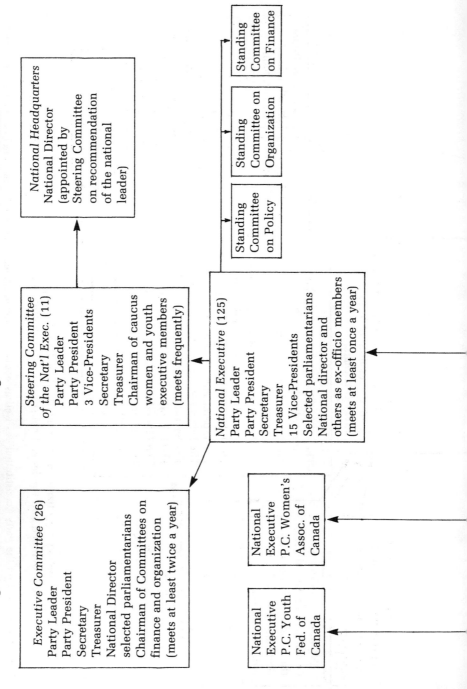

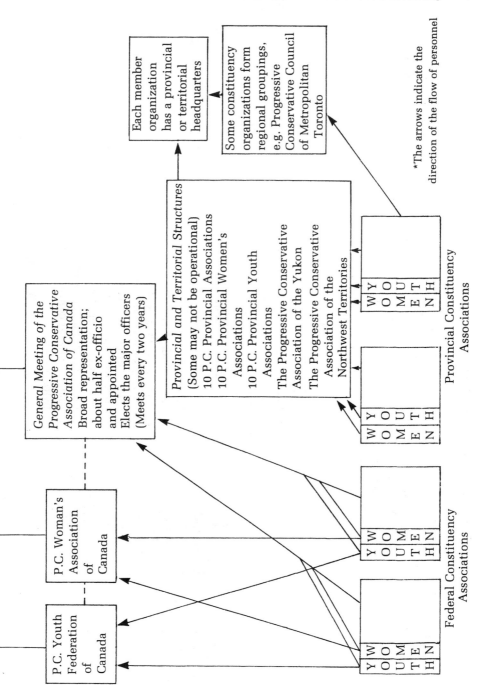

Each member organization has a provincial or territorial headquarters

Some constituency organizations form regional groupings, e.g. Progressive Conservative Council of Metropolitan Toronto

*The arrows indicate the direction of the flow of personnel

Provincial and Territorial Structures
(Some may not be operational)
10 P.C. Provincial Associations
10 P.C. Provincial Women's Associations
10 P.C. Provincial Youth Associations
The Progressive Conservative Association of the Yukon
The Progressive Conservative Association of the Northwest Territories

General Meeting of the Progressive Conservative Association of Canada
Broad representation; about half ex-officio and appointed
Elects the major officers
(Meets every two years)

P.C. Woman's Association of Canada

P.C. Youth Federation of Canada

Provincial Constituency Associations

Federal Constituency Associations

YOUTH WOMEN

YOUTH WOMEN

YOUTH WOMEN

YOUTH WOMEN

Figure 10-3. Constitution of the New Democratic Party*

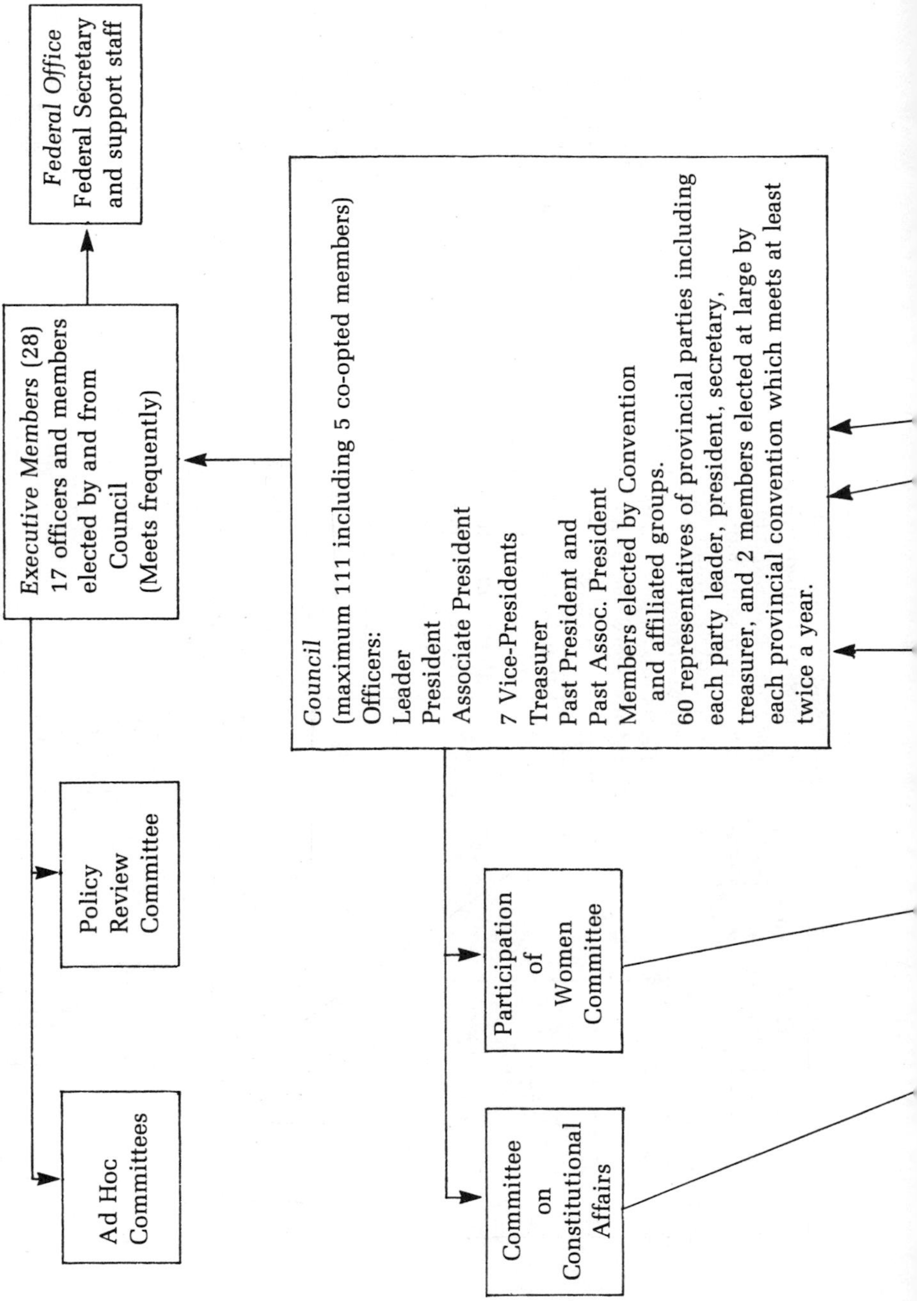

Federal Office
Federal Secretary and support staff

Executive Members (28)
17 officers and members elected by and from Council
(Meets frequently)

Policy Review Committee

Ad Hoc Committees

Council
(maximum 111 including 5 co-opted members)
Officers:
Leader
President
Associate President
7 Vice-Presidents
Treasurer
Past President and
Past Assoc. President
Members elected by Convention and affiliated groups.
60 representatives of provincial parties including each party leader, president, secretary, treasurer, and 2 members elected at large by each provincial convention which meets at least twice a year.

Participation of Women Committee

Committee on Constitutional Affairs

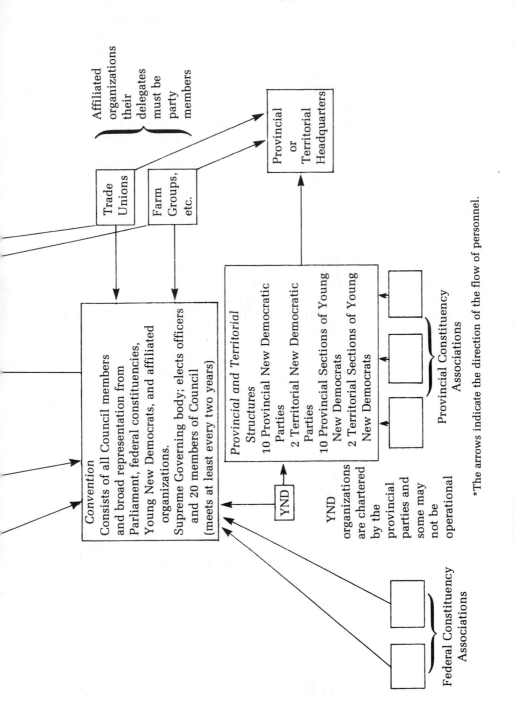

Affiliated organizations their delegates must be party members

Trade Unions

Farm Groups, etc.

Provincial or Territorial Headquarters

Convention
Consists of all Council members and broad representation from Parliament, federal constituencies, Young New Democrats, and affiliated organizations.
Supreme Governing body; elects officers and 20 members of Council (meets at least every two years)

Provincial and Territorial Structures
10 Provincial New Democratic Parties
2 Territorial New Democratic Parties
10 Provincial Sections of Young New Democrats
2 Territorial Sections of Young New Democrats

Provincial Constituency Associations

YND

YND organizations are chartered by the provincial parties and some may not be operational

Federal Constituency Associations

*The arrows indicate the direction of the flow of personnel.

successively led by three Central Canadians. The contrasting choices of Diefenbaker and Stanfield on the one hand and St. Laurent, Pearson, and Trudeau on the other may have enhanced the core-periphery cleavage. Between 1968 and 1972, the Conservative caucus employed skilled parliamentary debate to portray the Liberal government as insensitive to western needs. The Conservative Opposition identified itself repeatedly with western concerns, needled the government, and provoked it into apparent admissions of disinterest. The Liberal government became still more unpopular in the West and met near defeat in the general election in 1972. In the campaign of that year, David Lewis skillfully employed the "corporate welfare bum" rhetoric to enhance the left-right cleavage, the Liberal's right-wing image, and hence NDP fortunes by trotting out statistics to show substantial tax avoidance by large corporations; in contrast, T. C. Douglas achieved little national success via his witty, but general, attacks on Bay and "Jessie James St."

The six-week campaign period prior to the 1974 election illustrates how the mere declaration of party policy may provoke changes in mass sentiment. Robert Stanfield's celebrated commitment to "price and wage control" may have aroused anxiety in Ontario among trade unionists who, having learned to fear the Tories as the party of the right, switched from the NDP to the Liberals to forestall the Conservative victory.[1]

That leadership selection, campaigning, and policy-making can influence the political process at so many different stages and in so many ways makes it difficult to summarize their possible effects. It is also difficult to assess the political impact of campaigning and policy drafting because of the many types of campaign and policy activities. For example, there are national activities as opposed to sub-national, regional, or local activities. There are activities which take place between or during elections, as well as the activities of a party in opposition as opposed to one in power.

Despite their complexity, party activities can be distinguished according to whether they are controlled by a national party elite or by party activists below that level. Decisions made by national elites tend to mitigate political cleavages and diminish policy differences among the parties, while the reverse may be true when activities fall under the control of sub-national decision-makers.[2] One reason for the more moderate, integrative, and less polarized actions of national party elites is that national leaders have different goals, interests, and roles from regional or local leaders. One of the national leader's goals is to integrate the often incompatible components of his party and of his potential electorate. This task requires a certain amount of compromise, moderation, and obfuscation. To appeal too nakedly to any particular segment of the population risks losing existing support. The rational marketing strategy for any national party leader is to stake out a polar position on any cleavage only if a sizable and winning plurality of voters occupy that pole and also if the competing parties occupy the opposite pole.

The Formal Organization

The federal parties are formally organized as federations of provincial parties and special interest groups (see Figures 10-1 to 10-3).[3] The formal centrepiece of the organization chart of each national party is the convention. The conventions of the Liberal and Conservative parties select executives to act on their behalf. In the NDP, party officers are elected in convention. The remainder of the executive is chosen by the federal council, whose membership is selected by the convention and by the provincial parties. All the parties also possess a range of standing committees which report to the executive. For example, the Liberal constitution identifies standing committees on organization and constitution, on finance, on communications and publicity, and on policy. Finally, each party possesses a small bureaucracy of permanent officials who are responsible to the executives and to the parliamentary leader. The leading bureaucrats in the Liberal and Conservative parties are known as national directors following the language of interest groups and corporations, while the senior NDP bureaucrat is known as the federal secretary following the nomenclature of the European mass parties of the left.[4]

The standing committees are frequently moribund. However, to the extent that they exercise an influence, they probably enhance the position of the parliamentary leadership and help avoid the maintenance of severe and protracted differences among the parties. Members of the committees are appointed by the party executive, which in normal times would be sensitive to the leader's wishes. Committee members tend to have professional or upper status backgrounds and therefore have a stake in achieving any social change by increment and by negotiation. As amateurs, they may have little time or inclination to become involved in the traditional Canadian political cleavages or deviate greatly from the usually pragmatic goals set by the leader. Indeed, in the appointment of committee members, the party executive may seek a certain minimum likelihood of compliance.

For its part, the party executive moderates constitutional and behavioural biases. The Liberal, Conservative, and NDP constitutions all have regulations which protect bicultural and regional interests and which therefore help ensure that the parties adopt moderate positions on bicultural and regional matters. The Liberal constitution provides for equal francophone and anglophone representation among vice-presidents. The New Democratic party selects an associate president and an associate secretary from the cultural group not represented by the president and secretary. The constitution of the Progressive Conservative Association requires at least one vice-president "fluent in the official language which is not the 'mother tongue' of the President." Furthermore, the provincial and territorial parties have automatic representation on the executive. Thus, representation from every region is guaranteed, not merely from the regions in which the party achieves its electoral successes.

Nevertheless, party leaders do not leave it entirely to the constitution to assure that the views of party executives are compatible with their own. Generally, leaders and their advisors tend to become actively involved in grooming candidates for party office prior to each convention. A Liberal prime minister, for example, might reasonably expect to choose his own party president and trust his minions in the Prime Minister's Office (PMO) to look after his interests in the filling of lesser posts. However, in late 1975, Trudeau unilaterally appointed the party's new national director, to the chagrin of Liberal activists. By way of rebuke, the retiring president, Senator Gildas Molgat, made it known that he had not been consulted sufficiently by the prime minister during his presidential term, which included a federal election campaign. The election in convention of a successor to Molgat almost became an open contest between Senator Alasdair Graham, supported by the party activists, and Senator Keith Davey, co-chairman of the federal campaign committee in 1974 and Trudeau's personal preference. Davey did not contest the election and the Liberal party once again avoided a public demonstration of internal differences. However, Trudeau's disposition toward Graham need not differ from his apparent attitude towards Molgat.

Party constitutions also authorize the appointment of bureaucracies. Strong personality disputes at the time of the Conservative party's rejection of Diefenbaker's leadership in the 1960s embroiled the party bureaucracy in conflict. Normally, however, party bureaucrats, like members of standing committees, are loyal utilitarian servants of the party leader or at least of the dominant faction of the parliamentary party. Constitutionally, the national directors — federal secretary in the case of the NDP — are appointed by the party executives. Furthermore, the party bureaucrats do interact considerably with the party officers over organizational and related matters. On vital issues of policy and campaigning, however, the predominant influence lies with the parliamentary leadership; the authority of the executive over the party bureaucracy remains largely symbolic.

Allister Grosart, Conservative National Director under Diefenbaker, provides an example of the utilitarian outlook of party bureaucrats. During the 1957 election, Conservative strategy was to emphasize above all the role of the new leader. Party literature gave prominence to Diefenbaker while de-emphasizing the party. When Louis St. Laurent, the Liberal leader, complained that the Conservatives were not campaigning under their own name, Grosart sent a copy of his speech in a plain envelope to every Liberal candidate in the country. Grosart was undoubtedly pleased to see the theme appearing in the speeches of local Liberal candidates for it helped achieve Grosart's goal of portraying the Conservatives as a new party with a new populist image.[5]

While the constitutions of the three larger parties share a common centralizing tendency, there are nevertheless some differences. In particular, the NDP constitution accords a special significance to individual membership and states conditions for potential adherence. Applicants for membership must declare that they belong to no other party and that they accept and support the "constitution and principles" of the NDP. This particular provision not only acts as a symbolic rite of passage cementing the member's emotional links to the party, but the provision also permits the party elite to expel from time to time Communists and members of other sectarian left-wing organizations.

The NDP also specifies a complex dues structure. Individual membership dues and other personal contributions comprise the largest segment of party revenue. Formally, the supporter becomes the member of a provincial wing for a renewable fixed term and his fees are divided among the constituency, provincial, and federal levels of the party.

The constitutionally enshrined role for the member in the NDP may help account for his loyalty in the face of electoral misfortune at the federal level. This enshrined role may also account for the individualistic character of NDP delegates at conventions. For example, at the 1975 leadership convention, Ed Broadbent did not secure victory until the fourth ballot, although he had been acting parliamentary leader, had the combined support of the NDP provincial premiers, and received active support from leading members of the caucus, notably T. C. Douglas, the former national leader and longtime Saskatchewan premier. The individualism and occasional radicalism of delegates to NDP conventions is to some extent compensated by trade union representation. At the 1975 convention, almost one-eighth of the delegates belonged to the Steelworkers or United Automobile Workers unions. These delegates largely supported Broadbent just as they had largely supported Lewis at a previous leadership convention in preference to the more radical James Laxer.

In contrast to the case of the NDP, the Liberal and Conservative constitutions do not set membership qualifications or dues. Membership is sometimes more easily acquired in these parties. From time to time, local nomination meetings are held where memberships are sold frantically to bolster an aspirant's chance of success. Indeed, some candidates buy memberships to be distributed later to personal supporters for their nomination. Such irregular practices may occur occasionally when Liberal or Conservative fortunes are high and a particular constituency seems likely to elect the party's standard bearer. For the Conservative and Liberal parties, an apparently greater laxity may reflect the small historical role for members in the financing of party activities. Until and perhaps following the recent changes in government rules for party financing, the two major parties depended almost entirely on gifts from the 100 major corporations.

Just as the NDP has stricter notions of membership, it also holds conventions more regularly. Since the birth of the CCF in 1933, the party has required conventions at least once every two years. These conventions are regarded as the "supreme governing body" with "final authority in all matters of federal policy, program and constitution." Regardless of public opinion, the demands of electoral victory, or the presence or absence of charismatic candidates for party leadership, NDP conventions are held with regularity.

The Liberal party was actually the first to introduce the party con-

vention in this country. During the nineteenth century, party leaders
were chosen by the caucus if in opposition or by the Governor-General
if in power.[6] In 1919, a Liberal convention chose Mackenzie King as
leader and hence set a precedent for all parties to follow. However, the
Liberals did not meet again in convention for another generation and a
half — and then only to ratify King's personal choice as successor.
Liberal conventions became more frequent after the party lost power in
1957. Several Conservative conventions were held during their trou-
bled years in the 1940s and the 1960s. At the discretion of the party
executive, the Conservatives held general meetings (i.e. conventions)
in 1961, 1964, 1966, 1969, 1971, and 1974. At the gathering in 1971, the
Association passed a constitutional amendment requiring general
meetings every two years.[7] The Liberals held conventions approximately every two years after a constitutional amendment to that affect
in 1966.

At the time of Confederation, many Liberal and, especially, Conservative leaders were suspicious of democratic principles. However, a
century later the bureaucratic and parliamentary elites of both parties
are eager to involve their members in party affairs. Many see their
party's dependence on corporate subsidies as a necessary evil, rather
than as a desirable objective, and would like to augment membership
participation as a counterweight. For example, Liberal headquarters is
devoting more personnel to encouraging the participation and contribution of the mass members. From the Liberals' perspective, to acquire greater membership participation may be a means of demonstrating the party's ideological superiority over the allegedly more old-
fashioned and authoritarian Conservatives. For their part, the Conservatives feel that membership participation is more necessary for their
efforts because, at the federal level, they have come to have fewer allies
in the corporate world than the Liberals.

The expansion of the mass media may be another factor in the
Conservatives' and Liberals' new inclination to regular conventions
and membership participation. Party conventions — particularly leadership conventions — receive extensive reporting in the press and on
radio, and large segments are broadcast live and free on television.
Television provides an especially intimate link between thousands of
viewers and a party's internal life. With their personality conflicts,
build-up, climax, and denouement, conventions provide considerable
entertainment value. Party managers would be seriously amiss to overlook the public relations benefit of conventions.

While the mass media may be a factor in the development of party
conventions, they may also be a factor in the special influence of parliamentary elites. Although party constitutions treat all members as
equal, the parliamentary leaders have an extreme advantage in easier
access to mass communication. Like other citizens, party members receive most of their political information from the major dailies, from
radio, and from television. Consequently, the Ottawa-based parliamentary leader can reach his party's supporters much more easily than, say,
a party vice-president from Nova Scotia. Party newsletters are control-

led by the party elites, while the independent periodicals such as the left-socialist *Canadian Dimension* or left-liberal *Canadian Forum* have limited circulations. None of the parties provides channels of communication for their members that are less than fully loyal and controlled by the leaders.

When the parliamentary elites attend a convention, they begin not only with a communications advantage over any rivals, but they also begin with some other advantages. The Liberal and Conservative parties, in particular, permit large numbers of appointed committee members and appointed delegates-at-large to attend the conventions. Prior to the Conservative convention in 1967 at which Stanfield replaced Diefenbaker as leader, a party official announced that non-party participants in a policy conference sponsored by the party would be eligible to attend and vote for the party's future leader. Diefenbaker's partisans interpreted the attempt to broaden representation as an "establishment" device to weaken their candidate's position.[8] At recent Conservative and Liberal leadership conventions *ex officio* delegates constituted a significant minority of the participants.[9]

In summary, we argued that the constitutions of the three larger parties are fundamentally alike insofar as they reinforce the authority of the parliamentary leaders and insofar as they encourage the moderation of political cleavages. Some of the factors which contribute to the leader's authority and to a moderate political style are the existence of standing committees with appointed memberships, provisions to guarantee bicultural and regional representation at the executive level, the appointment of party bureaucrats, the absence of independent channels of communication within the parties, the presence of trade union delegates at NDP conventions. Of course, there are some party differences. The NDP has more rigid criteria for membership and more regular conventions. Until recent constitutional changes, the Liberal and Conservative elites were constitutionally free to hold national meetings at will.

Campaigning and Policy-Making

Two principle themes in the preceding section were that the constitutions of the parties tend to concentrate authority in the hands of the party leaders and that a number of constitutional attributes encourage moderation of party differences. The previous section also suggested that the national party elites are more inclined to mitigate political cleavages than the sub-national elites, who might exacerbate them. These arguments acquire greater validity as one's political analysis moves from the realm of constitutions to the domain of actual party behaviour. Behind the facade of constitutional decision-making lies a party organization which may or may not be constitutionally defined, but which nevertheless is almost always dominated by the parliamentary leader and his appointees. Despite the sometimes extreme sentiments of some sub-national elites within each party, the national leaders are able to use their extraordinary power to select party campaign styles and policy options which are essentially moderate in nature.

The power of the leader is most evident during campaigns. The decisions to highlight the "corporate welfare bum" theme in the 1972 NDP campaign and to emphasize the Conservatives' "wage-price freeze" in the 1974 election were made by the leaders on the advice of close associates. Furthermore, all party leaders have been prepared to enunciate positions which are far more moderate than many of their subordinates would prefer. This moderation has been especially true of Robert Stanfield, who forcefully committed his party to the bicultural program of the Liberal government even while the local campaigns of some Conservative candidates, particularly in the West, employed harshly anti-French themes. A similar portrait applies to the NDP, except that New Democrat candidates in the West may have exerted greater self-control in giving vent to their suspicions of Catholic Quebec. Conservative and New Democrat leaders have also been less willing to take advantage of western antipathy to Central Canada than their subordinates in the western provinces. In the case of the NDP, T. C. Douglas, David Lewis, and Ed Broadbent have all expressed less favourable sentiments towards the nationalization of industry than some party members desire and than most might find acceptable.

Both Stanfield and Lewis were repudiated by their parties' respective right and left-wings. Following the election of 1974, several Conservative MPs — called "Rednecks" by Stanfield admirers — protested the "socialist" direction of their leader. According to Tom Cossitt, MP, "there is a general feeling that the six or eight people who control the caucus and the party follow policies foreign to Conservative principles".[10] Earlier, part of the NDP's left faction split off to form the independent and soon-to-be defunct Waffle party. In the Liberal party, Prime Minister Trudeau has been more conciliatory towards criticisms from western and anglophone opposition MPs than some of the party's leaders from Central Canada. Jean Marchand, in particular, occasionally interpreted rejection or criticism as evidence of English backlash or bigotry.

The strategy of national party elites is not always to be conciliatory. If a sizable group in the electorate holds a polar view, a national party elite may claim that position especially if other parties hold opposite positions. David Lewis followed this course in 1972 when the NDP connected the Liberal government to the unpopular "corporate welfare bums." But this technique could not be successfully repeated a second time because by 1974 the NDP was identified in popular thinking with that very Liberal government.

The national Liberal elite has also taken polar campaign positions on political cleavages. Prior to and during the 1972 campaign, the Liberals appealed for anglophone support on the grounds that the government had allegedly overcome separatism by dealing firmly with the FLQ on the one hand and by making French Canadians feel at home in Ottawa on the other. The strategy failed partly because some English Canadians, now less concerned about separatism, felt less need to vote Liberal. The strategy also failed because the Conservatives refused to condemn the Liberals for being too conciliatory towards French Canada in their policy of making the public service more bilingual. Conservative strength lay in moderation. Stanfield refused to adopt the anti-French rhetoric of some of his predecessors. Finally, the Liberal campaign failed because, unlike their opponents, the Liberals did not introduce a new issue or cleavage from which they could gain. In contrast, the Conservatives made an issue out of the unfulfilled expectations created by Trudeau's promises of participatory democracy and the "just society" in 1968. The Liberal leader was portrayed as haughty, arrogant, insensitive, and uncaring.

With the Liberals' near defeat in 1972, George Elliott of MacLaren's Advertising left active Liberal politics. As principal secretary in the PMO, Martin O'Connell apparently helped rejuvenate party morale by diminishing the public profile of his office and by facilitating communication between the leader and the party. O'Connell contributed to the prime minister's new image of humanity and humility. As the 1974 election approached, Senator Keith Davey took charge, formally as chief campaign advisor. Government bicultural policy appeared to moderate with the removal of some francophone ministers from the limelight. In the 1974 campaign, the party refused to adopt a polar position among the traditional cleavages. Under Davey's prompting, the Liberals made an issue of "leadership," realising that the electorate regarded the reformed Trudeau more highly than his chief opponent. With the Conservatives' help, the Liberals also made an issue out of "price and wage control," suspecting that popular anxiety and Conservative disunity might be provoked and hoping that the Conservatives would not make a central theme of inflation itself.

While national leaders must be very careful before adopting extreme bicultural, sectional, or class positions, the same is not true for regional leaders or local candidates. With smaller, more homogeneous electorates sharing common ethnic or other prejudices, local and regional leaders encounter fewer risks in appealing to historic animosities or other base motives. In the 1974 election, for example, Conservative candidates in Manitoba expressed anti-French sentiments which could not conceivably be shared or countenanced by their leader.[11] Freed of national responsibilities, regional leaders and local candidates can arrange the most bizarre marriages and express the most incongruous views. Through most of the authoritarian, illiberal regime of Maurice Duplessis, many Liberal MPs maintained mutual non-aggression pacts with the *union nationale* Members sitting for the corresponding provincial constituencies. Federal Liberals were not to aid provincial Liberals, and *union nationale* personnel were not to work for the Conservatives. Conservative and NDP candidates in Quebec have sometimes made individual arrangements with local separatist groups. In 1963, the avowed national policy of the Liberal party was to install nuclear warheads in the anti-bomber Bomarc missile. Yet, many Quebec Liberals campaigned on a platform of no nuclear weapons.

Lester Pearson was presumably unconcerned so long as his francophone lieutenants kept a low profile in English Canada. In fact, there must be times when all national leaders cast a blind eye on the divergent and sometimes extreme views of local candidates because such tactics may add to the parties' fortunes. In Quebec, it has been a standard practice of federal Liberals to portray the Tories as militantly anti-French. In the 1974 campaign, Liberal advertisements in the French language referred to the Conservative leader as "Mister" Stanfield to emphasize his alien character. However, national leaders do not always cast a blind eye. Lester Pearson hastened the departure of Ralph Cowan, a francophobe MP from Toronto, while similar reasons prompted Stanfield to disavow the candidacy of Leonard Jones, the former Mayor of Moncton.

Cleverness in electoral strategy is not the only reason for the moderation of recent national party leaders. The leaders are simply very much alike. Except for Social Credit, they tend to be well educated, urbane, and undoubtedly more tolerant and open-minded than the population at large. Following the Canadian brahmin tradition, Trudeau, Stanfield, and Lewis all supplemented undergraduate experiences at elite Canadian universities with training at elite Anglo-American institutions. Stanfield and Trudeau went to Harvard, Lewis to Oxford as a Rhodes scholar. Party leaders tend to come from the core, but, even if they do not, they are obliged to live in the core and become exposed to its values in the course of their political careers.

The common educational background of the party leaders is important because of the well documented tendency in North America of highly educated people to hold liberal attitudes towards religion, ethnicity and race, political reform, and the welfare state.[12] Canadian party leaders possess the typical values of the modern liberal university. Trudeau preceded his political career as a professor, Lewis ended his career as a professor, and Stanfield is sometimes accused of being a misplaced professor. Nor is this professorial background mere happenstance. Trudeau's predecessor was a former professor, as are Lewis's and Stanfield's successors. This pattern of considerable educational achievement among contemporary party leaders is important because it contrasts with the relative absence of formal education among many spokesmen for extreme cultural, sectional, or ideological viewpoints. An exception to this generalization would be some of the academic spokesmen for the radical left in the NDP.

That national party leaders appear less willing to adopt extreme sectionalist, bicultural, or ideological positions than some of their followers has a bearing on the constitutional organization of the parties. If the internal structure of the parties were democratic, the national leaders would be obliged to adopt more divergent and less moderate positions than they do. However, formal constitutional appearances aside, the national parties, especially prior to and during election campaigns, are not glorious examples of participatory democracy. The *de facto* organization of the parties is autocratic and leaders feel under little pressure to make concessions to extremist policies advocated by their followers or even to follow policies adopted by party conventions. For their part, extremist subordinates in the parliamentary caucus of a

Figure 10-4.   Organizational Core of the
Liberal Party*

A. *Policy-Making*

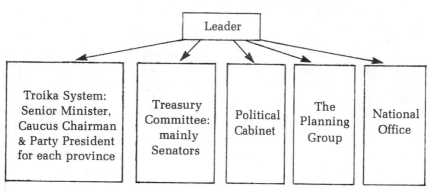

B. *Partisan Business between Elections*

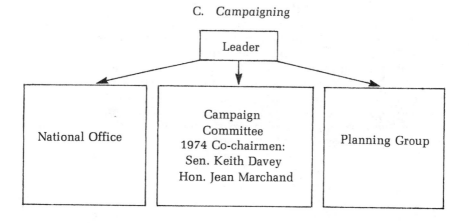

C. *Campaigning*

*Arrow indicates direction of appointment.

party or on a party's executive have little recourse except to express their disenchantment publicly through the media, a course of action which is unlikely to be popular among party loyalists.

The organization of the Liberal party illustrates well the power of the leader (see Figures 10-1 and 10-4). The party possesses an elaborately detailed democratic constitution in imitation of the European mass parties of the left, yet in practice the committee structure prescribed by the constitution is not even a facade behind which the parliamentary notables work. The standing committees which are defined by the constitution as vital are largely defunct, while the truly important committees are not mentioned in the constitution.

The national Liberal convention is supposed to exercise power either directly or indirectly through the executive or its offshoots. In practice, most power rests with the parliamentary leader, with his subordinates in the House of Commons, and particularly with his chosen colleagues in the Senate. In recent years, members of the upper house have controlled both the national executive and the financial function. From the late 1960s to be mid-1970s, the party presidency was held by five successive Senators. During the same period, Senators predominated in the vital treasury committee. Composed of Senators Stanbury, Godfrey, Hays, Riel, and other bagmen, the treasury committee's vital place in the Liberal hierarchy was never seriously threatened by the standing committee on finance. Senator Lafond is the party's chief financial representative under the new Election Expenses Act. Although constitutionally assigned responsibility for financial matters, the standing committee on finance has rarely met and has lacked a chairman for long periods. Even if the treasury committee were to bow to the standing committee, however, the leader's authority would not be seriously undermined because the constitution permits the leader to choose the chairman of that particular committee.

The Liberal constitution also provides for a standing committee on communications and publicity; however, its functions are largely performed by the national director and his staff and during elections by the campaign committee. Of course, Senator Davey, the national director, and the members of the campaign committee all receive their authority from the leader. During the 1974 election, a majority of the campaign committee belonged either to the Senate, the Cabinet, or the party office. A majority therefore possessed a personal obligation or, at least, an occupational link to the leader.

Because the ostensible purpose of a party is to win election in order to control policy-making, the Liberal constitution provides for a standing committee on policy. Between 1968 and 1972, the national party office also employed a director of policy research. However, the standing committee on policy is defunct and the policy advisory post was discontinued. The national office's policy advisory post may have been discontinued because of a belief that an excessively active role in policy-making might encourage electoral expectations that the Liberal government would not fulfil. Like its predecessors, the party's 1975 convention had a program and policy committee. However, the committee was not very independent of and therefore unlikely to embarrass the government since its chairman was an MP, its secretary was a functionary in the national office, and its membership included researchers from the Prime Minister's Office and the caucus research bureau. Of course, all convention committees are appointed by the convention co-chairmen, who are appointed by the leader in concert with the party President.

Another aspect of the structure of Liberal policy-making and campaigning is the "political cabinet." Ostensibly designed to facilitate communication between the government and the party, the meetings of the "political cabinet" are attended by the regular cabinet, party representatives, and the caucus chairman. The agenda is set by the national director and the principal secretary of the PMO. If the Liberals were truly a mass party, these meetings might be an appropriate occasion for the extra-parliamentary party to contribute to policy. However, the purpose of the "political cabinet" is primarily organizational and electoral. Apparently, policy questions are discussed less frequently than such issues as fund-raising, morale among party members, and the scheduling of party events. Furthermore, the outsiders invited to meetings of the "political cabinet" are campaign personnel such as the national director, who was Blair Williams prior to 1975, or Senator Keith Davey.

There may be some specific policy implications to Davey's attendance at meetings of the "political cabinet". The senator's leadership in the 1974 campaign is widely given credit for Liberal success. His high esteem within the party and his attendance at political cabinet suggest that the prime minister may feel very appreciative of his talents. When Davey's stature within the governing party is combined with his well-known nationalist views, expressed in his Senate Commission on the Mass Media, one may be forgiven for speculating whether the senator had any impact on the government's apparent reversal in 1975 of their long-term commitment to privileged tax protection for *Time* and *Readers' Digest*. It may not have even been necessary for Davey to lobby actively in order for his views to prevail, since parliamentary leaders feel a very special appreciation to their campaign advisors. Apparently, the cabinet committed itself to ending the special status for the two American publications as early as the 1974 election. However, the decision was not made public for fear of injecting an unnecessary issue into a smooth-running campaign.

Senator Davey's influence is also expressed through his membership in the "Planning Group." Formed as a result of the party's near debacle in 1972, the Group meets every two weeks. It includes among its members the party's national president, the national director, and Trudeau's principal secretary and press secretary. Jim Coutts, who has been an appointments secretary to Lester Pearson, a campaign adviser to Trudeau, a longtime associate of Davey and became Trudeau's principal secretary in 1975, was a member of the Planning Group before he became principal secretary. The Planning Group discusses campaign-related matters both between and during elections and makes suggestions with respect to appointments, patronage, volatile political issues, image-making, relations with the press, and regional problems.

If Davey exercises an occasional influence on government policy, this influence reflects his importance to Liberal fortunes and the prime minister's personal regard for him, rather than Davey's formal position in the Liberal party organization. More generally, little evidence can be found that individual Liberals have as great an impact on their government's policy as on their party's campaigning. One well-placed Liberal was quoted recently as saying that

> The party ought to function as a countervailing force to all the tech-nocratic advice that [the prime minister] gets from the high mucky-mucks in the civil service. Instead, its policy input is still minimal and it's mainly an electoral machine. . . . [13]

In practice, the Progressive Conservative party is no less au-thoritarian than that of the Liberals (see Figures 10-2 and 10-5). The leader appoints his own campaign staff, namely the national director, the chief of staff, and during "wartime" the campaign director. In 1972, Standfield's longtime campaign advisor in Nova Scotia, Finlay MacDonald, became the party's campaign director. In 1974, MacDonald became the leader's chief of staff, to be succeeded as campaign director by Malcolm Wickson. The Conservative leader also chooses the mem-bership of the treasury committee, which holds formal responsibility for money matters, as well as the membership of the finance committee of bagmen. In the realm of policy, the leader, of course, selects his own front benchers or shadow ministers and fills the posts in caucus. Fur-thermore, the leader chooses the various policy-making committees and policy research staffs. In recent years, Stanfield himself chaired the policy coordinating committee, which consists of approximately thirty parliamentarians, full-time researchers, elected Association officials, and outside experts. Professor Tom Symons chaired both the policy advisory committee, which solicits advice from a large reservoir of academics and businessmen, and the policy committee of the Conser-vative general meeting (convention). In practice, the leader's personal-ity determines the extent to which he consults the caucus and party officials in making his appointments. Stanfield in particular was more consultative than many of his predecessors.

The NDP is a more complicated case then either the Liberals or Conservatives. On the one hand, the internal activity of the party cor-responds well to the formal organization as described by the constitu-tion (see Figure 10-3). The federal secretary does retain responsibility for campaigning and the policy committee stipulated by the constitu-tion does function. The membership of the policy committee is chosen by an elected executive. However, in practice the extra-parliamentary party rarely threatens the supremacy of either the parliamentary lead-ership on its own or the parliamentary leadership in conjunction with the national office. In practice, the parliamentary leadership can ensure that its allies predominate within the national office and among the

Figure 10-5. Organizational Core of the
Progressive Conservative Party*

A. *Policy-Making*

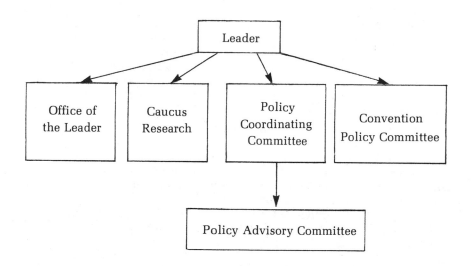

B. *Campaigning*

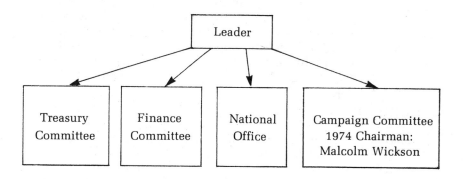

*Arrow indicates direction of appointment.

policy committees. Hence, for years, the party's policy chairman was Professor Charles Taylor, a protégé of David Lewis.

In principle, there is always a possibility that the parliamentary wing of the NDP may veer from socialist principles as defined by party convention. The extra-parliamentary wing might conceivably have to call the caucus to task. As Cliff Scotton, the party's federal secretary, acknowledged in an interview, "There is an understanding that it is the Secretary's duty to tell the leader if his policy is not the party's policy, but that has never happened."[14]

One reason for the relative absence of conflict in the federal NDP may be that the federal party is so far from power. Without exercising power, the parliamentary wing cannot be readily condemned for deviating from party policy. Another reason for the absence of conflict is that politicians normally prefer to avoid intra-party disputes over principle. Debates over principle are then replaced by the less volatile quarrels over priority or timing. For example, in 1944 the CCF government of Saskatchewan committed itself to the party policy on socialized medicine. By so doing, the government forestalled future criticisms of "betrayal" on the part of staunch party members. Yet, thirty years later, the NDP government has still not implemented all aspects of the 1944 commitment.

The general response of CCF-NDP governments to complaints from the extra-parliamentary wing that a given policy has not been implemented is to argue that there are other priorities or that there are insufficient resources. For example, in British Columbia then-Premier Dave Barrett did not actually express opposition to the party policy favouring a Women's Ministry. Barrett simply offered the view that the government had other priorities. When the extra-parliamentary wing continued to query the government, Barrett employed the special resources available to an incumbent government to overwhelm the opposition within his own party. According to one observer at the party's provincial convention, "Barrett stage-managed what amounted to a purge of those complaining officers, all of whom happened to be much more radical than the middle roaders in the government."[15]

Conclusion

The chapter suggested that some constitutional practices of the NDP differ from those of the Liberal and Progressive-Conservative parties. In particular, the NDP's origin as a movement party and its philosophical roots among the mass parties of the left may account for its more earnest treatment of the concept of party membership and of the concept of party convention. The New Democratic party's different roots may also explain why its formal constitution is a less misleading portrait of party workings than is the case for the two larger parties.

The differences among the parties are, however, outweighed by their similarities. The constitutions of the parties and especially their actual organization place an extraordinary concentration of power in the hands of the parliamentary leaders. Their special power enables parliamentary leaders to impose moderate policies on sometimes unwilling party memberships. We argued that the moderation characteristic of party leaders has its origins in their common high level of education and in their common desire for electoral fortune. Electoral gain is possible through the seduction of those voters who are most easily detached from other partisan loyalties and are least embroiled in traditional political cleavages. Furthermore, because all three parties are to some extent "omnibus" parties with disparate followings, to adopt other than a moderate stance at the national level risks alienating a segment of loyal followers.

Notes

1. Cliff Scotton, "1974 Federal Election," report to Federal Executive/Council, New Democratic Party, (Sept./Oct., 1974). For contrary evidence, see J. Pammet, J. Jenson et al., "The 1974 Election: A Preliminary Report," a paper presented to the meeting of the Canadian Political Science Association (Edmonton, 1975).

2. According to Henry Jacek, the results of a continuing study of local party activities in Hamilton demonstrates that "the small activist groups . . . are most intensely responding to the social cleavages in Canadian society." Jacek concludes that "[s]ocial cleavages are found to be the most salient among the active partisans and least important among the mass public." Thus, the brokerage functions usually attributed to parties are not performed, at least by local activists. See Henry J. Jacek, "Party Loyalty and Electoral Volatility: A Comment on the Study of the Canadian Party System," *Canadian Journal of Political Science*, VIII:1 (March, 1975), 144–145.

3. The information on formal party structure is based on the constitutions of the parties. *Constitution of the Progressive Conservative Association of Canada* (as amended March 17–18, 1974), PCHQ 955 (Amdt., March 1974). *Constitution of the Liberal Party of Canada, as amended at the Liberal Policy Convention, 1973. Constitution of the New Democratic Party as amended by the Federal Convention, 1973.*

4. In 1975, the senior Liberal and Conservative bureaucrats were Blair Williams and John Laschinger, respectively. In mid-year, Robin Sears succeeded Cliff Scotton as NDP Secretary. We are grateful to Mssrs. Laschinger, Scotton, and Williams for interviews with each. They had an opportunity to critique an earlier draft of this chapter, but are not responsible for the last.

5. For a handy, readable survey of Canadian electoral history, see J. Murray Beck, *Pendulum of Power* (Scarborough, Ont.: Prentice-Hall, 1968). Beck's work contains many references to and anecdotes about electoral tactics and the roles of party leaders and party bureaucrats.

6. See John C. Courtney, *The Selection of National Party Leaders in Canada* (Toronto: Macmillan, 1973).

7. For this and related information, we are grateful to Roy Norton, Progressive Conservative Headquarters.

8. James Johnston, *The Party's Over* (Don Mills: Longmans, 1971), 221.

9. J. Lele et al. state that 35% of Liberal delegates were *ex officio* while *ex*

officio delegates and delegates-at-large constituted 49% of Conservative delegates. See J. Lele, G. C. Perlin, and Hugh Thorburn, "The National Party Convention," in Hugh G. Thorburn (ed.), *Party Politics in Canada*, 3rd ed. (Toronto: Prentice-Hall, 1972), 109–111. However, John Laschinger, PC National Director, states that such a higher proportion is unlikely. For example, at the 1976 meeting no more than 802 of the 2600 delegates (31%) could belong to this category (interview, August 1975). The same tendency for the proportion of appointed delegates to decline was apparent at the 1975 Liberal convention. Of the 3014 delegates, 2374 (79%) were chosen by constituency associations. This group included constituency delegates, constituency presidents, MPs, and defeated candidates (interview with Blair Williams, Liberal National Director, September 1975).

10. *Ottawa Citizen* (April 14, 1975), 2.

11. See the article by Frances Russell in *Ottawa Journal* (July 16, 1974).

12. See E. C. Ladd, Jr., and S. M. Lipset, "Portrait of a Discipline," *Teaching Political Science*, II:2 (January 1975), 144–71, and "The Politics of American Sociologists," *American Journal of Sociology*, 78 (July 1972), 67–104. Responding to an earlier draft of this chapter, Cliff Scotton, the NDP Secretary, pointedly noted the differences in the social background of the leaders. He noted that Lewis left Byelorussia to escape pogroms and Bolshevism, arriving in Canada knowing neither English nor French. Stanfield and Trudeau were born to affluent manufacturing and entrepreneurial families (personal communication, August 1975).

13. Quoted in Christina Newman, "That big red machine is the Daveymobile," *The Globe and Mail* (July 7, 1975).

14. Interview (Ottawa, Spring 1975).

15. Paul Grescoe, "The Decency of Dave Barrett," *The Canadian Magazine* (April 19, 1975), 12.

 # SECTION V

Policy Dispositions (Outputs)

A large number of policy areas are important because they involve great expense (eg. National Defence) and/or because they are vital to the well-being of humanity (eg. the Environment). Two of the policy areas selected for attention in this work were chosen because they are directly related to significant political cleavages — namely, bicultural policy and redistributive policy (class cleavage). A third policy area, tariff and resources policy, was selected because the theme is a vital contemporary and historic issue and because it is linked to the geographic cleavage. Finally, foreign policy is included on account of its obvious significance.

A common approach to party policy is to compare platforms or attitudes. One of the fundamental principles of the social sciences is that to understand humanity requires the analysis of behaviour rather than merely intention or purpose. Accordingly, the chapters on party policy assess party dispositions wherever possible on the basis of actual behaviour rather than promises or declarations of intent.

CHAPTER 11
BICULTURAL POLICY
Conrad Winn

Introduction

The modern nation-state consists in principal of a geographically com-
pact people having a single culture, language, and faith. France is a
prototype because it possesses a predominant religion, a common language embodied in the name of the state, a concentration of industry
and government in the Paris core, and a contained geographical form.
The prospect of national survival is often bleak for peoples who, unlike
the French, are linearly dispersed and socially divided by differences
between language groups, races, and religions. Recent civil wars in
Pakistan, Nigeria, Viet-Nam, Rhodesia, and Northern Ireland attest to
the destructiveness of domestic cleavages.

Internal strife becomes especially severe when the divisions which
give rise to conflict reinforce rather than neutralize one another. In
Northern Ireland, for instance, the animosity between Protestants and
Roman Catholics is accentuated by disparities of wealth between the
two groups. In Canada, whose conditions can be compared to those of
Northern Ireland, the principal geographic, religious, linguistic, and
economic cleavages reinforce each other by virtue of the fact that the
French-speaking component is mainly Roman Catholic, mainly located
in Quebec, and less prosperous than the English-speaking protestant
population. Furthermore, unlike the population of France, Canada's
inhabitants are thinly dispersed and lack a single urban core. They
possess two historic and culturally different opposing centres in
Montreal and Toronto.

The unintegrated nature of Canadian society gives an extraordinary quality to the long existence of the Canadian state and to its
relatively high degree of internal peace. Yet, despite the relative absence of violent discord, bicultural tensions have been a central theme
in Canadian history. The elimination of binational distrust and the
achievement of "national unity" has been "Canada's major political
and intellectual obsession."[1] Party declarations on national unity have
been prominent in almost every federal election campaign.

Although the expressed attitudes of parties are readily available in
documents and in the press, it is nevertheless a complex matter to
identify their fundamental attitudes and dispositions. First, because of
the flexibility and pragmatism of the parties, individual party declarations may reflect more closely specific circumstances than long-term
preferences. Secondly, the expressed opinions of a party may not coincide perfectly with its policies while in office. If government policies

were influenced only by ministerial preferences, then policies would be a better gauge of essential party attitudes than declared intentions. On the other hand, government policies are influenced greatly by the values of public servants, who assist the drafting of legislation and control subsequent implementation. Thirdly, English-Canadian movement parties have tended to view themselves as regional parties without serious national ambitions and have therefore lacked a keen interest in, and a precise view of, English-French relations.

In terms of electoral behaviour, French-Canadians and Catholics have given disproportionate support to the Liberal party from the 1890s to the present while Conservatives have received disproportionate aid from the English-speaking protestant population. It has been generally assumed that this pattern of voter choice is reflected in the attitudes of the parties, that the Liberals have been moderately sympathetic to French-Canada, while Conservatives have been equally unsympathetic. The best evidence to support this interpretation exists in the realm of foreign policy, particularly among those issues relating to war and the British connection. However, even in foreign policy the evidence is by no means clear. Outside this domain, the evidence about the relative positions of the two parties is even more ambiguous. In domestic policy, Conservative actions have sometimes been unexpectedly favourable to French-Canada. Liberal policy has fluctuated considerably with more sympathetic records under English Liberal prime ministers than under French ones.

The following two sections of this chapter explore English-French relations in the foreign and domestic policies and attitudes of the Liberal and Conservative parties. The third section examines the attitudes of the movement parties, particularly the views of the NDP because of its keener interest in French-English relations.

Bicultural Character of Foreign Policy[2]

In foreign policy, the main conflict of interest between English- and French-Canada concerns the country's relations with Great Britain. As the Montreal daily, *La Presse*, has expressed it,

> We French Canadians belong to one country, Canada; Canada is for us the whole world; but the English-Canadians have two countries, one here and one across the sea.[3]

In practice, government policies and party declarations on the British connection appear to portray the Conservatives as more anglophile and less francophile than the Liberals. The strongest evidence to support this view arises from discord during both world wars over the adoption of compulsory military service. English-Canada was anxious to augment assistance to the beleaguered mother country while French-Canada was traditionally wary of such involvement. During the first conscription crisis, the predominantly Conservative coalition government enacted compulsory service in 1917, three years after the onset of fighting, while the official Liberal position remained resolutely opposed to conscription through the war. During the years of and preceding World War II, the Conservative party was publicly committed to conscription while the Liberals remained opposed. When the Liberal government finally invoked compulsory service in 1944, the Conservatives accused it of jeopardizing by its delay the safety of Canadian soldiers and the survival of the United Kingdom.

The Conservative view that Liberals have been willing to jeopardize Britain's position in time of military threat is not limited to conscription. Conservatives were sharply critical of the Liberal government's policy on the South African war at the turn of the century. Laurier's assistance to Britain was portrayed as lacklustre, insufficient, and therefore essentially disloyal. Liberal naval policies were seen in much the same light in the period of rearmament preceding World War I. Conservatives doubted the motives behind Laurier's act of 1910, authorizing the creation of a Canadian fleet independent of British authority. The suspicions of Conservatives were reinforced two years later, when their newly elected government introduced a bill to allocate $35 million for the construction of three British dreadnoughts. The measure was defeated in the predominantly Liberal Senate. In recent times, the St. Laurent government's early reaction against the British invasion of Suez in 1956 contrasted sharply with the attitudes of the Conservative opposition.

Evidence to support the view that Conservatives are more anglophile than Liberals can be drawn from the fields of diplomacy and trade as well as from military affairs. In the 1880s and 1890s, the two parties were opposed on the issue of commercial union with the United States. Both the Liberals, who favoured reciprocity, and the Conservatives, who rejected it, tended to construe the policy as a threat to the British connection. Although Laurier subsequently repudiated reciprocity, the traditionally greater preference of Conservatives for commerce with Britain appears to have persisted.[4] Thus, in the 1950s, the Conservative Party under John Diefenbaker condemned the Liberals for the decline in commerce between Canada and the United Kingdom.

The more anglophile nature of the Conservatives is also revealed in diplomacy. In 1935, the outgoing Bennett government advocated strong League of Nations sanctions in the light of fascist Italy's invasion of Ethiopia. The incoming King government promptly withdrew support for these sanctions. French-Canadian Catholics were thought to harbour sympathy for Italy on account of its ostensibly missionary purpose and its good relations with the Vatican. Subsequently, Mackenzie King declared that British commitments in World War II did not automatically involve Canada. The Conservatives cried foul.[5]

The preceding was constructed to present the strongest evidence in support of the traditional portrait of an anglophile Conservative party and a francophile Liberal party. However, the full spate of evidence is not so onesided. It is probably true that the private preferences of Liberal leaders have been less anglophile than those of Conservative leaders. It is likewise true that at any given point in time Liberal and

Conservative rhetoric tends to be pointed in the expected cultural direction. The same pattern of preferences probably emerges when the rhetoric and symbolism employed by a Liberal opposition in one parliamentary session is compared with the rhetoric and symbolism employed by a Conservative opposition in another session. However, when the actual policies of Conservative and Liberal governments are compared, the contrast between the two parties loses its starkness.

The argument that the two parties are not perfect mirror images of each other can be supported by the re-interpretation of those events which appear to uphold the orthodox view as well as by the introduction of new facts. First, contrary to orthodox expectations, Liberal governments have been responsible for important pro-British policies. Two of the most notable examples of Canadian assistance to Britain in this century were Laurier's imperial perference in trade and Mackenzie King's wartime grants and loans. The imperial preference artifically linked the Canadian market to the British economy, while Canadian aid to Britain in World War II amounted to thirty times the aid allocated to all other countries for the period.[6]

Secondly, although Conservatives condemned as disloyal Prime Minister King's rhetoric to the effect that British actions in World War II did not automatically commit Canada, King's assertions of independence were consistent with previous Conservative policy. During the first Great War, Prime Minister Borden had insisted that Canadian forces be commanded by Canadians and that Canada participate in the political management of the war. Furthermore, King's assertions of independence were limited mainly to rhetoric since his government subsequently assisted Britain in a spirit of great generosity.

Thirdly, Conservative and Liberal policies were remarkably alike even on the most controversial and divisive issue of conscription. Both parties adopted compulsory service in the end and both began its implementation by stealth and in increments during the early stages of fighting. Borden introduced the structure for national registration in 1916, while King implemented national registration as early as 1940 and adopted indefinite military service at home merely a year later. As leader of the opposition in World War I, Laurier did publicly oppose conscription. However, had his party been re-elected in 1911, Laurier's position might have been similar to King's in World War II. In order to retain the support of the English-speaking members of the Liberal caucus and cabinet, Laurier would have needed to implement conscription in one form or another.

The attention of this chapter has been devoted to binational differences between the major parties on war-related issues. While the policies of Conservative elites have tended to be anglophile, Liberal policies have not been consistently francophile. The lack of consistency among Liberal governments is especially evident in that aspect of foreign policy relating to external aid. English Liberal prime ministers appear to have been more sympathetic to French-Canadian interests in foreign assistance than have French Liberal prime ministers. Prior to Lester Pearson's ministries, Canadian aid was directed almost entirely to English-speaking countries. The anglophone nature of the aid program was very great under Louis St. Laurent, became less so under John Diefenbaker, and became much less so under Pearson. Diefenbaker's Conservative government established Canada's first assistance program to the former French colonies of Africa. Under Lester Pearson, the English Liberal, aid to Francophone countries burgeoned (see Table 11-1). Under Pierre Trudeau, the French Liberal, the proportion of aid to French-speaking countries has levelled off. This tentative pattern of greatest Francophone sympathies among English Liberal prime ministers becomes more evident in domestic policy, to be discussed below.

Table 11-1

Canadian External Aid Allocations to
ex-British and ex-French Colonies

	Ratio of Aid to Eng.-speaking countries divided by Aid to Fr.-speaking countries	Radio of Aid to Eng.-speaking Africa divided by Aid to Fr.-speaking Africa
1951–60	262	n.a.
1961–65	57	10.7
1965–66	16	3.1
1966–67	13	1.9
1967–68	10	1.6
1968–69	6	1.2
1969–70	4.9	.69
1970–71	3.4	.52
1971–72	3.9	.70
1972–73	2.9	.71

Source: Calculations based on Canadian International Development Agency annual reviews. Fiscal year 1972–3 is a CIDA estimate.

To be fair, international as well as domestic factors may have influenced Canada's external aid policy. It is probably true that French-speaking prime ministers were constrained from displaying open generosity to French-speaking countries. Likewise, it may be true that the governments of English Liberal prime ministers were not extraordinarily more pro-French in their aid policies than Conservative governments. Nevertheless, some of the variation in aid policy was affected by the late decolonization of the French empire as compared to the British and by the small number of ex-French dependencies prior to Diefenbaker and Pearson.

Domestic Policy

In the realm of spontaneous feelings and preferences, it seems reasonably clear that Conservative elected officials, particularly backbench MPs, have been less sympathetic to French Canada than their Liberal counterparts. In a survey of the House of Commons in 1962, Kornberg found that 67% of Liberal Members favoured the extension of "cultural dualism," while almost as many Conservatives were opposed.[7] Two years later, a study commissioned by the Royal Commission on Bilingualism and Biculturalism found that four-fifths of English-speaking Liberal MPs supported the installation of greater translation facilities in Commons committee rooms, while only half of the Conservatives held this view.[8]

Much of the Conservative animosity is rooted among the western MPs. However, for most of Canadian history the principal sources of anti-French sentiment in the Conservative party were located in Ontario. The main pressure for unilingually English, state schools in Ontario, Manitoba, Saskatchewan, and Alberta came from Ontario Orangemen. Likewise in the 1880s, the vigorous opposition to the Quebec Liberal government's Jesuit Estates Act arose among Conservative Orangemen from Ontario.[9]

In both the Liberal and Conservative caucuses, the decision-making elites have been remarkably independent of and almost oblivious to the sentiments of their followers. In an almost perverse way, the policies of Conservative leaders have been remarkably sympathetic to French Canada, while the policies of French-speaking Liberal leaders have been unexpectedly anglophile. For example, despite the demonstrable ambivalence, if not hostility, of Conservative MPs to simultaneous translation in Parliament, the major steps in this area were undertaken by John Diefenbaker's government. In general, governments headed by English Liberals have been most francophile in policy, while those headed by French-speaking Liberals have been frequently less francophile than governments led by Conservatives. It also seems generally true that all governments, irrespective of party or leader, have become more francophone in recent times.

Three factors appear to influence the nature of government policy. First, there exists a leadership paradox whereby the electoral needs of a party leadership are strikingly different from the needs of backbenchers. A backbencher's self-interest is satisfied by expressing aggressively the interests of his locality or region, while the needs of a party leadership are served by appealing to the interests of electors whose support cannot be taken for granted. So long as a party's base is by itself insufficient for election, the leadership must be more wary of causing disaffection among marginal voters than among loyal supporters. Thus, English-Protestant Conservatives, inherently suspect among French-Canadians and Catholics, must be cautious about alienating French-Canadians and Catholics and French Liberals, inherently suspect among English Protestants, must be cautious about alienating the latter group.[10]

Secondly, government policy is influenced by party elites, in that they view their public obligations in a more national framework than do backbenchers. Irrespective of their party and the emotional preferences of their followers, all governments in recent times have become sensitive to the threat posed by secessionist tendencies in Quebec and all have been subject to increasing pressures from Quebec for the redress of grievances. As a result, each government in the last generation has adopted some policies designed to appeal to French Canada and to undermine the popular basis of separatism. Because the separatist movement has grown continually in the past generation, successive federal governments have been obliged to devote greater and greater resources to redressing francophone grievances in what René Lévesque likes to call "Operation Panic." This growing separatism is probably the most important recent influence on federal policy — more important than the partisan composition of the cabinet or the ethnicity of the prime minister.

Thirdly, the greater sympathy for French Canada held by Liberal leaders, English and French alike, does bear some significance. Inter-party differences in the nature of personal feelings towards French Canada helps to explain why the policies of Conservatives have been more anglophone than the policies of English Liberals. However, personal sentiments could not have been predominant in the case of policies emanating from French-speaking Liberal leaders, who needed to be especially attuned to English-Canadian sensibilities.

A striking example of the impact of the leadership paradox on government policy involves party reactions to the Manitoba School crisis. Until the mid-nineteenth century, Manitoba had been settled largely by Quebeckers and its schools were mainly Catholic. In law, Protestant and Catholic school systems existed side by side. However, in response to waves of immigration from Ontario, the Manitoba government abolished Catholic schooling and established a unilingually English state system. Sir MacKenzie Bowell, the Conservative Prime Minister and a former Grand Master of the Orange Order, passed an order-in-council requiring the provincial government to give redress to the Catholic minority. Faced with Manitoba's refusal, Bowell convened Parliament to enact remedial legislation. Although the Catholic church was committed to redress, Laurier, the Catholic and French Canadian, publicly opposed the legislation on the apparent grounds that it transgressed provincial rights and that conciliatory "sunny ways" would be more appropriate. In fact, Laurier had been advised by Israel Tarte, his principal strategist, that the selection of a French-Canadian as Liberal leader was sufficient to carry Quebec and that any further attempts to conciliate Quebeckers would involve unnecessary electoral costs outside the province.

Laurier's vulnerability in defending French-Canadian interests in education appeared again in 1905 during the formation of the provinces of Saskatchewan and Alberta. The Prime Minister initially planned confessional schooling according to the Quebec pattern. But, seeing the prospects of turmoil among his English-speaking colleagues, he quickly adopted Manitoba's secular model.

The vulnerability of French-speaking Liberal prime ministers as defenders of French Canada and the strength of English Liberal prime ministers is evidenced in immigration policy, federal-provincial grants, and ministerial appointments. Immigration is a traditional concern among French Canadians. Because French-speaking immigrants are few in number and because non-French, non-British immigrants tend to settle in English communities, all forms of immigration threaten to tip the balance against French Canada. In 1944, the Quebec Legislative Assembly was so concerned about the prospect of mass post-war immigration that it passed a resolution threatening to boycott future immigration schemes. Yet, Laurier and St. Laurent, both francophone Liberals, administered two of the largest immigration ventures in Canadian history. Through the use of intensive advertising, steamship subisidies, and a system of agents abroad, the Laurier government induced 1.8 million foreigners to settle in Canada.

The volume of immigration under St. Laurent was smaller, but its ethnic character remained overwhelmingly British and non-French. A distinct administrative preference for British immigrants persisted. For Britons there existed more promotional campaigning, fewer formalities, shorter visa procedures, preferential transportation rates, more offices, and more officials. However, the Liberal government was afraid of limiting the British inflow. According to St. Laurent's Minister of Immigration, the government knew "damned well that the flow of immigrants was too big for Canada to digest", but if it "tried to stop the flow of British immigrants it would be the finish of the Liberal party in many Anglo-Saxon constituencies."[11]

The first serious attempts to augment the French-speaking component in immigration occurred during the Diefenbaker years. Immigration Minister Davie Fulton commissioned a study to explore the viability of attracting Franco-Americans from the northern states. Fulton's successor, Ellen Fairclough, made repeated overtures to Duplessis with the view to joint planning with Quebec. In terms of overseas spending to attract British and French immigrants, the imbalance in Britain's favour diminished slightly (Figure 11-1).

Under Pearson, the federal government displayed its greatest interest in stimulating French-speaking immigration. As a result of sustained overtures to the French government, immigration from France achieved a peak in 1967. The Pearson government also developed close relations with the Quebec Department of Immigration, giving generous subsidies to Quebec's Centres d'Orientation et de Formation des Immigrants. The imbalance in overseas spending between Britain and France was further reduced. Under Trudeau, the lower overseas spending imbalance achieved by Prime Minister Pearson persists, but there appear to be no further attempts to advance French interests in immigration.

Like the field of immigration, the field of federal-provincial grants gives evidence of the relative ineffectiveness of the French-speaking prime ministers. In the earlier period, Laurier was responsible for allocating approximately the same modest moneys to Quebec as his Conservative predecessors. In recent years, St. Laurent was far less successful at aiding Quebec than Lester Pearson and even less successful than John Diefenbaker. Trudeau has been no more successful than Pearson — possibly less so. Under St. Laurent, Quebec received an annual average of 5.7% of all federal-provincial conditional and unconditional grants (see Figure 11-2). Under Diefenbaker's Conservative government, Quebec's proportion rose to an average of 16.9%, with highs of

Figure 11-1. London/Paris Ratio of Foreign Service Expenditures of
Depts. of Citizenship and Immigration and Manpower

Source: Calculated from data in Appendix 6, Freda Hawkins, *Canada and
Immigration* (Montreal: McGill Queen's University Press, 1972).

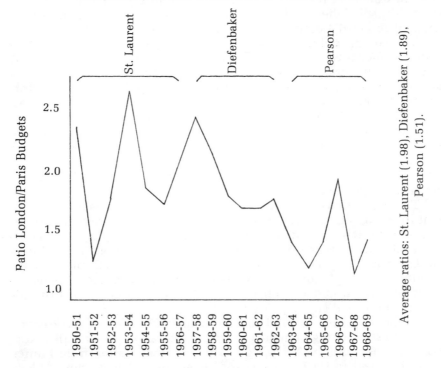

20.6% and 26.2% during the last two years in office. Federal largesse to
Quebec reached a peak under Pearson with a mean of 28.6%. The mean
proportion under Trudeau appears to have fallen about 1%.

The pattern of ministerial appointments also supports the thesis
about the greater effectiveness of English Liberal prime ministers. The
share of ministerial posts held by French-Canadians exceeded the
French-speaking portion of the population only twice: in Mackenzie
King's second ministry in 1926 and in Lester Pearson's ministries in
the 1960s.[12] Francophones held one-third of the posts at the beginning
of King's second ministry, while they held on the average almost two-
fifths of the positions under Pearson. By contrast, the French-Canadian
share under Laurier was only about one-fifth. The French-Canadian
share in Trudeau's first cabinet fell to below the French-Canadian
proportion of the population. The only significant exception to the rule
about the lesser effectiveness of French-speaking prime ministers involves Louis St. Laurent. Under his leadership, the francophone share
failed to drop, but instead rose slightly above the average for King's
ministries in the period 1935-48 (see Table 11-2). Apparently, St. Laur-

Table 11-2

Francophone and Catholic Share of
Federal Ministries, 1935–1972*

	% French	% Catholic
1935–48 (King)	26	34
1948–57 (St. Laurent)	28	34
1957–63 (Diefenbaker)	15	29
1963–68 (Pearson)	39	50
1968–72 (Trudeau)	27	45

*Calculations are not based on the proportion of ministers of a given language or religion, but rather on the proportion of time ministerial posts are held by that language or religion.

Figure 11-2. Quebec share of federal-provincial conditional and unconditional grants (%) for fiscal years 1953-54 to 1970-71.

Sources: Calculations Based on Mar. 1954-63 Historical Review Financial Statistics of Governments in Canada, Cat. 68-503 Table 17 and Mar. 1964-71 Federal Government Finance Cat. No. 680211, Tables 3 and 5.

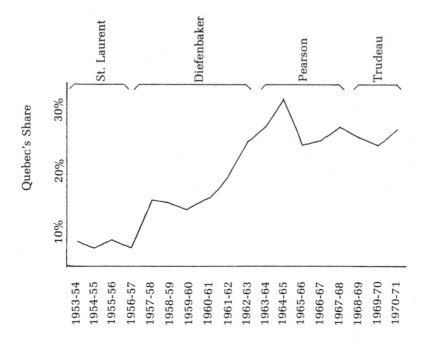

ent believed as a matter of principle that the French share of ministerial posts should approximate the French share in the population at large.

The arguments that there have been few fundamental differences in policies towards French Canada under Liberal and Conservative governments or that francophone prime ministers have not assisted their brethren with great effectiveness will not be pleasing to the eyes of English francophiles, especially those in the Liberal party. In reply, they may point to the obvious rise of French Canadians in the public service during the years of Trudeau as prime minister. Francophones until recently occupied positions of leadership ranging from head of CIDA to head of Air Canada and head of the RCMP. This is indeed a considerable change since a generation ago there were no French-Canadian deputy ministers in Ottawa. Furthermore, while the Liberal government identifies actively with its program of promoting French Canadians to responsible positions in the public sector, Tory backbenchers appear to be the main vehicle of protest for worried or hostile English-speaking civil servants.

Although Trudeau's commitment to a bicultural public service should obviously not be doubted, considerable credit for current programs should be assigned to his predecessors. The present program of requiring bilingual personnel in responsible positions is a direct outgrowth of policies established under Lester Pearson, including Pearson's well-known Royal Commission on Bilingualism and Biculturalism. Most significantly, the first great impetus for bilingualism in the public service came from John Diefenbaker. In 1962, the Glassco Commission on government organization called for an "increase in the extent of bilingualism among public servants" and warned that the public service was "not attracting and retaining enough highly qualified employees from French Canada."[13] A minority report by Commissioner Therrien painted a starker picture of the bicultural problem in the bureaucracy and urged that no efforts be spared to rectify the situation. At the end of the same year, Prime Minister Diefenbaker announced the creation of a Bureau of Government Organization, whose mandate would include the implementation of the bicultural recommendations of the Glassco Commision and especially (i.e. "with particular reference to") the views of Commissioner Therrien.

The orthodox portrait of Liberal governments as pro-francophone and Conservative governments as anti-francophone not only overlooks the bicultural contributions of Diefenbaker's rule, but it also overlooks the bicultural failures of Mackenzie King. In particular, the urgency for bicultural reform in the 1960s and 1970s resulted from the continual decline of the French fact in the bureaucracy during the mainly Liberal ministries after World War I. Between 1918 and 1946, the public service experienced an approximately 10% decline in francophone representation and the virtual disappearance of French-Canadians at the higher levels. Despite vigorous protest from the Montreal Chamber of Commerce and other sources, no serious remedies emerged from the King or St. Laurent governments.

Movement Parties

While the parliamentary parties have been preoccupied with the cultural cleavage, only those movement parties based in Quebec have had a keen interest. Both the Nationalists of Henri Bourassa during World War I and the *créditistes* of Réal Caouette were substantially motivated by the desire to redress French-Canadian grievances. The low interest in cultural issues among Progressives, CCFers, and Social Crediters prior to Caouette arose from intense commitments to their own special concerns and because their lack of electoral hope in Quebec provided little incentive to be concerned. To the extent that they were aware of cultural problems the Protestant leaders of the English movement parties were wary, if not directly suspicious, of Catholic Quebec.

Woodsworth and the other early CCF leaders did try hard to adopt fair-minded attitudes towards French Canada, but their puritan righteousness inhibited the development of much sympathy. The coolness of the CCF changed dramatically when the NDP was formed in 1961. The NDP became the first party to proclaim the "two nations" idea, whereby the special cultural interests of French Canada were formally recognized. Since that time, most attitude surveys of the Commons have shown New Deomocratic MPs to be at least as sympathetic to the linguistic and cultural needs of Quebec as members of the Liberal caucus.

The dramatic change in socialist attitudes deserves some explanation. One basic reason is that when the CCF became the NDP, electoral expectations rose greatly. In expectations and in subsequent performance, the NDP was a national party. Another influence was the newly affiliated Canadian Labour Congress. The leader of the predominantly English CLC was Claude Jodoin, a French-Canadian social democrat who was highly esteemed among CCF-NDP leaders. Another influence on the NDP's new attitudes came from a group of McGill University academics, especially from Charles Taylor and Michael Oliver. Professor Oliver, who became the first federal president of the party, founded the French Canada studies program at McGill and subsequently became research director for the Royal Commission on Bilingualism and Biculturalism. A final influence may have come from changed attitudes towards socialism in Quebec. After 1960, neither the Catholic Church nor the *union nationale* exercised sufficient political supremacy to enforce their deep hostility to socialism.

Conclusion

The main concern of the chapter was to explore the orthodox view that the Conservative and Liberal parties are respectively anglophile and francophile in policy. The best evidence to support this view was found to be that aspect of foreign policy relating to the British connection. However, even the evidence in this domain was not straightforward. While in opposition, the parliamentary parties made symbolic declarations consistent with the orthodox view. However, when in office, the policies of the two parties converged, even on the conscription controversies.

In the domain of domestic policy, the Conservative party was not found to be consistently anglophile. Furthermore, French-speaking Liberal prime ministers appeared to be the weakest defenders of French-Canadian interests. This weakness was attributed to an electoral vulnerability resulting from the smaller French-speaking base of voters.

To be fair, Canadian history does not go back far enough to support this interpretation with any certainty. There have been too few Conservative, English Liberal, and French Liberal prime ministers to permit statistical reliability. Nonetheless, at a minimum the evidence raises some doubt about the orthodox view of Conservative-Liberal differences.

The English-Canadian movement parties were shown to be uninterested in binational questions. The new interest in French Canada acquired by the NDP was described and then attributed to increased electoral hopes and to the influence of the CLC and several McGill intellectuals. It is of course difficult to be certain about NDP policies, since the party has not won power at the federal level and since bicultural issues are insufficiently important in the western provinces to justify using provincial NDP policies as a gauge of potential policies at the federal level.

Finally, it was suggested that the threat of separatism and the need to redress francophone grievances influences policy more than the partisanship of government or the ethnicity of prime ministers.

Notes

1. John Porter, *The Vertical Mosaic* (Toronto: University of Toronto Press, 1968), 369.

2. For a more comprehensive review of the foreign policies of the parties, see Chapter 14, by Garth Stevenson.

3. Quoted in J. Bartlet Brebner, *Canada: A Modern History* (Ann Arbor, Michigan: University of Michigan Press, 1959), 372.

4. For a review of the parties' attitudes towards trade and the tariff, see Chapter 13, by John Weir.

5. The traditional interpretation of Prime Minister King's reticence to openly support Britain in its conflict with the Axis powers is based on King's alleged concern for French-Canadian sensibilities. However, a perusal of the King diaries made public in 1975 suggests that King was not too concerned about French Canada, but did express some curious pro-Nazi sympathies, at least before the outbreak of hostilities in 1939. For example, on Tuesday, June 29, 1937, his diary read: ". . . I feel more and more how far-reaching in the interest of the working classes are the reforms being worked out in Germany, and how completely they are on the right lines." Quoted in *Ottawa Citizen*, (January 11, 1975), 25.

6. Michel Brunet, *Canadians et Canadiens* (Montreal: Fides, 1954), 145. See also Chapter 13.

7. Allan Kornberg, *Canadian Legislative Behavior* (Toronto: Holt, Rinehart & Winston, 1967), 123.

8. David Hoffman and Norman Ward, *Bilingualism and Biculturalism in the Canadian House of Commons* (Ottawa: Queen's Printer, 1970), 215.

9. The Jesuit Estates Act was devoted primarily to compensating the Jesuit Order for holdings that had passed to the Crown as a result of the Order's dissolution by the Church.

10. A notable exception to this rule occurred in 1957, when the Conservative party deliberately ignored Quebec during the election campaign. However, the Conservative victory was small and tenuous. Although the Conservatives received a greater number of seats than the Liberals, their proportion of the popular vote was smaller. For a discussion of the impact of electoral law on election outcomes, see Chapter 7.

11. J. W. Pickersgill, quoted in G. A. Rawlyk, "Canada's Immigration Policy, 1945–62," *Dalhousie Review*, XLII:3 (1962), 295.

12. See Richard Van Loon, "The Structure and Membership of the Canadian Cabinet," Internal Research Project of the Royal Commission on Bilingualism and Biculturalism (Oct. 1966) and especially Frederick W. Gibson (ed.), *Cabinet Formation and Bicultural Relations* (Ottawa: Queen's Printer, 1970). See also Richard Van Loon and Michael Whittington, *The Canadian Political System*, 2nd ed. (Toronto: McGraw-Hill Ryerson, 1976), 312–35, passim.

13. Royal Commission on Government Organization, *Report* (Ottawa: Queen's Printer, 1962). See 28–29, 67–77, and 348. See also the excellent analysis in V. Seymour Wilson, "Language Policy," in G. Bruce Doern and V. Seymour Wilson (ed.), *Issues in Canadian Public Policy* (Toronto: Macmillan, 1974), 253–85.

CHAPTER 12
REDISTRIBUTIVE POLICY

Douglas McCready and Conrad Winn

We gratefully acknowledge the assistance of Professors Irwin Gillespie and Michael Whittington, Carleton University, and of Max Saltsman, MP.

Introduction

In the literature on party cleavages in Canada, the left-right cleavage receives considerable attention. However, the bicultural cleavage and to some extent the geographic cleavage are more relevant to the electorate.[1] Academics probably ascribe a special importance to class because they are less regional, less ethnocentric, more secular, and more universalist than the population at large. Among academics, there is a certain consensus that electoral democracy derives at least part of its meaning from conflict over the allocation of wealth.[2]

If there is a dominant view about the redistributive nature of the parties, it is that the policies of the NDP achieve the most egalitarian distribution of wealth, while the policies of the Liberal and Conservative parties are equally non-egalitarian. Mallory, Dawson, Taylor, Porter, and others seem to hold this view.[3] Peter Newman entitled one of his essays on the parties "The Lack of Conservative-Liberal Differences in Canadian Politics".[4] In the 1960s John Meisel wrote that "there is very little difference between the Conservatives and the Liberals with regard to their attitudes towards the welfare state and towards the role of free enterprise in the Canadian economy."[5] Some observers do believe that the major parties are different.[6] However, beyond a few disagreements about the major parties, there is a general consensus that the NDP is the most redistributive of them all.

The thesis of this chapter is that the redistributive behaviour of all the parties does not differ significantly.[7] Although no quantitative evidence about beliefs, intentions, or symbols among federal parties exists,[8] we do not dispute the possibility of significant differences in this domain. We intend to argue that there are few systematic differences in output.

One problem in making statements about the distributive character of the parties is to disentangle general party characteristics from the temporary behaviour of parties in specific time periods. Attitudes and policies can change dramatically. In the 1870s, for instance, the Conservatives sponsored considerable progressive legislation, while the Liberals vehemently opposed trade unions. A generation later, the roles were reversed (see Chapter 2, Parliamentary Parties).

A more serious problem than time period is the problem of separating rhetoric from performance. Many observers implicitly assume that expressed attitudes are an accurate guide to performance and that their own impressions present an accurate portrait of these expressed attitudes.[9] However, to our knowledge, no systematic quantitative studies of party statements in the federal system exists, nor are there any systematic quantitative studies of party output that corroborate a thesis supporting party differences.

Another problem is to disentangle party dispositions towards the role of the public sector from party dispositions towards the distribution of personal wealth. There is no automatic connection between the size of the public sector and the inequality of personal income; for example, the Canadian nationalization of the U.S. oil companies might increase the long-term income of the government. However, the expected increase in government revenue would not necessarily diminish class differences because government expenditures are not necessarily redistributive. One of the many consequences of such a nationalization might be to redistribute income away from the upper status professionals conducting research at the parent firm in the U.S. and towards researchers who are Canadian or willing to locate in Canada.

A final problem is the conundrum of evidence or data. Because the minor parties including the NDP and Social Credit have never governed in the federal system, federal government output is irrelevant to assessing their performance. In fact, the federal monopoly of the major parties makes provincial government output and explicit policy positions by the federal parties a less imperfect means of comparing the potential performance of the federal parties.

A null thesis which includes the NDP may come as no surprise to specialists in public policy, but it may seem novel to specialists in parties and elections and shocking to some socialist supporters of the NDP. Much of what passes for advances in science are simply the transfer of discoveries from one field of inquiry to another. An important function of this chapter is therefore to communicate some of the findings in the fields of public finance and public policy.

The next section presents some general evidence — cross-national and Canadian — in support of the null thesis. The following section examines individual policy domains such as health care and education. The section explores some constraints on redistribution that result from the practical limitations on redistribution and from philosophical confusion among the parties.

Some Relevant Canadian and Foreign Literature

A large cross-national literature is devoted to discovering the factors which influence the size and pattern of government expenditures. For our purposes, however, this literature poses several dilemmas. First, little is actually known about the redistributive nature of most government expenditures. Little empirical evidence exists to show whether individual categories of expenditures such as health and education tend to benefit the poor, the rich, or the population in general. Secondly, few studies have examined the role of political parties. Most works have looked at economic or social change rather than at the impact of political factors. As a result, considerable evidence shows that wealthy countries have disproportionately large governmental budgets. However, few facts tell of the impact of the partisan or ideological composition of governments. Thirdly, there are few studies of Canada.

In Canada, the literature on parties and redistributive expenditures consists mainly of the work of David Falcone, Dale Poel, and David Campbell.[10] Falcone conducted an analysis of federal expenditures from Confederation to the present. Falcone, Poel, and Campbell examined provincial allocations in recent decades. The findings of all three researchers suggest that Canadian parties have not had a discernible impact on the distribution of income. It is possible of course that these findings are fortuitous. It is conceivable that Canadian parties do influence the patterns of expenditures, but that these patterns are obscured by factors which have not yet been detected.[11]

In the absence of other Canadian research to corroborate the null thesis, the most effective way of responding to the possibility of chance findings is to compare Canadian research with research in other countires. To this end, we will review briefly the foreign research on government expenditures. In general, the foreign research which examines the role of parties or ideology finds little evidence of their influence on the nature of redistributive outputs. In general, the foreign research which does not consider the question of parties is able to explain a substantial portion of the variation in government expenditures without any reference to parties.

Falcone's work on federal government outputs in Canada is monumental.[12] For the period 1867–1968, he examined a range of legislative outputs which included annual expenditures on social welfare and the number and types of distributive bills. Falcone's purpose was to see whether socio-economic changes such as urbanization were sufficient to explain outputs or whether political factors such as the party in power and party competitiveness bore an influence as well. Falcone concluded that government policies were almost entirely influenced by socio-economic change. As the country became more populous, industrialized, and urbanized, there was an accompanying increase in general government expenditures, in welfare expenditures, and in the number of distributive measures affecting labour and agriculture. Also, the number of distributive measures affecting business decreased. Falcone's statistical analysis showed no inherent differences in the distributive or redistributive behaviour of Liberal and Conservative governments.

Falcone's research has not been restricted to the federal level. In a more recent work, he studied the impact of socio-economic and political variables on health policy in the provinces.[13] His socio-economic variables included per capita income and the proportion of the workforce in manufacturing. His political variables included the amount of legislative and electoral support possessed by the Liberals, Conservatives, Social Credit and NDP. Measures of health care included health expenditures per capita and the number of days spent in hospitals per capita. From his statistical analysis, Falcone found no relationship between support for any party and health expenditures.

Along with Falcone, Poel was among the first to undertake a quantitative analysis of government expenditures in Canada.[14] He set out to compare Canadian provincial policies with American state policies. An American study had shown that there existed two distinct aspects of state expenditures: those on services such as highways and those on education and welfare. Both types of expenditures were higher in affluent states, while expenditures on welfare and education were also higher in states with competitive party systems. Lack of electoral security seemed to encourage state governments to augment their expenditures on education and welfare.

In his Canadian analysis, Poel examined net provincial expenditures on education, welfare, mothers' allowance, highways, and natural resources as well as other measures of government output. He found no distinction between welfare and education and other types of expenditures. Instead, he found that all types of expenditures varied together and that total expenditures were influenced primarily by the economic development of the province.[15]

That the types of government expenditure did not vary from province to province implies that Canadian parties do not vary on a left-right basis. Of course, it is possible that left-wing or redistributive parties simply have a propensity for all kinds of expenditures. Poel's table of provincial expenditures does not suggest such a phenomenon (see Table 12-1). Poel himself discovered a statistical relationship between per capital income and provincial expenditures. In addition to the role of wealth, a glance at Table 12-1 suggests the importance of regionalism. On the average, three of the four highest spending provinces are western. Together, regionalism and economic development seem to explain the high spending patterns of British Columbia and Alberta under allegedly "free enterprise" Social Credit and Progressive Conservative parties. As for Saskatchewan, there was actually a slight, but statistically insignificant, decline in its rank among spending provinces under the CCF-NDP in 1951 and 1961 as opposed to the "free enterprise" Liberals in 1941 and 1966.

Because of the importance of Saskatchewan where the NDP has governed for long periods of time, it is fortunate that one of Falcone's students conducted a statistical analysis of expenditures in that province.[16] Campbell examined expenditures on general government services, health, social welfare, transportation, and other sectors. He tested for statistically significant differences in expenditures after Ross Thatcher's "free enterprise" Liberals returned to power in 1964. He found no such differences. Campbell did not test for differences after the NDP won its first election in 1944 because he attributed the obvious increases in Saskatchewan's expenditures in the mid-forties to a general increase in government activity across Canada. However, because the conventional view suggests significant party differences in this period, a test should be undertaken to see whether increases in Saskatchewan were indeed no greater than elsewhere, but such a test will need to await reliable data.

Table 12-1

Provincial Factor Scores on Poel's
General Policy Factor
(ranked within years)

1966	Score	1951	Score
Alta.	2.113	B.C.	.037
P.Q.	1.731	Alta.	−.437
Nfld.	1.709	Ont.	−.500
Sask. (Lib.)	1.498	Sask. (NDP)	−.516
P.E.I.	1.408	N.S.	−.632
B.C.	1.282	N.B.	−.637
Ont.	.984	Man.	−.670
Man.	.921	P.E.I.	−.731
N.B.	.653	Nfld.	−.784
N.S.	.539	P.Q.	−.912

1961	Score	1941	Score
Alta.	.917	B.C.	−.848
B.C.	.709	Sask. (Lib.)	−1.045
Sask. (NDP)	.689	Man.	−1.047
Man.	.423	Ont.	−1.054
P.Q.	.360	Alta.	−1.068
Ont.	.283	N.S.	−1.284
Nfld.	.133	P.Q.	−1.420
P.E.I.	.121	N.B.	−1.448
N.B.	.013	P.E.I.	−1.453
N.S.	−.037		

Note: each factor score is a measure of the province's governmental expenditures.

Now that the essential Canadian literature has been reviewed, it is appropriate to turn to the foreign literature. Among foreign studies are three components relevant to our purposes. First, there is a long-established tradition identified with the nineteenth-century economist Adolph Wagner.[17] The Wagner school holds that government expenditures increase more quickly than the rate of economic growth and that this pattern is explained by the nature of economic change. Secondly, there is a body of literature which argues that government expenditures are influenced by the degree to which there exists competitive electoral conflict. Thirdly, there is a small literature which examines the partisan or ideological nature of government. In general, the literature in all three domains of foreign research conforms with our position. Of course, evidence about cross-national behaviour or about behaviour within other countries cannot prove the null thesis for Canada. However, foreign evidence can disprove an alternative thesis that a universal tendency for parties to influence expenditures is obscured in the Canadian case by undetected, extraneous, or confounding variables.

The first component of foreign research to consider is Adolph Wagner's "law of expanding state expenditures." For Wagner, the main cause of increasing government intervention was apparently industrialization. Industrialization required governments to intervene where technological investments outstripped the capacities of private enterprises. Industrialization also provided the high personal incomes which stimulated demand for cultural and welfare services.

Wagner's interpretation has been severely criticized and amended. To take an extreme case, Falcone has argued that data which show the continual growth of government expenditures need not be attributed to economic factors. According to Falcone, the relative growth of the public sector may result from the socialization of successive generations of public servants to the belief that government services should grow.[18] Indeed, the public at large may have been socialized to new expectations about government.

Whatever the merits of Wagner's particular interpretation, few economists have disputed his empirical observations about ever-increasing government expenditures. A classic study of expenditures among the American states showed that 72% of the variation in public expenditures were associated with per capita income, population density, and urbanization.[19] A similar study in Canada accounted for 78% of the variation in provincial expenditures.[20] A major cross-national study of the determinants of social security programs found that the best predictor of the extent of social security was a country's economic development.[21]

For our purposes, Wagner's developmental thesis is helpful because it is incompatable with an extreme ideological or partisan interpretation of expenditures. If parties are crucial, the level of expenditures should change abruptly when one government is replaced by another. However, the increases described by the developmental theorists are continuous and incremental rather than disjunctive.

A second component of foreign research on government expenditures concerns the significance of party competition. The theory holds that evenly matched parties are obliged to promise and eventually implement welfare and other services in order to bolster their electoral positions. The theory is supported by a large number of quantitative studies among the American states[22] and by one major cross-national study.[23]

For our purposes, the theory of party competitiveness is important because it is incompatible with a thesis purporting to explain expenditures in terms of the ideologies of governments. If ideology or partisanship did explain output, the competitiveness of party systems would not matter. The logic of the partisan or ideological thesis decrees that a secure left-wing government would be more likely to extend welfare services than an insecure one. However, the data on competitiveness suggests that secure governments, irrrespective of ideology, are less likely to extend such services than insecure governments.

The third and last component of foreign research on expenditures consists of those few studies which are more closely related to the issue of partisanship or ideology. There have been a few studies of the impact of ideology on government expenditures or income inequality among the American states, but the results are inconclusive.[24] The only major study of the impact of ideology is the cross-national work of Frederic Pryor. Comparing a sample of communist and non-communist countries, he failed to discover many intrinsic differences in patterns of expenditure. For example, Marxist ideology would hold that the mass of workers would only find their fullest educational experiences in a "socialist" system. However, Prior demonstrated that there were no significant differences between the two systems in the level of school enrolments and that enrolment was almost entirely explicable in terms of the economic development of the individual country.[25]

Pryor concluded that "a number of general economic features . . . underlie the differences in public consumption expenditures between nations that are related neither to the system of property ownership nor to the method of resource allocation." Pryor also concluded that "the policy dilemmas facing decision makers of public consumption expenditures are quite similar in all nations, regardless of system."[26]

It could be argued that the comparison of communist and non-communist countries has no bearing on socialist and non-socialist parties within non-communist countries. Fortunately, some cross-national data exist on social mobility to permit comparisons between countries with long traditions of socialist government and countries without such traditions. If a strong ideological thesis is to hold true, the rate of social mobility should be higher in Sweden, for example, than in the United States. Because of the long reign of the socialist movement in Sweden, there should be a greater likelihood in that country than in the United States that the offspring of workers would rise to elite positions and that the offspring of elite families would decline in social standing.

The opposite is closer to the truth. There are no striking differences in social mobility among the middle and working classes in Sweden, Denmark, and the United States. However, at the elite level a much higher degree of inherited status exists in Sweden and Denmark than in the United States.[27] Of course, this does not prove that socialism accentuates class barriers. It is conceivable that the barriers to mobility might have been greater in Sweden and Denmark without the presence of socialist parties. However, the known facts about social mobility do imply that parties lack a determining impact.

To summarize, we began this section by reviewing some recent quantitative studies of expenditures in Canada. Neither the federal studies of Falcone, nor the provincial studies of Falcone and Poel, nor the Saskatchewan study of Campbell found evidence to reject the null thesis. As a check against the possibility of chance findings, we turned to the foreign literature. We looked to the foreign literature in order to discover if parties always tended to possess a determining influence. If no such universal tendency existed, it would be more difficult to argue that the Canadian findings were accidental. In fact, we found no conclusive evidence in the foreign literature that would support a partisan theory of expenditure.

The Thesis of Partisanship

Despite the weight of evidence in favour of the null thesis, the belief that parties do influence the distributive nature of government output is unlikely to disappear. On the one hand, the theorists of partisanship can regain confidence by arguing that existing data analysis is misleading. They can argue that it is less important to know how much is spent in a large field, such as health, than it is to know how much is spent on individual programs which are thought to help specific social strata. On the other hand, the thesis of partisanship can retain its momentum so long as four important assumptions about policy-making are not refuted: that the welfare state redistributes income greatly and that attitudes towards the welfare state are therefore important; that politicians can affect the distribution of income because they understand the distributional effects of their policies; that left-wing or redistributive politicians lack non-redistributive goals which might frustrate the achievement of their redistributive objectives; and that left-wing politicians are necessarily willing to require their constituents to pay the costs of redistribution.

There is some validity to the criticism of existing data analysis. In the field of health, for example, a progressive policy could differ from a regressive one in the proportion of expenditures which served the lower strata rather than in the total volume of expenditures. An ideal method of comparing the distributive effects of the parties would involve a comparison of the changes in net personal incomes under different governments. However, such data are unavailable for the provinces.

Another solution to the dilemma would be to analyze government pension plans, family allowances, and other individual programs whose distributive effects can be estimated. However, a comprehensive analysis of the distributive effects of government programs would be beyond our present resources. Nevertheless, a partial survey of programs is presented below in the context of an evaluation of the first premise of partisanship theory, that the welfare state redistributes wealth significantly.

Any study of government expenditures is fraught with uncertainty because reliable comparative data are available for few programs of which the impacts on society are known. However, government expenditures are only one aspect of the government's distributive role. Taxation is the other aspect. On the revenue side, strong evidence shows that the sales tax is comparatively regressive and the income tax, comparatively progressive (see Figure 12-1). If the thesis of partisanship is true, a left-wing government should depend less on sales tax and more on income tax when compared with a right-wing government.

Figures 12-2 and 12-3 portray the dependence of the western provinces on revenue from sales and income taxes. Only the behaviour of the western provinces is shown in order to exclude the effects of different regional practices. In general, the graphs show no evidence of inherent party differences. All four provinces increased their dependence

Figure 12-1. The Distributive Character of Selected Taxes

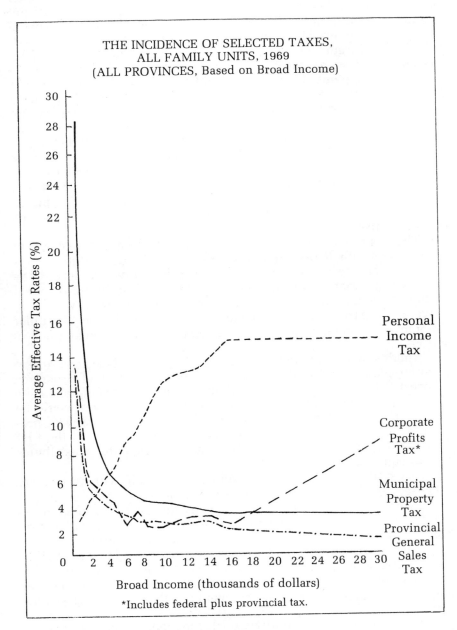

THE INCIDENCE OF SELECTED TAXES,
ALL FAMILY UNITS, 1969
(ALL PROVINCES, Based on Broad Income)

Source: Allan M. Maslove, *The Pattern of Taxation in Canada*, Economic Council of Canada (Ottawa: Information Canada, 1972), 76.

Figure 12-2. Revenue from the personal income tax as a proportion of total provincial revenue (exclusive of federal transfer payments): western provinces, fiscal years ending in 1963-72.*

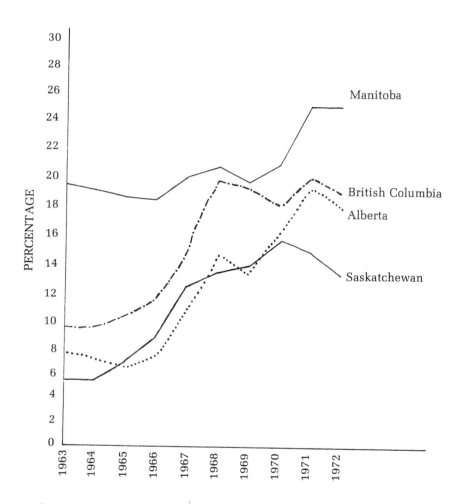

Source: Dominion Bureau of Statistics, *Provincial Government Finance* (title varies) (Ottawa: Queen's Printer, various years).

*Prior to 1962-63, the western provinces did not levy their own personal income tax, but received transfers in lieu of doing so.

Figure 12-3. Revenue from the Retail Sales Tax as a Proportion of Total Provincial Revenue (exclusive of Federal Transfer Payments): Western Provinces, Fiscal Years ending in 1953-72.

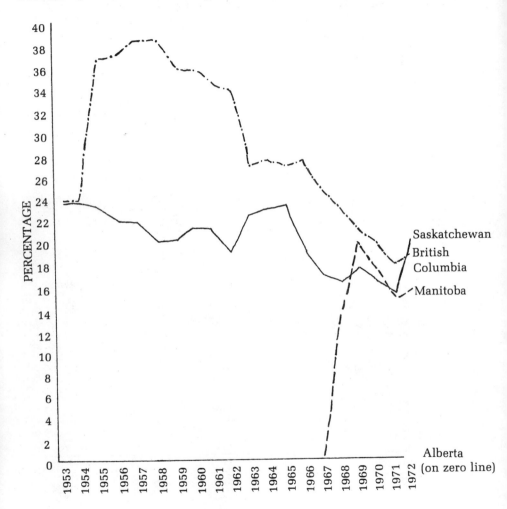

Source: Dominion Bureau of Statistics, *Historical Review: Financial Statistics of Canada 1952-62* (1963) and Provincial Government Finance (title varies) (Ottawa: Queen's Printer).

on income tax simultaneously. In the case of Saskatchewan, the province's dependence on income tax actually increased more under Liberal governments than under the CCF-NDP simply because the Liberal party was in power in the more recent period between 1964 and 1971.

Figure 12-3 on sales tax shows a similar pattern of no inherent differences among the parties. Social Credit governments occupied the extremes, British Columbia being the most dependent on revenue from sales tax and Alberta having no sales tax at all. The case of Saskatchewan does not seem to show partisan pattern.

It is undoubtedly true that existing quantitative studies of government expenditures have some significant weaknesses. However, that the pattern of government revenues also conforms with the null thesis should be an added stimulus for partisans of partisanship theory to bring forth evidence in their own support. At this point, we turn to the four unconfirmed premises which appear to underlie the partisanship thesis.

Although little systematic evidence corroborates the assertion, it is probably true that the spokesmen for the NDP are more sympathetic to the welfare state.[29] From this assertion, it is often inferred that the New Democrats do, or would, redistribute wealth more sharply *on the assumption that the welfare state does redistribute wealth substantially.* In fact, the welfare state as we know it does not redistribute wealth greatly. A number of government programs thought to be progressive are in fact neutral or regressive. Furthermore, many government programs not explicitly redistributive may be regressive rather than neutral.

The simplest method of assessing the redistributive performance of government programs is to compare the Lorenz curves of income before and after government taxes and transfers (see Figure 12-4). If the welfare state has accomplished a redistribution of wealth, the plot of family incomes should be substantially closer to equality (i.e. the diagonal) after taxes and transfers than before. In fact, for the middle and lower strata the plot is slightly closer to the diagonal. However, the incomes of the wealthiest 6% seem to be unaffected by the government's alleged redistributive role. So much for the "Robin Hood" image of the welfare state!

The limited redistributive achievements of the welfare state can be understood once it is accepted that low income families are less likely to use many government services. In the case of transportation, for example, the poor are less likely to own a vehicle, but, if so, are less likely to travel. Although roads are constructed and maintained to serve travel demand irrespective of social class, the lower strata are probably served less because their demand is less. Expenditures on transportation become even more regressive as a result of expenditures on air travel, since air travellers are less likely to belong to the lower strata.

A similar situation applies to education. The NDP has always favoured low university tuitions because of a conviction that there

Figure 12-4. Distribution of Income* to family units before and after
governmental taxes and transfer, Canada, 1969.

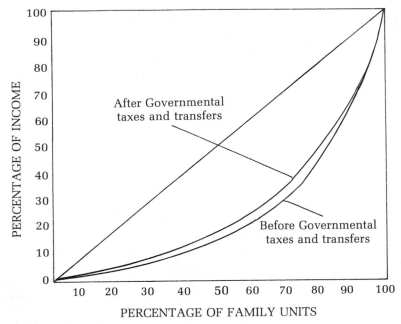

PERCENTAGE OF FAMILY UNITS

*Income includes money and non-money income.

Source: Allan M. Maslove, The Pattern of Taxation in Canada (Ottawa: Information
Canada, 1974), 20-21, 34-35, 132-35. Reprinted by permission of Information Canada.

should not be financial barriers to education. However, expenditures
on university and other post-secondary programs are regressive since
the children of lower income families are less likely to enroll. A cost-
benefit study of post-secondary education in Ontario showed that costs
and benefits were about equal for those earning less than $3000, but
that the effect was regressive for all other families (see Table 12-2).

Even those social programs which are allegedly the keystone of the
welfare state are not necessarily redistributive. The CCF-NDP and
left-wing members of the Liberal party have rushed to claim credit for
the adoption of family allowances, unemployment insurance, and government pension plans. The family allowances, however, were regressive for most of their existence.[30] Until 1974, they were regressive
because they were nontaxable. Family allowances were of greater value
to high earners than low simply because high earners were exempt
from higher rates of taxation. Unemployment insurance is not especially progressive. To the extent that it is financed by premiums, un-

employment insurance may be neutral. In recent years, high unemployment rates have obliged the federal government to draw upon general revenue with the result that the plan might be slightly progressive for middle and high income people. However, unemployment insurance has regressive aspects as well. Employees in well-paid occupations, such as in the construction industry, tend to have high rates of unemployment and therefore receive greater benefits. Unemployment "rip-off"'s among middle-class students and housewives have been indicated.[31] Finally, because unemployment premiums are tax deductible, the premiums are actually more costly for low income earners than for high. Government pension plans include a similar source of regressivity. Furthermore, these pensions are of greater assistance to high income earners because they live longer.

Table 12-2

Redistributive Effects, All Post-Secondary Institutions
(Ontario, 1968–1969)

	Under $3000	$3000-4999	$5000-6999	$7000-9999	$10,000 and over
Cost	8.86	16.58	23.65	22.66	28.25
Benefit	8.98	12.24	19.94	24.93	33.91
Net Gain	+.12	−4.34	−3.71	+2.27	+5.66

Source: *Cost and Benefit Study of Post-Secondary Education in Ontario, School Year 1968–69: A Study Prepared for the Commission on Post-Secondary Education in Ontario* (Toronto: Queen's Printer, 1972), 82, 86.

Government-paid medical care constitutes another program which is not necessarily progressive. Studies in Manitoba, Saskatchewan, and Ontario suggest that the lower strata have lesser rates of usage, while the contrary seems to be true in Montreal.[32] Montreal's pattern may stem from its high population of low status immigrants, who by their active nature may be more inclined to use government facilities. Montreal also has a high concentration of physicians. In the absence of much knowledge about the effects of medicare, an intelligent guess might be that health services are progressive when the supply of services is sufficiently great. As for physicians, the introduction of socialized medicine has caused a vast increase in their personal income. The incomes of physicians in Saskatchewan under the CCF-NDP increased substantially.

The purpose of the preceding discussion was not to demonstrate that the programs of the welfare state were regressive. Some services are indeed redistributive. Social welfare disbursements and old age supplements are examples of effective redistributive programs. Our purpose was merely to show that neither the welfare state as a whole nor all of its individual programs were extraordinarily progressive. Consequently, a party's apparent attitude towards the welfare state is not a good indicator of the party's likely effects on the distribution of income.

A second assumption underlying the faith of those who believe that parties have a predictable impact on the distribution of income is *that politicans understand the distributive effects of their policies.* If politicians can understand the effects of their policies, they might be able to consciously affect the distribution of incomes. However, it is not likely that either politicians or others understand fully the implications of most policies. For example, how likely is it that Saskatechwan doctors would have demonstrated in the streets against medicare if they had known that their incomes would rise by 28% or more?[33]

A good example of the failure of politicians to understand the distributive effects of their policy is the NDP attitude towards the Women's Liberation Platform. Of all the parties, the NDP is probably the most sympathetic. Some of the party's affinity for the women's movement comes from its socialist opposition to a discriminatory practice by which women receive less pay for the same work men perform. It is, however, a paradox that any government policy which can guarantee to women equal pay for equal work is actually regressive. A basic reason is that well trained women tend to be paired with better trained, high status mates. If women in the workforce are treated fairly, two processes are likely to occur. A relative depression will occur in the incomes of males with lesser training and lower status, while the gap between the incomes of well and poorly trained women will increase. The net result will be greater inequality of income among families. The inequality will be particularly large because the women who presently face the greatest discrimination and have the most to gain are in the high status "managerial" and "technical" occupations.

Evidence that women in the high status occupations are subject to the greater discrimination comes from a study by Slyvia Ostry. After taking into consideration the lesser education, ages, and working times of women, Ostry found that those in low status categories such as "labourers," "craftsmen," and "sales" received approximately the same rewards as men. However, women in the "managerial" and "technical" categories faced income deficiencies of 25–35%.[34]

It is possible and in our view desirable to introduce the practice of equal pay for equal work without making family incomes more unequal. The solution is simple enough — increase the rates of income taxation for two earner families with high combined incomes. Joint returns may be an answer. The NDP has advocated the more regressive solution, of equal pay without an accompanying change in income tax laws. This paradox can be explained most simply this way: the New Democrats have not understood fully the implications of their policy.[35]

In addition, the NDP has supported the government's tax amendment to exempt childcare expenses incurred so that women can work. The net effect of this policy is regressive since deductions discriminate in favour of those who earn higher incomes.[36] Instead of being based on regressive deductions, a genuinely left-wing policy would consist of tax credits which are larger for families with low incomes.

A third assumption underpinning the belief that parties consciously affect the redistribution of wealth is that *politicians lack non-distributive goals which conflict with their attitudes towards the goal of equality of income.* In Canada, few right-wing politicians openly admit that they advocate an unequal pattern of income. Therefore, the task remains to assess whether left-wing politicians have goals which are incompatible with redistribution.

In fact, the first goal of all politicians — to secure election — places a hindrance in the path of left-wing politicians seeking greater equality of wealth. All parties, left or right, require leaders with higher education and social standing in order to maximize their electoral support. As a result, the leaders of all Canadian parties share a similar class background. Table 12-3 shows the Blishen socio-economic status (SES) scores for the recent NDP, Social Credit, Liberal, and PC cabinets in the western provinces. The federal party elites are not compared because the SES of Conservative and NDP elites would be artificially low, if only because the SES of any party is low when the party is remote from power. When this phenomenon is taken into consideration, the similarity among the western cabinets becomes all the more striking. The Social Credit governments of Bennett and Manning in British Columbia and Alberta were the longest and therefore would be expected to manifest the highest SES scores. The Liberal government of Thatcher and the NDP governments of Barrett, Schreyer, and Blakeney tended to be of shorter duration.

Table 12-3

Blishen Scores for the Provincial Cabinets
of the Western Provinces[37]

	NDP	SC	PC	L.
Highest 60% of Blishen's Occupations	68%	75%	73%	66%
Lowest 40% of Blishen's Occupations	32%	25%	27%	34%

Note: The Blishen scale is a measure of socio-economic status. See Bernard R. Blishen et al, *Canadian Society*, 3rd edition (Toronto: Macmillan, 1971), 495–507.

The NDP attitude towards war veterans also illustrates the conflict between a non-redistributive goal and the goal of greater equality of income. Led by Stanley Knowles, its House leader, the party believes that veterans continue to deserve special considerations such as subsidized farm mortgages. Knowles has pointed to the plight of elderly veterans who may need land on which to retire. In fact, it would be the better-off veterans who would reap the greatest benefits from subsidized ownership.

A fourth assumption is that *left-wing politicians are willing to incur, or oblige their constituents to incur, the costs of redistribution.* At a minimum, the redistribution of wealth could require greater initiative, imagination, and capacity on the part of the government bureaucracy. At a maximum, the redistribution of income might involve social disturbance, higher overall costs, and a decline in the quality of the public's well-being.

The introduction of socialized medicine illustrates some of the impediments to economic equality. The incomes of physicians rose greatly in all provinces. All governments apparently felt powerless to limit doctors' incomes for electoral and economic reasons. They were apprehensive of the electoral wrath of the medicine men, who continued to possess as much mass psychological influence in industrialized North America as in pre-industrial Africa. As for economic considerations, a ceiling on doctors' salaries would risk an outflow of physicians, who had been trained at provincial expense. These considerations affected the NDP in Saskatchewan as much as they did the other parties in other provinces.

None of Canada's provinces has seriously faced the question of controlling doctors' ability to extract income from the public treasury. To do so could provoke the ire of doctors and irritate the sensibilities of civil servants who might feel threatened by administrative change. Furthermore, serious administrative supervision of physicians' accounts would require a substantial increase in government personnel and resources. As one provincial Health official confided to the authors, "There is no way we can verify the truthfulness of practitioners' accounts. We hardly have enough administrative capacity simply to pay them."

In England, a Labour Member of Parliament estimates that inner London has a half a million more patients than people: "These are people who simply do not exist — an army of ghosts. At the moment these phantoms are probably costing the health service £500,000 (about $1,300,000) in inner London alone."[38] In Canada, some provincial governments deliberately cast a blind eye to the billing practices of their doctors. Unethical practices are permitted and sometimes encouraged so that the incomes of doctors can rise without a corresponding change in the stated fee structure and therefore without causing offence to segments of the press and public. So long as free migration between provinces is permitted, no single provincial government can readily reduce the salaries of doctors. So long as easy emigration to the United States continues, any federal government would be limited in its ability to restrain the incomes of any profession.

Conclusion

We argued that there were few, if any, continuous differences in the distributive policies of the parties. The chapter began with a review of the large-scale quantitative analyses of Falcone, Poel, and Campbell. Their studies of provincial and federal output in Canada showed no inherent partisan differences. Because the Canadian findings might have been fortuitous, we turned to the foreign literature to see whether the Canadian null findings were at variance with discoveries elsewhere. In fact, the cross-national and intra-national research on other countries was compatible with the conclusion that parties lacked historically distinguishable impacts on the distribution of income.

We acknowledged the validity of one powerful criticism of previous policy research, that the categories being examined were too large to identify distributive effects. For example, we agreed that right-wing and left-wing governments could spend the same amounts on health care, but the health programs of the latter might serve the lower strata better.

We therefore turned to a detailed study of revenue under different provincial governments in the West. Our data on provincial revenue from the sales and income taxes showed no inherent party patterns. Our analysis concerned only the western provinces in order to exclude the effect of regional characteristics. Among all the provinces, however, it is curious that the first party to rely on a revenue from income tax was the *union nationale* of Quebec. The nationalist government of Maurice Duplessis had simply no alternative source of additional revenue. In a similarly curious way, the parties with the least regressive patterns of revenue were the "free enterprise" Socreds and Progressive Conservatives of Alberta. Apparently, Alberta possesses enough wealth not to require the additional revenue of a sales tax.

In order to disprove the thesis of partisan differences in government expenditures, we examined four assumptions about political behaviour that underpin its logic. We strove to invalidate these assumptions by examining individual government programs. Generally, we argued that partisan attitudes towards the welfare state were poor indicators of a party's redistributive behaviour because the welfare state did not redistribute greatly. Specifically, we showed that family allowances and some other key programs of the welfare state had regressive aspects.

We freely recognize that our analysis has many limitations. It is conceivable that mere statistical analysis overlooks important phenomena. Perhaps left-wing governments appoint left-wing judges who side with labour in contract disputes. The effects on the distribution of income could be real, if not easily measured. Furthermore, how does one measure the socialization effects of left-wing parties? Perhaps the influence of the left is first and foremost on social attitudes rather than directly on government output.

We are not totally certain about the real relationship between partisanship and redistributive policy. By presenting a forceful argument in favour of a null thesis, we hoped to rekindle debate rather than end it. However, so long as people claim that there are important redistributive differences among the parties, it is only fair to insist that they present some evidence.

Notes

1. See Chapter 1, above, passim.

2. Anthony Downs, *An Economic Theory of Democracy* (New York: Harper and Row, 1957).

3. J. R. Mallory, "The Structure of Canadian Politics," in Hugh Thorburn (ed.), *Party Politics in Canada* (Toronto: Prentice-Hall, 1967); R. MacGregor

Dawson, *Democratic Government in Canada* (Toronto: University of Toronto Press, 1969), 123; Charles Taylor, *The Pattern of Politics* (Toronto: McClelland and Stewart, 1970), 14; John Porter, *The Vertical Mosaic* (Toronto: University of Toronto Press, 1969), 366–416. See also Paul Fox, "Politics and Parties in Canada," in Fox (ed.), *Politics: Canada*, 3rd ed. (Toronto: McGraw-Hill, 1970), 223–26.

4. Peter C. Newman, "The Lack of Conservative-Liberal Differences in Canadian Politics" in Gordon Hawkins (ed.), *Order and Good Government* (Toronto: University of Toronto Press, 1965).

5. "Recent Changes in Canadian Parties" in Thorburn, *Party Politics*.

6. Alford assumes that the Liberals are more redistributive than the Conservatives, while Smith argues the converse. See Robert Alford, *Party and Society: The Anglo-American Democracies* (Chicago: Rand McNally, 1963), and Denis Smith, "Prairie Revolt, Federalism, and the Party System" in Thorburn, *Party Politics*.

7. In the passages that follow, "distributive" policies are those which involve transfer of wealth to and/or from any social group or stratum. "Redistributive" policies transfer wealth to the lower strata.

8. For a pioneering quantitative study of provincial party beliefs, see Koula Mellos, "Quantitative Comparison of Party Ideology," *Canadian Journal of Political Science* (December 1970), 540–58. For a non-quantitative study of party ideologies, see W. Christian and C. Campbell, *Political Parties and Ideologies in Canada* (Toronto: McGraw-Hill Ryerson, 1974).

9. See, for example, William Christian and Colin Campbell, *Political Parties and Ideologies in Canada* (Toronto: McGraw-Hill Ryerson, 1974) and Thomas L. Burton, *Natural Resource Policy in Canada* (Toronto: McClelland and Stewart, 1972), especially 113–33. In his analysis of the Liberal party, Burton does distinguish between "its promises and its performance" (p. 124), but he does not apply the same standard of measure to his analysis of Conservative and NDP policies.

10. David J. Falcone, "Legislative Change and Output Change: A Time-Series Analysis of the Canadian System," (Doctoral Dissertation, Duke University, 1974); David J. Falcone and Michael S. Whittington, "Output Change in Canada: A Preliminary Attempt to Open the 'Black Box'," a paper presented to the Annual Meetings of the Canadian Political Science Association (June 1972); David Falcone and William Mishler, "Canadian Provincial Legislatures and System Outputs: A Diachronic Analysis of the Determinants of Health Policy", a paper presented at the annual convention of the (U.S.) Southern Political Science Association (November 1974); Dale H. Poel, "Canadian Provincial and American State Policy: A Qualitative Explication of an Empirical Difference," a paper presented at the Annual Meetings of the Canadian Political Science Association (June 1972); and David B. Campbell, "Ideology and Public Policy: A Time-Series, Quasi-Experimental Analysis of the Saskatchewan Case," (Honours B.A. thesis, Carleton University, 1974). For a review of the economics literature involving the quantitative analysis of government expenditures in Canada, see Richard M. Bird, *The Growth of Government Spending in Canada* (Toronto: Canadian Tax Foundation, 1970), Chapters 2 and 3.

11. It is possible for expenditures to be influenced by interprovincial agreements. For example, it is difficult for education systems to vary greatly

because of agreements between provinces about standards for transfer students. See D. J. McCready "Federal Education Grants, 1945–1967: Economic Development in New Brunswick" (Ph.D. thesis, University of Alberta, 1973).

12. "Legislative Change and Output Change."

13. Falcone and Mishler, "Canadian Provincial Legislatures."

14. "Canadian Provincial and American State Policy."

15. Among political variables, Poel found that ministerial salaries, an indicator of "professionalism," was a modest predictor of provincial expenditures.

16. Campbell, "The Saskatchewan Case". Professor Michael Whittington was the supervisor of this Carleton thesis, but he credits Professor Falcone with much of the direction. Two additional studies are Marsha A. Chandler and William M. Chandler, "Parliamentary Politics and Public Policy in the Canadian Provinces," a paper presented at the meetings of the U.S. Mid-West Political Science Association (April 1974) and David Siegal, "Determinants of Provincial Budgets — Fiscal Year Ended March 31, 1973," a term paper submitted to Professor David Falcone, Carleton University (April 1974). The former paper claims to show that left-wing governments spend slightly more on social welfare, while the latter paper claims to show that the governments of the major parties spend more on education than governments of the minor parties. Otherwise, no major relationships between party in power and type of expenditure are alleged to exist. These studies are less relevant to our task than the ones discussed in the text because no attempt is made to identify the net effects of party independent of economic development, regional culture, and other confounding variables. The analysis of Chandler and Chandler is especially confounded by their failure to control for the effects of historical period (eg. recent governments spend more on welfare than earlier governments).

17. For a discussion of Wagner's thought, see Alan T. Peacock and Jack Wiseman, *The Growth of Public Expenditures in the United Kingdom* (Princeton: Princeton University Press, 1961), 16–19; and Richard M. Bird, *The Growth of Government Spending in Canada* (Toronto: Canadian Tax Foundation, 1970), 69–88.

18. "Legislative Change."

19. Soloman Fabricant, *The Trend of Government Activity in the United States Since 1900* (New York: National Bureau of Economic Research, Inc., 1952), 123–31.

20. Nicholas Michas, "Variations in the Level of Provincial-Municipal Expenditures in Canada: An Econometric Analysis" (Doctoral dissertation, University of Illinois, 1967).

21. Phillips Cutright, "Political Structure, Economic Development, and National Social Security Programs," *American Journal of Sociology*, 70 (March 1965), 540–43.

22. R. I. Hofferbert, "The Relation Between Public Policy and Some Structural and Environmental Variables in the American States," *American Political Science Review*, 60 (1966), 73–82; Ira Sharkansky and Richard Hofferbert, "Dimensions of State Politics, Economics, and Public Policy," ibid., 62 (September 1969), 867–79; Richard E. Dawson, "Social Development, Party Competition, and Policy" in W. N. Chambers and W. D. Burham, (ed.), *The American Party Systems* (Toronto: Oxford University Press, 1969), 203–37.

23. Phillips Cutright found a statistical association between social security

programs and a "political representativeness index." However, his index was really another measure of competitiveness. For example, a country received 2 points if its largest party had less than 70% of the seats in the lower chamber while a country received 1 point if the largest party possessed more than 70% of the seats and its nearest rival, less than 2% of the seats. See Cutright, "Political Structure, Economic Development, and National Social Security Programs."

24. See Elliott R. Morss, J. E. Friedland, and S. H. Hymans, "Fluctuations in State Expenditures: An Econometric Analysis," *Southern Economic Journal*, 33 (April 1967), 496–517, and Thomas R. Dye, "Income Inequality and American State Politics," *American Political Science Review*, 63 (March 1969), 157–62. Elliott et al. suggest that Republicanism might be associated with low redistributive expenditures, but their data is ambiguous. Dye suggests that support for the Democratic Party is associated with high income inequality.

25. Frederic L. Pryor, *Public Expenditures in Communist and Capitalist Nations* (London: George Allen and Urwin, 1968), 190–95.

26. Ibid., 285.

27. The indices of association for fathers and sons among professionals, proprietors and managers are 9.559 (Denmark), 8.122 (Sweden) and 3.295 (United States). The comparable scores for Japan, France, and French Quebec are 3.277, 5.715, and 6.275. See S. M. Miller, "Comparative Social Mobility", *Current Sociology*, 9:1 (1960), 54.

28. We acknowledge our gratitude to Mrs. C. Higginson, Carleton Political Science Department, for preparing these figures.

29. See Allan Kornberg, *Canadian Legislative Behaviour* (Toronto: Holt, Rinehart and Winston, 1967), 124ff.

30. George Drew's opposition to family allowances illustrates the non-ideological nature of some attitudes towards redistributive measures. Former premier of Ontario and leader of the federal Conservatives, Drew expressed his view in the form of a question put to Harry Nixon, the last Liberal premier of the province: "Why should Ontario pay for Quebec's f—ing?" Larry Zolf, "The New Shape of Canadian Politics, or How to Make the Lynch Mob Work for You," *Saturday Night* (December 1975), 18.

31. This has been suggested at various times by Max Saltsman, and by Reuben Baetz of the Canadian Council on Social Development. However, in the absence of empirical verification, it is difficult to know how pervasive the "rip-offs" are.

32. P. Enterline, "Distribution of Medical Services Before and After 'Free' Medical Care," *New England Journal of Medicine*, 289 (Nov. 1973), 1174; G. Beck, "Economic Class and Access to Health Services," *International Journal of Health Services* (Winter 1972); W. D. Eckstrand, "Patterns of Medical and Hospital Care in Manitoba 1970," White Paper on Health Policy, Appendix to vol. II (November 1972).

33. Department of National Revenue, *Taxation Statistics* (Ottawa: Queen's Printer, various years).

34. Ostry, *The Female Worker in Canada* (Ottawa: Dominion Bureau of Statistics, 1966), 44.

35. In October 1974, Winn asked David Lewis, then leader of the New Democratic party, if he could find fault with the preceding analysis and if he

had heard the argument before. Mr. Lewis replied in the negative to both questions.

36. While daycare expenditures may not distribute income in a left-wing direction, the daycare environment appears to socialize shildren to non-left-wing values. The socialist utopia usually emphasizes the values of cooperation (witness the *Cooperative* Commonwealth Federation), the peaceful resolution of conflict (J. S. Woodsworth's pacifism), and the avoidance of "rugged individualism." Ironically, it seems that early daycare experiences socialize children to be less cooperative, more aggressive, and less tolerant of frustration than children reared in the home. See J. Conrad Schwartz et al, "Infant Day Care: Behavioral Effects at Preschool Age," *Developmental Psychology*, X:1 (1974), 502–6.

37. Computed in April 1974, the scores were based on the occupations of the contemporary NDP, Conservative, NDP, and NDP governments in British Columbia, Alberta, Saskatchewan, and Manitoba and on the occupations of the respective preceding Social Credit, Social Credit, Liberal, and Conservative cabinets. From a term paper authored by Bruce Comens (Wilfrid Laurier University, Spring 1974).

38. Marcus Lipton MP quoted in *Kitchener-Waterloo Record* (May 25, 1974), 31.

CHAPTER 13
TRADE AND RESOURCE POLICIES
John Weir

Introduction

No man in Canada has been more inconsistent than the man who has
faithfully followed either party for a generation.[1]

It is common to construct a stereotype of each political party in Canada
and to illustrate the consistency with which the party has adhered to its
announced political ideologies. According to the portrait usually presented, the Conservative party in Canada has stood for high tariffs and a
strong link with the United Kingdom, usually referred to as the "British
connection". The Liberals are portrayed as being in favour of free trade
and economic integration with the United States, often called "continentalism". The CCF-NDP is pictured as socialist and, in recent years,
anti-American. Like most stereotypes, these positions do not stand up
well under closer scrutiny. If we examine the various economic
policies, particularly the trade and resource policies of the parties in
Canada, it becomes apparent that at any particular time the parties'
economic programs have been quite similar to one another and often
quite unlike the policies which each has advocated in the past. Despite
political rhetoric, all parties have been pragmatic in their responses to
Canada's economic needs and resource development.

This paper concentrates on what was done when parties were in
power; it pays only scant attention to what was said in opposition or
during election campaigns. Since the CCF-NDP and Social Credit parties have never held power at the federal level, we say little about their
attitudes towards the tariff, a matter of exclusively federal jurisdiction.
When other issues, such as resource policies, are dealt with, the CCF-
NDP and Social Credit record in the relevant provinces is discussed.
There is probably another side to each of the stories told here, but we
shall leave such presentations to those who prefer to examine political
beliefs rather than the legacies of governments. Our theme throughout
is that events and circumstances, more than party ideologies, have
molded policy and we have collected evidence to support this thesis.

Once Sir John A. Macdonald's National Policy was in place there
was no turning back. The CPR had been built and no one was about to
tear it up. Much of Canadian industry was established under the umbrella of a tariff and no major party in or out of power was going to
attempt to dismantle it. The West was settled: grain and other agricultural products had to be moved to market, regardless of the party col-
ours flying over Ottawa. Most of the industrial policies implemented
by one party have at one time or another been amended by the other
and, when one abstracts from the requirements of the times, little in

any of these policies can be branded as uniquely Liberal, Conservative, CCF-NDP, or Social Credit.

Each of Canada's major industries has had particular difficulties to overcome. In most cases a major determinant of Canada's economic policy with respect to a particular industry has been the policy prevailing in the United States. At any particular time these industries have reached different stages of development, so that the policies appropriate for one were not necessarily appropriate for others. Some were based on non-renewable resources; others, like manufacturing, had no such constraint.

The paper is divided into three parts. The first section traces the tariff policies of the federal governments since Confederation. The second section deals with resource exports and discusses newsprint, nickel, water, natural gas and petroleum. The third section examines contemporary attitudes towards government intervention in the resource sector, and looks at recent government behaviour at the federal and provincial levels. This third section places particular emphasis on the record of the NDP governments in three provinces. Finally, the conclusion draws the findings together, and reiterates the theme. Since tariffs are exclusively a federal matter, the CCF-NDP and Social Credit parties are not discussed in relation to this topic.

The Tariff

"The National Policy"

While Sir John A. Macdonald is best remembered as the architect of Canada's National Policy, it is not often emphasized that before its adoption Macdonald was an advocate of reciprocity with the United States. When the Washington Treaty was signed in 1871 between the United States and Great Britain, Macdonald attended to argue for a restoration of the reciprocal trade arrangements which had existed between Canada and the United States in the period 1854–1866. Because of the constitutional problem, Canada was unable to sign treaties on its own behalf. Since the British, for reasons of their own, did not back Macdonald in his battle against northern U.S. manufacturing interests, they were at least partially responsible for his failure to increase North-South reciprocal trade. Canada got very little of what it wanted during those particular negotiations; Macdonald was obliged to turn to protectionism.[2]

For Macdonald and perhaps for others, a policy of tariff protection was a second best solution to Canada's trade problem. In fact, considerable evidence shows that Macdonald endorsed tariffs so that they could be used later as a bargaining device to reinstate freer trade. When he was leader of the Opposition in 1878, Macdonald introduced a motion to Parliament advocating higher tariffs which he said could later be negotiated away.[3] A year later he tidied up some of his ideas and revealed what has become known as the "National Policy." According to the National Policy, Canada's economic development was to proceed on the tripod of high tariffs, a transcontinental railway system, and settlement of the West. Not everything in the National Policy was new.

For the most part it endorsed practices already in position. Prior to Macdonald's articulation of the National Policy, a transcontinental railway had been promised to British Columbia, there were people living on the prairies, and Canada had a tariff system, albeit primarily for revenue as opposed to protection. On several occasions after the adoption of the National Policy, the Conservatives made formal overtures for freer trade with the United States. They were rebuffed. It is also significant that, even though there had been periodic changes in the government until 1898, the Canadian Tariff Act contained in various forms an open invitation for freer trade negotiations with the United States.[4]

Laurier's Conversion

Despite an initial reluctance, the Liberal party gradually accepted Macdonald's National Policy in its entirety. At their party convention in 1893 — the first of its kind in Canada — the Liberals endorsed a program of fairly broad reciprocity with the United States.[5] At the time, the Conservatives advocated a more restricted type of reciprocity. Within a couple of years the Liberals changed their position from unrestricted to restricted reciprocity. Laurier was elected in 1896 on a low tariff program, but in fact did little to change the level of the tariff. He realized quickly that unilateral tariff reductions were not in Canada's interest and that reciprocal arrangements with the United States were not possible at that particular time. In 1897, the Liberal government increased duties on many products, introduced tariff preferences for the United Kingdom, and withdrew Canada's standing invitation for reciprocity discussions. While these measures retaliated against the United States Dingley tariff of 1897,[6] it is significant that the first post-Confederation attempt to use the tariff to divert trade towards Britain was made by the so-called Continentalists, not by the party of the British connection.

Laurier became convinced that trade negotiations with the United States were not likely to bear much fruit. After unsuccessful visits to that country's capital, he is quoted as having said, "There will be no more pilgrimages to Washington, we are turning our hopes to the old Mother Land."[7] At the Imperial Conference in 1906 Laurier remarked in the same vein:

> There was a time when we wanted reciprocity with the United States, but our efforts and our offers were put aside. We have said goodbye to that trade and we now put all our hopes upon British trade.[8]

However, Laurier was not prepared to go all the way. In 1907, when a British delegation offered Canada imperial free trade, Laurier declined the offer on the grounds that Canada could not afford to lose the revenue generated by the existing tariffs.[9] Ironically, half a century later, Conservative Prime Minister John Diefenbaker found himself in a similar situation. An anglophile in rhetoric, he advocated trade diversion from the United States to the United Kingdom. Yet, when the British proposed free trade as a method of accomplishing such a switch, Diefenbaker, like Laurier, turned it down.

To Laurier's Liberals, the British preference was at least in part an attempt to increase traffic on the nation's railway system. Trains moved from West to East loaded with agricultural products destined for European markets, but the East-West traffic had been disappointing. The British preference was an attempt to increase this traffic by encouraging the importation of products from Great Britain rather than the United States.[10] In his analysis of the Canadian tariff, during the Laurier years, John McDiarmid made the following observations: "British preferences and the intermediate tariff notwithstanding, Canadian commercial policy during this period of economic expansion was fundamentally nationalistic."[11]

Laurier's attitude towards the railways also evidences his endorsement of the National Policy. In the railway debates of 1903, he strongly advocated a second transcontinental railway and disagreed with the Conservatives only on the matter of who should own it and how it should be financed. The following quotation suggests the degree to which Laurier was committed to the East-West as opposed to North-South Trade:

> Already they are at work opening the long dormant soil; already they are at work sowing, harvesting and reaping . . . We consider that it is the duty of all those who sit within these walls by the will of the people, to provide immediate means whereby the products of those new settlers may find an exit to the ocean at the least possible cost, and whereby, likewise, a market may be found in this new region for those who toil in the forests, in the fields, in the mines, in the shops of the older provinces. Such is our duty; it is immediate and imperative . . . Heaven grant that it be not already too late; heaven grant that whilst we tarry and dispute, the trade of Canada is not deviated to other channels, and that an ever vigilant competitor does not take to himself trade that properly belongs to those people who acknowledge Canada as their native or adopted land.[12]

The Reciprocity Election

Rather than for his support of the National Policy, Laurier is mostly remembered for his attempt in 1910-11 to restore reciprocity. There is no denying that for the purposes of the election campaign of 1911 the parties adopted opposing attitudes on this issue. It is difficult to say exactly how the Conservatives would have reacted had they been in power when President Taft, fearing a trade war with Canada, made overtures for freer trade. As an Opposition party, the Conservatives launched an all-out attack on Laurier's attempt to restore reciprocity. Opposition to the reciprocity, however, was not confined to Conservative ranks: eighteen prominent Liberals, including Clifford Sifton, a former Liberal cabinet minister, bolted the party and gave their support to the Conservatives. Fortunately for those who opposed reciprocity, prominent government people in the United States made statements to the effect that they felt reciprocity would hasten the day when the two countries would be united politically. Another factor in Laurier's defeat on the issue was his insistence that any agreement should be implemented by legislation in both countries, as opposed to being enacted by a treaty. The issue was therefore before the people for an unusually long period of time and became quite emotional. It is not clear why Laurier insisted on this scenario, but it is probable that, recalling the fate of Macdonald in earlier reciprocity negotiations, he chose the legislative approach to circumvent the requirement of having Great Britain as a signatory of any agreement which might have been implemented via a treaty.

An analysis of the results of the negotiations with the United States suggests that the agreement reached would have fitted the prevailing policies in either party. It was by no means an agreement for free trade, since it included natural products and only a selected number of manufactured items.[13] However, the content of the agreement had very little to do with the campaign and Laurier has gone down as the Father of Continentalism.

In their study of party values, Christian and Campbell argue that the Liberals have historically endorsed continentalist policies:

> The goal of greater economic integration with the United States has . . . been pursued by Laurier in the reciprocity campaigns of 1891 and 1911, by King in the 1938 trade agreement with the U.S., by St. Laurent and Howe in the resource export boom of the 1950s, by Pearson in the Automobile Pact of 1965 and by the Trudeau government in its original inclination to continental sharing of energy resources. The logical end of such policies . . . has been obscured to, or obscured by, many Liberal politicians.[14]

However, by his actions and some of his statements, Laurier was committed to the National Policy, albeit partly of necessity. His response to Taft's overtures indicates that he saw certain advantages in increasing North-South trade in particular kinds of goods — exactly what both parties had tried to do for years. As will be demonstrated, the other examples cited by Christian and Campbell to illustrate how the parties have differed in their behaviour simply do not support their case.

With the exception of World War I, when the tariffs were raised for revenue purposes, from the time Macdonald instituted the National Policy until 1930, tariff levels in Canada remained remarkably constant. Each party tinkered with the tariffs on particular items, but their general level remained about the same. During the 1920s, the Liberals did lower slightly the tariff in such sectors as agricultural machinery, but at the same time increased the significance of the British preference.[15] It is easy to marshal any number of quotations to suggest that after 1911 parties agreed that the tariff should be reasonable or moderate. One from Thomas White, the Conservative minister of finance in 1914, will suffice:

> The evils of a high protective tariff are too well known to make it necessary that I should discuss them here. The tariff of Canada has not been a high tariff but one affording a moderate degree of protection only.[16]

The Great Depression

A major departure from the traditional practices of both parties took place in the 1930s in response to declining world trade. While it is usually assumed that R. B. Bennett's Conservative budget of September 1930 was the departure point, C. A. Dunning's Liberal budget of a few months earlier started the change in direction. The protectionist policies of both parties during the 1930s were inconsistent with their positions of the past, but quite in keeping with the tenor of the times. Most countries, particularly the United States through the Hawley-Smoot tariff of 1930, were moving to higher tariffs in an attempt to insulate themselves from the depression. In May 1930, the Liberals adopted a retaliatory policy towards the United States in an act which included measures to implement countervailing duties against the United States and extended the British preference.[17] Again, the Liberals used the tariff in an attempt to divert trade from the United States and towards Britain.

During the federal election campaign of 1930, R. B. Bennett, the Conservative leader, advocated higher tariffs. It was during this campaign that he made his reference to using the tariff as a method of blasting a way into world markets.[18] After defeating the Liberals, the Conservatives imposed tariffs unlike anything Canada had previously experienced, but not dramatically out of line with those being imposed at the time by other countries. Bennett condemned the Liberals because they had not insisted that Britain be required to reciprocate by giving concessions to Canada in return for the preferred position she was granted. Shortly after he implemented his tariff legislation, Bennett went to England and proposed what might be viewed as an English-speaking Zollverein: Canada and other parts of the British Empire would increase their tariffs against the rest of the world and thereby encourage trade amongst themselves. The British were not too receptive to this notion and responded with a typically English "humbug".[19]

In 1932, tariffs between the United Kingdom and Canada were nevertheless reduced under the Ottawa agreement. Two years later, Bennett requested that negotiations be initiated in keeping with the U.S. Trade Agreements Act of that year, which gave the President power to lower tariffs under certain conditions. By 1935 when his government was defeated by the Liberals, Bennett had nearly completed negotiations for a trade agreement with the United States. The agreement, which was signed one month after the Liberals took office, followed the lines negotiated by Bennett. Under this agreement and one which followed it in 1938, duties were substantially reduced by both countries. While the granting of lower tariffs to the United States naturally extended the work Bennett had begun in 1934, the treaty granted to the United States for the first time the status of a Most Favoured Nation, a significant implication. Instead of being assigned the higher general rates of tariff, the United States benefited from the lower category applied to treaty countries. This, however, was still an inferior position compared to the rates granted to Great Britain.[20]

Since it was the Liberals who established the discrimination against the United States when they instituted the British preference in 1897, since it was they who extended the discrimination in 1923 and 1930, and since Bennett had started trade negotiations with the United States in 1934, it certainly cannot be argued that the signing of agreements in 1935 and 1938 was merely another contrived Liberal step down the logical road to continentalism.

In the early 1930s the Conservatives defended their policy of high tariffs by pointing to the increase in the number of U.S. subsidiaries operating in this country as a consequence of their higher tariffs. The Conservatives later criticized the lower Liberal tariffs of the 1935 and 1938 agreements because they resulted in a withdrawal of branch plants. The Conservatives cited the cessation of operations by Studebaker and a scaling down of activities by Hudson-Essex to illustrate their case.[21] Since firms tend to set up factories to manufacture their products in markets to which tariffs prevent them from exporting goods, the Conservatives were correct in linking changes in foreign investment to tariff policies. However, they did not seem to appreciate that a couple of decades later such investment would be viewed by many as the main vehicle of continental economic integration. This is not to imply that the Liberals were any more astute on the issue, for their policies of British Preference had invited U.S. firms to come to Canada to serve the British market. When the foreign investment issue finally became a political problem in the 1960s, the party policies were as similar as they had been on the tariff.

One Last Fillip

After the 1930s, the tariff ceased to be a political issue in Canada and its administration was handed to a tariff board.[22] The parties seemed to accept the existing level of protection. As Eric Kierans has put it, "During election campaigns, the Liberals insist that tariffs cannot be raised, and the Conservatives insist that they cannot be lowered."[23] However, one event in 1957 deserves further comment.

In that year, Prime Minister Diefenbaker announced that he intended to divert 15 per cent of Canada's imports to the United Kingdom. Under the rules of the General Agreement on Tariffs and Trade, to which both Canada and Britain subscribed, discriminatory tariffs were specifically forbidden but free trade areas were permitted. Being receptive to the notion of diversion, yet wishing to abide by the principles of GATT, the British proposed that tariffs between the two countries be reduced gradually to zero so that a free trade area would be created. According to Peter Newman, "Diefenbaker was so vehement in condemning the idea that he insisted that the final communique of the meeting not even mention his reaction. . ." Newman goes on to point out:

> Ironically enough, the only legislative action that the Diefenbaker government took vis-a-vis Britain was to increase Canadian tariffs on British woolens and rubber footwear, and to alter upward the valuation method on British cars.[24]

Resource Exports: Some Case Studies

This section deals with the country's policies towards exports and concentrates mainly on the practices followed by the parties with respect to natural resources. As will become clear, resource policies in Canada have been more clearly delineated by provincial boundaries than by party lines. The British North America Act assigns jurisdiction over natural resources to the provinces, but gives authority on matters of interprovincial and international trade to the federal government. The Act also divides taxing powers between the federal government and the provinces. This constitutional division of powers has been at the centre of resources policy conflicts between the provincial and federal governments ever since Confederation, but the intensity of the jurisdictional dispute has varied from one resource industry to another.

In cases such as pulp and paper where the industry is spread throughout the country and much of the output is destined for export, regional disputes have been less acute. In the case of petroleum and natural gas, however, where one region of the country produces a resource product which can be either exported to the United States or to another party of the country, the federal government must arbitrate between the desires of the producing and consuming regions of the country. Another issue which complicates resource policies is the relative monopoly position of the particular Canadian industry vis-a-vis the North American continent. Whether or not Canada's objectives with respect to a resource are consistent with the objectives of the United States is also of concern.

For these reasons it is not surprising, then, that it is difficult to discern a resource policy which embodies the ideology of a particular party. Each resource industry has had particular conditions associated with it; collecting these policies together gives the general impression that federal policies have been largely in the realm of *ad hocery*. One theme does emerge, however: all political parties have persistently attempted to increase the degree to which resources are processed in Canada. This policy is quite consistent with that of the tariff, which was primarily designed to create jobs in Canada.

Newsprint and Nickel[25]

Around the turn of the century, as U.S. timber stands were being rapidly depleted, Canada's forests were being used to supply raw material to the United States for processing into paper, especially newsprint. Between 1891 and 1902, the non-party government of British Columbia and the Liberals in Ontario, Quebec, and Ottawa passed tax and export legislation designed to encourage pulp processing in Canada. In 1909 the United States offered to reduce the tariff on low grade paper on the proviso that the provinces remove their restrictions. When the Canadians refused to budge on the issue, the United States retaliated with an additional duty against Canadian paper. One effect of the retaliatory duty was an increase in the price of newsprint in the

United States. As a result of a campaign waged by the newspaper industry in that country the United States duty was removed in 1913. Since that time newsprint production has developed into one of Canada's largest industries.

The issues here are clear: the United States preferred Canadian pulpwood to finished newsprint, but, since its own pulp resources were vanishing rapidly, Canada got essentially what it wanted. In the case of this industry with no inter-regional conflicts in Canada, the position of the producing provinces was easily supported by the federal government. It is probably only incidental that two of the involved provinces as well as Ottawa had Liberal governments at the time: the objective of establishing increased processing appealed to all of the parties.

The difficulties encountered in attempting to increase domestic nickel processing contrast sharply with the smooth implementation of increased processing in the pulp and paper industry. By 1890, the Canadian Copper Company, a U.S. controlled firm, had developed Canada's nickel industry to the point where it was a major supplier of nickel ore to the United States. Because it had refineries in the United States, Canadian Copper was opposed to processing ore in Canada. It pleaded successfully with the United States to retain duties on refined nickel while reducing those on nickel ore and matte.

In order to encourage nickel refining in Canada, the federal Liberal government passed legislation in 1897 allowing for an export duty on ore and matte. However, because Canadian Copper threatened to leave Canada if the duty was imposed, the legislation was not proclaimed. Two years later, the Liberal government of Ontario unsuccessfully petitioned Ottawa to apply the duty and, during the election of 1902, both major parties advocated increased nickel processing in Canada. After the Liberals were re-elected in the province they did pass an act which would have imposed a tax on exports of unrefined nickel ore, but, like its counterpart in Ottawa, the act was not proclaimed because of political pressure from the industry.

In the early years of World War I before the United States was a belligerent, rumours circulated that Canadian ore processed in the United States had been shipped to Germany by submarine. Supported by outraged Canadian opinion, the Conservative governments in Ottawa and Ontario threatened to nationalize the American firm unless it agreed to process nickel in Canada. Canadian Copper finally complied and opened a Canadian refinery in 1918.

Once again there seems to be little difference between the policies of the major political parties with respect to this resource. The relative monopoly position of the corporation involved in the industry was able to frustrate the wishes of the Canadian Liberal government. The desires of the government conflicted with those of the United States and in a peacetime atmosphere Canada was unable to take the drastic action necessary to force compliance. Changed circumstances later permitted the Conservatives to achieve what the combined efforts of the Ontario and federal Liberals had been unable to accomplish.

The St. Lawrence Seaway

Since 1907, all federal Liberal and Conservative governments have accepted Laurier's policy that exports of energy must be licensed. As a matter of principle, the federal government must be satisfied that exports will be surplus to Canada's immediate and long-term needs. In practice, it has proved difficult to assess Canada's requirements in relation to available supplies; consequently, estimates of surplus quantities have often proved unreliable.

One of the most bitter controversies over energy exports took place in 1937 when MacKenzie King's Liberal government denied Mitchell F. Hepburn's Liberal government of Ontario permission to export hydro power to New York. At the time, the federal government was considering President Roosevelt's proposal for a joint U.S.-Canada program to develop the power and navigation potential of the entire St. Lawrence system. Hepburn opposed this massive project, preferring to export power from expanded facilities at Niagara Falls. He argued that the larger scheme would not be economically sound and would ruin the country's railroads.

The United States saved King the embarrassment of having to choose between the Hepburn and Roosevelt proposals by refusing to accept short-term Ontario power. This incident was only one among many which manifested the animosity between the two Liberal leaders.[26] The case illustrates, however, that federal-provincial differences on energy matters can be quite marked and that party blood is not always thick enough to prevent open rift between party leaders in Ottawa and the provinces. The project was shelved during World War II. Construction was finally begun in 1954, with the official backing of both major parties at the federal level and cooperation from the Conservative and *union nationale* governments of Ontario and Quebec respectively.[27]

The Columbia River Treaty

Soon after they attained power in 1957, the Conservatives were made painfully aware that Ottawa's preferences on energy development in a particular province are constrained by the desires of provincial governments and the United States. Talks between the United States and Canada on the development of the power potential of British Columbia's Columbia River were begun by the Liberals in 1947. By 1959 it appeared that a series of dams would be built on the upper Columbia high in the mountains of the province to provide hydro power to serve both British Columbia and the United States. The dams would also serve to control seasonal flows and so prevent flooding in the United States.

British Columbia's Social Credit premier, W. A. C. Bennett, objected to the whole concept of dams on the north end of the Columbia River and forced the Conservatives in Ottawa to accept his plan for a series of three dams on the river, close to the United States' border. When the Columbia River Treaty was signed by Prime Minister Diefenbaker and President Eisenhower early in 1961, it contained provisions which were to make the Columbia, in the words of E. Davie Fulton, Canada's chief negotiator, "the next major source of hydro power to supply British Columbia's requirements."

Bennett, however, did not agree to the provisions on power rights and refused to endorse the treaty. He insisted on a settlement whereby the United States would take all of the power for a thirty- to sixty-year term and in return give British Columbia sufficient capital to finance a completely different project involving the Peace River.[28] Fulton charged that Bennett's plan for long-term exports would grant the United States "the greatest windfall since the purchase of Manhattan Island."[29] Eventually, the Conservative government reversed Canada's traditional policy and stated that "large-scale, long-term contracts for the export of power surpluses ... should now be encouraged."[30] Diefenbaker's government was defeated before the Columbia Treaty came up for debate. However, in 1964 the Pearson Liberal government negotiated a protocol which gave Bennett essentially what he wanted and went along with the concept of long-term power exports.

The 1961 Columbia River Treaty set several important precedents in the field of energy policy. It was the first in a series of hydro developments in Canada installed primarily for the export of power to the United States. Others, including the controversial James Bay project, soon followed. The Treaty also departed from the usual practices of water management as outlined by the Boundary Waters Treaty, negotiated by Laurier's Liberals in 1909. The established practice has been that each country retained control of waters flowing through its territory. Any diversions or attempts to regulate flows which subsequently passed through the other country were subject to the terms of the 1909 treaty, which provided machinery for the settlement of conflicts. The Columbia River Treaty, however, totally ignored the previous practices and placed the Canadian portion of the Columbia basin under international control, but left the American portion under American control. In addition, the 1961 legislation provided no machinery for the settlement of disputes. Thus, the Columbia River Treaty, signed by the Conservatives and assented to by the Liberals, has serious implications for Canadian sovereignty and further evidences lack of choice between the two parties on the issue of continentalism.

While the Liberals and Conservatives might both have preferred a different Columbia River agreement, neither party was able to salvage many of its principles or objectives in their respective dealings with the provincial Social Credit premier. This case illustrates that the policies of the federal parties can be modified beyond recognition in the course of battles with the provinces.

Natural Gas and Petroleum

In 1951 the Social Credit government of Alberta and the federal Liberal government agreed to allow the export of natural gas to the United States. By 1953, however, the federal government had decided to apply the principles of the 1907 Electricity Act to future exports of natural gas. Ottawa insisted that Canada's present and future needs be satisfied before any additional quantities be assigned to exports. In practice this policy meant that gas from the prairies would have to be available to Ontario and a pipe line was needed to carry it.

Canada's Minister of Trade and Commerce, the American-born C. D. Howe, insisted that the line follow an all-Canada route north of the Great Lakes. On the condition that the line be built, permission was granted to allow the export of a specified amount of additional gas. The proposed route was so expensive, however, that the federal Liberal government agreed to build the so-called "Canadian Bridge" north of Lake Superior via a joint crown corporation with the Conservative government of Ontario. The American-owned Trans Canada Pipe Line Company was to build the section across the prairies and later take over the section built by the crown. When the Federal Power Commission of the United States refused permission for the gas to enter that country, the financial viability of the whole project was threatened and the Liberal government decided to lend Trans Canada $80 million to finance the venture and ensure its completion on schedule.

In an effort to accelerate the project, the Liberals limited parliamentary debate on the loan to Trans Canada and invoked closure. The Conservatives directed their opposition mainly at the procedures used by the Liberals in forcing the loan legislation through parliament. Some Conservatives suggested that an alternative ought to be adopted so that the project could be carried out without government aid and by a Canadian firm.[31] The CCF-NDP argued that, since the government was financing the entire project and actually building part of it, the government ought to undertake the whole venture as a state enterprise. The Social Credit members from oil-producing Alberta backed the Liberal government. Whatever differences might have occurred, this issue regarding resource policies became largely obscured by the overriding resentment the Liberals caused by invoking closure on the debates.

Much in this case conjures up memories of controversies over the building of the CPR. The issues there also involved government assistance to a privately financed public utility, an all-Canadian route north of the Great Lakes, and the ultimate defeat of a government.[32] This time, however, the Liberals instead of the Conservatives were in trouble. The effect of the U.S. Federal Power Commission's rejection of Canada's request to sell the gas in the United States is another example of how Canada has had to accommodate itself to the policies of that country in determining its own resource policies.

During their years in opposition, the Conservatives did not seem to object to any particular Liberal energy projects, but they did suggest that the Liberal solution to the whole question of energy and resources was piecemeal and that an overall energy policy was needed. One of the first acts of the Diefenbaker Government was to appoint the Borden Royal Commission to examine the whole question of energy. As a result of Borden's recommendations, all markets west of the Ottawa Valley were to be served by Canadian crude, whereas areas east of the Ottawa Valley were to be served from off-shore sources. The Borden Commission also recommended the establishment of a National Energy Board. This was to be a non-political agency which would determine Canada's future energy requirements and decide what quantities of various types of energy were to be available for export at any particular time.

The establishment of this agency was supported by the Conservatives, the Liberals, and the CCF-NDP.[33] The basic principle in determining surplus quantities was the same as that which had governed energy exports since 1907. Until the past few years, the National Energy Board depoliticized the energy question in much the same way that the Tariff Board had removed an earlier issue from Canadian politics. The present controversy over energy revolves around the problem of determining the quantities which ought to be exported, the prices which ought to be charged for these exports, and how the revenues from energy and resource sales ought to be shared among the companies involved and the people living in different parts of Canada. More will be said about this issue when this chapter discusses resource problems as they relate to the provinces.

Contemporary Issues

Christian and Campbell refer to the export boom of the 1950s as a phenomenon uniquely Liberal that further indicated the Liberals' continentalism. In fact, there was little fundamental difference between positions of the major parties during the 1950s and 1960s. It is true that the policies of the Liberals during the period between World War II and their defeat in 1957 actively promoted resource exploration and exports by means of tax laws. But the Conservatives, who took power in 1957, offered only more of the same.

Diefenbaker's vision of the North and his "roads to resources" program plus his proposals for tax incentives merely extended existing Liberal policies. Some Conservatives, such as Alvin Hamilton, did believe there was a fundamental difference between their policies and those of the Liberals, in that they wanted a more rational approach to resource exports. To Hamilton, an apparent Red Tory and nationalist, a rational approach implied a continental resources pact with the United States.[34] While such a program might have some merit, it surely cannot be viewed as a significant alternative to what Christian and Campbell have referred to as the Trudeau Government's "original inclination to continental sharing of energy resources." Under present conditions of world shortages of resources, any such pact would likely be contingent upon the United States granting Canada access to markets for manufactured goods; hence, the countries might after all become partners in a sort of reciprocity treaty. While the countries appear to be still playing the same game, the 65 years since Laurier have given the United States and Canada a chance to "change ends."[35]

Crown Corporations, Resources, and Rents

Thus far, we have devoted little space to the policies of the third parties.

There is an obvious difficulty in commenting on national policies of minor parties that have never held federal power: what opposition parties say they are going to do and what they actually do when confronted with the realities of office are often quite different. The CCF-NDP, as has been suggested above, expressed more concern about the export of raw materials than have the major parties.[36] This position probably stems from their socialist roots, but even the way that party has articulated its belief in socialization has been modified over the years. Their philosophy seemed to moderate with respect to nationalization as the party became more preoccupied with social services and placed less emphasis on the question of ownership (see Chapter 3, Fragment and Movement Parties).

The Regina Manifesto of 1933 proclaimed boldly, "No CCF government will rest content until it has eradicated capitalism and put into operation the full programme of socialized planning. . ."[37] By 1956, however, the official emphasis of the party had shifted and the Winnipeg Declaration of that year supported "equality and freedom, a sense of human dignity, and an opportunity to live a rich and meaningful life . . . for everyone."[38]

During the 1960s the so-called Waffle group, a nationalist and socialist minority in the NDP, advocated policies more similar to the manifesto of 1933 than that of 1956. In the early 1970s the influential Ontario NDP expelled its Waffle element and the position outlined in 1961 by veteran socialist MP Stanley Knowles is now unchallenged:

> It is the objectives that count and these objectives determine the extent to which democratic socialists advocate public ownership or other ways of enlarging the public sector of our economy. . .[39]

Anyone, regardless of party affiliation, could agree with such a pragmatic approach to the problem of the influence of the public sector. Indeed, it seems that both major parties have behaved in just such a manner. In the early 1920s, Robert Borden's Conservative government merged a number of small and inefficient railroads into what we now know as the government-owned Canadian National Railways. In 1938 King's Liberal government established the state-owned Trans Canada Airlines, now Air Canada, since private capital was not interested in establishing a national airline in Canada. During World War II, King's Liberals founded Polymer Corporation because Canada needed rubber production in a hurry. One could point to many other such ventures at the federal level and to numerous examples of state-run enterprises in the various provinces to illustrate that all parties have been willing on occasion to enter directly into business to achieve their goals.[40]

By 1971, Liberal cabinet minister Eric Kierans resigned because he believed that prevailing government policies had led to corporate exploitation of the resource sector. He referred to Canada's federal and provincial resource policies as an invitation to other countries to "come and gut us."[41] Probably one of the most significant events leading to recent changes in party resource attitudes was a speech made by Kierans to the Canadian Economics Association at Memorial University in Newfoundland in June of that year. In that speech and subsequent amplifications of it, Kierans argued that Canada had failed to collect its economic rents from resource industries. Economic rents are profits in excess of those required to attract new capital into an industry. His argument was based on classical Ricardian economic theory and appealed so much to Canada's custodians of the "dismal science" that they gave him a standing ovation.[42] This type of analysis has triggered a movement by the federal and provincial governments towards greater activity in the resource sector, through both the taxation system and direct government enterprise.

Influential provincial politicians of various governing parties have articulated the emphasis which all parties now place on resource ownership and economic rent. Saskatchewan's NDP Premier Allan Blakeney has said, "The people of Saskatchewan own the oil." His mineral resources minister has added, "Private industry . . . had their chance and they blew it." The Conservative Premier of Alberta, Peter Lougheed, has remarked, "We have to give a greater opportunity for Albertans to participate as risk takers in the development of our resources." John White, Ontario's Treasurer, has insisted, ". . . it is only fair that we secure for the people a higher return from our natural resources." Quebec's Liberal Finance Minister, Raymond Garneau, has said, "The government is reassessing . . . the revenues Quebec is entitled to as the owner of resources. . ."[43]

From 1973 to 1975, Quebec's Liberal Government, the Conservative Governments of Ontario and Alberta, and the NDP Governments of Manitoba, Saskatchewan, and British Columbia substantially increased — in most cases doubled — their taxes on resource industries. A unique feature of these "super royalties" is that taxes are calculated on the increased value of sales due to price increases, whereas previously royalties were fixed in relation to quantities, i.e. so much a barrel, a ton, etc. The change is clearly an attempt on the part of these governments to collect what Kierans had referred to as economic rent. To paraphrase what University of Chicago economist Milton Friedman has said about the economic teachings of John Maynard Keynes, "We are all Kieransians now."

The new method of calculating royalties has led to a conflict between the provinces and the federal Liberal government, which also has been trying to increase its revenues from the resource industries. The federal government has inisted that, unlike royalties based on quantities, royalties based on selling prices are not deductible as a corporate expense for the purposes of calculating federal corporate income tax. If the federal government prevails, corporations would suffer double taxation in provinces which persist in calculating royalties on sales. The federal government insists that some of the economic rent in question ought to go to all the people of Canada through its income tax and redistribution system; the provinces involved would prefer to keep the revenues for their own uses. The federal Liberals have also introduced legislation which would give Ottawa the power to establish prices for oil and natural gas. As will be seen below, some provinces already have legislation which they claim empowers them to set such prices. As a matter of fact, all of the provinces with the exception of the Liberal-governed Nova Scotia, which has few natural resources, have united in an attempt to move the federal government from its present positions. Quebec, a resource-rich province with a Liberal government, opposed the federal Liberal position. The federal opposition parties, especially the Conservatives, have attempted to turn the issue into one of provincial rights and have supported the position of the provinces.[44]

In a speech to a symposium on Canada's non-renewable resources in 1974, sponsored by the *Financial Post*, Darcy McKeough, Ontario's minister of energy, spoke of the changing role of government in energy matters:

> ... the halcyon days of 'laissez-faire' ... are finished ... The evidence is all around us. It may be a matter of some regret to an audience such as this, but I think ... that it should be recognized that this is a developing social phenomenon and not simply a product of the attitudes of socialist governments in three provinces of Canada. The electors of Alberta have never flirted with socialism but ... the people are observing with approval the increasing involvement of their government in the development and execution of energy planning. This is true of Quebec, it is true of Ontario.[45]

McKeough is correct in sensing that the Canadian people are receptive to considerable government intervention in the resources sector; for example, in a *Financial Times* survey of business executives conducted in 1974, close to 70% of those polled approved of the Canada Development Corporation's having purchased a controlling interest in Texasgulf Inc., an American-owned mining firm with operations in Canada. The survey also revealed that over 60% of the executives approved of the federal Liberal government's plan to establish a national petroleum corporation, which would compete with the private firms in that industry.[46] The Canadian consensus in favour of government intervention is remarkable if one considers that the respondents in the *Financial Times* survey were businessmen rather than university professors or the population at large.

The Ontario minister was also accurate in his assessment that the NDP governments of Manitoba, Saskatchewan, and British Columbia, the Conservative governments of Ontario and Alberta, as well as the Liberal government of Quebec were all employing similar strategies of intervention in their resource policies.

In 1973, Eric Kierans handed his commissioned *Report on Natural Resources Policy in Manitoba* to Premier Ed Schreyer's NDP government. The report recommended that the Manitoba government conduct all future mining exploration and extraction in the province and that it should tax the existing mining companies out of business within ten years.[47] Schreyer, who once declared, "I am not a socialist," was quick to dissociate himself from the report and to assure business that it was not government policy.[48] After a year's study of the report, the Manitoba government substantially increased taxes on the mining industry, made regulations about in-province processing and increased government involvement in exploration. Rather than taxing the private companies out of business, however, the NDP government assured them of a return on investment commensurate with the nature of their undertakings.[49] Schreyer's policies turned out to be no more socialist than those of other resource provinces such as Ontario and Alberta. It is perhaps because of Schreyer's lack of commitment to socialism that the more radical NDP members, such as Professor Cy Gonick, have gradually withdrawn from his Government.[50]

Because of his reluctance to involve the province's crown corporation "Sask Oil" more deeply in the affairs of industry, NDP Premier Allan Blakeney of Saskatchewan has come under fire for lack of commitment to socialism. Under pressure from the Waffle wing of the provincial party, Saskatchewan's NDP government passed legislation in the 1970s which enabled the corporation to engage in such activities as producing, refining, buying, selling, and exploring in the petroleum and natural gas industries. In practice, however, "Sask Oil" has been confined to exploration activities in joint ventures with private firms. Kim Thorson, minister of mineral resources has said, "The crown [oil] corporation should operate in the same manner as other companies . . . in joint ventures with other companies."[51] The federal Liberal government has taken this stance in its northern exploration activities as a member of the Panartic Oils consortium, in which it has 45% equity. The Waffle has been extremely critical of Blakeney's government for abandoning its socialist principles with respect to oil and natural gas. The Waffle would prefer the government to nationalize the entire industry.

Not surprisingly, Alberta's Premier Lougheed has been harshly criticized within his own party — even within his cabinet — for interfering too much with private business. Alberta has benefited from increased revenues from oil and natural gas sales to other provinces and to the United States. His government has ploughed much of the money back into investments which it hopes will keep the province prosperous after its conventional oil reserves are depleted. Like Saskatchewan, Alberta has enacted legislation designed to permit it to control the sales and prices of its oil and natural gas. It has established the Alberta Energy Company, which eventually will be 50% privately owned, to act as a major investor in Alberta business ventures such as the Syncrude tar sands project. The company will also invest in Interprovincial Steel and Pipe, a company in which the Saskatchewan NDP government also has an interest. Alberta also has acquired control of Pacific Western Airlines. Despite all of this involvement in business, Lougheed still insists that he remains a true-blue supporter of free enterprise.[52]

In a relatively short period, Dave Barrett's NDP government in British Columbia made some dramatic changes in the resource sector of the province. The government purchased Ocean Falls town and papermill because it was to be abandoned by the previous owners. The province also acquired control of Canadian Cellulose Limited in order to prevent the company from being taken over by the U.S. controlled

International Telephone and Telegraph Company. The NDP retained the same management. In 1975, the company continued to be directed by nine businessmen, four of whom lived outside of Canada. This resource-rich province also purchased shares in B. C. Telephone Company, a Vancouver bus line, and a number of other companies. Barrett, however, was careful to insist that the province welcomed private capital and travelled to several countries in an effort to persuade foreigners to invest in British Columbia.

Many feared that the NDP government would nationalize Westcoast Transmission Company, the province's monopoly gas carrier. Instead, Barrett purchased less than 15% of the company and established B.C. Petroleum Company, which has power to buy and sell natural gas in a manner similar to its counterparts in other provinces such as Alberta and Saskatchewan.

Barrett's short-lived government seemed determined to obtain a high price for the province's resources. Nevertheless, rhetoric to the contrary, the former NDP government seemed willing to sell them to the highest bidder, usually the United States. For instance, before Barrett came to power, he condemned Social Credit Premier Bennett's proposals to build transportation facilities into the northern interior of the province. As premier, however, Barrett did just that in order to tap resources which hitherto had been safely out of reach and therefore made them available to the world.[53]

Barrett had the style and his rich province had lots of money to invest in the province's development. His government managed to escape the scathing criticism of the party's left wing. But, with the exception of his auto insurance scheme in which a crown company had a complete monopoly, his resource schemes had parallels in the other provinces and their extent was probably more a function of "ability of pay" than of a "desire to own".

It is indeed difficult to make fundamental distinctions between what Lougheed calls "state capitalism" and the "democratic socialism" of Schreyer, Blakeney, and Barrett. However, it is clear that none of these governments would satisfy the standards of the Regina Manifesto or the Waffle.

Conclusion

This paper demonstrated that, allowing for circumstances of particular times and industries, parties have differed little with respect to trade and resources. Since only the Conservatives and Liberals have held power at the national level, much of this chapter was devoted to their policies. In situations where it was possible to judge NDP practices at the provincial level, that party also governed in a pragmatic rather than an ideological manner.

On the issue of the tariff, both major parties have had to accept the reality that the U.S. must be Canada's largest trading partner. Both parties have shown a willingness to engage in negotiations to expand that trade and both have turned to increased trade with the United

Kingdom whenever the United States resisted such trade deals.

The newsprint and nickel industries illustrate that both major parties have attempted to encourage more processing in Canada, while the United States has preferred to import unprocessed raw materials from Canada. Success in achieving their objectives with respect to processing has been more a function of the economic circumstances of the industries involved than it has been of party ideologies.

The St. Lawrence Seaway and the Columbia River developments illustrate the extent to which provincial governments can frustrate federal attempts to develop the country's energy potentials along certain lines. The St. Lawrence Seaway points out how difficult it is for a party to have a national policy even when it governs at the federal level and in the involved province. The Columbia River Treaty shows how a province can effectively change the federal policy of both major parties.

The natural gas and petroleum industries also illustrate the federal and provincial interaction and compromise which take place on resource matters. In the 1970s, the Conservatives, who were in power in the producing province of Alberta and in the consuming province of Ontario, had particular problems in balancing between the desires of each province and the needs of the nation. They turned the issue into one of provincial rights to divert attention from the energy issue. All parties now seem committed to obtaining greater economic rents from the resource sectors.

- The main purpose of the argument was to demonstrate the similar nature of the policies implemented by all the parties. When in power, all parties appeared to be influenced by questions of feasibility, feasibility in terms of international relations, of technical considerations, and of popular belief about desirable levels of government intervention or taxation. This pragmatic reality not only invalidates the Christian and Campbell argument about the alleged continentalism of the Liberals and the nationalism of the Conservatives, but it also invalidates any suggestion that party policies reflect directly different geographic or class bases of support.

Notes

1. Sir John Willison, Ottawa correspondent for the *Times of London* (1920), as quoted by Peter C. Newman in *MacLean's* (May 5, 1962).

2. For a readable account of Macdonald's position on the Washington Treaty, see Bruce Huchison, *The Struggle for the Border* (Don Mills, Ontario: Longmans, Windfammer edition, 1970), 397–420.

3. L. Ethan Ellis, *Reciprocity 1911: A Study in Canadian-American Relations* (New York: Greenwood Press, Publishers, 1968), 3.

4. Ibid., 4–7. See also O. J. McDiarmid, *Commercial Policy in the Canadian Economy* (Cambridge, Mass.: Harvard University Press, 1946), 208.

5. J. M. Beck, *Pendulum of Power: Canada's Federal Elections* (Scarborough, Ontario: Prentice Hall, 1968), 72.

6. Ellis, *Reciprocity*, 5.

7. Quoted by Ellis, *Reciprocity*, 5.

8. Quoted in D. Owen Carrigan, *Canadian Party Platforms 1967–1968* (Toronto, Ontario: Copp-Clark Publishing Company, 1968), 66.

9. McDiarmid, *Commercial Policy*, 227.

10. W. A. MacKintosh, *The Economic Background of Dominion-Provincial Relations: A Study Prepared for the Royal Commission on Dominion-Provincial Relations* (Ottawa: King's Printer, 1939), 36.

11. McDiarmid, *Commercial Policy*, 238.

12. *House of Commons Debates* (1903), 7659–60.

13. For a more detailed discussion of these points see Ellis, *Reciprocity*, 187–96; D. C. Masters *Reciprocity, 1846–1911* (Ottawa: The Canadian Historical Association Booklets, no. 12, 1969), 16–18; and McDiarmid, *Commercial Policy*, 227–38.

14. W. Christian and C. Campbell, *Political Parties and Ideologies in Canada* (Toronto: McGraw-Hill Ryerson, 1974), 46.

15. MacKintosh, *Economic Background*, 83–84.

16. Thomas White, Conservative Minister of Finance, *House of Commons Debates*, III (1914) 2452.

17. McDiarmid, *Commercial Policy*, 272–73.

18. Beck, *Pendulum*, 191–200.

19. Richard Wilbur, *The Bennett Administration 1930–1935* (Ottawa: The Canadian Historical Association Booklets, no. 24, 1969), 5–6.

20. McDiarmid, *Commercial Policy*, 209–305; Wilbur, *Bennett Administration*, 10.

21. *House of Commons Debates* (1939), 3349–50.

22. Beck, *Pendulum*, 218.

23. Eric W. Kierans, *Challenge of Confidence: Kierans on Canada* (Toronto: McClelland and Stewart, 1967), 71.

24. Peter C. Newman, *Renegade in Power: The Diefenbaker Years* (Toronto: McClelland and Stewart, The Carleton Library no. 70, 1973), 267–270.

25. This analysis relies heavily on Hugh G. J. Aitken, "The Changing Structure of the Canadian Economy: With Particular Reference to the Influence of the United States," in Aitken, Deutsch et al., *American Impact on Canada* (Durham, N.C.: Duke University Press, 1959), 13–21.

26. Neil McKenty, *Mitch Hepburn* (Toronto: McClelland and Stewart, 1967), 147–56.

27. Carrigan, *Party Platforms*, 189, 289. *Canada Year Book*, 1959, 823–25.

28. For general background see: Peter C. Newman, *Renegade*, 119–20. Philip Sykes, *Sellout: The Give Away of Canada's Energy Resources* (Edmonton, Alberta: Hurtig Publishers, 1973), 48–68. For a detailed analysis of the political positions involved, see John M. McMenemy, "The Columbia River Treaty 1961–1964: A Study of Opposition and Representation in the Canadian Political System" (doctoral dissertation, University of Toronto, 1969).

29. Quoted in Newman, *Renegade*, 120.

30. *Ibid.*

31. The political picture became clouded when a Canadian firm offered to build the line with no government assistance. Howe turned down this alternative on the grounds that its promoter wanted to further increase the volume of exports and that he had neither contracts at the producing and distributing

ends of the project nor options to buy the necessary pipe.

For background, see Hugh G. J. Aitken, "Changing Structure," 27–33; John N. McDougall, "Oil and Gas in Canadian Energy Policy," in G. Bruce Doern and V. Seymour Wilson (ed.), Issues in Canadian Public Policy (Toronto: Macmillan, 1974), 115–33; Freeman Lincoln, "Frank McMahon's Pipe Dream," in Fortune (January 1958), 146–48, 168–72. Newman, Renegade, 37–44.

32. For a fascinating account of the political and economic problems associated with the construction of the Canadian Pacific Railroad see, Pierre Berton, The Last Spike (Toronto: McClelland and Stewart, 1974).

33. Carrigan, Party Platforms, 219, 237, and 245.

34. Alvin Hamilton, A Resource Policy For Canada, 1964: A Paper Prepared for the National Conference on Canadian Goals (mimeographed, Fredericton, September 9–12, 1964).

35. In Laurier's time, and until quite recently, Canada was trying to persuade the United States to buy resource products and the United States wanted access to Canadian markets for finished goods. Under present circumstances the United States wants Canada's resources, such as natural gas, and Canada has become reluctant to sell them. It seems reasonable to expect that one price Canada might extract from the United States in exchange for resources is a market for Canadian finished goods.

36. For an analysis of the avowed resource policies of the Conservative, Liberals, and CCF-NDP, see Thomas L. Burton, Natural Resource Policies in Canada: Issues and Perspectives (Toronto: McClelland and Stewart, 1972), Chapter 5.

37. From the CCF Program adopted at Regina, Sask. (July 1933), as reprinted in Carrigan, Party Platforms, 127.

38. From the Winnipeg Declaration of Principles of the CCF (1956), as reprinted in Carrigan, Party Platforms, 215.

39. Stanley Knowles, The New Party (Toronto: McClelland and Stewart, 1961), 33.

40. Philip Mathias, Forced Growth: Five Studies of Government Involvement in the Development of Canada (Toronto: James Lewis and Samuel, 1971), 1–14.

41. As quoted in Sykes, Sellout, 24.

42. The author witnessed Kierans' speech at Memorial University. A later version of the theme was presented in Kingston on June 2, 1973, and subsequently published. See Eric Kierans, "Canadian Resources Policy", The Canadian Forum, (June-July, 1973).

43. All quotations from The Financial Times of Canada (Montreal, April 15, 1974).

44. Globe and Mail (Toronto, Nov. 15 and Dec. 7, 1974).

45. Darcy McKeough, Ontario Minister of Energy, Remarks to the Financial Post International Symposium on Canada's Non-renewable Resources (mimeographed, Toronto, March 26, 1974).

46. Financial Times of Canada (Montreal, March 18, 1974).

47. Globe and Mail (Toronto, January 12 and 19, 1974).

48. Time (July 9, 1973).

49. Globe and Mail (Toronto, March 22, 1974).

50. Financial Times of Canada (Montreal, June 4, 1973).

51. Analysis and quotation from John Richards "Sask Oil: A Modest contribution Towards a New Energy Policy," *The Canadian Forum* (June-July, 1973).

52. *Financial Post* (Toronto, September 14, 1974).

53. *Financial Post* (Toronto, January 26, 1974). *Financial Times* (Montreal, March 18, 1974). *Globe and Mail* (Toronto, February 15, 1974).

CHAPTER 14
FOREIGN POLICY
Garth Stevenson

Introduction

Although Canada has had a foreign policy in the formal sense for only a little more than half a century, it has interacted with the world outside its borders throughout its history. Interactions with the United Kingdom and the United States in particular have shaped the course of Canadian development. Canadians have defined their own identity by distinguishing themselves from these older and larger nations, but at the same time have patterned themselves after them, as they did in adopting British parliamentary government and American federalism. Political decisions by Canadians have affected the volume and the composition of Canada's trade with the United Kingdom and the United States. Canada's military defence was traditionally based on collaboration with the United Kingdom that after 1940 was supplemented and gradually replaced by collaboration with the United States. Since Canadians have engaged in controversy over these matters for as long as their political parties have existed, the orientations of the major parties towards Canada's external relations (which is perhaps a more useful and more Canadian term than "foreign policy") can be traced back long before the formal commencement of Canadian diplomacy after World War I.

Historians have produced two conventional interpretations of how Canadian parties differ in their approach to Canada's external relations. The first, which might be called the "Whig" interpretation, is based on the assumption that Canadian history was a natural and inevitable progression from colonialism to the status of a sovereign, democratic, and self-governing nation. According to this view domestic political reforms and a gradual loosening of the imperial ties with Britain were logically related, and the thrust in this direction was mainly provided by the Liberal party. The Conservatives, on the other hand, are depicted as resisting Canada's natural evolution, clinging to imperial ties, and failing to appreciate Canada's true destiny as a basically North American nation.[1]

The second conventional interpretation, which may be called the Red Tory interpretation, arose in reaction to the first. According to this view, the evolution from "colony to nation" was merely a transition from a British to an American sphere of influence. The Liberals, either deliberately or because they were too blind to see what was happening, cut Canada loose from its ties with Britain at the very time when those ties were most needed to resist the fatal attraction of the United States.

The Conservatives tried bravely to resist the onslaught of continentalism, but, by the time they returned to office in 1957 after a long absence, the damage had been done.[2]

Despite the bitter mutual hostility of their respective proponents, these two interpretations of the history of Canadian foreign policy are curiously alike. In fact, one merely mirrors the other, transforming the heroes into villains and vice versa, but conveying the same general impression of the actual facts. Both interpretations magnify and distort the real differences between the Liberal and Conservative parties. Both implicitly attribute to the parties a degree of consistency, homogeneity, and ideological coherence which neither one has ever displayed. Both ignore or supress any evidence which might cast doubts on their oversimplified assumptions. Both beg the question as to whether political parties really exercise decisive influence on Canadian foreign policy at all. In short, both conventional interpretations are good propaganda but bad history and bad social science.

Although parties may have predispositions in the area of foreign policy, little is known about the extent, if any, to which they influence foreign policy. Foreign policy, under the British and Canadian forms of government, is the prerogative of the Crown, which means that Parliament need be consulted only when the expenditure of money is required. Canadian treaties are customarily tabled in Parliament, but do not require legislative ratification as do treaties in the United States. Largely for this reason, the Standing Committee on External Affairs and National Defence in the House of Commons is far less influential than its counterparts in both houses of the U.S. Congress. The only politically identified actors involved in making Canadian foreign policy are the members of the cabinet, yet even they must share their power with a permanent and highly influential civil service.

Until the 1970s, the influence of the civil service was probably greater in Canadian foreign policy than in other areas of policy because foreign service officers, as in most western countries, tended to be regarded as an elite group in the civil service and because they control sources of information about the external environment. As a result, ministers tended to defer to their views, the more so since foreign policy was normally assumed to have little effect on the outcomes of elections. The influence of the bureaucracy is almost always on the side of adherence to existing foreign policies, usually justified on the grounds that other governments would be distressed by any break with tradition. Particularly in a middle power sensitive to the views of stronger neighbours and allies, this bureaucratic influence tends to lessen the perceptible differences between the foreign policies of the two parties which have held office at the federal level. Conversely, the foreign policy of the New Democratic party appears more distinctive because its lack of electoral success has prevented it from being exposed to bureaucratic influences. The experience of British Labour governments suggests, however, that an NDP government might differ little from previous governments in its conduct of Canadian foreign policy.

Red Tories tend to assume a different relationship between bureaucratic and political elites in the making of Canadian foreign policy. They assume that the Liberals took over the Department of External Affairs during the long period of Liberal government from 1935 to 1957 and that this fact, rather than bureaucratic inertia and sensitivity to foreign opinion, explains the bureaucracy's penchant for close ties with the United States, regardless of which party is in office. In actual fact it would be more accurate to say that the civil servants took over the Liberal party, rather than the other way around. The party's traditional foreign policy had been one of minimal committments and a modest role in world affairs. In the last years of his life Mackenzie King struggled unsuccessfully to maintain this tradition against the efforts of the foreign service officers, particularly Norman Robertson and Lester Pearson, both of whose views on foreign policy resembled those of Borden and Bennett more than those of King.[3] Pearson's entry into the cabinet and King's retirement marked the defeat of King's efforts to maintain the Liberal tradition.

Over the next twenty years, in the course of which Pearson was successively Secretary of State for External Affairs, Leader of the Opposition, and Prime Minister, the concept of Canadian foreign policy which he had acquired as a non-partisan civil servant tended to be attributed to the party which he had subsequently joined. Certainly the party was quick to adopt Pearson's views, as shown by its dramatic about-face on the question of nuclear weapons in January 1963, but this turnaround only suggests the extent to which the party was subordinated to the leader. It is arguable that the association between Pearsonian-bureaucratic foreign policy and the Liberal party was accidental and that Pearson might as easily have become a Conservative had the Conservative party held office in 1948.[4] The true Liberal tradition may not be Pearsonian, but the anti-Pearsonism implicit in the Trudeau government's "Foreign Policy for Canadians" papers, which derided the Pearsonian notion of Canada as a "helpful fixer" in world affairs.

The case of Pearson epitomizes a problem in discussing the foreign policies characteristic of Canadian political parties: the extreme importance of individual personalities. Between 1918 and 1976, only fourteen persons held the offices of Prime Minister and Secretary of State for External Affairs.[5] On the basis of a sample consisting of six Conservatives and eight Liberals, it may be hazardous to make sweeping generalizations about "Conservative" or "Liberal" foreign policies. (By way of contrast, a student of American foreign policy could study the voting behaviour of several thousand senators and congressmen over the same period of time.)

This recital of difficulties is not intended to discourage the reader, but only to emphasize that what follows must be a rather tentative and speculative appraisal of the foreign policies of the Canadian political parties. It is nonetheless interesting to examine and compare the foreign policies of the parties and the exercise may cast some fresh light on Canadian foreign policy itself.

Most of what follows will deal with policies towards the United Kingdom and the United States, not only because of their continuing importance in Canada's external relations, but also because the historical antecedents of attitudes and policies towards them can be traced back long before Canada began to conduct its own foreign policy. A third section of the paper deals, in somewhat more impressionistic fashion, with the actions of Canadian parties towards other countries and regions of the world whose impact on Canada has been more recent and less profound. Only the Liberal, Progressive Conservative, and New Democratic parties will be considered, since regional parties, past and present, have taken little interest in foreign policy.

The British Connection

In the minds of most Canadians, the Liberal and Conservative parties are clearly distinguished by their attitudes towards the United Kingdom. Conservatives are seen and see themselves as defenders of the monarchy, the British connection, and the Commonwealth. John A. Macdonald's famous pledge, "A British subject I was born, a British subject I will die", still seems to express a Conservative sentiment, as shown by the party's response to the Suez crisis of 1956 and its resistance to the adoption of the maple leaf flag in 1964–65. By contrast, the Liberal party appears to hold these sentiments less intensely, or not at all, and even to flirt with republicanism.

These stereotypes have some basis in fact for at least two reasons. First, the late Victorian mystique of crown and empire, with its overtones of racism and militarism, appealed more to Conservatives than to Liberals, not only in Canada, but also in the United Kingdom itself. The second reason, which has more relevance to our time, is that the Conservatives have remained a predominantly English-Canadian party, while the Liberal party has been much more influenced by its large contingent of French-speaking members. While French-speaking Canadians long accepted the British connection for essentially pragmatic reasons, they have been understandably unable to feel the emotional attachment to the United Kingdom that many English Canadians still feel. There have been some fervent monarchists and anglophiles in the Liberal party, such as former Governor-General Vincent Massey, but their influence has been diluted ever since Quebec became the party's political stronghold in the federal election of 1896.

As noted at the outset of this chapter, the Whig interpretation of Canadian history identifies the Liberal party with the achievement of Canadian autonomy and the transition from empire to commonwealth, while the Conservatives are viewed as perpetually eager to fight Britain's wars and to follow the lead of British foreign policy. Neither perception is completely accurate. As early as 1885, Sir John A. Macdonald refused to assist a British government (admittedly it was a British Liberal government!) by sending troops to the Sudan. According to Donald Creighton, the old chieftain "remained unsympathetically aloof" from the interventionist sentiment in the country on this occasion.[6]

In the decade after World War I, Canada began to acquire an international status distinct from the British empire, signing its own treaties, launching its own diplomatic service, and having its new status explicitly recognized at the Imperial Conference of 1926, Mackenzie King took the credit and Red Tory revisionists have assigned him the blame for these developments; however, it was actually the Conservative Robert Borden who had taken the decisive step by insisting that Canada be represented at the Paris Peace Conference, that it sign the Treaty of Versailles, and that it become a member of the League of Nations. Even the opening of a legation in Washington was agreed to in principle before Mackenzie King took office in 1921, although it did not actually take place until 1927. Moreover, some Liberals opposed these developments. W. S. Fielding, the former finance minister who was King's most serious rival for the succession to Laurier, criticized Borden for demanding that Canada have separate representation at the peace conference and warned of the danger of making Canada a separate nation.[7]

King, however, continued the process of disengaging Canada from the British Empire and he refused to support Britain in a confrontation with Turkey in 1922. Arthur Meighen, the Conservative leader at the time, is generally remembered for having said that Canada should be "ready, aye, ready" at Britain's side in confronting the Turks. Less generally remembered is that Meighen was deliberately quoting the precise words used by Sir Wilfrid Laurier, the Liberal leader in 1914. King's cautious policy seemed more in tune with the nation's mood after the grim experiences of wartime. Anglo-Turkish relations improved after the fall of British Prime Minister David Lloyd George and the Conservative party of Canada acquired a reputation for questionable and unpopular foreign policies that has not been entirely dispelled after half a century.[8]

Although King was following in the footsteps of Borden when he championed the cause of Canadian autonomy, the two differed, in that Borden (and later R. B. Bennett) thought that autonomy should be used to play an active role in international affairs, while King's main concern was to avoid incurring obligations and commitments by too close an association with British diplomacy. This stance was sound political strategy in the 1920s because support for an isolationist foreign policy was one of the few points of agreement between the Quebec Liberals, whose support had given King the party's leadership, and the Prairie Progressives, who sustained his minority government in the House of Commons.

Britain's decline as a world power has diminished the likelihood that its foreign policy will contribute to controversy among Canadian politicians. One of the last occasions on which it did so — and on which the Liberals and Conservatives had the opportunity to act out their traditional stereotypes — was the Suez crisis of 1956. The Liberal government of Louis St. Laurent refused to support British policy towards Egypt, just as Mackenzie King had refused to support a similar British policy towards Turkey in 1922. The Conservative opposition argued at the time, and in the election campaign a few months later, that Canada should have given full support to British policy, as had Australia and New Zealand. Actually the Liberal governemnt's policy was not anti-British, since it assisted the British in retreating gracefully from an enterprise which they were not strong enough to pursue, but St. Laurent's statement that "the supermen of Europe" could no longer hope to dominate the world was resented by many Conservative anglophiles.

Anglo-Canadian relations have been economic as well as political: the evidence from this aspect of the relationship reinforces the impression created by the political aspect that Conservatives are somewhat more pro-British than Liberals, but the difference is not entirely clearcut. Macdonald's National Policy was rather ambiguous in this regard, since it relied on British capital and British markets but protected Canadian industry from British, as well as American, competition. Laurier's Liberal government was the first to grant a tariff preference to British goods, a practice which has been continued down to the present. Britain could not reciprocate at the time, since it had no tariffs and adhered to the principle of free trade, but, as its competitive advantage weakened, it abandoned the principle and in 1932 a system of reciprocal tariff preference among all parts of the British Empire came into existence, with the encouragement of R. B. Bennett's Conservative government in Ottawa. Partly because of the preferences and partly because other countries responded to the depression by raising barriers against Canada's exports, the proportion of Canada's trade conducted within the empire increased sharply during the few years of Bennett's government.

By 1957, after more than two decades of Liberal government, the importance of Britain as a trading partner had sharply declined, but this change resulted from Britain's economic decline rather than from Liberal policies. In the aftermath of World War II, Britain had to devalue the pound and restrict imports to avoid bankruptcy. Its share of Canada's exports fell from 42% in 1935 to 17% in 1956, while its share of Canada's imports fell from 21% to 9%. John Diefenbaker promised to reverse this trend when he brought the Conservative party back into office. This goal could be seen as a fulfillment of Conservative tradition and had particular significance for the prairie region, the prime minister's political base, which still relied on British markets for its grain. An increase in the British preference had been one of the demands of the Progressive party, which had swept the Prairies after World War I.

The goal of increasing economic ties with Britain was not achieved and the attempt to achieve it had the ironic result of worsening relations between the two countries. Acceptance of a British offer to negotiate complete free trade between the two countries was judged to be politically unfeasible by the Conservative government. Subsequently the government opposed Britain's attempt to join the European

Economic Community, which it realized would mean the end of the preferential tariff system if it succeeded. Sentimental regard for the Commonwealth and concern for the economic interests of Western Canada both contributed to the government's policy. The Liberal opposition, on the other hand, was less emotionally attached to the Commonwealth and its political base was in Quebec and urban Ontario, which had little interest in the British market. For most Liberals, the Commonwealth took second place to the post-war concept of an "Atlantic Community", which they argued would be strengthened by Britain's entry into the European community.[9] When Britain eventually did join the community, on its third attempt, the Liberals were back in office and the Canadian government welcomed the success of the British application.

The attitudes of the CCF-NDP towards the British connection can be summarized quite briefly. In Canada as elsewhere, the left has opposed militarism and imperialism. Since World War II this position has led them to be critical of the United States, but before the war it led the CCF to be critical of the United Kingdom, then viewed as the country most likely to draw Canada into imperialist adventures. The CCF was thus even more isolationist in its prewar foreign policy than Mackenzie King, but it was never really anti-British, since it modelled itself after the British Labour party. Continuing ties with the Labour party, interest in the developing countries of the Commonwealth, a belief that the British connection somehow serves to distinguish Canada from the United States, and the large number of British-born Canadians among its members and supporters, have all contributed to pro-British tendencies in the New Democratic party. Although the NDP supported the maple leaf flag, it has never called for the abolition of Canada's constitutional ties to the British Crown, nor has it even considered adopting that position.

The American Presence

The United States has always loomed so large in the consciousness of Canadians that attitudes towards that country have had implications for almost every area of Canadian life, not just for foreign policy. The United States has been a source of economic and cultural influences which may be welcomed or feared, a model to be emulated or an example to be shunned. Canadian attitudes towards the United States are thus well documented and can be traced back long before Canada began to conduct its own foreign policy. For our purposes it is useful to distinguish four aspects of these attitudes: general attitudes towards the United States as a society, views on Canadian-American trade and the tariff, views on American ownership of Canadian industry, and views on military collaboration with the United States.

The Red Tory explanation for the orientations of Canadian parties towards the United States suggests that Liberals are most sympathetic towards that country because the United States embodies their liberal individualistic values. On the other hand it is argued that both Conservatives and socialists are less pro-American because their "collectivist" view of society and politics differs from American liberal individualism.

This view has a certain plausibility and appears to be partially confirmed by the record of Canadian history, but it has become questionable whether the parties still differ ideologically — if they ever did — in the way assumed by the theory. Although the Progressive Conservative party still has a few Red Tories, the party as a whole seems to be losing its traditional collectivism, such as it was, and becoming more like the Republican party in the United States, with its cult of individual initiative and free enterprise. [10] On the other hand many Liberals in recent years have become disillusioned with the United States, which no longer seems to qualify as the prototype of a liberal society. This disillusionment seems to be particularly great in southern Ontario, probably because of its geographical proximity to American social problems, and results in the sort of liberal nationalism associated with the *Toronto Star*, *Maclean's*, and the Committee for an Independent Canada.

In the nineteenth century there was a more clear-cut ideological distinction between Conservatives and Liberals, reflected in differing views of the United States. Conservatives tended to believe that the American Civil War was "in some sense, the inevitable bloody outcome of mob rule and presidential despotism". [11] They emphasized the contrasting virtues of tradition, order, and stability under constitutional monarchy. The Reformers or Liberals were more sympathetic to American democracy and their electoral stronghold in those days was in rural southwestern Ontario, whose inhabitants were described by John A. Macdonald as "Yankees and Covenanters, in fact the most yeasty and unsafe of populations". [12] The suspicion that the Liberal party harboured subversive republicans and annexationists was exploited by the Conservatives in election campaigns, notably those of 1861, 1891, and 1911. As late as 1943 the Liberal speaker of the Ontario legislature actually predicted that Canada would eventually join the United States and Mackenzie King believed that the statement had contributed to the Liberal party's loss of the provincial election in that year. [13]

Until after World War II any concern about the influence of the United States on Canadian life seemed to be expressed by Conservatives rather than by Liberals. An example of a policy brought about by such concern was the establishment of a public broadcasting network by R. B. Bennett's government so as to lessen the influence of American commercial radio. In the last years of his life, however, Mackenzie King appeared to recognize that the United States had replaced Britain as the imperial power and privately expressed apprehension about its growing influence on Canada. [14] More recently prominent Liberals, such as Vincent Massey, Walter Gordon, Eric Kierans, Gerard Pelletier, and Marc Lalonde, have recommended measures to halt the Americanization of Canada. Even greater apprehension about American influence has been expressed by the New Democratic party. The Conservatives can no longer be identified as the party of resistance to continentalism.

The impression that Conservatives were anti-American and Liberals pro-American was reinforced for many years by the contrasting views of the major parties concerning the protective tariff. From the 1870s until the 1930s, this issue was probably the most important in Canadian federal politics. Since its effect was to encourage manufacturing in Canada by discouraging the import of finished products from Canada's nearest neighbour, the tariff became a symbol of Canada's determination to remain separate from the United States. Sir John A. Macdonald's Conservatives had returned to office in 1878 on a program of railway-building, immigration, and industrialization through protective tariffs: the National Policy. This platform reinforced Conservative support in urban industrial areas where the tariff meant jobs for the worker and profits for the businessman. As Ontario was the province most suited for industrialization, it eventually became the Conservative stronghold. The Liberals, a more predominantly rural party, opposed high tariffs because protectionism increased the cost of goods purchased by the farmer without expanding his markets. This policy won support for the Liberals in the Maritimes and later in the West. In 1891 the Liberals fought an election on a platform of "unrestricted reciprocity", or free trade with the United States. They were defeated in large part because Macdonald, fighting his last campaign, charged that the "veiled treason" of reciprocity was a prelude to annexation by the United States. The Liberals subsequently abandoned reciprocity and gained fifteen years of power, but in 1911 Prime Minister Laurier again espoused reciprocity and fought another election in the issue. Robert Borden, the Conservative leader, accused the Liberals of "continentalism" — one of the earliest uses of this word — and Laurier was defeated. In 1948 there were secret discussions of continental free trade between Canadian and American officials, but Mackenzie King decided on reflection that the Liberal party could not risk the political consequences of being associated with this policy for a third time.[15]

In recent years Canadian nationalists have worried less about commodity imports from the United States and more about American direct investment. For a long time neither Conservatives nor Liberals appeared to regard American ownership of Canadian industry as any cause for concern. Conservative high-tariff policies deliberately encouraged American firms to establish branch plants in Canada, although they benefited Canadian-owned firms as well. Liberal low-tariff policies, on the other hand, encouraged American direct investment in the natural resource industries and the shipment of Canadian raw materials to the American market. Not until about 1955 did representatives of either traditional party discover that "foreign ownership" was, or should be, a political issue. George Drew and John Diefenbaker both expressed some concern on behalf of the Progressive Conservatives, but Mr. Diefenbaker did little about it while in office. Walter Gordon, the Liberal Minister of Finance from 1963 until 1965, was convinced that American ownership in Canada should be reduced, but he had little success in winning the Liberal party to his point of view. Both parties today appear to be internally divided on the importance of this issue and even more on what should be done about it. Clear differences of opinion between the two parties are almost impossible to discover.

In contrast to the traditional parties, the Labour Members of Parliament for Winnipeg, J. S. Woodsworth and A. A. Heaps, expressed concern about American ownership of Canadian industry as early as 1928.[16] The need to reduce American control of the economy has been a major theme of NDP statements and speeches, although, bearing in mind the American affiliations of the industrial trade unions which support the party, NDP spokesmen usually deny that they are "anti-American". A party of the left is inevitably concerned about foreign-controlled business as a corollary of its conviction that all big business should be strictly regulated, if not controlled, by the state. American-owned business in particular attracts resentment because American foreign policy and certain features of American society have become distasteful to most New Democrats.

Military collaboration between Canada and the United States has existed only since 1940. In the nineteenth century the United States was regarded as a potential mimitary antagonist, rather than as an ally. The Department of National Defence actually produced a contingency plan for war against the United States as late as 1921 and retained it until 1933.[17] The Canadian-American alliance began under the Liberal government of Mackenzie King, seemingly logical since the Liberals were traditionally the more pro-American party and since Mackenzie King himself had worked in the United States as a labour consultant for the Rockefellers. Perhaps more surprising, the Conservatives did not really oppose military collaboration with the United States, either then or later. Even the contrast between King's refusal to accept British entanglements and his willingness to sign military agreements with President Roosevelt attracted relatively little criticism. In 1957, a Progressive Conservative government accepted an even closer Liberal negotiated military relationship with the United States in the shape of NORAD, placing most of Canada's air force under American command.

What explains this shift in position on the part of a party which had traditionally had little affection for the United States? One reason was that since the United Kingdom was now also an ally of the United States, military ties with the latter country no longer appeared as disloyalty to the British connection.[18] A second reason, after 1945, was the strong anti-communist and anti-Soviet sentiment in the Progressive Conservative party. A third reason was the traditionally close ties between the Tories and the armed forces. George Drew, who led the party from 1948 until 1956, was a colonel in the reserves. Almost every member of the Diefenbaker cabinet was a war veteran, including a Major-General (Pearkes), four lieutenant colonels, an air force wing commander, four majors, and several commissioned with lesser rank. After 1945, the defence establishment supported close ties with the United States as strongly as they had once supported the British connection and the party followed their example.

A fourth reason for the new attitude of the Conservatives was probably a long-term change in the structure of the Canadian economy and the erosion of the economic interests which had underlain the old Conservative policy of building barriers against the United States. In the past Canada had financed its chronic trade deficit with the United States by selling more to Britain than it purchased from that country. After 1945 Britain was economically too weak to absorb its normal share of Canadian exports. Canada made up for this loss by seeking American markets and importing American capital to pay for its imports of goods from the United States. American firms moved in to develop Canada's mineral resources for American needs and to buy up the manufacturing industries established under the National Policy. Although these changes took place under a Liberal government, their greatest political impact was on the Conservative party because the business community in Ontario, the party's traditional stronghold, now identified its interests with the United States rather than with the British connection and the National Policy.

—   The Diefenbaker government's quarrel with the United States over nuclear warheads may seem to cast doubt on these observations, but in fact the episode illustrates the changes noted above. It took a series of disagreements with the Kennedy administration on China, Cuba, disarmament, the Organization of American States, the British application to enter Europe, and the nuclear warheads to reveal that a residue of the party's traditional anti-American sentiments remained. Yet the crisis also revealed that the party could no longer be held together, much less re-elected, on such sentiments. It is interesting that all three of the ministers who resigned over this issue had held high military rank during World War II. In addition George Hees was a graduate of the Royal Military College and a member of the Ontario economic elite created by the National Policy. Pierre Sévigny was the son of one of Borden's ministers, and Douglas Harkness represented Calgary, once the home of R. B. Bennett but transformed beyond recognition by the post-war influx of American capital. Such men now refused to serve in a government on bad terms with Washington.

After their defeat in 1963, the Progressive Conservatives seem to have taken this lesson to heart by becoming even more pro-American than the Liberals. The change began even while Mr. Diefenbaker retained the leadership and accelerated after he was succeeded by Robert Stanfield. Under Stanfield's leadership the Conservatives argued that both the foreign and economic policies of the Liberal government were causing friction with the United States, an ironic reversal of the positions taken by the two parties in 1963. A number of leading Conservatives publicly defended American objectives in Southeast Asia during the late 1960s and early 1970s. Conservative MP Jack Mackintosh cast the only vote in the House of Commons against a government resolution condemning American nuclear testing in the Pacific in 1971.

While the Conservatives are becoming more pro-American, the Liberals appear since 1968 to have moved in the opposite direction. Possibly, as suggested earlier in this chapter, the Liberals are simply returning to their traditional policy of minimizing foreign commitments and obligations. Possibly they are responding, with characteristic opportunism, to their assessment of public opinion. The election of Pierre Trudeau as leader of the party may also explain the change. Although never anti-American in any real sense, Trudeau had bitterly criticized Pearson and the Liberal party for espousing the acquisition of nuclear warheads in 1963 and had publicly announced his intention to vote NDP in the 1963 election.[19] The continentalist right wing of the Liberal party strongly opposed Trudeau's election as leader. Paul Hellyer, who had persuaded Pearson to change his position on nuclear warheads and became Pearson's Minister of National Defence, eventually resigned from the Trudeau cabinet and joined the Conservative party.

Although the CCF accepted military collaboration with the United States in the post-war period, the New Democratic party has been more critical of Canada's participation in military alliances. The NDP strongly opposed any Canadian involvement in the possession or possible use of nuclear weapons, making this a major issue in its 1963 election campaign. New Democrats also criticize the United States for using its military and economic power to uphold the status quo in Latin America and Asia. Nonetheless, the NDP did not clearly advocate withdrawal from military ties with the United States until 1969.

The Outer World

Canadian foreign policy took a long time to emerge from almost exclusive preoccupation with Britain and the United States. Since World War II, however, Canada has become much more involved with the outer world through diplomatic relations, external aid programs, and active participation in the Commonwealth, NATO, and the United Nations. Some evidence of different partisan orientations towards the outer world has therefore emerged, although it is more scant than the evidence regarding attitudes towards the British connection and the American presence.

Orientations of the parties towards the outer world can best be described in terms of their sympathy or antipathy towards particular foreign countries. Sympathetic feelings have been directed towards a variety of countries and for a variety of reasons. Antipathetic feelings have been directed towards dictatorships of the right and of the left, but more frequently and consistently the latter.

The Conservative party's favourable sentiments towards the United Kingdom have tended to spill over on to other members of the Commonwealth and Conservative interest in the Commonwealth has survived the Commonwealth's transition from a group of white dominions to a multiracial association of mainly developing countries. The party's interest in closer ties with the Commonwealth Caribbean can be traced back as far as the Borden government. More recently, the Diefenbaker government found allies among Asian and African Commonwealth members in its battle to keep Britain out of the European community. Although British Conservatives had by this time lost interest in the Commonwealth, Canadian Conservatives had not. Concern for the survival of the Commonwealth probably led Prime Minister Diefenbaker to side with the African and Asian members in their insistence that South Africa could not remain a member unless it accepted the principle of racial equality.

Favourable sentiments towards particular countries in the outer world are somewhat harder to discern in the case of the Liberal party, but the party has tended, because of its strong support among French Canadians and other Roman Catholics, to be sympathetic towards countries in which Roman Catholicism is the dominant religion. This factor contributed to Mackenzie King's timid policy regarding sanctions against fascist Italy following the invasion of Ethiopia. Italy was a Roman Catholic country and Mussolini enjoyed good relations with the Vatican in 1935.[20] On a more positive note, the Liberals have been somewhat more interested in Latin America than the other parties. French Canadians have traditionally felt an affinity with Latin America, in common opposition to Protestant, Anglo-Saxon, and materialist influences in the western hemisphere. It was also the Liberal government of Pierre Trudeau that first exchanged ambassadors with the Vatican, an initiative criticized by some non–Roman Catholic Canadians.

New Democrats tend to sympathize, as might be expected, with governments which are left-wing without being communist. This category encompasses a wide range, from Scandinavian social democrats to radical third world regimes like Tanzania and, prior to its overthrow, Allende's Popular Unity government in Chile. Radical Arab governments are the exception to the rule, largely because Israel's governing party, like the NDP itself, belongs to the Socialist International.

One country which has been an object of antipathy on the part of all three parties is the Union of Soviet Socialist Republics, but the parties differ to some extent in the intensity with which they hold these sentiments and in the conclusions which they draw from them.

As might be expected, the most pronounced and consistent antipathy towards the Soviet regime has been displayed by the Conservative party; this hostility can be traced back to the early days both of Soviet communism and of Canadian foreign policy. Sir Robert Borden's government was one of several which sent troops to Russia in the aftermath of the Bolshevik revolution in a futile effort to overthrow the new regime. At about the same time, the issue of Canadian-Soviet relations became associated with the fear of domestic subversion. Borden and his successor, Arthur Meighen, apparently believed that the Winnipeg General Strike of 1919 was a "Bolshevik" uprising and R. B. Bennett expressed similar fears about some of the manifestations of unrest during the depression which coincided with his term of office.

The anti-communist and anti-Soviet tradition was maintained when the Conservatives next came to power in 1957. Prime Minister Diefenbaker was no farther to the right than his party on this issue and in fact had opposed declaring the Communist party of Canada illegal in 1948 when most Conservatives favoured this measure.[21] However, his term of office was marked by much anti-Soviet rhetoric, the most famous instance being his speech at the United Nations in 1960. Admittedly these were some of the coldest years of the Cold War, but an additional reason for the government's anti-Soviet stance was its popularity among certain ethnic groups, particularly the Ukrainians, who were well-represented among Conservative MP's and those who voted for them. Some Conservative candidates in 1962 went so far as to suggest that the Liberal party and its leader were "soft on communism".[22] More recently, some Conservatives have criticized Mr. Trudeau for his efforts to improve Canadian-Soviet relations.

Despite the anti-Soviet stance of the Diefenbaker government, it was more moderate in its attitude towards the Communist regimes of China and Cuba. Trade with both was encouraged, in spite of American disapproval. A cynic might note that Tibetans were less numerous than Ukrainians on the Canadian prairies and that wheat farmers, who appreciated the Chinese market, were more numerous than either. Since the policy of the Kennedy administration in the United States was to improve relations with the Soviet Union while maintaining a hard line against the newer and supposedly more militant regimes, these facts contributed to the deterioration of Canadian-American relations.

Although the Liberals are also anti-communist, they appear to be somewhat more flexible than the Conservatives in their attitude towards the Soviet Union. In any event the Communist party of Canada must have thought so at the end of World War II, when it called for a union of all "progressive forces", a category in which it included the Liberals, against the threat of a Conservative revival. The Gouzenko affair and the Cold War ended this brief honeymoon, but Lester Pearson, anti-communist though he was, became in 1955 the first NATO foreign minister to visit Moscow. In the following year the Liberals extended most favoured nation status to the USSR, a step over which the United States was still hesitating nearly two decades later.

Prime Minister Trudeau made serious efforts to improve Soviet-Canadian relations despite the invasion of Czechoslovakia a few months after he took office. He also showed signs of not taking either NATO or NORAD very seriously. The Conservatives were extremely critical of two remarks made by Mr. Trudeau when he visited the USSR: one in which he said that Canada needed ties with the USSR to balance the overwhelming influence of the United States and the second to the effect that nationalist terrorism was no more praiseworthy in the Ukraine than in Quebec. The possibility of any prominent Conservative making either of these remarks in private, let alone in public, is remote enough to be disregarded.

It might be expected that the NDP, as a party of the left, would be less hostile to the Soviet Union and other Communist regimes than the business-oriented parties. In fact, however, the NDP has been so fearful of being associated in the public mind with communism that it has made great efforts to emphasize its lack of sympathy with communist parties and regimes. A revealing — and ridiculous — example of this fear occurred when Premier Barrett of British Columbia visited Western

Europe in 1973 and met the leaders of various left-wing parties; Mr. Barrett announced that François Mitterand, the socialist leader in France, was not on his calling list because Mitterand had committed the unpardonable sin of forming an electoral alliance with the communists.[23]

Electoral expediency, however, is not the whole explanation for the anti-communist stance of the NDP. Communists and social democrats are competitors rather than allies; that both see the working class as their natural constituency exacerbates the conflict between them. The bitter struggle between communists and CCF supporters for control of the labour movement, although long since resolved by the total defeat of the communists, has left a legacy of anti-communism in the unions and in the NDP itself. Thus, it is not surprising that the NDP waited until 1969 before it finally advocated withdrawal from NATO, nor that the party's foreign policy critic in Parliament retained his role despite his public opposition to the change of policy.

The NDP is the only one of the major parties that has displayed real and consistent antipathy towards dictatorships of the right. The Liberal attitude towards Mussolini has already been referred to; the Conservatives opposed him because he threatened the British Empire, not for ideological reasons. Both traditional parties supported the appeasement of Hitler and changed their views only when it became clear that he threatened the security of Canada itself. In more recent times only the NDP has publicly objected to the presence of Portugal and Greece in NATO, although Lester Pearson wrote in his memoirs that he had opposed the inclusion of Portugal when the alliance was established.[24] The Trudeau government launched a major Canadian aid program in Indonesia, where a right-wing dictatorship had recently gained power after a brief but bloody civil war. Later the government was criticized by the NDP for its prompt recognition of the counter-revolutionary regime in Chile.

In summary it can be said that the parties do have different approaches to foreign policy and that these differences reflect their history, ideology, the personalities of their leaders, and the economic, social, and cultural groups from which they draw support. The differences, however, are not extreme; in practice, they are diluted by expediency, bureaucratic pressure, and the lack of direct party influence on policy-making. By and large the continuity of Canadian foreign policy and the consensus which supports it are more striking than the differences between the parties.

Notes

1. "Whig" interpretations of Canada's external relations can be found in Bruce Hutchison, *The Incredible Canadian* (Toronto: Longmans, 1952), A. R. M. Lower, *Colony to Nation*, 3rd edition (Toronto: Longmans, 1959), and Frank H. Underhill, *In Search of Canadian Liberalism* (Toronto: Macmillan, 1961).

2. The term "Red Tory" — akin to the Tory Democracy as epitomized by Benjamin Disraeli — was employed by Gad Horowitz in "Tories, Socialists,

and the Demise of Canada," *Canadian Dimension*, II:4 (May-June 1965). This article is a review of George Grant, *Lament for a Nation* (Toronto: McClelland and Stewart, 1965), which is a classic statement of the Red Tory position. See also Donald Creighton, *Canada's First Century* (Toronto: Macmillan, 1970).

3. J. W. Pickersgill and D. F. Forster, *The Mackenzie King Record: 1947–1948* (Toronto: University of Toronto Press, 1970), 133–153, 176–177.

4. Pearson was actually accused of being a Tory and of setting his principles aside to join the Liberal cabinet. See his *Memoirs*, II (Toronto: University of Toronto Press, 1973), 4–5.

5. In chronological order: Borden, Meighen, King, Bennett, St. Laurent, Pearson, Diefenbaker, Smith, Green, Martin, Trudeau, Sharp.

6. Donald Creighton, *John A. Macdonald: The Old Chieftain* (Toronto: Macmillan, 1955), 410.

7. Roger Graham: *Arthur Meighen: The Door of Opportunity* (Toronto: Clarke, Irwin, 1960), 224.

8. According to a Canadian Institute of Public Opinion poll released on April 15, 1967, three times as many Canadians associated the Liberal party as associated the Conservative party with "a sound foreign policy."

9. The United States supported the British application and France opposed it for essentially the same reason.

10. George Grant sees this as the reason why Diefenbaker's government was unable to implement policies of increasing Canadian independence (Grant, *Lament for a Nation*, 13–20).

11. Donald Creighton, *John A. Macdonald: The Young Politician* (Toronto: Macmillan, 1952), 320.

12. Quoted in R. M. Hamilton, *Canadian Quotations and Phrases* (Toronto: McClelland and Stewart, 1952), 154.

13. J. W. Pickersgill: *The Mackenzie King Record, 1939–1944* (Toronto: University of Toronto Press, 1960), 517–519, 569.

14. J. W. Pickersgill, *The Mackenzie King Record: 1939–1944*, 644–645; J. W. Pickersgill and D. F. Forster, *The Mackenzie King Record: 1947–1948*, 265, 269–270.

15. J. W. Pickersgill and D. F. Forster, *The Mackenzie King Record: 1947–1948*, 259–273.

16. H. F. Angus (ed.), *Canada and Her Great Neighbor* (New York: Russell and Russell, 1970), 334–336.

17. James Eayrs, *In Defence of Canada: From the Great War to the Great Depression* (Toronto: University of Toronto Press, 1964), 70–78.

18. It could be argued, of course, that a de facto Ango-American alliance existed long before 1940 and that the notion of a British counterweight to American influence was therefore intrinsically fallacious. This argument is presented by Glen Frankfurter, *Baneful Domination: The Idea of Canada in the Atlantic World* (Don Mills: Longmans, 1971).

19. See his article "Pearson ou l'abdication de l'esprit," *Cité Libre*, 56 (April 1963).

20. This episode is discussed in Lester B. Pearson, *Memoirs*, I, (Toronto: University of Toronto Press, 1972), 92–101. It is interesting that the future Liberal prime minister preferred the Conservative to the Liberal policy in 1935 and was prepared to say so in retrospect.

21. Peter C. Newman, *Renegade in Power* (Toronto: McClelland and Stewart, 1963), 25.

22. Peyton V. Lyon, *Canada in World Affairs: 1961–1963* (Toronto: Oxford University Press, 1968), 69–71.

23. *The Globe and Mail*, (June 6, 1973).

24. Lester B. Pearson, *Memoirs*, II, 45, 55.

CHAPTER 15
CONCLUSION

Summary

In describing the patterns of genesis and cleavage in the party system, Sections I and II demonstrated some significant differences among the parties. The chapters on party origins suggested that the major parties were characteristically more flexible than the minor parties and that this difference could be attributed in part to their parliamentary origins. The chapters on political cleavages showed how Canada possessed the cultural, geographic, and class cleavages prevalent in industrial countries. In other political systems, the cultural cleavage may assume a religious vs. secular form (eg. pro-clerical vs. anti-clerical in Italy). The cleavage may be expressed as a dispute between an established religion and a non-established religion (eg. Anglicans vs. nonconformists in England) or between particularists and universalists (eg. racists and Vietnam hawks vs. non-racists and Vietnam doves in the United States). Like Belgium and other bicultural countries, Canada exhibits the peculiarly bicultural mode of cultural conflict at the input stage in her party system.[1]

According to the input-throughput-output model employed in the organization of the text, Canada's cleavages are transformed by the representational process (elections and mass communications) discussed in Section III and by the internal organization of the parties examined in Section IV. The transformation effectively diminishes differences. Each chapter on party policy suggests that there are few systematic differences to distinguish the output of one party from another.

The curious failure of Canada's cleavages to be reflected in party policy raises four vital questions: how does Canada compare with other countries? what is the relative importance of the factors which cause the absence of systematic differences in output? is the absence of systematic philosophical differences in party output a desirable phenomenon? if this situation is not desirable, as we will argue below, what kinds of political changes can be undertaken to provide voters with philosophically meaningful choices?

In all frankness, these questions can be tackled only in an intuitive fashion. There is simply too little knowledge about Canada, not to mention other countries, to be certain about valid cross-national comparisons. Without knowing which national party systems offer the voter the most philosophically distinct choices, it is difficult to estimate the relative impacts of cleavage patterns, mass communications, party organizations, and other factors on the nature of these choices.

In an analogous way, the absence of knowledge about the social impacts of policies makes it difficult to link individual policies to specific political philosophies. To the extent that political philosophies express class interests, it is virtually impossible for individuals of a given political philosophy to hold an intelligent view of a public policy or program without knowing which social strata benefit most or least from that policy or program.

Even in a wealthy, highly educated country like Canada, the process of policy-making is in some ways no more advanced today than a century ago. As Robert Jackson and Michael Atkinson have pointed out in their incisive study of the making of legislation, a considerable share of policy-making is a reactive response to short-term contingencies.[2] The government therefore does not have the time to await studies of the impact of proposed changes. Once policy is adopted, the beliefs which guided it are assumed to be true and are left untested. The longer the delay in subjecting the policy to empirical verification, the more serious the consequences and the greater the fear of discovering that the policy may not serve the intended purpose.

Although not a uniquely federal matter, socialized medicine illustrates our point well. Some cabinet ministers and senior policy-makers understand the possibilities for abuse provided by the public health plans. In the picturesque words of one bureaucrat, "medicare is a license for larceny." Fee for service provides physicians with an incentive to encourage unnecessary use of services. So long as physicians are permitted to own the medical buildings in which pharmaceutical, laboratory, and other services are located, there is an additional conflict of interest. On the one hand, physicians exercise an unsupervised influence over the demand side of the economic process. On the other hand, they retain the power to limit the supply side in both the kinds and number of medical practitioners trained for the marketplace. Thus, physicians possess legally an economic monopoly which, if enjoyed by businessmen, would yield fines and/or imprisonment.

Health ministers and officials sometimes lament the situation in private, but they are frightened to act. An attempt to merely study public health practices runs the risk of an embarrassing exposure at the hands of opposition parties. Governments are sometimes queezy about employing reform-minded academics for fear that research findings will reach the eyes of the opposition leaders before reaching the eyes of the cabinet.

The weakness of political parties appears to be a crucial factor in the absence of knowledge about the social consequences of government policies. Compared to British parties, Canadian parties possess very few independent resources in the domains of research and policy-making. Canadian politicians are typically amateurs or professional politicians with strong local roots. David Lewis, past leader of the New Democratic party, is a rare exception in his rise from a career with the party's national office. By contrast, Denis Healey, R. A. Butler, and other Labour and Conservative leaders spent periods as central party researchers before rising to cabinet or shadow cabinet positions in Britain.

The research weakness of Canadian parties means that they have only limited capacities to criticize government programs on a sustained basis. Our parties tend to be reactive. If the government says "white," the opposition says "black," or vice-versa. There is therefore no incentive for governing parties to commission extensive research on the effects of their programs. In contrast to philosophical debate, "black vs. white" debates can be handled easily without preparation. There is furthermore every incentive for governments to prevent research of the kind being discussed. To commission research incurs a risk of valuable ammunition falling into the hands of the opposition.

Having discussed some of the reasons for the absence of information about policy impacts, we now turn to the first of the four basic questions which arise from our studies. Despite a lack of reliable cross-national data, it seems reasonably clear that the policy output of Canada's parties is less distinguishable than those of other political systems. In Italy and Israel, for example, obvious gulfs separate the parties in their attitudes towards economic equality and economic systems and in their attitudes towards religion. Even Great Britain offers a party system with philosophical differences. In spite of criticisms from the left that Labour has been co-opted by conservative civil servants, the party retains a distinct method of handling trade union relations, wildcat strikes, and other economic issues associated with class conflict.

Although it is possible to suggest that the Canadian party system offers fewer philosophical differences than other systems, the absence of cross-national data makes it difficult to explain why. One reason for the absence of policy differences, especially left-right or class differences, is that the left-right cleavage is simply weaker in this country than elsewhere. If the left-right cleavage is weak, it is only reasonable to expect modest differences in output.

Nevertheless, all the throughputs do combine to diminish even further the strength of the class cleavage. As Cairns showed in his classic study of elections, the first-past-the-post electoral rules increase the importance of regional conflicts at the expense of class conflict.[3] To take the NDP, for example, the loss of a few thousand votes in its strongholds in British Columbia or Saskatchewan would not be compensated by an equivalent increase in support in Quebec or the Maritimes.

The system of mass communications also diminishes the strength of the class cleavage. One factor is that some of the media tend to be regional in focus and tend therefore to accentuate regional and bicultural divisions at the expense of class. Regionalism is a marked trait of the Radio-Canada television network, where the often alleged separatist sympathies of its staff may help explain the Quebec-centered character of its news reporting.

Another factor in the impact of mass communications on the class cleavage is that the media are business enterprises seeking profit and avoiding cost. In order to minimize cost, the media depend as much as they can on U.S. wire services for copy for the women's, sports, entertainment, and financial pages, not to mention the essential news pages.

As we indicated in the chapter on the mass media, the American content of Canadian news is so overwhelming that the reporting of Canadian foreign policy is exceeded not only by the reporting of American foreign policy, but also by the reporting of American domestic politics. Some newspapers even rely on United States sources for background stories on Canada.

One consequence of the American pre-eminence in Canadian news may be to exacerbate the bicultural cleavage by encouraging English Canadians to perceive greater similarities between themselves and Americans and therefore to perceive greater differences between themselves and French-Canadians. This identification was probably a more serious problem when Kennedy was president because the good news from south of the border did outweigh the bad. Another consequence of the American pre-eminence in news may be to deprive Canadian citizens and politicians alike of sufficient information to identify and interpret some of the avowed philosophical characteristics of the political parties.

The media not only control costs by depending on American sources, but they also control costs by employing staffs which lack both numbers and highly specialized training. The journalist who is poorly schooled or who has but a generalist's training is simply no match for the well educated finance minister supported by an army of top-flight researchers. Nor is the journalist permitted the resources or time to consult independent authorities. At best, the journalist reports accurately the minister's statements, leaving intact the habitual euphemisms, circumlocutions, and misleading inferences. At worst, the reporter forgets the content of the minister's address and emphasizes the drama, the personalities involved, and the emotional context. The press feels comfortable emphasizing personalities, drama, and confrontation at the expense of issues because the former approach does not require specialized knowledge or understanding and allegedly has audience appeal.[4]

In recent years, the leading newspapers of the United States have come to devote greater resources for the purpose of research. For example, Seymour Hersh, of the *New York Times* is authorized to spend a month or longer on an individual story, such as domestic espionage by the Central Intelligence Agency. In Canada, very few journalists, even senior ones, are not burdened with the daily humdrum of 500-word submissions. During the 1974 federal election, Anthony Westell sought a more modest change at the *Toronto Daily Star*. Instead of accepting party pronouncements at face value and reporting them instantaneously, the *Star*'s Ottawa bureau chief chose to subject the pronouncements to dispassionate analysis and evaluation. The newspaper's publishers insisted on a more flamboyant, instantaneous style. Westell and two colleagues resigned in apparent despair.

The superficial character of contemporary journalism appears to influence the party system in two ways. In a direct sense, many parliamentarians base their parliamentary debates on decisions of newsworthiness by the press. These parliamentarians view the press in a utilitarian way. If the press responds well to a line of questioning by according front page attention, then this line of questioning is a profitable one to pursue. For example, during the 1972 election, the NDP did not plan its campaign around the "corporate welfare bum" slogan, but changed its strategy after the CBC and other media responded favourably to the new rhetoric.

Mass communications influence the character of the party system in an indirect sense as well. Because the media fail to interpret events and policies for the public, the public is left unequipped to pass judgment. Ideally, the press should include in the body of its reporting the views of academics and other experts as a means of measuring the truthfulness of statements reported in the news. Some of the media make some attempt to employ experts in documentaries or for the purpose of background analysis. However, none of the media employ experts systematically in the vital domain of news. In the absence of this kind of intellectual assistance, large segments of the public remain unable to assess government programs in terms of their own self-interest and in terms of the self-interest of others. As a result, neither electors nor parliamentarians see the budgetary and legislative process as a "win-or-lose" situation. There is no notion that expenditures in one segment of the population may be borne by taxes on another or that expenditures in one sector may reduce options in another. On the contrary, government budgets are seen as limitless reservoirs from which an increasing variety and volume of needs can and ought to be satisfied.

It is rare to find a party opposed to a given expenditure. Instead, parties compete with each other in efforts to promise subsidies which may be indiscriminant or, at least, incompatible with the party's philosophic conception of just rewards. Thus, the Conservative party, the historic party of tradition, Protestantism, and the work ethic, advocated a guaranteed income plan which included healthy young males remaining outside the work force by choice, not through impediment. The alleged party of the middle class, the Liberals, exempted from income tax the interest from bank deposits and other sources normally available to the rich only. The NDP, the intended party of the working class, advocated subsidies on milk, veterans' mortgages, and on other goods and services which would be of modest benefit to low income earners because their lack of capital and information limits their ability to take advantage of government programs.

There is an incentive for parties to promise assistance to almost any segment of the electorate in the hope of augmenting support. Because the mass public is so uninformed by the media there is little risk that the promise of support to one segment of the electorate would alienate another, already loyal, segment. The effect is a non-ideological style of discourse among the parties. As Jackson and Atkinson describe House of Commons proceedings, "most parliamentarians seem unable to structure debate ... around competing party policies or philosophies."[5] Jackson and Atkinson also find, "the parties often converge in their attitudes toward sectional and ethnic cleavages and traditional left-right divisions seem inappropriate to the discussion of many political issues."[6]

While Canadian cleavages, especially the class cleavage, are mitigated by the intellectual impoverishment of the media, they are also mitigated by the impoverishment of the parties. None of the parties possess serious, effective research arms. The few researchers in the employ of the parties are utilized for short-term contingencies rather than long-term analysis. A party researcher is employed typically to read and summarize the government's budget or find data to corroborate a policy already adopted by the party's leader, caucus, or convention. Occasionally, a party, particularly one in opposition, will sponsor a brief conference of "thinkers" to create new policies. The parties assume that they understand the effects of current programs and that it is therefore a comparatively simple task to develop new ones. However, as the astute parliamentarian Max Saltsman has stated frequently, few Members of Parliament do understand the impacts of existing government programs. A leading member of the NDP, Saltsman has attempted to coax and cajole his party into devoting more energy to understanding the entire government process.

One of Saltsman's favourite examples of the need to understand rather than merely advocate is the Unemployment Insurance Act. The characteristic left-wing or redistributive position has been to make it easier to receive benefits by shortening the waiting period, by permitting pregnancy as a qualification for receiving benefits, and by including highly paid seasonal workers such as the westcoast fishermen. Saltsman argues that, if reliable data were available, the data might show that weaker qualifications actually cause a regressive distribution of benefits. Saltsman suspects that wealthy employees — well paid seasonal workers or females with high family incomes — are the most able and prepared to remain on unemployment insurance. Following this argument to its logical conclusion, we are convinced that the parties' inability and unwillingness to allocate resources for research purposes undermines their ability to offer coherent alternatives consistent with their avowed beliefs.

The Nature of Our Concern

In our view, the absence of coherent philosophical differences is undesirable because the legitimacy of electoral democracy appears to be thereby undermined. The absence of systematic ideological differences is also undesirable because this absence appears to be a factor in the evolution of two objectionable features of our political economy: a large, growing public sector accompanied by an unequal distribution of income and wealth.

As matters of principle, we possess an enormous confidence in the benefits of electoral democracy and the parliamentary system. At a minimum, elections do provide a choice of personnel and do set constraints on the whimsicality and authoritarianism of public officials.

Nevertheless, in our view, the legitimacy or public acceptance of democratic elections is not well served by parties which fail to offer meaningful, systematic alternatives. We would not for a moment suggest that the Canadian system be somehow remade into a replica of the polarized, stalemated systems of Italy and France, where the parties are sometimes incapable of the most elementary gestures of cooperation. We are concerned because our federal parties have already been supplanted by other agencies as the effective opposition to the national government. The Economic Council of Canada, Statistics Canada, the Consumers' Association of Canada, Pollution Probe, provincial governments, CBC-TV's *Ombudsman*, and other institutions and interest groups are already significant sources of criticism of government policy. Most of these non-party groups, whether independent-minded federal agencies or provincial governments, have research facilities which far exceed those at the disposal of the opposition parties.

It is easy, therefore, to see how popular respect for Parliament can be eroded. The less than great reverence for parliamentary institutions is not helped by the lack of resources available to the opposition nor by the failure of the opposition to offer an alternative program. En masse, the vast number of interest groups and agencies outside the federal Parliament must appear as a random source of commentary. It is by offering a systematic alternative to the government that the opposition parties can distinguish themselves from the many non-party spokesmen and therefore claim a privileged role in the eyes of the public.

While we suspect that the parties' lack of intellectual resources undermines their ability to compete for attention, we also suspect that their weakness may explain the undesirable direction of government policy — towards a greater public sector without a greater social equality. With classical liberalism and the modern political right, we share a mistrust of large governments. At a minimum, we refuse to believe that public officials are intrinsically more benevolent than private ones. In the North, for instance, we have not noticed a remarkable transformation of white bureaucrats into socially enlightened individuals in their dealings with natives merely because they were employees of government. Nor have we found labour-management relations in the Post Office, for example, to be more enlightened than labour-management relations in, say, Labatts Breweries or ALCAN. Furthermore, we are concerned that the unplanned expansion of government services and subsidies injects sources of irrationality and inefficiency into the economy. At a maximum, we fear the totalitarian possibilities of large governments. We note that libertarian systems, whether ideologically socialist as in Sweden or ideologically capitalist as in the United States, have moderate public sectors.

With traditional socialism, we believe in the value of a measure of social equality consistent with the obligation of all able members of society to contribute. At a minimum, some degree of social equality is required for cohesion and public order. At a maximum, an egalitarian society is pleasant, compassionate, and makes efficient use of its manpower.

Table 15-1

Policy Options

	Social Equality	Social Inequality
Small Public Sector	I	II
Large Public Sector	III	IV

Table 15-1 portrays four basic policy options. Recent Canadian development appears to be in the direction of quadrant IV, a situation of increased government activity and stabilized social inequality. While admitting frankly a comparative lack of evidence, we speculate that the contemporary direction of Canadian policy is related to the intellectual weakness of the parties. The philosophical cornerstones of the Canadian left are social equality and government intervention. The philosophical cornerstones of the right are autonomy from government and the rewarding of private effort. From intellectual weakness and sometimes from electoral self-interest as well, both the left and right have failed to set the parameters or criteria by which the growth of the public sector is to be assessed. Thus, the civil service has been free to satisfy the sometimes indiscriminant public demand for government services and bureaucratic desires for empire-building. The left has been content to accept government intervention on the assumption that government intervention somehow assures social equality. The right has been prepared to set aside its predilections against government activity in the knowledge that its natural constituency, the middle and upper strata, is confident that it can receive a sizeable share of government beneficence.

Some Proposals for Reform

In the preceding discussion, we expressed several values: the importance of cohesive, identifiable parties as ends in themselves, as a means of augmenting the legitimacy of Parliament, as a means to achieving some degree of social equality, and as a means to controlling the expansion of the public sector. The last objective is the easiest to achieve. The expansion of the public sector is bound to slow down quickly, if only because of popular resistance to greater taxation. Even Jim Laxer, the Waffle spokesman and left-wing socialist, has drawn attention to the likelihood of a taxpayers' revolt.[7] Furthermore, as the knowledge grows that the welfare state does not guarantee the welfare of the lower strata, there is likely to be less pressure from the left in the NDP and the major parties for the holus-bolus expansion of government.

As for our other values, we propose three reforms which may be necessary, but not necessarily sufficient, conditions for their achievement. There will need to be a change in the structure of parliamentary debate to give greater play to party differences and an increase in the research and intellectual capacities of both the individual parties and the mass media.

The organization of parliamentary business should be changed to reflect more closely the central importance of the parties.[8] First, the passage of bills which provoke no inter-party controversy should be accelerated by sending them to a Second Reading Committee. The time saved by this reform could then be devoted to matters which provoke genuine disagreements. The parties would have more opportunity to display the full nature of their differences.

Secondly, the Government should provide Parliament with its legislative schedule much farther in advance than the customary week. The opposition parties would thus have more time to prepare coherent criticisms. In particular, the opposition parties would have more time to prepare criticisms congruous with the alternative philosophical outlooks to which they lay claim.

Thirdly, a considerable amount of time should be allocated for debate on the government's overall budget and not merely for debate on the estimates of individual departments. The effect of debate on departmental estimates alone must be to diminish systematic party differences and augment government spending. Because our culture values "positive" discourse more highly than "negative" discourse and, because of electoral self-interest, parliamentarians are unlikely to call for a reduction in a department's budget. Instead, all opposition parties tend to lament that a given departmental budget has overlooked a certain program or a certain group's needs. The cry of the opposition is more often that the government has "not done enough" rather than that it "has done too much." In addition to providing the opposition with more opportunity to debate the Government's budget, some consideration might be given to allowing each major opposition party to present beforehand its own "counter-budget." More than other changes in legislative practice, this innovation might encourage the opposition to be better prepared for financial debate.

A reform in the structure of parliamentary debate does not by itself assure an improvement in the content of debate or a change in the public's perceptions of the parties and of government policy. The crux of the problem is that the capacities of the parties and of the media to participate effectively and intelligently in the political system have lagged far behind the importance of the political system. Over the last century, the proportion of the public sector has grown from virtually nil to almost half of the total economy. Consequently, almost no private economic or organized cultural activities can be considered without reference to government policy. In foreign policy, the world has contracted to the extent where the outbreak of conflict on any part of the globe threatens the potential well-being of the most remote settlement in this country.

During the same period of one hundred years, there has also been a growth in the capacity of parties and the media to process information. However, even without full-proof data, it is probably accurate to say that the capacities of the parties and of the media to process information have not kept up with the increased pace and importance of information. Each of the parties now employ a handful of full-time researchers. However, this handful is no match for the huge, well trained bureaucracy. A century ago, the bureaucracy was small and possessed the inefficiency of a patronage-ridden institution. The legislator's role was sufficiently simple to be considered a part-time occupation.

The comparative inability of the parties to process information and conduct research independently of the public bureaucracy inhibits their ability to influence policy once they are in power. This kind of reasoning influenced Prime Minister Trudeau to expand the resources of the Prime Minister's Office as well as the resources of the two larger opposition parties. However, the few hundreds of thousands of dollars allocated to the opposition are insufficient, even if well intended. If parliamentary democracy is to provide a choice of policies as well as personnel, then the parties must have significant abilities to conduct research and proffer alternative remedies. This capacity can only be developed outside the confines of the public bureaucracy. At present, the slim resources available to the parties do not even enable parliamentarians to frame effectively the kinds of questions for the parliamentary order paper that are needed to discover the impacts of existing government programs. Because modern government operations are so complex, the parties need assistants with advanced training in the social and physical sciences merely to pose the right questions.

Following Trudeau's precedent, the government and Parliament should expand much further the monies allocated to the parties for research. The expansion should be low simply because the small scale of present research activities provides the parties with only a modest ability to absorb and plan increased allocations. However, if parties are to become independent sources of policy, they must have resources in the many millions of dollars and not in the thousands.

Like the parties, the media have not developed the intelligence resources in proportion to society's need. Over the last century, the proportion of the gross national product devoted to mass communications has remained approximately constant.[9] However, there has been an enormous increase in the share of the expenditure devoted to technology and a corresponding decline in the share expended on human resources. As a result, the media are able to process more and more information, but not necessarily with more and more intelligence.

Along with the development of technology, the last century has witnessed a cultural change whereby traditional notions of excellence and the "just price" in the market place have been replaced by notions of quantitative efficiency, "market" quality, and "market" price. In news reporting, there are usually choices between an immediate report and a profound report, between a quickly given opinion and an analysis, between dramatic images and structured explanation, between capsule reports dictated by events and the planned treatment of events, between problem exposure and problem solution, and between conflict presentation and conflict resolution. In each of these dichotomies, the first alternative represents the economic choice while the second represents the socially desirable choice. It is by opting for the first series of choices that the media can employ fewer journalists, that they can employ less well trained and therefore less costly journalists, and that they can even avoid the employment of journalists altogether by relying on wire services.

The Canadian Radio-Television Commission understands well some of the unfortunate consequences of contemporary media practices. As the CRTC has declared in a general statement about all broadcasting services,

> ... the development of the means of transmission and broadcasting in Canada has not been accompanied by an adequate corresponding development of the means of production and processing; nor has there been a sufficient increase in the identification and promotion of talent. [10]

A chairman of the CRTC was even more blunt, for he argued that there is "a squandering of technology when we all are engulfed by each others' monetary problems yet have no idea where the other lives, or what he feels."[11]

Although the CRTC understands many of the problems, their solutions have been few and slow in coming. The major achievement has been to increase Canadian content by means of regulation. This method has demonstrably increased Canadian music content and has been a boon to the music and recording industries. On the other hand, to require Canadian content without providing funds does not necessarily assure good programming, the obvious case of television entertainment.[12]

Increasing Canadian content generally may have a positive effect on the political system by strengthening a sense of Canadian identity. However, the CRTC's regulations will not guarantee a flow of intelligible information so that the public and its elected representatives can understand the nature of the parties and perceive the political system in terms of choices and alternative policies.

For political broadcasting to improve, three reforms must be undertaken: to reduce our dependence on foreign wire services and U.S. networks, to integrate English and French news programs on the CBC, and to increase the quality of Canadian reporting. If Canadians are to become interested in and learn more about Canadian events, our media must depend less on foreign, especially American, sources. The reaction of the CRTC to a problem of this kind would normally be to reduce foreign sources of information by regulation because regulation comes directly within the purview of the Commission. However, broadcasting regulations would not change the nature of the print media, nor would regulations by themselves guarantee an increased quality of Canadian information.

A sensible solution would not directly limit or prohibit the use of foreign sources, because foreign sources would be useful as a supplement to an expanded Canadian service. Foreign sources might be useful as a check against Canadian cultural biases or news management. A sensible policy would change income tax regulations to provide the media with incentives to employ more Canadian reporters across this country and abroad and to boost the resources of Canadian news cooperatives. Thus, the media might be permitted greater than 100% deductions on expenses devoted to Canadian sources (eg. 130%) and less than 100% deductions for foreign sources (eg. 70%). A direct subsidy to the media or to any of the cooperatives would be a poor solution because CBC news illustrates the timidity which might evolve. Expanded foreign coverage would enable Canadians to see the world through their own eyes as well as through the eyes of Americans, while an expanded domestic coverage might enable Canadians to see their own country through other than the eyes of Montrealers and Torontonians.

Of course, Canadians do not see the world through the eyes of Montrealers and Torontonians at the same time. The English and French networks of the CBC are quite isolated from each other. This separation is quite a significant problem because it undoubtedly strengthens the bicultural cleavage at the expense of class cleavage. At the stage of policy output, the bicultural cleavage can split the country seriously, while the class cleavage would, if ever manifested, offer some meaningful alternatives.

As a means to getting the CBC to serve bicultural unity rather than division, Pierre Berton has suggested that the CRTC oblige the Corporation to unify its national news programs and that the English and French programs have the same scripts. To implement this change at once would probably cause major disturbance because anglophones and francophones would learn too quickly the depth of the differences which separate them. However, it would make a great deal of sense to require the CBC to integrate its programs in staged increments, beginning with a common foreign news section, for example. Ironically, the shared dependence of the English and French networks on the American networks for their foreign television news would make this task less difficult than the task of amalgamating radio news, where the francophones rely on Agence France Presse.

Finally, we reach the intractable problem of improving the quality of Canadian reporting. Part of the solution may be achieved by providing an incentive for the media to devote greater resources to Canadian reporting. However, funds are not the only factors. The communications industry is a wealthy one. In the famous phrase of Lord Thomson of Fleet, to own a television station is to possess a "license to print money." Furthermore, recent American experiences show that an investment in research can be profitable if it leads to audience-catching articles of a muckraking nature. Consequently, the willingness of the Canadian media to accept mediocrity must be a reflection of themselves as much as evidence of objective economic constraints.

Notes

1.   For a survey of the comparative politics literature on political cleavages, see Conrad Winn, "Spatial Models of Party Systems: An Examination of the Canadian Case" (doctoral dissertation, University of Pennsylvania, 1972), Chapter 2.

2. Robert J. Jackson and Michael M. Atkinson, *The Canadian Legislative System* (Toronto: Macmillan, 1974), 61.

3. For a discussion of Cairns's work, see above, Chapter 6.

4. As Graham Spry, the dean of broadcasting, has often said, Journalism schools will not provide an effective remedy for the undertrained journalism profession. To report economic policy requires an economics training; to report science policy requires a science training; journalism schools provide neither. We acknowledge and appreciate our long conversation with him in December 1974.

5. *The Canadian Legislative System*, 93.

6. ibid., 190.

7. Quoted in *The Ottawa Citizen*, (December 13, 1974), 2.

8. For a more adequate discussion of Parliamentary reform, see Jackson and Atkinson, *The Canadian Legislative System*, Chapter 9.

9. For U.S. data, see Maxwell E. McCombs, "Mass Media in the Market-place," *Journalism Monographs* (August 1972). We are grateful to Prof. Peter Johansen of the Carleton School of Journalism for sharing his insights with us on the subject of media reform, but we do not hold him responsible for our conclusions. See Johansen's "Televising Parliament," *Journal of Canadian Studies*, VIII:4 (November 1973), 39–50.

10. Canadian Radio-Television Commission, "Canadian Broadcasting, A Single System: Policy Statement on Cable Television," (July 16, 1971), 37.

11. Pierre Juneau, "International Broadcasting: Diversity or Uniformity?" Address to Conference on International Communications and Institutions (March 23–24, 1973), 11.

12. Our comment is not intended to denigrate the CRTC, since communications policy is subject to many departments and the federal government does not possess an international reputation for inter-departmental cooperation.

Appendix I*

*Numbers of seats and votes are percentages rounded to the nearest figure.

[1]The first election was not so much a competition between parties as between coalitions for and against Confederation. However, the Macdonald coalition was the nascent Conservative party.

[2]Support for Nationalist candidates (autonomistes) is included in these totals.

[3]Support for Unionist candidates is included in these totals.

Election Year	Total Seats	Conservative		Liberal		Progressive		Social Credit		Reconstruction		Créditiste	
		Vote	Seats	Vote	Seats	Vote	Seats	Vote	Seats	Vote	Seats	Vote	Seats
1867[1]	181	50	60	49	40								
1872	200	50	52	49	48								
1874	206	45	32	54	67								
1878	206	53	68	45	32								
1882	211	53	65	47	35								
1887	215	51	59	49	40								
1891	215	52	57	46	42								
1896	213	46	41	45	55								
1900	213	47	38	52	62								
1904	214	47	35	52	65								
1908	221	47	38	51	61								
1911	221	51[2]	61	48	39								
1917	235	57[3]	65	40	35								
1921	235	30	21	41	49	23	28						
1925	245	46	47	40	40	9	10						
1926	245	45	37	46	52	5	8						
1930	245	49	56	45	37	3	5						
1935	245	30	16	45	71	9 (CCF)	3	4	2	9	0.4		
1940	245	31	16	51	74	8	3	3	4				
1945	245	27	27	41	51	16	11	4	5				
1949	262	30	16	49	74	13	5	4	4				
1953	265	31	19	49	64	11	9	5	6				
1957	265	39	42	41	40	11	9	7	7				
1958	265	54	78	34	18	9	3	2	0				
1962	265	37	44	37	37	14 (NDP)	7	12	11				
1963	265	33	36	42	49	13	6	12	9				
1965	265	32	37	40	49	18	8	4	2			5	3
1968	264	31	27	45	59	17	8	1	0			5	5
1972	264	35	41	38	41	18	12					8	6
1974	264	35	36	42	53	15	6					5	4

Appendix II

General Elections	Party forming the Government following General Elections	Prime Ministers of Canada
1867	"Conservative"[1]	Macdonald
1872	Conservative	Macdonald
		Mackenzie (Lib.) 1873
1874	Liberal	Mackenzie
1878	Conservative	Macdonald
1882	Conservative	Macdonald
1887	Conservative	Macdonald
1891	Conservative	Macdonald
		Abbot 1891-2
		Thompson 1892-4
		Bowell 1894-6
		Tupper 1896
1896	Liberal	Laurier
1900	Liberal	Laurier
1904	Liberal	Laurier
1908	Liberal	Laurier
1911	Conservative	Borden
1917	"Conservative"[2]	Borden
		Meighen 1920
1921	Liberal (minority)	King
1925	Liberal (minority)	King
		Meighen (Cons.) 1926 (minority)
1926	Liberal	Bennett
1930	Conservative	King
1935	Liberal	King
1940	Liberal	King
1945	Liberal	King
		St. Laurent 1948
1949	Liberal	St. Laurent
1953	Liberal	St. Laurent
1957	Conservative (minority)	Diefenbaker
1958	Conservative	Diefenbaker
1962	Conservative (minority)	Diefenbaker
1963	Liberal (minority)	Pearson
1965	Liberal (minority)	Pearson
		Trudeau 1968
1968	Liberal	Trudeau
1972	Liberal (minority)	Trudeau
1974	Liberal	Trudeau

[1]The election of 1867 was, in effect, a referendum on Confederation and, though it was not a party victory, the "Macdonald coalition" was the Conservative party.

[2]While the election of 1917 was won by a "Unionist" coalition of Conservatives and Liberals, the Government was effectively the Conservative party.

INDEX

Aberhart, William, 36-37
Action Canada, 30-31, 34-35
Activists (party), see Party personnel and parties by name.
Advertising agencies, 123-125, 128n, 181n
Agnew, Spiro, 72, 74, 124
Air Canada, 75, 121-122, 202, 241
Alberta, 30-31, 34-38, 41-44, 56, 72, 74, 82-83, 92, 103, 123, 197-198, 209, 217, 221, 223, 227n, 238-239, 242-244, 246
Alford, Robert, 98, 224n
Allan, Hugh, 21
American expansionism, 24-25, 257-259
American Federation of Labour-Congress of Industrial Organization (AFL-CIO; US), 106
Anglicans, 156, 267
Anglo-Scottish Canadians, 92, 146
Anti-Asian sentiment, 88n, 103, 110n, 116, 127n
Anti-Catholic sentiment, 14-17, 110-111n, 180, 197-198, 203
Anti-clericalism, 10, 14-19, 53-55, 267
Anti-combines legislation, 20-21
Anti-English sentiment, 18
Anti-French sentiment, 14-19, 51-58, 67-68, 103, 180-182, 197-198
Anti-semitism, 53, 69n, 72, 83, 87n, 103, 110-111
Argue, Hazen, 159
Asian Canadians, 88n, 103, 110n, 115-116
Atkinson, Michael, 268, 271
Atlantic Community, 25, 80, 256
Austin, Jack, 163
autonomistes, see the Nationalists.
Autonomy bill (1905), 31, 56

Baldwin, G. W. (Jed), 5
Baldwin, Robert, 16, 54
Barrett, Dave, 188, 221, 244-245, 263-264
Bay Street, see Economic elite.
Beauharnois Scandal, see Corruption.
Beck, J. Murray, 46n
Benjamin, Les, 162
Bennett, R. B., 4-5, 12, 34, 194, 233-234, 252, 254-255, 257, 260, 262
Bennett, W. A. C., 221, 237-238, 245
Berton, Pierre, 131, 278
Bicultural cleavage,
  attitudes to economic progress as a reflection of, 15, 50-53
  attitudes to representative government as a reflection of, 50-53
  assimilation as a solution to, 51-53, 55, 68
  bilingualism and, 18-19, 32-33, 63, 197, 202
  (mass) communication system and, 53, 57, 137, 144, 146-148, 270, 278
  the Conquest as origin of, 14, 50-51, 55, 67
  conscription and, 17-18, 32, 56-57, 75, 193-195
  Conservative party support on, 1, 3, 14-19, 32, 37-38, 54-57, 63-67, 84, 156-158, 180-181, 193, 253
  cultural animosity derived from geographic, religious, linguistic, and economic cleavages, 15-19, 50-57, 92, 103, 197

education policy as a reflection of, 17, 31, 33, 55-58, 63, 197-198
electoral behaviour as a result of, 14-19, 31-33, 51, 53-68
electoral system and, 54, 58-61, 116, 120-121, 126
emmigration as a reflection of, 61
French nationalism, 14-19, 31-33, 50, 52-53, 56-57, 67-68
impact within the parties of, 14-19, 31-33, 37-39, 55-68, 75, 156-159, 164, 175, 180-182, 192-205, 271
input in party system, 1, 49, 68, 267
Irish Canadian attitudes on, 63
legislative behaviour as a result of, 14-19, 33, 50-57
Liberal party support on, 1, 3, 14-19, 30-33, 54-57, 63-68, 156-158, 180-181, 193, 253
linguistic component, 18-19, 32-33, 51, 55-56, 63
Lord Durham on, 50, 53
NDP strategy on, 39, 67, 159
Northwest Rebellion and, 15-16, 55, 58
Orange Order, 15, 17, 55-57, 63, 197-198
party leadership and, 14-19, 54-55, 63-68, 158-159, 197-198
Quebec basis of Conservative and Liberal party pre-eminence, 14-19, 54-55, 63-68
religious component of, 10, 14-19, 51-63, 156-157, 164
Royal Commission on Bilingualism and Biculturalism, 33, 50, 197, 202, 204
Bicultural policy,
  anglophone Liberal leaders compared to francophone Liberal leaders, 197-204
  as a basis of Conservative and Liberal party pre-eminence, 14-19, 54-55, 63-68, 145
  bilingualism, 18-19, 32-33, 63, 197, 202
  CCF-NDP attitudes on, 203-204
  conscription and other military policies as, 17-18, 31-32, 54-57, 75, 193-195
  Conservative and Liberal leaders' attitudes on, 14-19, 31-33, 37-38, 54-57, 63-67, 180-181, 194-203
  Conservative and Liberal private members' attitudes on, 18-19, 196-197
  Conservative party attitudes on, 14-19, 32, 37-38, 55-57, 180, 193-203
  education policy as, 17, 31, 33, 55-58, 63, 197-198
  external aid policy as, 55, 195-196
  federal-provincial grants as, 199-200
  foreign policy as, 18, 31-32, 55-57, 193-196, 204, 253
  fundamental party dispositions in contrast to declared intentions on, 192-204
  Glassco (Royal) Commission on Government Organization and, 202-203
  immigration policy as, 51-52, 56, 198-199
  Liberal party attitudes on, 14-19, 31-33, 55-57, 63-68, 193-203
  ministerial appointments as a reflection of, 54, 68, 75, 200-202
  movement party attitudes on, 37-39, 203-204
  output in party system, 191
  public service appointments as a reflection of, 68, 75, 202-203